CONTENTS

KT-468-156

Clockwise from top: Astronomical Clock; Charles Bridge statues; ...ejn Palace; Mucha's window, St Vitus Cathedral; Old Town Square. Previous page: Cha... ...idge.

PRAGUE

With some six hundred years of architecture virtually untouched by natural disaster or war, few other European capitals look quite as beautiful as Prague. Straddling the winding River Vltava, with a steep wooded hill to one side, the city retains much of its medieval layout, and its rich mantle of Baroque, Rococo and Art Nouveau buildings have successfully escaped the vanities and excesses of modern redevelopment.

Buildings on the Old Town Square

View of the castle from Charles Bridge

When to visit

Prague is very popular, which means that the streets around the main sights are jam-packed with tourists for much of the year. If you can, it's best to avoid the summer months, when temperatures sometimes soar above 30°C, and you have to fight your way across Charles Bridge. The best times to visit, in terms of weather, are May and September. The winter months can be very chilly in Prague, but if you don't mind the cold, the city does look good in the snow and the crowds are manageable. Christmas and New Year are perfect as there are Christmas markets right across town, and plenty of mulled wine and hot punch to keep you warm.

Physically, Prague may have weathered the twentieth century very well but it suffered in other ways. The city that produced the music of Dvořák and Smetana, the literature of Čapek and Kafka and modernist architecture to rival Bauhaus, was forced to endure a brutal Nazi occupation. Prague had always been a multiethnic city, with a large Jewish and German-speaking population – in the aftermath of the war, only the Czechs were left. Then for forty years, during the Communist period, the city lay hidden behind the Iron Curtain, seldom visited by Westerners. All that changed in the 1990s, and nowadays Prague is one of the most popular European

city break destinations, with a highly developed tourist industry and a large expat population who, if nothing else, help to boost the city's nightlife.

Prague is divided into two unequal halves by the river, which meanders through the heart of the capital and provides the city with one of its most enduring landmarks, Charles Bridge. Built during the city's medieval golden age, this stone bridge, with its parade of Baroque statuary, still forms the chief link between the more central old town, or Staré Město, on the right bank, and Prague's hilltop castle on the left. The castle is a vast complex, which towers over the rest of

What's new

It's not so much what's new, but what's reopening soon in Prague that's big news. The National Museum (p.81) spent several years under scaffolding before its grand doors swung open again in 2018, and the same is true of the Museum of Decorative Arts (UPM; p.76), which has undergone a complete makeover. Artisan food is now big in the Czech capital with places like *Naše maso* (p.69) pleasing the city's sworn carnivores. Prague is adding tram lines at a frantic pace and construction of blue metro line D from Náměstí Míru is underway.

the city and supplies the classic picture-postcard image of Prague. Spread across the slopes below the castle are the wonderful cobbled streets and secret walled gardens of Malá Strana, little changed in the two hundred years since Mozart walked them.

With a population of just one and a quarter million, Prague (Praha to the Czechs) is relatively small as capital cities go. It originally developed as four separate self-governing towns and a Jewish ghetto, whose individual identities and medieval street plans have been preserved, to a greater or lesser extent, to this day. Almost everything of any historical interest lies within these compact central districts, and despite the twisting matrix of streets, it's easy enough to find your way around between the major landmarks. If you do use public transport, you'll find an extensive and picturesque tram network and a futuristic Soviet-built metro system that rivals most German cities. Price rises over the last decade mean Prague is no longer the budget destination it once was. However, one thing you can be sure of is that the beer is better and cheaper than anywhere else in the EU.

Where to...

Shop

Pařížská, in **Josefov**, is home to the city's swankiest stores, among them branches of the international fashion houses. Celetná in **Staré Město**, and Na příkopě on the border of **Nové Město**, also specialize in luxury goods. The city's most modern department store is the multistorey My národní on **Národní**. Czechs have had their own malls – known as *pasáže* – since the 1920s, and new ones continue to sprout up. The mother of all malls is Palladium, on **Náměstí Republiky**, housed in a castellated former army barracks. For more offbeat, independent shops you need to explore the cobbled side streets of Staré Město and Nové Město.

OUR FAVOURITES: Truhlář marionety p.50. Art Deco p.66. Bric a Brac p.66.

Eat

As in many cities, the main thoroughfares in Prague aren't the best places in which to find somewhere to eat and drink. One or two grand Habsburg-era cafés survive on the main junctions of the city centre, but for the most part, the best cafés and restaurants are hidden away in the backstreets. There's a particularly acute dearth of decent places in and around Prague Castle and **Hradčany**, while expensive restaurants predominate in **Malá Strana**. For a much wider choice of cafés, and of cuisine, head to **Staré Město** and the streets of **Nové Město** just south of Národní.

OUR FAVOURITES: Lehká hlava p.69. Naše maso p.69. Café Slavia p.92.

Drink

Given that the Czechs top the world league table of beer consumption, it comes as little surprise to find that Prague is a drinker's paradise. Wherever you are in the city, you're never very far from a pub or bar where you can quench your thirst. **Staré Město** has the highest concentration of pubs and bars, but if you're looking for one of the city's new microbreweries or for a traditional Czech pub (**pivnice**), you'll need to explore the residential streets of **Nové Město**, **Vinohrady** or **Holešovice**. Look out, too, for the many alfresco drinking spots beside the river, on one of the islands, or in one of the city's many public parks.

OUR FAVOURITES: U černého vola p.39. Prague Beer Museum p.70. U zlatého tygra p.71.

Go out

Prague's often excellent theatre and concert venues are all very centrally located in **Staré Město** and **Nové Město**; the same is true for most small and medium-scale jazz and rock venues. **Žižkov** has more late-night pubs and bars than anywhere else, plus a smattering of gay and lesbian venues. One area that's up-and-coming for nightlife is **Holešovice**, in particular the old industrial and market area to the east of the metro line – the warehouse spaces here already house several of the city's newest clubs and venues. **Wenceslas Square** remains the traditional centre of Prague's seedier side.

OUR FAVOURITES: AghaRTA Jazz Centrum p.71. Roxy p.71. Lucerna Music Bar p.89.

Prague at a glance

TROJA

Holešovice p.118. Home to Prague's impressive museum of modern art, the Veletržní Palace, and Výstaviště, its old-fashioned trade fair grounds.

Stromovka

BUBENEČ

VÝSTAVI

Prague Castle p.32. Prague Castle (Hrad) contains the city's cathedral, the old royal palace and gardens, and a host of museums.

Hradčany p.40. The district immediately outside the castle gates is a wonderfully quiet quarter filled with old palaces.

LETNÁ

Letenske sady

Chotkovy sady

HRADČANY

Prague Castle

Cathedral of sv Víta

Valdštejn Palace

Vojanovy sady

JOSEFOV

Old Jewish Cemetery

Kinský Palace

Černín Palace

Loreta

sv Mikuláš

Karluv Most (Charles Bridge)

Týn Ch

Staré Město Town Hall

Strahov Monastery

Panny Marie Vítězné

MALÁ STRANA

KAMPA

Museum Kampa

STARÉ MĚSTO

PETŘÍN

Palác Adria

sv Voršila

Malá Strana p.46. A picturesque district squeezed between Prague Castle and the river, with twisting cobbled streets, Baroque palaces and secret walled gardens.

National Theatre

Nové M Town H

NOVÉ MĚ

Staré Město p.60. The medieval hub of the city, Staré Město ("Old Town") has a huge number of pubs, bars and restaurants packed into its labyrinthine layout.

Palacký Monument

Emauzy Monastery

Botani zahra

SMÍCHOV

VYŠEHR

sv Petr & Pavel

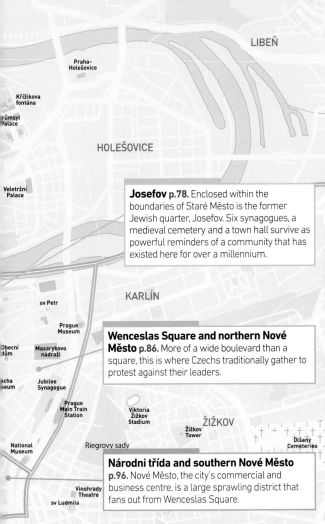

LIBEŇ

Praha-Holešovice

Křižikova fontána

růmysl Palace

HOLEŠOVICE

Veletržní Palace

Josefov p.78. Enclosed within the boundaries of Staré Město is the former Jewish quarter, Josefov. Six synagogues, a medieval cemetery and a town hall survive as powerful reminders of a community that has existed here for over a millennium.

KARLÍN

sv Petr

Prague Museum

Obecní Dům   Masarykovo nádraži

acha seum   Jubilee Synagogue

Wenceslas Square and northern Nové Město p.86. More of a wide boulevard than a square, this is where Czechs traditionally gather to protest against their leaders.

Prague Main Train Station

Viktoria Žižkov Stadium

ŽIŽKOV

Žižkov Tower

Olšany Cemeteries

National Museum   Riegrovy sady

Národni třída and southern Nové Město p.96. Nové Město, the city's commercial and business centre, is a large sprawling district that fans out from Wenceslas Square.

Vinohrady Theatre

sv Ludmila

a Amerika Fák Museum)

Vyšehrad, Vinohrady and Žižkov p.108. The fortress of Vyšehrad was one of the earliest points of settlement in Prague; Vinohrady and Žižkov are rather grand late nineteenth-century suburbs.

NUSLE

17 Things not to miss

It's not possible to see everything that Prague has to offer in one trip – and we don't suggest you try. What follows is a selective taste of the city's highlights, from Baroque architecture to modern art.

∧ Charles Bridge
p.54
Decorated with extravagant ecclesiastical statues, this medieval stone bridge is the city's most enduring monument.

< Old Town Square
p.60
The city's showpiece square, lined with exquisite Baroque facades and overlooked by the town hall's famous astronomical clock.

> Prague Main Train Station
p.81
Fight your way through the subterranean modern station and you'll find Josef Fanta's newly renovated 1909 station.

< **Stavovské divadlo**
p.64
The city's chief opera house has a glittering interior and many Mozart associations.

> **Convent of St Agnes**
p.64
Gothic convent that provides the perfect setting for the National Collection of Medieval Art.

> **Vyšehrad**
p.104
This old Habsburg military fortress is now a great escape from the busy city.

< **Prague Castle**
p.26
Towering over the city, the castle is the ultimate picture-postcard image of Prague.

∨ **UPM**
p.76
A treasure trove of Czech applied art, ranging from Meissen porcelain and Art Nouveau vases to avant-garde photography.

THINGS NOT TO MISS

< Obecní dům
p.84
Built in 1911 with the help of
leading Czech artists, this is the
city's finest Art Nouveau edifice.

∨ Church of sv Mikuláš
p.41
Prague's finest Baroque church,
whose dome and tower dominate
the skyline of Malá Strana.

THINGS NOT TO MISS

< **Wenceslas Square**
p.80
The modern hub of Prague, this sloping boulevard has been the scene of countless protests over the centuries.

∨ **Strahov Monastery**
p.38
Strahov boasts two monastic libraries with fantastically ornate bookshelves and colourful frescoes.

Day One in Prague

Prague Castle p.26. From Hradčanské náměstí, the square outside the main castle gates, you get an incredible view over Prague.

Cathedral of sv Víta p.26. Occupying centre stage in the castle's vast precincts is the city's Gothic cathedral.

Old Royal Palace p.29. Visit the palace's vast, rib-vaulted Vladislav Hall.

Story of Prague Castle p.29. Get the lowdown on past goings-on at Prague's most famous attraction – and learn a lot about Czech history in the process – at this modern exhibition.

Golden Lane p.31. Built in the sixteenth century for the imperial guards, these tiny little cottages situated hard against the fortifications are now one of the most popular sights in the castle.

Lunch p.33. *Villa Richter*, situated in the middle of the castle vineyards, has superb views across the rooftops and river to Staré Město.

Church of sv Mikuláš p.41. This prominent Malá Strana landmark, below the castle, is Prague's most ornate Baroque church.

Charles Bridge p.54. Prague's famous medieval stone bridge is packed with people and lined with Baroque statues.

Museum Kampa p.46. This art gallery houses a permanent collection of two Czech artists: Kupka, a pioneer in abstract art, and the cubist sculptor Gutfreund.

Dinner p.51. Try the intimate French restaurant, *Café de Paris*, or for a more grandiose setting, head for the *Savoy*.

Cathedral of sv Víta

Old Royal Palace

Savoy

Day Two in Prague

Obecní dům p.84. Book yourself on the morning tour round this cultural centre, an Art Nouveau jewel built in 1911.

Church of sv Jakub p.63. Enjoy one of Prague's finest ecclesiastical interiors at this huge Old Town church, with Prague's second-longest nave and a gruesome tale of theft and punishment.

Týn Church p.62. This giant Gothic church's twin, unequal towers preside over Old Town Square.

Old Town Square p.60. Prague's spectacular square boasts a parade of Baroque facades, giant statue of Jan Hus and interactive astronomical clock.

Apple Museum p.58. One of the world's best computer technology museums is hidden in the backstreets between the Old Town Square and Charles Bridge.

Lunch p.69. *Maitrea* is a smart, cave-like vegetarian restaurant near the Týn Church.

Pinkas Synagogue p.75. Pay your respects to the 77,297 Czech Jews killed in the Holocaust, whose names cover the walls of this sixteenth-century synagogue.

Old Jewish Cemetery p.75. An evocative medieval cemetery in which the crowded gravestones mirror the cramped conditions in the ghetto.

Old-New Synagogue p.73. This thirteenth-century synagogue is the oldest active synagogue in Europe and one of Prague's earliest Gothic buildings.

Dinner p.69. Try *Lokál* for a homely, traditional Czech meal with great service and fresh Pilsner Urquell beer.

Obecní dům

Old Town Square

Lokál

Communist Prague

Despite forty-odd years of Communism, the regime left very few physical traces on the city. However, if you know where to look there are several understated – and one or two ironic – memorials to the period.

Kinský Palace p.61. It was from the balcony of this Baroque palace that Klement Gottwald proclaimed the 1948 Communist takeover.

Museum of Communism p.83. It took an American expat to group together the city's only collection of Communist memorabilia.

Jan Palach and Jan Zajíc Memorial p.80. In 1969, two young men took their own lives in protest against the Soviet invasion of the previous year. A simple plaque memorializes them.

Jan Palach Memorial

Národní p.92. A simple bronze memorial commemorates the demonstration of November 17, 1989, which sparked the Velvet Revolution. An annual gathering takes place here on that date.

Memorial to the Victims of Communism p.48. Olbram Zoubek's striking memorial at the floor of Petřín hill pays tribute to the thousands who were imprisoned, executed and went into exile.

Míčovna p.32. Seek out the hammer and sickle added to this Renaissance building in the Royal Gardens by the Communist restorers.

Museum of Communism

Metronome, Letná p.112. Take in the view from the metronome, which stands in the place where the world's largest Stalin statue once stood.

Žižkov Hill p.112. Once used as a Communist mausoleum, the Žižkov monument still boasts lashings of Socialist Realist decor.

Olšany cemeteries p.108. Pay your respects to the Red Army soldiers who lost their lives liberating the city in May 1945.

Kinský Palace

Kids' Prague

Most kids will love Prague, with its hilly cobbled streets and trams, especially in summer when the place is alive with street performers and buskers. Prague Castle, with its fairytale ramparts and towers, rarely disappoints either.

Funicular p.49. The funicular at Újezd, which takes you effortlessly to the top of Petřín hill, is part of the public transport system and a great way to start a day's sightseeing.

Museum of Miniatures p.38. Kids will love this unusual museum with its tiny creations. Have fun looking through the magnifying glasses at Anatoly Konenko's miniature masterpieces.

Petřín p.48. The Mirror Maze is a guaranteed hit with kids of all ages, and if you need to wear them out even more, get them to walk up the mini-Eiffel Tower for top views.

Changing of the Guard p.27. Prague Castle's armed guards are dressed like toy soldiers, and at noon every day they put on a bit of a show to a melancholic modern melody.

Tram #22 p.132. This tram takes you from Prague Castle, round a hairpin bend and across the river to Karlovo náměstí, a short walk from the PPS terminal.

Boat trip p.132. From April to September, you can take a 45-minute boat ride from PPS terminal near Palackého all the way to Troja, home of the zoo.

Prague Zoo p.118. Prague Zoo has had a lot of money spent on it, and it shows: modern enclosures, sensitive landscaping and everything from elephants to zebras.

Truhlář marionety p.50. Prague is awash with puppets, but some of the best and most authentic are available at this small Malá Strana shop. A great souvenir for the kiddies.

Tram #22

Changing of the Guard

Petřín

Green Prague

For a tightly-packed, medieval city Prague boasts a lot of green spaces, many dating back to the Czech capital's earliest days. Today these are welcome places to unfurl the picnic blanket and escape the tourist crush.

Terraced Palace Gardens p.44. The pretty terraced gardens below Prague Castle offer sweeping views of the city.

Stromovka p.117. Large leafy park which extends between the Výstaviště and the chateau of Troja.

Royal Gardens p.32. Prague Castle's formal gardens are famous for their disciplined crops of tulips.

Petřín p.48. This wooded hill on Prague's left bank provides a spectacular viewpoint over the city and has several popular attractions.

Valdštejnská zahrada

Slovanský ostrov p.95. The three leafy islands in the middle of the River Vltava are great places to picnic as you watch the river's swan population. The most easily accessible is the Slovanský ostrov with its grand, Habsburg-era cultural centre.

Kampa p.40. The southern end of Kampa island is a large park, a perfect central location for picnicking fun and sunbathing.

Botanic Gardens p.118. The highlight of Prague's tranquil Botanic Gardens is the Fata Morgana glasshouse with its tropical plants and butterflies.

Rotunda of St Martin, Vyšehrad>

Vyšehrad p.104. This towering Habsburg fortress south of the centre is a superb place to escape the busy city.

Valdštejnská zahrada p.44. The formal Renaissance gardens adjoining the Valdštejn Palace are populated by freely-roaming peacocks.

Žižkov Hill p.109. This huge area of parkland a short walk from the city centre is the ideal spot to flee the crowds.

Botanic Gardens

Baroque & Art Nouveau Prague

If there are two artistic and architectural styles that define the Czech capital, they are the ornate duo of Baroque and turn-of-the-century Art Nouveau, the first dominating Malá Strana, the second found mostly in the New Town.

Loreto church p.37. A sumptuous Baroque pilgrimage complex with frescoed cloisters, a Black Madonna, and a stunning array of reliquaries and monstrances.

Church of sv Mikuláš p.41. The city's most impressive Baroque church, with its distinctive green dome and tower.

Strahov Monastery p.38. Strahov boasts two monastic libraries with fantastically ornate bookshelves and colourful frescoes.

Charles Bridge statues p.54. It's the (mostly) Baroque statues that make this medieval bridge so unforgettable – the originals are spread around various museums.

Prague Main Train Station p.81. Forget the modern, underground section, and head straight for the newly renovated 1909 Art Nouveau station, designed by Josef Fanta.

Mucha Museum p.83. Dedicated to Alfons Mucha, the Czech artist best known for his Art Nouveau Parisian posters.

Obecní dům p.84. One of Europe's finest Art Nouveau edifices, decorated by the leading Czech artists of the day.

Mucha's Window – St Vitus' Cathedral p.26. Alfons Mucha's Art Nouveau stained-glass window in St Vitus Cathedral dates from the mid-1920s.

Klementinum p.58. This huge Baroque complex with its libraries, chapels and famous Astronomical Tower is best explored on a tour.

Obecní dům

Prague Main Train Station

Loreto church

PLACES

Stained glass by Mucha, Obecní dům

Prague Castle

Prague's skyline is dominated by the vast hilltop complex of Prague Castle (Pražský hrad), which looks out over the city centre from the west bank of the River Vltava. There's been a royal seat here for over a millennium, and it continues to serve as headquarters of the Czech president, but the castle is also home to several of Prague's chief tourist attractions: the Gothic Cathedral of sv Víta, the late medieval Old Royal Palace, the diminutive and picturesque Golden Lane and numerous museums and galleries. The best thing about the place, though, is that the public are free to roam around the atmospheric courtyards and take in the views from the ramparts from early in the morning until late at night.

Cathedral of sv Víta

MAP p.28, POCKET MAP C11
Third courtyard. April–Oct Mon–Sat
9am–5pm, Sun noon–5pm; Nov–March
closes 4pm. Entry included with Prague
Castle ticket.

Begun by Emperor Charles IV (1346–78), the **Cathedral** has a long and chequered history and wasn't finally completed until 1929. Once inside, it's difficult not to be impressed by the sheer height of the nave, and struck by the modern fixtures and fittings, especially the **stained-glass windows**, among them Alfons Mucha's superb *Cyril and Methodius* window, in the third chapel in the north wall, and František Bílek's wooden altar, in the north aisle.

Of the cathedral's numerous side chapels, the grand **Chapel of sv Václav** (better known as Wenceslas, of "Good King" fame), by the south door, is easily the main attraction. The country's patron saint was killed by his pagan brother, Boleslav the Cruel, who later repented, converted,

Prague Castle main gate

and apparently transferred his brother's remains to this very spot. The chapel's gilded walls are inlaid with over a thousand semi-precious stones, set around ethereal fourteenth-century frescoes of the Passion; meanwhile, the tragedy of Wenceslas unfolds above the cornice in sixteenth-century paintings.

The highlight of the ambulatory is the **Tomb of St John of Nepomuk**, a work of Baroque excess, sculpted in solid silver with free-flying angels holding up the heavy drapery of the baldachin. On the lid of the tomb, back-to-back with John himself, a cherub points to the martyr's severed tongue. Before you leave, check out the Habsburgs' sixteenth-century marble **Imperial Mausoleum**, in the centre of the choir, surrounded by a fine Renaissance grille. Below lies the claustrophobic **Royal Crypt**, resting place of emperors Charles IV and Rudolf II, plus various other Czech kings and queens.

You can also climb the cathedral's **Great Tower** (daily: April–Oct 10am–6pm; Nov–March 10am–5pm; closed in bad weather; 150Kč), from the south aisle. Outside the cathedral, don't forget to clock the **Golden Gate**, above the south door, decorated with a remarkable fourteenth-century mosaic of the Last Judgement.

Visiting the castle

The castle precincts are open daily (April–Oct 5am–midnight; Nov–March 6am–11pm ☎ 224 372 423, ⊛ www.hrad.cz). There are two main types of **multi-entry ticket** available for the sights within the castle. The **long tour** ticket (350Kč) gives you entry to most of the sights within the castle, including the Cathedral of sv Víta, the Old Royal Palace, the Basilica and Convent of sv Jiří, the Prague Castle Picture Gallery and Golden Lane. The **short tour** (250Kč) only covers the Cathedral of sv Víta, the Old Royal Palace, the Basilica of sv Jiří, and Golden Lane. Castle tickets are valid for two days and are available from various ticket offices. Temporary exhibitions, such as those held in the Imperial Stables and Riding School, all have separate admission charges.

Most people **approach the castle** from Malostranská metro station by taking the steep short cut up the Staré zámecké schody, which brings you into the castle from the rear entrance to the east. A better approach is down Valdštejnská, and then up the more stately Zámecké schody, where you can stop and admire the view, or up the cobbled street of Nerudova, before entering the castle via the main gates. From April to October, you might also consider coming up through Malá Strana's wonderful terraced gardens (see p.44), which are connected to the castle gardens. Alternatively, you can take tram #22 from Malostranská metro, which deposits you at the Pražský hrad stop outside the Royal Gardens to the north of the castle.

The hourly **Changing of the Guard** at the main gates is a fairly subdued affair, but every day at noon there's a much more elaborate parade, accompanied by a modern fanfare.

There are a couple of cafés within Prague Castle at which you can grab a coffee and a snack, though you'd be better off outside the castle precincts.

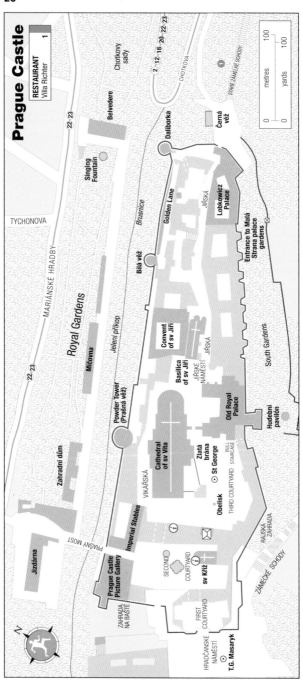

Prague Castle

RESTAURANT	
Villa Richter	**1**

Alfons Mucha's Cyril and Methodius window in the cathedral

Old Royal Palace (Starý královský palác)

MAP OPPOSITE, POCKET MAP C11
Third courtyard. Daily: April–Oct 9am–5pm; Nov–March 9am–4pm. 140Kč.
The **Old Royal Palace** is a sandwich of royal apartments, built one on top of the other by successive princes and kings of Bohemia, but left largely unused for the past three hundred years. It was in the **Vladislav Hall**, with its remarkable, sweeping rib-vaulting which forms floral patterns on the ceiling, that the early Bohemian kings were elected, and that every president since 1918 has been sworn into office. From a staircase in the southwest corner, you can climb up to the Bohemian Chancellery, scene of Prague's **second defenestration**, when two Catholic governors, appointed by Ferdinand I, were thrown out of the window by a group of Protestant Bohemian noblemen in 1618. A quick canter down the Riders' Staircase will take you to the Gothic and Romanesque palace chambers containing "**The Story of Prague Castle**", an interesting, if overlong, exhibition on the development of the castle through the centuries.

Powder Tower (Prašná věž)

MAP OPPOSITE, POCKET MAP C10
Vikářská. Daily: April–Oct 9am–5pm; Nov–March 9am–4pm. 70Kč.
The **Powder Tower** is where Rudolf II's team of alchemists were put to work trying to discover the secret of the philosopher's stone. It now houses an exhibition on the history of the Castle Guard.

Basilica of sv Jiří

Basilica of sv Jiří

MAP p.28, POCKET MAP C10–C11
**Jiřské náměstí. Daily: April–Oct 9am–5pm;
Nov–March 9am–4pm.**

Don't be fooled by the basilica's russet-red Baroque facade; inside is Prague's most beautiful Romanesque building, meticulously scrubbed clean and restored to re-create something like the honey-coloured stone basilica that replaced the original tenth-century church in 1173. The double staircase to the chancel is a remarkably harmonious late Baroque addition and now provides a perfect stage for chamber music concerts. The choir vault contains a rare early thirteenth-century painting of the *New Jerusalem from Revelation*, while to the right of the chancel are sixteenth-century frescoes of the burial chapel of sv Ludmila, Bohemia's first Christian martyr and grandmother of St Wenceslas.

Good King Wenceslas

Disappointingly, there's very little substance to the story related in the nineteenth-century English Christmas carol, "Good King Wenceslas looked out". For a start, **Václav (Wenceslas)** was only a duke and never a king (though he did become a saint); he wasn't even that "good", except in comparison with the rest of his family; Prague's St Agnes fountain, by which "yonder peasant dwelt", wasn't built until the thirteenth century; and he was killed a good three months before the Feast of Stephen (Boxing Day) – the traditional day for giving to the poor, hence the narrative of the carol.

Born in 907, Václav inherited his title aged 13. His Christian grandmother, Ludmila, was appointed regent in preference to Drahomíra, his pagan mother, who subsequently had Ludmila murdered in 921. On coming of age in 925, Václav became duke in his own right and took a vow of celibacy, intent on promoting Christianity throughout the dukedom. Even so, the local Christians didn't take to him, and when he began making conciliatory overtures to the neighbouring Germans, they persuaded his pagan younger brother, Boleslav the Cruel, to do away with him. On September 20, 929, Václav was stabbed to death by Boleslav at the entrance to a church just outside Prague.

Convent of sv Jiří (Jiřský klášter)

MAP p.28, POCKET MAP C10
Jiřské náměstí.

Bohemia's earliest monastery was founded in 973 by Prince Boleslav II and his sister Mlada, who was its first mother superior. A fire in 1142 resulted in the addition of the main apse and two steeples which are still in place today, while the Early Baroque period saw it given its striking facade. In the eighteenth century invading troops devastated the building, with later architects seeking to revive its original Romanesque style. Until 2012 the convent held an art collection from the National Gallery, but at the time of writing there were no plans to reopen it.

Golden Lane (Zlatá ulička)

MAP p.28, POCKET MAP D10
Daily: April–Oct 9am–5pm; Nov–March 9am–4pm.

A seemingly blind alley of brightly coloured miniature cottages, **Golden Lane** is by far the most popular sight in the castle, and during the day the whole street is crammed with sightseers. Originally built in the sixteenth century for the 24 members of Rudolf II's castle guard, the lane takes its name from the goldsmiths who followed a century later. By the nineteenth century, the whole street had become a kind of palace slum, attracting artists and craftsmen, its two most famous inhabitants being Nobel Prize-winning poet Jaroslav Seifert, and Franz Kafka, who came here in the evenings to write short stories during the winter of 1916.

Lobkowicz Palace (Lobkovický palác)

MAP p.28, POCKET MAP D10
Jiřská 3 ⓦ lobkowicz.com. Daily 10am–6pm. 275Kč.

Appropriated in 1939 and again in 1948, and only handed back in the late 1990s, the Lobkowicz Palace now houses an impressive selection of the Lobkowicz family's prize possessions (with audio-guide accompaniment), including original manuscripts by Mozart and Beethoven, old musical instruments, arms and armour and one or two masterpieces such as a Velázquez portrait, Pieter Brueghel the Elder's sublime *Haymaking* from the artist's famous cycle of seasons, and two views of London by Canaletto.

Golden Lane (Zlatá ulička)

South Gardens (Jižní zahrady)

MAP p.28, POCKET MAP C11
Daily: April & Oct 10am–6pm; May & Sept 10am–7pm; June & July 10am–9pm; Aug 10am–8pm. Free.

These gardens, which link up with the terraced gardens of Malá Strana (see p.44), enjoy wonderful vistas over the city. Originally laid out in the sixteenth century, the gardens were remodelled in the 1920s with the addition of an observation terrace and colonnaded pavilion, below which is an earlier eighteenth-century *Hudební pavilón* (music pavilion). Two sandstone obelisks further east record the arrival of the two Catholic governors after their 1618 defenestration from the Royal Palace (see p.29).

Royal Gardens (Královská zahrada)

MAP p.28, POCKET MAP C10
Daily: April & Oct 10am–6pm; May & Sept 10am–7pm; June & July 10am–9pm; Aug 10am–8pm. Free.

Founded by Ferdinand I in 1530, the **Royal Gardens** are smartly maintained, with fully functioning fountains and immaculately cropped lawns. It's a popular spot, though more a place for admiring the azaleas and almond trees than lounging around on the grass. Set into the south terrace – from which there are unrivalled views over to the cathedral – is the Renaissance **ball-game court** (Míčovna), occasionally used for concerts and exhibitions. The walls are tattooed with sgraffito and feature a hammer and sickle to the side of one of the sandstone

Royal Gardens

Filigree ironwork at the Belvedere

half-columns, thoughtfully added by restorers in the 1950s.

Prague Castle Picture Gallery (Obrazárna pražského hradu)

MAP p.28, POCKET MAP C11
Second courtyard Ⓦ kulturanahrade.cz.
Daily: April–Oct 9am–5pm; Nov–March 9am–4pm. 100Kč.

The remnants of the **Imperial Collection**, started by Rudolf II, are housed here. Among the collection's finest paintings is Rubens' richly coloured *Assembly of the Gods at Olympus*, an illusionist triple portrait of Rudolf II and his Habsburg predecessors that's typical of the sort of tricksy work that appealed to the emperor. Elsewhere, there's an early, very beautiful *Young Woman at Her Toilet* by Titian, and Tintoretto's *Flagellation of Christ*, a late work in which the artist makes very effective and dramatic use of light.

Belvedere (Kralovský letohrádek)

MAP p.28, POCKET MAP D10
Mariánské hradby 1. Tues–Sun 10am–6pm. Free.

Prague's most celebrated Renaissance building is a delicately **arcaded summerhouse** topped by an inverted copper ship's hull, begun by Ferdinand I in 1538 for his wife, Anne (though she didn't live long enough to see it completed). The Belvedere's exterior walls are decorated by a series of lovely figural reliefs depicting scenes from mythology, while the interior is normally in use as a venue for exhibitions of contemporary art. However, the main attraction here can be found in the palace's miniature formal garden – the **Singing Fountain** gets its name from the musical sound the drops of water make when falling in the metal bowls below.

Restaurant

Villa Richter

MAP p.28, POCKET MAP D10
Staré zámecké schody 6 ☏ 702 205 108,
Ⓦ www.villarichter.cz. Daily 11am–11pm.

Set amid the castle vineyards, just outside the Black Tower (Černá věž), *Villa Richter* has three separate places one on top of the other: the *Piano Nobile* serves up classy duck, beef and seafood dishes (600–700Kč); below, the *Piano Terra* specializes in Bohemian standards (180–500Kč); and *Panorama Pergola* is the perfect place to sample some Czech wines and soak up the view.

Hradčany

Hradčany – the district immediately outside Prague Castle – is replete with ostentatious Baroque palaces built on an ever-increasing scale. The monumental appearance of these palaces is a direct result of the great fire of 1541, which destroyed the small-scale medieval houses that once stood here and allowed the Habsburg nobility to transform Hradčany into the grand architectural showpiece it still is. Nowadays, despite the steady stream of tourists en route to the castle, it's also one of the most peaceful parts of central Prague, barely disturbed by the civil servants who work in the area's numerous ministries and embassies. The three top sights to head for are the Šternberg Palace, with its collection of Old Masters; the Baroque pilgrimage church of Loreto and the ornate libraries of the Strahov Monastery.

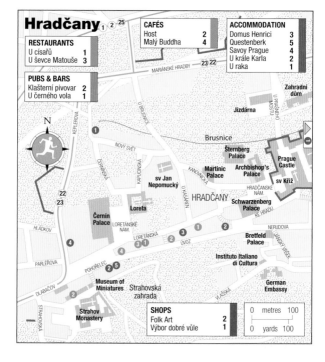

Hradčany 1 2 25

RESTAURANTS
U císařů	1
U ševce Matouše	3

PUBS & BARS
Klašterní pivovar	2
U černého vola	1

CAFÉS
Host	2
Malý Buddha	4

ACCOMMODATION
Domus Henrici	3
Questenberk	5
Savoy Prague	4
U krále Karla	2
U raka	1

SHOPS
Folk Art	2
Výbor dobré vůle	1

0 metres 100
0 yards 100

View over Malá Strana from Hradčany

Hradčanské náměstí

MAP OPPOSITE, POCKET MAP B11
Hradčanské náměstí fans out from the castle gates, surrounded by the oversized palaces of the old Catholic nobility. The one spot everyone heads for is the ramparts in the southeastern corner, which allow an unrivalled view over the red rooftops of Malá Strana, and beyond. Few people make use of the square's central green patch, which is heralded by a wonderful giant green wrought-iron lamppost from the 1860s and, behind it, a Baroque plague column. The most noteworthy palaces on the square are the **Schwarzenberg Palace**, at no. 2, with its over-the-top sgraffito decoration, and the sumptuous, vanilla-coloured Rococo **Archbishop's Palace**, opposite.

Šternberg Palace

MAP OPPOSITE, POCKET MAP B11
Hradčanské náměstí 15 Ⓦ ngprague.cz. Tues–Sun 10am–6pm. 220Kč.

The elegant, early eighteenth-century **Šternberg Palace** is now an art gallery housing **European Old Masters** from the fourteenth to the eighteenth century. It's a modest collection, though the handful of masterpieces makes a visit here worthwhile, and there's an elegant courtyard café.

The ground floor contains several superb Cranach canvases, plus one of the most celebrated paintings in the whole collection: the *Feast of the Rosary* by Albrecht Dürer, one of Rudolf II's most prized acquisitions, which he had transported on foot across the Alps to Prague.

The highlights of the first floor include Dieric Bouts' *Lamentation*, a complex composition crowded with figures in medieval garb; two richly coloured Bronzino portraits; and Jan Gossaert's eye-catching *St Luke Drawing the Virgin*, an exercise in architectural geometry and perspective. Before you head upstairs though, don't miss the side room (11) containing Orthodox icons from Venice, the Balkans and Russia.

The second floor boasts a searching portrait of old age by Tintoretto, a wonderfully rugged portrait by Goya and a mesmerizing *Praying Christ* by El Greco. Be sure to admire the Činský kabinet, a small oval chamber smothered in gaudy Baroque Chinoiserie, and one of the palace's few surviving slices of original decor. Elsewhere, there is a series of canvases by the Brueghel family, a Rembrandt, and Rubens' colossal *Murder of St Thomas* (room 30).

Schwarzenberg Palace

MAP p.34, POCKET MAP B11
Hradčanské náměstí 2 ⓦ ngprague.cz.
Tues–Sun 10am–6pm. 220Kč.

The most outrageous, over-the-top, sgraffitoed pile on Hradčanské náměstí, **Schwarzenberg Palace** now houses a collection of **Czech Baroque art**, of only limited interest to the non-specialist. Chronologically, you should begin on the second floor, where you get a brief glimpse of the overtly sensual and erotic Mannerist paintings that prevailed during the reign of Rudolf II (1576–1612). The rest of the gallery is given over to the art that spearheaded the Counter-Reformation in the Czech Lands: paintings by the likes of Bohemia's Karel Škréta and Petr Brandl, and the gesticulating sandstone sculptures of Matthias Bernhard Braun and Ferdinand Maximilian Brokof.

Martinic Palace

MAP p.34, POCKET MAP B11
Hradčanské náměstí 8.

Compared to the other palaces on the square, the **Martinic Palace** is a fairly modest pile, built in 1620 by one of the governors who survived the second defenestration (see p.29). Its rich sgraffito decoration, which continues in the inner courtyard, was only discovered during restoration work in the 1970s. On the facade, you can easily make out Potiphar's wife making a grab at a naked and unwilling Joseph. The interiors contain some exceptionally well-preserved Renaissance art as well as providing a glimpse of the lifestyle enjoyed by the palace's original owners. Lovely Late Renaissance painted ceilings and frescoes give new meaning to the term wall art, and there's a nice display of typical furnishings from the Renaissance era. Sadly, today it is only open during events.

Černín Palace

MAP p.34, POCKET MAP A11
Loretánské náměstí 5. Closed to the public.

Loretánské náměstí is dominated by the phenomenal 135m-long facade of the **Černín Palace**, decorated with thirty Palladian half-columns and supported by a row of diamond-pointed rustication. Begun in the 1660s, the building nearly bankrupted future generations of the Černín family, who were eventually forced to sell the palace to the Austrian state in 1851, which converted it into military barracks.

Černín Palace

Since 1918, the palace has housed the **Ministry of Foreign Affairs**, and during World War II it was, for a while, the Nazi Reichsprotektor's residence. On March 10, 1948, it was the scene of Prague's third – and most widely mourned – defenestration. Only days after the Communist coup, **Jan Masaryk**, the only son of the founder of Czechoslovakia, and the last non-Communist in the cabinet, plunged to his death from the top-floor bathroom window of the palace. Whether it was suicide (he had been suffering from bouts of depression, partly induced by the political developments in Czechoslovakia at the time) or murder will probably never be satisfactorily resolved, but for most people Masaryk's death cast a dark shadow over the newly established regime. Jan Masaryk's story is the subject of a 2017 feature film, *A Prominent Patient*, which looks at his life and death and what he might have achieved had he lived longer.

Loreto

MAP p.34, POCKET MAP A11
Loretánské náměstí 7 ⓦ loreta.cz. Daily 9am–5pm. 150Kč.

The outer casing of the **Loreto** church was built in the early part of the eighteenth century – all hot flourishes and Baroque twirls, topped by a bell tower that clanks out the hymn "We Greet Thee a Thousand Times" on its 27 Dutch bells. The focus of the pilgrimage complex is the **Santa Casa** (a mock-up of Mary's home in Nazareth), built in 1626 and smothered in a rich mantle of stucco depicting the building's miraculous transportation from the Holy Land. Pride of place within is given to a limewood statue of the Black Madonna and Child, encased in silver.

Loreto church

Behind the Santa Casa, the much larger **Church of the Nativity** has a high cherub count, plenty of Baroque gilding and a lovely organ replete with music-making angels and putti. As in the church, most of the saints honoured in the **cloisters** are women. Without doubt, the weirdest of the lot is St Wilgefortis (Starosta in Czech), whose statue stands in the final chapel of the cloisters. Daughter of the king of Portugal, she was due to marry the king of Sicily, despite having taken a vow of virginity. God intervened and she grew a beard, whereupon the king of Sicily broke off the marriage and her father had her crucified. Wilgefortis thus became the patron saint of unhappily married women, and is depicted bearded on the cross (and easily mistaken for Christ in drag).

You can get some idea of the Loreto's serious financial backing in the church's **treasury**, whose master exhibit is a tasteless Viennese silver monstrance, studded with diamonds taken from the wedding dress of Countess Kolovrat, who made the Loreto sole heir to her fortune.

Nový svět

MAP p.34, POCKET MAP A11

Nestling in a shallow dip in the
northwest corner of Hradčany,
Nový svět provides a glimpse
of life on a totally different
scale. Similar in many ways to
the Golden Lane in the Hrad –
but without the crowds – this
picturesque cluster of brightly
coloured cottages is all that's left
of Hradčany's medieval slums,
painted up and sanitized in
the eighteenth and nineteenth
centuries.

Strahov Monastery

MAP p.34, POCKET MAP A12
Strahovské nadvoří 1 Ⓦ strahovmonastery
.cz. Libraries: Daily 9am–noon & 1–5pm;
120Kč. Gallery: Daily 9–11.30am &
noon–5pm; 120Kč.

The Baroque entrance to the
Strahov Monastery is topped by
a statue of St Norbert, who
founded the order in 1140 and
whose relics were brought here
in 1627. The church, which was
remodelled in Baroque times, is
well worth a peek for its colourful
frescoes relating to St Norbert's
life, but it's the monastery's
two ornate Baroque **libraries**
(*knihovny*) that are the real reason
for visiting Strahov.

The **Philosophical Hall** has
walnut bookcases so tall they
almost touch the frescoes on the
library's lofty ceiling, while the

paintings on the low-ceilinged
Theological Hall are framed by
wedding-cake-style stuccowork.
Look out, too, for the collection
of curios in the glass cabinets
outside the library, which
features shells, turtles, crabs,
lobsters, dried-up sea monsters,
butterflies, beetles and plastic
fruit. There's even a pair of
whales' penises displayed
alongside a narwhal horn,
harpoons and a model ship.

The monastery's collection of
religious art, displayed in the
Strahov Gallery (*obrazárna*)
above the cloisters, contains
one or two gems: a portrait of
Emperor Rudolf II by his court
painter, Hans von Aachen, plus
a superb portrait of Rembrandt's
elderly mother by Gerrit Dou.

Museum of Miniatures

MAP p.34, POCKET MAP A12
Strahovské nadvoří 11 Ⓦ muzeumminiatur
.cz. Daily 9am–5pm. 100Kč.

The (appropriately) small **Museum
of Miniatures** displays forty or
so works by the Russian **Anatoly
Konenko**, including the smallest
book in the world, a thirty-page
edition of Chekhov's *Chameleon*.
Among the other miracles of
miniature manufacture are the
Lord's Prayer written on a human
hair; a caravan of camels passing
through the eye of a needle; and
a flea bearing golden horseshoes,
scissors, and a key and lock.

Strahov Monastery

Shops

Folk Art

MAP p.34, POCKET MAP A12
Pohořelec 7. Daily 10am–9pm.

Specializes in a variety of handcrafted textiles including tablecloths, scarves and purses.

Výbor dobré vůle

MAP p.34, POCKET MAP D10
Zlatá ulička 19. Daily 9am–5pm.

All the crafts in this tiny shop in the Hrad are made by disabled children, and profits go to the Olga Havlová Foundation, set up by Václav Havel's late wife to help them. Hrad ticket required.

Cafés

Host

MAP p.34, POCKET MAP B11
Loretánská 15. Mon–Sat 11.30am–10pm, Sun 11.30am–9pm.

Down an inconspicuous flight of steps off Loretánská, this well-hidden restaurant has stupendous Malá Strana views from its glass front, a mix of Czech and safe-bet international mains (350–500Kč) and a 175Kč lunch menu.

Malý Buddha

MAP p.34, POCKET MAP A12
Úvoz 46. Tues–Sun noon–10pm.

Typical Prague teahouse decor, with a Buddhist altar in one corner and good vegetarian Vietnamese snacks on the menu. A very useful Hradčany haven.

Restaurants

U císařů (The Emperor)

MAP p.34, POCKET MAP B11
Loretánská 5 ☏ 220 518 484. Daily 10am–midnight.

Upmarket medieval place serving up hearty, meaty Czech dishes,

Malý Buddha

as well as trout, butterfish and fondue for 400Kč and upwards.

U ševce Matouše (The Cobbler Matouš)

MAP p.34, POCKET MAP A11
Loretánské náměstí 4 ☏ 220 514 536. Daily 11am–11pm.

Fried pork steak served with potato salad (300Kč) is the speciality of this former cobbler's, which is one of the few half-decent places to eat in the castle district.

Pubs and bars

Klašterní pivovar (The Monastery Brewery)

MAP p.34, POCKET MAP A12
Strahovské nádvoří 1. Daily 10am–10pm.

Tourist-friendly monastic brewery, offering their own light and dark St Norbert beers and Czech pub food.

U černého vola (The Black Ox)

MAP p.34, POCKET MAP A11
Loretánské náměstí 1. Daily 10am–10pm.

Great traditional Prague pub doing a brisk business serving huge quantities of popular light beer Velkopopovický kozel to thirsty local workers, soaked up with a few classic pub snacks.

Malá Strana

Malá Strana, Prague's picturesque "Little Quarter", sits below the castle and is in many ways the city's most entrancing area. Its many peaceful, often hilly, cobbled backstreets have changed very little since Mozart walked them during his frequent visits to Prague between 1787 and 1791. They conceal a whole host of quiet terraced gardens, as well as the wooded Petřín Hill, which together provide the perfect inner-city escape in the summer months. The Church of sv Mikuláš, by far the finest Baroque church in Prague, and the Museum Kampa, with its unrivalled collection of works by František Kupka, are the two major sights.

Malostranské náměstí

MAP p.42, POCKET MAP D11

Malostranské náměstí, Malá Strana's arcaded main square, is dominated and divided in two by the Baroque church of sv Mikuláš (see opposite). Trams and cars wind their way across the cobbles below the church, regularly dodged by a procession of people heading up the hill to the castle. On the square's north side at no. 18, distinguished by its two little turrets and rather shocking pistachio and vanilla colour scheme, is the **dům Smiřických**, where, in 1618, the Protestant posse met to decide how to get rid of Emperor Ferdinand's Catholic governors: whether to attack them with daggers, or, as

they eventually attempted, to kill them by chucking them out of the window of the Old Royal Palace (see p.29).

Parliament

MAP p.42, POCKET MAP D11
Sněmovna 4 ⓦ www.psp.cz.
The Czech parliament occupies a Neoclassical palace that served as the provincial Diet in the nineteenth century. Later it housed the National Assembly of the First Republic in 1918, the Czech National Council after federalization in 1968, and, since 1993, it has been home to the **Chamber of Deputies** (Poslanecká sněmovna), the (more important) lower house of the Czech parliament. To find out more,

View of the Church of sv Mikuláš

House sign on Nerudova

visit the **information centre** at Malostranské náměstí 6 (Mon–Fri 9am–4pm).

Church of sv Mikuláš

MAP p.42, POCKET MAP C11–D12
Malostranské náměstí Ⓦ stnicholas.cz.
Daily: March–Oct 9am–5pm; Nov–Feb 9am–4pm. 90Kč.

Towering over the whole of Malá Strana is the Baroque **Church of sv Mikuláš** (St Nicholas), whose giant green dome and tower are among the most characteristic landmarks on Prague's left bank. Built by the Jesuits in the early eighteenth century, it was their most ambitious project yet in Bohemia, and the ultimate symbol of their stranglehold on the country. Nothing about the relatively plain west facade prepares you for the overwhelming High Baroque interior. The vast fresco in the nave portrays some of the more fanciful miraculous feats of St Nicholas, while the dome at the east end of the church is even more impressive, thanks, more than anything, to its sheer height. Leering over you as you gaze up at the dome are four terrifyingly oversized and stern Church Fathers, one of whom brandishes a gilded thunderbolt, leaving no doubt as to the gravity of the Jesuit message. It's also possible to climb the **tower** (daily: April–Sept 10am–10pm; March & Oct 10am–8pm; Nov–Feb 10am–8pm; 90Kč) for fine views over Malá Strana and Charles Bridge.

Nerudova

MAP p.42, POCKET MAP C11
The busiest of the cobbled streets leading up to the castle is **Nerudova**. Historically, this was the city's main area for craftsmen, artisans and artists, though the shops and restaurants that line Nerudova now are mostly aimed at tourists heading for the castle. Many of the houses that line the street retain their medieval barn doors and peculiar pictorial house signs. One of Nerudova's fancier buildings, at no. 5, is the **Morzin Palace**, now the Romanian Embassy, its doorway supported by two Moors (a pun on the owner's name). Meanwhile, opposite, two giant eagles hold up the portal of the **Thun-Hohenštejn Palace**, now the Italian Embassy. Further up the street, according to legend, Casanova and Mozart are said to have met up at a ball given by the aristocrat owners of no. 33, the Bretfeld Palace.

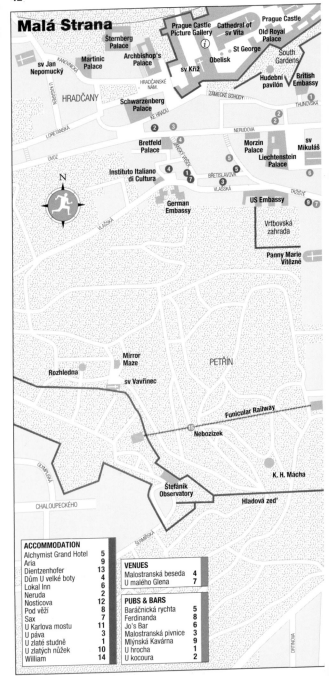

Malá Strana

Prague Castle
Prague Castle Picture Gallery
Cathedral of sv Víta
Old Royal Palace
St George
South Gardens
British Embassy
Hudební pavilón
Obelisk
sv Kříž
Sternberg Palace
Martinic Palace
Archbishop's Palace
sv Jan Nepomucký
HRADČANY
HRADČANSKÉ NÁM.
ZÁMECKÉ SCHODY
THUNOVSKÁ
Schwarzenberg Palace
KE HRADU
KANOVNICKÁ
U KASÁREN
LORETÁNSKÁ
ÚVOZ
Bretfeld Palace
Instituto Italiano di Cultura
NERUDOVA
Morzin Palace
sv Mikuláš
Liechtenstein Palace
JÁNSKÝ VRŠEK
BŘETISLAVOVA
VLAŠSKÁ
US Embassy
TRŽIŠTĚ
German Embassy
VLAŠSKÁ
Vrtbovská zahrada
Panny Marie Vítězné
N
Mirror Maze
PETŘÍN
Rozhledna
sv Vavřinec
Funicular Railway
Nebozízek
K. H. Mácha
OLYMPIJSKÁ
CHALOUPECKÉHO
Štefánik Observatory
Hladová zeď'
ŠERMÍŘSKÁ
DRTINOVA

ACCOMMODATION

Alchymist Grand Hotel	5
Aria	9
Dientzenhofer	13
Dům U velké boty	4
Lokal Inn	6
Neruda	2
Nosticova	12
Pod věží	8
Sax	7
U Karlova mostu	3
U páva	1
U zlaté studně	10
U zlatých nůžek	10
William	14

VENUES

Malostranská beseda	4
U malého Glena	7

PUBS & BARS

Baráčnická rychta	5
Ferdinanda	8
Jo's Bar	6
Malostranská pivnice	3
Mlýnská Kavárna	9
U hrocha	1
U kocoura	2

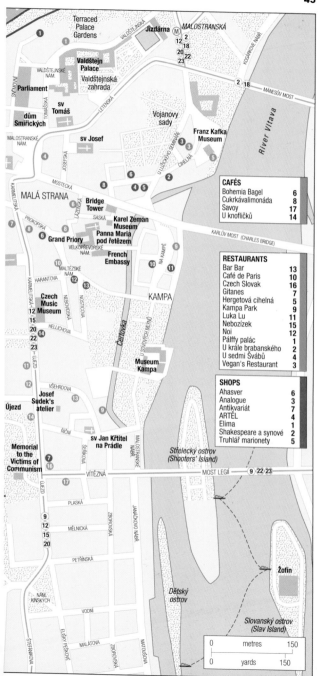

Terraced Palace Gardens

VALDŠTEJNSKÁ

Jizdárna

MALOSTRANSKÁ

M

2
12
18
20
22
23

Valdštejn Palace

VALDŠTEJNSKÉ NÁM.

Valdštejnská zahrada

Parliament

LETENSKÁ

2 18

MÁNESŮV MOST

sv Tomáš

dům Smiřických

MALOSTRANSKÉ NÁM.

Vojanovy sady

sv Josef

Franz Kafka Museum

River Vltava

MOSTECKÁ

MALÁ STRANA

Bridge Tower

Karel Zeman Museum

Panna Maria pod řetězem

Grand Priory

KARLŮV MOST (CHARLES BRIDGE)

French Embassy

VELKOPŘEVORSKÉ NÁM.

MALTÉZSKÉ NÁM.

KAMPA

Czech Music Museum

12
15
20
22
23

HELLICHOVA

ÚJEZD

Museum Kampa

VŠEHRDOVA

Josef Sudek's atelier

Újezd

sv Jan Křtitel na Prádle

Memorial to the Victims of Communism

VÍTĚZNÁ

Střelecký ostrov (Shooters' Island)

MOST LEGIÍ

9 22 23

PLASKÁ

9
12
15
20

MĚLNICKÁ

PETŘÍNSKÁ

Žofín

NÁM. KINSKÝCH

VODNÍ

Dětský ostrov

Slovanský ostrov (Slav Island)

MALÁTOVA

CAFÉS	
Bohemia Bagel	6
Cukrkávalimonáda	8
Savoy	17
U knoflíčků	14

RESTAURANTS	
Bar Bar	13
Café de Paris	10
Czech Slovak	16
Gitanes	7
Hergetová cihelná	5
Kampa Park	9
Luka Lu	11
Nebozízek	15
Noi	12
Pálffy palác	1
U krále brabanského	2
U sedmi Švábů	4
Vegan's Restaurant	3

SHOPS	
Ahasver	6
Analogue	3
Antikvariát	7
ARTĚL	4
Elima	1
Shakespeare a synové	2
Truhlář marionety	5

0	metres	150
0	yards	150

Valdštejn Palace

MAP p.42, POCKET MAP D11
Valdštejnské náměstí 4 Ⓦ senat.cz.
Tours: April, May & Oct Sat & Sun
10am–5pm; June–Sept Sat & Sun
10am–6pm. Free.

Built in the 1620s for **Albrecht von Waldstein**, commander of the Imperial Catholic armies of the Thirty Years' War, the Valdštejn Palace was one of the first and largest Baroque palaces in the city. Nowadays, it houses the Czech parliament's upper house, or **Senate** (Senát), whose sumptuous Baroque chambers can be visited on a guided tour at the weekend in warmer months.

Karel Zeman Museum

MAP p.42, POCKET MAP D12
Saská 3 Ⓦ muzeumkarlazemana.cz.
Daily 10am–7pm. 200Kč.

Czech animator, director and special effects innovator **Karel Zeman** influenced a generation of filmmakers and technicians, from George Lucas and Steven Spielberg to Tim Burton and Terry Gilliam. This museum covers the director's entire filmography. Exhibits detail the **special effects** techniques used in individual movies, each accompanied by a video showcasing their use. Best of all is the interactive nature of the museum: visitors can record themselves in front of a rear-projected image or film a shoot through a 3D model.

Valdštejnská zahrada (Palace Gardens)

MAP p.42, POCKET MAP D11
April, May & Oct Mon–Fri 7.30am–6pm;
June–Sept Mon–Fri 7.30am–7pm, Sat & Sun 10am–7pm. Free.

Valdštejn Palace's **formal gardens** are accessible from the palace's main entrance, and also from a doorway in the palace walls along Letenská. The gardens' focus is a gigantic Italianate **sala terrena**, a monumental loggia decorated with frescoes of the Trojan Wars, which stands at the end of an avenue of sculptures. In addition, there are a number of peacocks, a pseudo grotto along the south wall, with quasi-stalactites, and an aviary of eagle owls.

Terraced Palace Gardens

MAP p.42, POCKET MAP D10
Valdštejnská. Daily: April & Oct 10am–6pm; May–Sept 10am–7pm. 100Kč.

A great way to reach the Hrad is via Malá Strana's Baroque **Terraced Palace Gardens**, on the steep slopes where the royal vineyards used to be. Dotted with

The sala terrena in the Valdštejn Palace's gardens

urns and statuary, they command superb views over Prague. From Valdštejnská, you enter via the Ledeburská zahrada, gardens which connect higher up with the castle's own South Gardens (see p.32).

(see p.32).

Franz Kafka Museum

MAP p.42, POCKET MAP E11
Cihelná 2b ⓦ kafkamuseum.cz.
Daily 10am–6pm. 200Kč.

This museum offers a fairly sophisticated rundown of the life and works of the Czech–German writer **Franz Kafka** (1883–1924). The first section includes photos of the old ghetto into which Kafka was born; an invoice from his father's shop, with the logo of a jackdaw (*kavka* in Czech); copies of his job applications, requests for sick leave; one of his reports on accident prevention in the workplace; and facsimiles of his pen sketches. Upstairs, audiovisuals and theatrical trickery are used to explore the torment, alienation and claustrophobia Kafka felt throughout his life and expressed in his writings. On a lighter note, don't miss David Černý's **Pissing Figures** (Čůrající postavy) statue in the courtyard outside, which features two men urinating into a pool shaped like the Czech Republic.

Maltézské náměstí

MAP p.42, POCKET MAP D12
Maltézské náměstí is one of a number of delightful little squares between Karmelitská and the river. At the north end is a plague column, topped by a statue of St John the Baptist, but the square takes its name from the Order of the Knights of St John of Jerusalem (now known as the Maltese Knights). In 1160 they founded the nearby church of **Panna Maria pod řetězem** (St Mary below-the-chain), so-called because it was the Knights'

Franz Kafka Museum, Pissing Figures

job to guard the Judith Bridge (predecessor to Charles Bridge). Only two bulky Gothic towers are still standing and the apse is now thoroughly Baroque, but the nave remains unfinished and open to the elements.

John Lennon Wall

MAP p.42, POCKET MAP D12
The pretty little square of **Velkopřevorské náměstí** echoes to the sound of music from the nearby Prague conservatoire, its northern limit marked by the garden wall of the Grand Priory of the Maltese Knights. Here, following John Lennon's death in 1980, Prague's youth established an ad hoc shrine smothered in graffiti tributes to the ex-Beatle. The running battle between police and graffiti artists continued well into the 1990s, with the society of Maltese Knights taking an equally dim view of the mural, but a compromise has now been reached and the wall's scribblings legalized. While you're in the vicinity, be sure to check out the love padlocks which have been secured to the railings of the nearby bridge.

Kampa

MAP p.42, POCKET MAP D13–E12

Heading for **Kampa**, the largest of the Vltava's islands, with its cafés, old mills and serene riverside park, is the perfect way to escape the crowds. The island is separated from the left bank by Prague's "Little Venice", a thin strip of water called **Čertovka** (Devil's Stream), which used to power several millwheels until the last one ceased to function in 1936. For much of its history, the island was the city's main washhouse area, a fact commemorated by the church of **sv Jan Křtitel na Prádle** (St John-the-Baptist at the Cleaners) on Říční. It wasn't until the sixteenth and seventeenth centuries that the Nostitz family, who owned Kampa, began to develop the northern half of the island; the southern half was left untouched, and today is laid out as a public park, with riverside views across to Staré Město. To the north, the oval main square, **Na Kampě**, once a pottery market, is studded with slender acacia trees and cut through by Charles

View of Kampa from Charles Bridge

Bridge, to which it is connected by a double flight of steps.

Throughout Kampa, look out for the high-water marks from the devastating flood of 2002 – water reached first-floor rooms here.

Museum Kampa

MAP p.42, POCKET MAP D13–E13

U Sovových mlýnů 2 ⓦ museumkampa.cz. Daily 10am–6pm. 240Kč.

Housed in an old riverside watermill, **Museum Kampa** is dedicated to the private art collection of Jan and Meda Mládek. As well as temporary exhibitions, the stylish modern gallery also houses the best of the Mládeks' collection, including a whole series of works by the Czech artist **František Kupka**, seen by many as the father of abstract art. These range from early Expressionist watercolours to transitional pastels like *Fauvist Chair* from 1910, and more abstract works, such as the seminal oil painting, *Cathedral and Study for Fugue in Two Colours*, from around 1912. The gallery also displays a good selection of Cubist and later interwar works by the sculptor **Otto Gutfreund** and a few collages by postwar surrealist Jiří Kolář.

Vrtbovská zahrada

MAP p.42, POCKET MAP C12

Karmelitská 25 ⓦ vrtbovska.cz. April–Oct daily 10am–6pm. 65Kč.

One of the most elusive of Malá Strana's many Baroque gardens, the **Vrtbovská zahrada** was founded on the site of the former vineyards of the Vrtbov Palace. Laid out on Tuscan-style terraces, dotted with ornamental urns and statues of the gods by Matthias Bernhard Braun, the gardens twist their way up the lower slopes of Petřín Hill to an observation terrace from where there's a spectacular rooftop perspective on the city.

Church of Panny Marie Vítězné

Church of Panny Marie Vítězné

MAP p.42, POCKET MAP C12–D12
Karmelitská 9 Ⓦ pragjesu.info. Mon–Sat
8.30am–7pm, Sun 8.30am–8pm. Free.

Surprisingly, given its rather
plain exterior (it started life as a
German Protestant church), the
church of **Panny Marie Vítězné**
(Our Lady of Victory) houses
a high-kitsch wax effigy of the
infant Jesus as a precocious
3-year-old, enthroned in a glass
case. Attributed with miraculous
powers, this image, known as the
Bambino di Praga (or Prazské
Jezulátko), became an object of
international pilgrimage and
continues to attract visitors,
mainly Catholics from southern
Europe and Poland. The *bambino*
boasts a vast personal wardrobe
of expensive swaddling clothes
– approaching a hundred
separate outfits at the last count
– regularly changed by the
Carmelite nuns. A small number
of these outfits is on display in a
miniscule museum, which can
be found up the spiral staircase
in the south aisle, including a
selection of his velvet and satin
overgarments sent from all over
the world.

Czech Music Museum

MAP p.42, POCKET MAP D12–D13
Karmelitská 2 Ⓦ nm.cz. Wed–Mon
10am–6pm. 120Kč.

Housed in a former nunnery,
the permanent collection of the
Czech Music Museum (České
muzeum hudby) begins with a
crazy cut-and-splice medley of
musical film footage from the
last century. Next up is August
Förster's pioneering quarter-tone
grand piano from 1924 – you
can even listen to Alois Hába's
microtonal *Fantazie no. 10*,
composed for, and performed
on, its three keyboards. After
this rather promising start, the
museum settles down into a
conventional display of old central
European instruments, from a
precious Baumgartner clavichord
and an Amati violin to Neapolitan
mandolins and a vast contrabass
over 2m in height. Best of all is the
fact that you can hear many of the
instruments on display being put
through their paces at listening
posts in each room.

Josef Sudek's Atelier

MAP p.42, POCKET MAP D13
Újezd 30 ⓦ sudek-atelier.cz. Tues–Sun
noon–6pm. 10Kč.

Hidden behind the buildings on the east side of the Újezd is a faithful reconstruction of the cute little wooden garden studio, where **Josef Sudek** (1896–1976), the great Czech photographer, lived with his sister from 1927. Sudek moved out in 1958, but he used the place as his darkroom to the end of his life. The twisted tree in the front garden will be familiar to those acquainted with the numerous photographic cycles he based around the studio. The building itself has only a few of Sudek's personal effects and is now used for temporary exhibitions of other photographers' works.

Memorial to the Victims of Communism

MAP p.42, POCKET MAP D14
Újezd/Vítězná.

In 2002, the Czechs finally erected a **Memorial to the Victims of Communism**. The location has no particular resonance with the period,

Memorial to the Victims of Communism

but the memorial itself has an eerie quality, especially when illuminated at night. It consists of a series of statues and self-portraits by sculptor **Olbram Zoubek**, standing on steps leading down from Petřín Hill behind, each in varying stages of disintegration. The inscription at the base of the monument reads "205,486 convicted, 248 executed, 4500 died in prison, 327 annihilated at the border, 170,938 emigrated".

Petřín

MAP p.42, POCKET MAP A13–C13
The hilly wooded slopes of **Petřín**, distinguished by the Rozhledna (see opposite), a scaled-down version of the Eiffel Tower, make up the largest green space in the city centre. The tower is just one of several exhibits which survive from the **1891 Prague Exhibition**, whose modest legacy also includes the hill's funicular railway (see opposite). At the top of the hill, it's possible to trace the southernmost perimeter wall of the old city, popularly known as the **Hunger Wall** (Hladová zeď). Instigated in the 1460s by

The funicular railway

Štefánik Observatory

MAP p.42, POCKET MAP B14–C14
Ⓦ observatory.cz. Tues–Sun, times
vary. 65Kč.

At the top of the hill, the Hunger
Wall (see opposite) runs southeast
from the funicular to Petřín's
Štefánik Observatory. The small
astronomical exhibition inside is
hardly worth bothering with, but
if it's a clear night, a quick peek
through either of the observatory's
two powerful telescopes is a treat.

Rozhledna

MAP p.42, POCKET MAP B13
Ⓦ petrinska-rozhledna.cz. Daily: March &
Oct 10am–8pm; April–Sept 10am–10pm;
Nov–Feb 10am–6pm. 150Kč.

Petřín's most familiar landmark is its lookout tower,
or **Rozhledna**, a miniature,
octagonal version of the Eiffel
Tower, a mere fifth of the size
of the original. It was built after
members of the Czech Hiking
Club visited Paris in 1889 – so
taken were they with the Paris
tower that they decided to build
a copy in Prague. Many see it
as a tribute to the city's strong
cultural and political links with
Paris at the time.

The view from the public
gallery is almost the best in
the capital – at least when the
weather cooperates.

Mirror Maze (Bludiště)

MAP p.42, POCKET MAP B13
Ⓦ petrinska-rozhledna.cz. Daily: March &
Oct 10am–8pm; April–Sept 10am–10pm;
Nov–Feb 10am–6pm. 90Kč.

The **Mirror Maze** is housed in a
mini neo-Gothic castle complete
with mock drawbridge. As well
as the maze, there is an action-
packed, life-sized **diorama** of the
victory of Prague's students and
Jews over the Swedes on Charles
Bridge in 1648. The humour of
the convex and concave mirrors
that lie beyond the diorama is so
simple it has both adults and kids
giggling away.

Emperor Charles IV, it was much
lauded at the time as a great
public work which provided
employment for the burgeoning
ranks of the city's destitute (hence
its name); in fact, much of the
wall's construction was paid for
by the expropriation of Jewish
property.

Funicular railway

MAP p.42, POCKET MAP B13–C13
The **funicular railway** (lanová
dráha) up to Petřín departs
from a station just off Újezd
and runs every 10–15min (daily
9am–11.30pm); ordinary public
transport tickets and travel
passes are valid on the service.
At the Nebozízek stop halfway
up, where the carriages pass
each other, you can get out and
soak up the spectacular view
at the Nebozízek (Little Auger)
restaurant (see p.52); the top
station is closest to the Mirror
Maze and Rozhledna.

Though the entire journey is
only 510m long, and lasts just a
few minutes, it saves you a lot of
legwork.

Shops

Ahasver

MAP p.42, POCKET MAP D12
Prokopská 3. Tues–Sun 11am–6pm.

A delightful little shop selling antique gowns and jewellery, as well as paintings, porcelain and glass.

Analogue

MAP p.42, POCKET MAP C12
Vlašská 10. Mon–Fri 10am–7pm, Sat noon–6pm.

The future is analogue at this tiny temple to all things non-digital, where they specialize in film photography.

Antikvariát

MAP p.42, POCKET MAP D13
Újezd 26. Mon–Fri 11am–6pm.

Small second-hand bookshop that also sells old film and theatre posters.

ARTĚL

MAP p.42, POCKET MAP D12
U lužického semináře 7. Daily 10am–7pm.

Specializing in handcrafted Bohemian crystal glassware, the shop is a treasure-trove of unique pieces decorated with lovely motifs.

Cafés on Kampa

Elima

MAP p.42, POCKET MAP C12
Janský vršek 5. Daily 10am–6pm.

This tiny little shop in the backstreets sells beautiful, inexpensive, handmade Polish pottery from Boleslawiec (Bunzlau).

Shakespeare a synové

MAP p.42, POCKET MAP E12
U lužického semináře 10. Daily 11am–7pm.

Don't be deceived by the tiny frontage; this is a wonderful, large, rambling and well-stocked English-language bookstore. A perfect spot in which to while away some time.

Truhlář marionety

MAP p.42, POCKET MAP D12
U lužického semináře 5. Daily 10am–9pm.

Prague is awash with cheap, and frankly quite gawdy, puppets, but the Truhlář family are a cut above the rest. Wooden marionettes off the peg from 1600Kč – bespoke from 12,000Kč.

Cafés

Bohemia Bagel

MAP p.42, POCKET MAP D12
Lázeňská 19 ⓦ bohemiabagel.cz. Mon–Fri 7.30am–6pm, Sat 7.30am–7pm.

Malá Strana branch of the successful self-service chain (a favourite with Prague's foreign residents) situated close to Charles Bridge, serving filled bagels, all-day breakfasts, soup and chilli.

Cukrkávalimonáda

MAP p.42, POCKET MAP D12
Lázeňská 7. Daily 9am–7pm.

Very professional and well-run café, serving good brasserie-style dishes, as well as coffee and croissants, with tables overlooking the church of Panna Maria pod řetězem.

Savoy

MAP p.42, POCKET MAP D14
Vítězná 5. Mon–Fri 8am–10.30pm, Sat &
Sun 9am–10.30pm.

An L-shaped Habsburg-era café
from 1893 with a superb, neo-
Renaissance ceiling; you can just
have a coffee or a snack if you
want, but it doubles as a very good
restaurant, with mains (including
lots of seafood) from 400Kč.

Restaurants

Bar Bar

MAP p.42, POCKET MAP D13
Všehrdova 17 ☎ 257 312 246. Mon–Sat
11am–11pm, Sun noon–10pm.

Funky cellar restaurant serving
healthy Czech and European
dishes. The short menu (around
200Kč) includes turkey breast,
salmon and *tortellini*.

Café de Paris

MAP p.42, POCKET MAP D12
Maltézské náměstí 4 ☎ 603 160 718.
Daily 11.30am–midnight.

A cosy, family-run restaurant
based on Geneva's famous *Café de
Paris*. The short menu's signature
dish is beef entrecôte in a creamy
sauce composed to a secret recipe
(379Kč); there's a tofu version, too.

Czech Slovak

MAP p.42, POCKET MAP D14
Újezd 20 ☒ czechslovak.cz. Daily
noon–11.30pm.

Upmarket return to the halcyon
days of Czechoslovak cuisine with
its twenty first-century white and
black decor, up-lit in neon purple.
Mains (250–350Kč) include
dishes from across the former
Czechoslovakia.

Gitanes

MAP p.42, POCKET MAP C12
Tržiště 7 ☎ 257 530 163. Daily noon–
midnight.

A surreal interior and well-executed
Mediterranean food inspired

Savoy

by Dalmatian and Montenegrin
cuisine. Mains 200–700Kč.

Hergetová cihelná

MAP p.42, POCKET MAP E11
Cihelná 2b ☎ 296 826 103. Daily
noon–1am.

Slick restaurant serving Tiger
prawn starters, plus pasta and
risotto, and the odd traditional
Czech dish (around 500Kč).
The riverside summer terrace
overlooks Charles Bridge.

Kampa Park

MAP p.42, POCKET MAP E12
Na Kampě 8b ☎ 296 826 102. Daily
11.30am–1am.

Pink house exquisitely located
right by the Vltava on Kampa
Island, with a superb fish
and seafood menu (mains
600–900Kč), top-class service
and tables outside in summer.

Luka Lu

MAP P.42, POCKET MAP D13
Újezd 33. Daily 11am–midnight.

This Serb restaurant specialising
in grilled Balkan meat dishes
(200–400Kč) is touting for the most
colourful Prague restaurant award,
its art-filled walls competing with
floorboards, ceiling and fittings
painted in the brightest of hues.

Nebozízek (Little Auger)

MAP p.42, POCKET MAP C13
Petřínské sady 411 ☏ 257 315 329. Daily
11am–11pm.

Situated at the halfway stop on the
Petřín funicular, the view from
Nebozízek is superb; there's an
outdoor terrace and a traditional
Czech menu with game dishes
from around 300Kč.

Noi

MAP p.42, POCKET MAP D13
Újezd 19 ☏ 257 311 411. Daily 11am–1am.

A stylish, atmospheric restaurant
dishing out some of the tastiest,
spiciest Thai food in Prague (mains
200–300Kč), though it's not great
for vegetarians. There's a lovely
courtyard patio round the back.

Pálffy Palác

MAP p.42, POCKET MAP D11
Valdštejnská 14 ☏ 257 530 522. Daily
11am–11pm.

The restaurant occupies a grand
candle-lit room on the first floor
of an old Baroque palace, and
features a wonderful outdoor

Pálffy Palác

terrace from which you can
survey the red rooftops of Malá
Strana. The international menu is
renowned for its creative dishes
(500–700Kč).

U krále brabantského

MAP p.42, POCKET MAP C11
Thunovská 15. Mon 11am–10pm,
Tues–Thurs & Sun 11am–11pm, Fri &
Sat 11am–midnight.

This rough, medieval tavern –
which claims to be Prague's oldest
– has been serving platters of meat
and jugs of ale since 1375. Everyone
from King Václav IV to Jaroslav
Hášek is said to have eaten here.

U sedmi Švábů (The Seven Swabians)

MAP p.42, POCKET MAP C11
Janský vršek 14 ☏ 257 531 455. Daily
11am–11pm.

Named after the Grimm brothers'
tale, this torch-lit tavern serves up
traditional Czech beer and food
(165–495Kč) to the occasional
accompaniment of medieval
shenanigans from fire breathing
to sword fighting.

Vegan's Restaurant

MAP p.42, POCKET MAP C11
Nerudova 36. Daily 11.30am–9.30pm.

A vegan "old Bohemian feast"
would seem to be an impossibly
incompatible culinary pairing to
pull off, but the mix of buckwheat,
millet, barley, mushrooms and
vegetables is tasty and filling.
Other meat-free options (175–
230Kč) include curries, veggie
burgers and fruit dumplings.

Pubs and bars

Baráčnická rychta

MAP p.42, POCKET MAP C12
Na tržiště 23 ⊛ baracnickarychta.cz.
Daily 11.30am–11.30pm.

Všebaráčnická rychta (as it's
also known) is a nostalgia-
inducing, wood-panelled beer

hall dedicated to keeping things traditionally Czech in Malá Strana. One of the few 1930s Modernist buildings in the area.

Ferdinanda

MAP p.42, POCKET MAP C12
Karmelitská 18. Mon–Sat 11am–11pm, Sun 11am–5pm.

The Ferdinand brewery's second pub in Prague has four brews on tap (both their dark and the pale lager 11° are delicious). Good lunch menu (Mon–Fri).

Jo's Bar

MAP p.42, POCKET MAP C12
Malostranské náměstí 7. Daily noon–midnight.

Jo's is the city's original American backpacker hangout. Though it no longer has quite the same vitality, it remains a good place to meet other travellers. There's a club downstairs.

Malostranská pivnice

MAP p.42, POCKET MAP E11
Cihelná 3. Daily 11am–midnight, Fri & Sat 11am–1am.

Be warned: they spot tourists a mile away, but for excellent Pilsner, as well as dark Kozel beers in a quiet courtyard, this *pivnice* is hard to beat.

Mlýnská kavárna

MAP p.42, POCKET MAP D13
Všehrdova 14 (entry from Kampa Park). Daily noon–midnight.

This quiet spot on Kampa Island attracts journalists, politicians and artists, all hanging out around a rough wooden table, at the large bar, or on the terrace.

U hrocha (The Hippopotamus)

MAP p.42, POCKET MAP C11
Thunovská 10. Daily noon–10.30pm.

A close-knit bunch of locals fill this small, smoky Czech *pivnice*, which is located close to the British Embassy and serves Pilsner Urquell.

U kocoura (The Cat)

MAP p.42, POCKET MAP D11
Nerudova 2. Daily noon–10.30pm.

The most famous Czech pub on Nerudova inevitably attracts tourists, but the locals come here too for the Pilsner Urquell and Budvar, plus the obvious Czech stomach-fillers.

Venues

Malostranská beseda

MAP p.42, POCKET MAP D11
Malostranské náměstí 21 ☎ 257 409 123, ⓦ malostranska-beseda.cz. Daily 5pm–midnight.

This authentically Czech venue started life as Malá Strana's original town hall, a function it served until 1748. Refurbished a decade ago, it's one of the best places to catch local rock and big beat bands, from both Prague and the countryside.

U malého Glena (Little Glenn's)

MAP p.42, POCKET MAP D12
Karmelitská 23 ⓦ www.malyglen.cz. Live music nightly 7.30pm–1am.

The tiny downstairs stage at *U Malého Glena* hosts an eclectic mix of Latin jazz, bebop and blues. There's a cover charge of 150–200Kč.

U malého Glena

Staré Město

Staré Město – literally the "Old Town" – is Prague's most central, vital ingredient. The busiest restaurants and pubs are here, and during the day a gaggle of shoppers and tourists fills its complex and utterly confusing web of narrow byways. Yet despite all the commercial activity, there are still plenty of residential streets, giving the area a lived-in feel that is rarely found in European city centres. At the heart of the district is the Old Town Square (Staroměstské náměstí), Prague's showpiece main square, easily the most magnificent in central Europe, and a great place to get your bearings before heading off into the labyrinthine backstreets. The best approach is from the city's most famous medieval landmark, the statue-encrusted Charles Bridge.

Charles Bridge (Karlův most)

MAP p.56, POCKET MAP E12

Bristling with statuary and crowded with people, **Charles Bridge** is by far the city's most famous monument. Built in the fourteenth century by Charles IV, the bridge originally featured just a simple crucifix. The first sculpture wasn't added until 1683, when **St John of Nepomuk** appeared. His statue was such a propaganda success that the Catholic church authorities ordered another 21 to be erected between 1706 and 1714. Individually, only a few of the works are outstanding, but taken collectively, set against the backdrop of the Hrad, the effect is breathtaking.

The bridge is now one of the city's most popular places to hang out, day and night: the crush of sightseers never abates during the day, when the niches created by the bridge-piers are occupied by souvenir-hawkers and buskers,

Charles Bridge at night

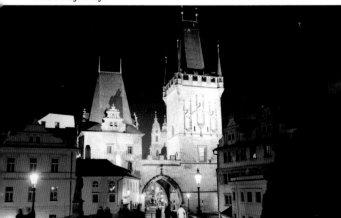

Church of sv František z Assisi

but at night things calm down a bit, and the views are, if anything, even more spectacular.

You can climb both of the mighty Gothic **bridge towers** for a bird's-eye view of the masses pouring across. The one on the Malá Strana side (daily: April–Sept 10am–10pm; March & Oct 10am–8pm; Nov–Feb 10am–6pm; 90Kč) features two unequal towers, connected by a castellated arch, which forms the entrance to the bridge. The Staré Město one (same hours and entry fee) is arguably the finer of the two, its eastern facade still encrusted in Gothic cake-like decorations from Peter Parler's workshop.

Church of sv František z Assisi (St Francis of Assisi)

MAP p.56 POCKET MAP F12
Křížovnické náměstí.

Built in the 1680s for the Czech **Order of Knights of the Cross with a Red Star** (the original gatekeepers of the bridge), the interior of this half-brick church is covered in rich marble and gilded furnishings and dominated by its huge dome, decorated with a vast fresco of

The Last Judgement and rich marble furnishings.

Charles Bridge Museum (Muzeum Karlova mostu)

MAP p.56, POCKET MAP F12
Křížovnické náměstí 3
ⓦ muzeumkarlovamostu.cz. Daily: May–Sept 10am–8pm; Oct–April 10am–6pm. 170Kč.

Those with an interest in stone-masonry and engineering will enjoy the exhibition; everyone else will probably get more out of the archive film footage.

Church of sv Salvátor (St Saviour)

MAP p.56, POCKET MAP F12
Křížovnické náměstí.

The facade of the **Church of sv Salvátor** prickles with saintly statues which are lit up attractively at night. Founded in 1593, it marks the beginning of the Jesuits' rise to power and is part of the Klementinum (see p.58). Like many Jesuit churches, its design copies that of the Gesù church in Rome; it's worth a quick look, if only for the frothy stucco plasterwork and delicate ironwork in its triple-naved interior.

Staré Město

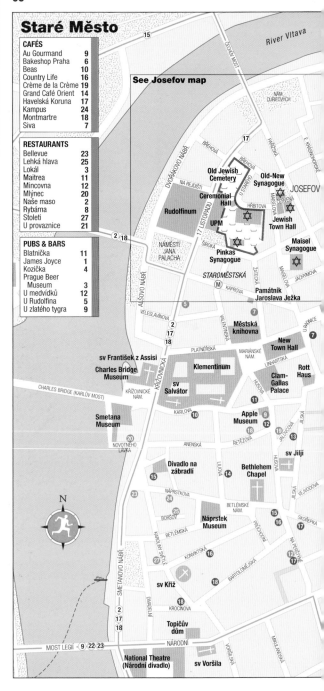

CAFÉS

Au Gourmand	9
Bakeshop Praha	6
Beas	10
Country Life	16
Crème de la Crème	19
Grand Café Orient	14
Havelská Koruna	17
Kampus	24
Montmartre	18
Siva	7

RESTAURANTS

Bellevue	23
Lehká hlava	25
Lokál	3
Maitrea	11
Mincovna	12
Mlýnec	20
Naše maso	2
Rybárna	8
Století	27
U provaznice	21

PUBS & BARS

Blatnička	11
James Joyce	1
Kozička	4
Prague Beer Museum	3
U medvídků	12
U Rudolfina	5
U zlatého tygra	9

River Vltava

ČECHŮV MOST

See Josefov map

NÁM. CURIEOVÝCH

E. KRÁSNOHORSKÉ

BŘEHOVÁ

17

PAŘÍŽSKÁ

BŘEHOVÁ

DVOŘÁKOVO NÁBŘ.

NA REJDIŠTI

U STAREHO

Old Jewish Cemetery

Old-New Synagogue

JOSEFOV

ČERVENÁ

MAISELOVA

Ceremonial Hall

HŘBITOVA

Rudolfinum

17 LISTOPADU

UPM

Jewish Town Hall

2 18

NÁMĚSTÍ JANA PALACHA

ŠIROKÁ

Pinkas Synagogue

Maisel Synagogue

MAISELOVA

JÁCHYMOVA

ALŠOVO NÁBŘ.

STAROMĚSTSKÁ

ŽATECKÁ

M KAPROVA

Památník Jaroslava Ježka

VELESLAVÍNOVA

2
17
18

5

7

VALENTINSKÁ

Městská knihovna

7

U RADNICE

PLATNÉŘSKÁ

MARIÁNSKÉ NÁM.

New Town Hall

sv František z Assisi

Charles Bridge Museum

KŘIŽOVNICKÁ

Klementinum

LINHARTSKÁ

Clam-Gallas Palace

Rott Haus

CHARLES BRIDGE (KARLŮV MOST)

KŘIŽOVNICKÉ NÁM.

sv Salvátor

KARLOVA

HUSOVA

Smetana Museum

10

Apple Museum

9

18 12

19

13

JALOVCOVA

JILSKÁ

20

NOVOTNÉHO LÁVKA

ANENSKÁ

ŘETĚZOVÁ

sv Jiljí

HUSOVA

Divadlo na zábradlí

15

LILIOVÁ

14

Bethlehem Chapel

BETLÉMSKÉ NÁM.

JILSKÁ

VEJVODOVA

N

23

NÁPRSTKOVA

24

25

BORŠOV

Náprstek Museum

15

16

SKOŘEPKA

17

27

KARLOVY LÁZNĚ

BETLÉMSKÁ

KONVIKTSKÁ

16

PROKOPSKÁ

BARTOLOMĚJSKÁ

12

17

SMETANOVO NÁBŘ.

sv Kříž

18

KROCÍNOVA

DIVADELNÍ

2
17
18

Topičův dům

NÁRODNÍ

VORŠILSKÁ

MIKULANDSKÁ

MOST LEGIÍ 9 22 23

National Theatre (Národní divadlo)

sv Voršila

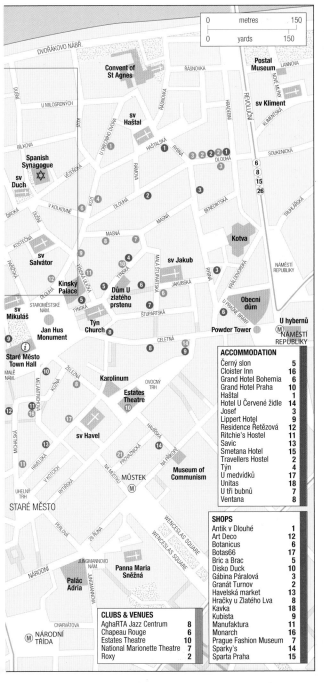

ACCOMMODATION

Černý slon	5
Cloister Inn	16
Grand Hotel Bohemia	6
Grand Hotel Praha	10
Haštal	1
Hotel U Červené židle	14
Josef	3
Lippert Hotel	9
Residence Řetězová	12
Ritchie's Hostel	11
Savic	13
Smetana Hotel	15
Travellers Hostel	2
Týn	4
U medvídků	17
Unitas	18
U tří bubnů	7
Ventana	8

SHOPS

Antik v Dlouhé	1
Art Deco	12
Botanicus	6
Botas66	17
Bric a Brac	5
Disko Duck	3
Gábina Páralová	10
Granát Turnov	2
Havelská market	13
Hračky u Zlatého Lva	8
Kavka	18
Kubista	9
Manufaktura	11
Monarch	16
Prague Fashion Museum	7
Sparky's	14
Sparta Praha	15

CLUBS & VENUES

AghaRTA Jazz Centrum	8
Chapeau Rouge	6
Estates Theatre	10
National Marionette Theatre	7
Roxy	2

Karlova

MAP p.56, POCKET MAP F12

As the quickest route between
Charles Bridge and the Old Town
Square, the narrow street of
Karlova is packed with people day
and night, their attention divided
between the souvenir shops and
not losing their way as the street
zigzags to the river. With Europop
blaring from several shops, jesters'
hats and puppets in abundance,
and heaps of dubious jewellery on
offer, the whole atmosphere can
be a bit oppressive in the height
of summer – a more peaceful
alternative is to head through the
Klementinum's courtyards.

Klementinum

MAP p.56, POCKET MAP F12
Karlova 1 ⓦ klementinum.com. Daily:
April–Oct 10am–5pm; Nov–March
10am–4pm. 220Kč.

As they stroll down Karlova, few
people notice the **former Jesuit
College** on the north side of the

Puppets for sale on Karlova

street, which covers a huge area
second in size only to the castle.
The Habsburg rulers summoned
the Jesuits to Prague in 1556 to
help bolster the Catholic cause in
Bohemia, and put them in charge
of the entire education system,
only to expel them in 1773. The
complex now belongs to the state
and Charles University and houses,
among other things, the **National
Library**. Aside from the ornate
Mirrored Chapel (Zrcadlová
kaple), a choice classical music
venue, the Klementinum's most
easily accessible attractions are
open to the public on a 45-minute
guided tour (in English). The most
spectacular sight is the **Baroque
Library**, a long room lined with
leather tomes, whose ceiling is
decorated with one continuous
illusionistic fresco praising secular
wisdom, and whose wrought-iron
gallery balustrade is held up by
wooden barley-sugar columns.
Upstairs, at roughly the centre
of the Klementinum complex, is
the **Astronomical Tower**, from
which there's a superb view over
central Prague. The weather has
been recorded here since 1775,
one of the world's longest periods
of continual meteorological
observation.

Apple Museum

MAP p.56, POCKET MAP F12
Husova 21 ⓦ applemuseum.com.
Daily 10am–10pm. 290Kč.

Just off Karlova, the medieval
lanes of Prague's Old Town
provide an unlikely location
for one of the world's best
computer technology museums.
Established in 2015 using items
from private collections, the
Apple Museum is unmissable,
even for those with an aversion
to Macs, iPads and iPhones.
Guided – aptly enough – by your
smartphone, the exhibition is the
definitive Apple collection, with
everything from Steve Jobs' New
Balance trainers and the very

The Rott Haus, Malé náměstí

first Apple I computer to chunky 1990s printers and a section on Pixar, founded by Jobs in 1986.

New Town Hall (Nová radnice)

MAP p.56, POCKET MAP F12–G12
Mariánské náměstí 2.

The most striking features of the rather severe **New Town Hall** are the two gargantuan Art Nouveau statues which stand guard at either corner of the building. The one on the left, looking a bit like Darth Vader, is the "Iron Knight", mascot of the armourers' guild; to the right is the caricatured sixteenth-century Jewish sage and scholar, **Rabbi Löw**. According to legend, Löw was visited by Death on several occasions, but escaped his clutches until he reached the ripe old age of 97, when the Grim Reaper hid in a rose innocently given to him by his granddaughter. He is also credited with creating the Golem, a mute Frankenstein's monster type of figure, which periodically ran amok in Prague (see p.77).

Since 1945 the building has been the seat and official residence of the mayor of Prague.

Malé náměstí

MAP p.56, POCKET MAP G12

A little cobbled square at the eastern end of Karlova, **Malé náměstí** was originally settled by French merchants in the twelfth century and is home to the city's first apothecary, **U zlaté koruny** (The Golden Crown), which was opened by a Florentine in 1353 at no. 13. The former pharmacy boasts beautiful chandeliers and a restored Baroque interior, though it's now a jeweller's. The square's best-known building is the russet-red, neo-Renaissance **Rott Haus**, originally an ironmonger's shop founded by V.J. Rott in 1840. Its facade is smothered in agricultural scenes and motifs inspired by the Czech artist Mikuláš Aleš. At the centre of the square stands a fountain dating from 1560 which retains its beautiful, original wrought-iron canopy; sadly, however, it is no longer functioning.

Smetana Museum (Muzeum Bedřicha Smetany)

MAP p.56, POCKET MAP E12–F12
Novotného lávka 1 ⓦ nm.cz. Mon & Wed–Sun 10am–5pm. 50Kč.

Housed in a gaily decorated neo-Renaissance building on the riverfront, the **Smetana Museum** celebrates the life and work of the most nationalist of all the great Czech composers, Bedřich Smetana. His greatest success as a composer was *The Bartered Bride*, which marked the birth of Czech opera, but he was forced to give up conducting in 1874 with the onset of deafness, and eventually died of syphilis in a mental asylum. Unfortunately, the museum fails to capture much of the spirit of the man, though the views across to the castle are good, and you get to wave a laser baton around in order to listen to his music.

Clam-Gallas Palace (Clam-gallasův palác)

MAP p.56, POCKET MAP F12–G12
Mariánské náměstí 2. Open for concerts only.

Despite its size, the **Clam-Gallas Palace** is easy to overlook in

a narrow space. It's a typically lavish Baroque affair, with big and burly *Atlantes* supporting the portals. The palace's doors are open exclusively for concerts, with regular performances in the Opera Barocca series (ⓦ operabarocca.cz).

Staroměstské náměstí (Old Town Square)

MAP p.56, POCKET MAP G11–G12

Easily the most spectacular square in Prague, **Staroměstské náměstí** is the traditional heart of the city. Most of the brightly coloured houses look solidly eighteenth century, but their Baroque facades hide considerably older buildings. Over the centuries, the square has seen its fair share of demonstrations and battles: the **27 white crosses** set into the paving commemorate the Protestant leaders who were condemned to death on the orders of the Habsburg Emperor in 1621, while the patch of green grass marks the neo-Gothic east wing of the town hall, burned down by the Nazis on the final day of the Prague Uprising in May 1945. Nowadays, the square is lined with café tables in summer and packed with a Christmas market in winter, while tourists pour in all year round to watch the town hall's astronomical clock chime, to sit on the benches in front of the Hus Monument, and to drink in the atmosphere of this historic showpiece.

Staré Město Town Hall (Staroměstská radnice)

MAP p.56, POCKET MAP G12
Staroměstské náměstí 1.

The Staré Město **Town Hall** occupies a whole sequence of houses on Staroměstské náměstí, culminating in an obligatory wedge-tower with a graceful Gothic oriel window. You can

House facade on Staroměstské náměstí

Astronomical Clock

check out the historical halls and a few rooms that survived World War II, including two former prison cells (Mon 11am–6pm, Tues–Sun 9am–6pm; 100Kč); it's fun to climb the tower too (Mon 11am–7pm, Tues–Sun 9am–7pm; 250Kč). You can also visit the medieval chapel, which has patches of original wall painting, and wonderful grimacing corbels at the foot of the ribbed vaulting. If you get here just before the clock strikes the hour, you'll be able to watch the Apostles going out on parade.

Astronomical Clock

MAP p.56, POCKET MAP G12
Staroměstské náměstí 1. Daily, on the hour 9am–9pm.

By far the most popular sight on Staroměstské náměstí is the town hall's fifteenth-century **Astronomical Clock**, whose hourly mechanical dumbshow regularly attracts a large crowd of upward-gazing tourists. Little figures of the Apostles shuffle along, bowing to the audience, while perched on pinnacles below are the four threats to the city as perceived by the medieval mind: Death carrying his hourglass and tolling his bell, the Jew with his moneybags (since

1945 shorn of his stereotypical beard and referred to as Greed), Vanity admiring his reflection, and a turbaned Turk shaking his head. Beneath the figures, four characters representing Philosophy, Religion, Astronomy and History stand motionless throughout the performance. Finally, a cockerel pops out and flaps its wings to signal that the show's over; the clock then chimes the hour and the crowds drift away.

Kinský Palace

MAP p.56, POCKET MAP G11
Staroměstské náměstí 12 Ⓦ ngprague.cz.
Tues–Sun 10am–6pm. 150Kč.

The largest secular building on Staroměstské náměstí is the Rococo **Kinský Palace**, which is perhaps most notorious as the venue for the fateful speech by the Communist prime minister, **Klement Gottwald**, who walked out onto the grey stone balcony one snowy February morning in 1948, flanked by his Party henchmen, to celebrate the Communist takeover with thousands of supporters packing the square below. The top two floors house a permanent collection of Asian art, plus temporary exhibitions.

STARÉ MĚSTO

Jan Hus Monument

MAP p.56, POCKET MAP G12
Staroměstské náměstí.

The colossal **Jan Hus Monument** features a turbulent sea of blackened bodies – the oppressed to his right, the defiant to his left – out of which rises the majestic moral authority of Hus himself, a radical religious reformer and martyr from the fifteenth century. On the 500th anniversary of his death, in 1915, the statue was unveiled, but the Austrians refused to hold an official ceremony; in protest, Praguers covered the monument in flowers. Since then it has been a powerful symbol of Czech nationalism: in March 1939, it was draped in swastikas by the invading Nazis, and in August 1968, it was shrouded in funereal black by Praguers, protesting at the Soviet invasion.

The inscription along the base is a quote from the will of pioneering educator John Comenius, one of Hus's seventeenth-century followers. It includes Hus's most famous dictum, *Pravda vítězí* (Truth Prevails), which also appears on the Czech president's official banner.

Church of sv Mikuláš

MAP p.56, POCKET MAP G11–G12
Staroměstské náměstí. Daily noon–4pm.

The destruction of the east wing of the town hall in 1945 rudely exposed the Baroque church of **sv Mikuláš**, built for the Benedictines in 1735. The south front is decidedly luscious, with blackened statuary at every cornice; inside, however, it's a much smaller space, theatrically organized into a series of interlocking curves. It's also rather plainly furnished, partly because it was closed down by Joseph II and turned into a storehouse, and partly because it's now owned by the very "low", modern, Czechoslovak Hussite Church. Instead, your eyes are drawn sharply upwards to the impressive stuccowork, the wrought-iron galleries and the trompe l'oeil frescoes on the dome.

Týn church (Týnský chrám)

MAP p.56, POCKET MAP G12
Celetná 5 ⊕ tyn.cz. Mon–Sat 10am–1pm & 3–5pm, Sun 10am–noon. Free.

The mighty **Týn church** is by far the most imposing Gothic structure in the Staré Město. Its two irregular towers, bristling with baubles, spires and pinnacles, rise like giant antennae above the arcaded houses which otherwise obscure its facade, and are spectacularly lit up at night. Inside, the church has a lofty, narrow nave punctuated at ground level by black and gold Baroque altarpieces. One or two original Gothic furnishings survive, most notably the pulpit and the fifteenth-century baldachin, housing a winged altar in the north aisle. Behind the pulpit, you'll find another superb

Týn church

Týn courtyard

winged altar depicting John the Baptist, dating from 1520. The pillar on the right of the chancel steps contains the red marble tomb of **Tycho Brahe**, court astronomer to Rudolf II.

Týn courtyard

MAP p.56, POCKET MAP G11

Hidden behind hulking Týn church is the **Týn courtyard**, also known by its German name, **Ungelt** (meaning "No Money", a pseudonym used to deter marauding invaders), which, as the trading base of German merchants, was one of the first settlements on the Vltava. Later, it was transformed into a palace, only to fall into disrepair during the decades of communist rule. The complex has now come full circle and is once again home to various shops, restaurants and hotels – and the Dominicans, who can often be seen crossing its cobbles.

Church of sv Jakub

MAP p.56, POCKET MAP H11

Malá Štupartská 6. Daily 9.30am–noon & 2–4pm. Free.

Before entering this imposingly large church, make sure you admire the distinctive bubbling, stucco portal above the main entrance. The church's massive Gothic proportions – it has the longest nave in Prague after the cathedral – make it a favourite venue for organ recitals and other concerts. After the great fire of 1689, Prague's Baroque artists remodelled the entire interior, adding huge pilasters, a series of colourful frescoes and over twenty side altars.

The church has close historical links with the butchers of Prague, who are responsible for the thoroughly decomposed and time-shrivelled human forearm you'll see hanging high up on the west wall, on the right as you enter. It has been here for over four hundred years now, ever since a thief tried to steal the jewels of the Madonna from the high altar. As the thief reached out, the Virgin supposedly grabbed his arm and refused to let go. The next day the congregation of butchers had no option but to lop it off, and it has hung there as a warning ever since.

Church of Sv Jakub

Shops

Antik v Dlouhé

MAP p.56, POCKET MAP H11
Dlouhá 37. Mon–Fri 10am–7pm, Sat &
Sun noon–6pm.

Great antique shop with many
authentic items that will fit in a
suitcase, though it does specialize
in spectacular light fittings and
First Republic chrome tube chairs.

Art Deco

MAP p.56, POCKET MAP G12
Michalská 21. Mon–Sat 2–7pm.

A stylish antiques trove made up
of clothes, hats, mufflers, teapots,
glasses, clocks and art from the
first half of the twentieth century.

Botas 66

MAP p.56, POCKET MAP G13
Skořepka 4. Mon–Sat 11am–7pm, Sun
11am–5pm.

The products of this communist-
era sneaker company have been
brought back from the dead,
reproduced in garish hues and
sold as "retro".

Art Deco

Botanicus

MAP p.56, POCKET MAP H11
Týn 3. Daily 10am–8pm.

Czech take on the UK's Body Shop,
with a more folksy ambience. Dried
flowers, handmade paper and fancy
honey are sold alongside natural
soaps and shampoos.

Bric a Brac

MAP p.56, POCKET MAP G11
Týnská 7. Daily 10am–6pm.

Absolutely minute antiques store,
packed to the rafters with trinkets.
The central location means that
prices are quite high, but it's worth
visiting for the spectacle alone.
The owner also runs a larger place
round the corner.

Disko Duck

MAP p.56, POCKET MAP F12
Karlova 12. Daily 12.30–6.30pm.

With some five thousand records
in stock, ranging from house, hip
hop, r'n'b and techno to electro,
jungle and breakbeat, Disko Duck
are bound to have something you
didn't even know that you needed.

Gábina Páralová

MAP p.56, POCKET MAP H11
Jakubská 14. Mon–Fri noon–7.30pm,
Sat 11am–5pm.

Czech designer Gábina Páralová
creates casual outfits with surprising details and lively twists. Her
shop is a good place to get a fresh
look at the Czech fashion scene.

Granát turnov

MAP p.56, POCKET MAP H11
Celetná dlouhá 28. Daily 9am–7pm.

The best place to get hold of
some exquisite Bohemian garnet
jewellery, made in North Bohemia.

Havelská Market

MAP p.56, POCKET MAP G12
Havelská. Mon–Fri 8am–6pm, Sat &
Sun 9am–6pm.

Open-air market stretching the
full length of the arcaded street
of Havelská, selling fruit, flowers,

U medvídků (The Little Bears)

MAP p.56, POCKET MAP G13
Na Perštýně 7. Mon–Sat 11.30am–11pm, Sun 11.30am–10pm.

A Prague beer hall going back to the thirteenth century and still much the same as it always was (make sure you turn right when you enter, and avoid the bar to the left). The Budvar flows freely, and the food is reliably Bohemian.

U rudolfina

MAP p.56, POCKET MAP F11
Křížovnická 10. Daily 11am–11pm.

A proper Czech *pivnice* serving beautifully kept Pilsner Urquell and typical pub grub, very close to Charles Bridge.

U zlatého tygra (The Golden Tiger)

MAP p.56, POCKET MAP F12
Husova 17. Daily 3–11pm.

Small central *pivnice*, always busy with locals and tourists trying to get a seat; the late writer and Bohemian, Bohumil Hrabal, was a semi-permanent resident.

Clubs and venues

AghaRTA Jazz Centrum

MAP p.56, POCKET MAP G12
Železná 16 ☏ 222 211 275, ⓦ agharta.cz.
Daily 7pm–1am.

A great central jazz club, with a mix of Czechs and foreigners, a consistently good programme of gigs and a round-the-year festival that brings in some top acts. Cover charge 250Kč.

Chapeau Rouge

MAP p.56, POCKET MAP H11
Jakubská 2 ⓦ www.chapeaurouge.cz.
Mon–Thurs noon–4am, Fri noon–6am, Sat 4pm–6am, Sun 4pm–3am.

Centrally located, multi-floor, good-time club, with a blood-red bar on the ground floor (free entry) and two dancefloors above

Roxy

featuring either DJs or live bands. Cover charge 50–100Kč.

Estates Theatre (Stavovské divadlo)

MAP p.56, POCKET MAP H12
Ovocný trh 1 ☏ 224 901 448, ⓦ narodni–divadlo.cz.

Known for its Mozart connections, Prague's oldest opera house has a glorious nineteenth-century interior and puts on a mixture of theatre, ballet and opera (with English subtitles). Building tours are available outside of performance times.

National Marionette Theatre

MAP p.56, POCKET MAP F11
Žatecká 1 ☏ 224 819 322, ⓦ mozart.cz.

It could be corny but this is actually good fun – Mozart's operas performed by giant marionettes. They do an early kids' show of *The Magic Flute*.

Roxy

MAP p.56, POCKET MAP H11
Dlouhá 33 ☏ 224 826 296, ⓦ roxy.cz.
Daily from 7pm.

Roxy is a great little venue: a laidback, rambling old theatre with a programme ranging from arty films and exhibitions to top live acts and DJ nights. Cover varies from free to 250Kč.

Josefov

The old Jewish ghetto district of Josefov remains one of the most remarkable sights in Prague and an essential slice of the city's cultural heritage. Although the warren-like street plan of the old ghetto was demolished in the 1890s – to make way for avenues of luxurious five-storey mansions – six synagogues, the Jewish Town Hall and the medieval cemetery still survive. They were preserved under the Nazis as a record of communities they had destroyed. To this end, Jewish artefacts from Czechoslovakia and beyond were gathered here, and today make up one of the most comprehensive collections of Judaica in Europe.

Památník jaroslava ježka

MAP BELOW, POCKET MAP G11
Kaprova 10 Ⓦ nm.cz. Tues 1–6pm. 20Kč.
If you happen to be in the Josefov area on a Tuesday afternoon, it's worth taking the opportunity to visit the **Památník Jaroslava**

Ježka, which occupies one room of the first-floor flat of the avant-garde composer Jaroslav Ježek (1906–42), at Kaprova 10. It's a great way to escape the crowds, hear some of Ježek's music, and admire the Modrý pokoj (Blue

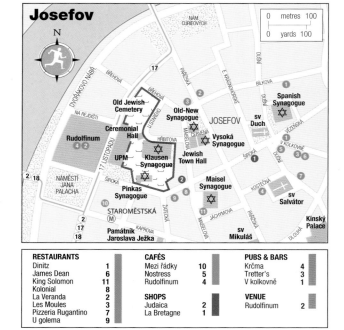

RESTAURANTS		CAFÉS		PUBS & BARS	
Dinitz	1	Mezi řádky	10	Krčma	4
James Dean	6	Nostress	5	Tretter's	3
King Solomon	11	Rudolfinum	4	V kolkovně	1
Kolonial	8				
La Veranda	2	SHOPS		VENUE	
Les Moules	3	Judaica	2	Rudolfinum	2
Pizzeria Rugantino	7	La Bretagne	1		
U golema	9				

Old-New Synagogue

Room), with its functionalist furniture and grand piano, in which he did his composing.

Náměstí Jana Palacha

MAP OPPOSITE, POCKET MAP F11

On the Josefov riverfront is **Náměstí Jana Palacha**, previously known as Red Army Square and embellished with a flowerbed in the shape of a red star (now replaced by an anonymous circular vent), in memory of the Soviet dead who were temporarily buried here in May 1945. The building on the east side of the square is the Faculty of Philosophy, where Jan Palach (see p.80) was a student (his bust adorns a corner of the building).

Old-New Synagogue (Staronová synagoga)

MAP OPPOSITE, POCKET MAP G11
Červená 2. Mon–Fri & Sun: April–Oct 9am–6pm; Nov–March 9am–4.30pm. 200Kč.

The **Old-New Synagogue** (**Staronová synagoga** or Altneuschul) got its strange name from the fact that when it was built it was indeed very new, though eventually it became the oldest synagogue in Josefov. Begun in the second half of the thirteenth century, and featuring a wonderful set of steep, sawtooth brick gables, it is, in fact, the oldest functioning synagogue in Europe, one of the earliest Gothic buildings in Prague and still the religious centre for Prague's Orthodox Jews. To get to the **main hall**, you must pass through one of the two low vestibules from which women watch the proceedings through narrow slits. Above the entrance is an elaborate tympanum covered in the twisting branches of a vine tree, its twelve bunches of grapes representing the tribes of Israel. The simple, plain interior is mostly taken up with the elaborate wrought-iron cage enclosing the bimah in the centre. The tattered red standard on display was originally a gift to the community from Emperor Ferdinand II for helping fend off the Swedes in 1648.

Visiting Josefov's sights

All the major sights of Josefov – the Old-New Synagogue, Old Jewish Cemetery, the Ceremonial Hall, the Maisel, Pinkas, Klausen and Spanish synagogues – are part of the **Jewish Museum** (ⓦ jewishmuseum.cz) and covered by an **all-in-one ticket**, available from any of the quarter's numerous **ticket offices** (main office at U staré školy 1). This costs 500Kč including the Old-New Synagogue, or 330Kč without. **Opening hours** vary but are basically daily (except Sat and Jewish holidays April–Oct 9am–6pm and Nov–March 9am–4.30pm).

Jewish Town Hall

Jewish Town Hall (Židovská radnice)

MAP p.72, POCKET MAP G11
Maiselova 18. Not open to the public.

The **Jewish Town Hall** is one of the few such buildings in central Europe to survive the Holocaust. Founded and funded by Mordecai Maisel, minister of finance to Rudolf II, in the sixteenth century, it was later rebuilt as the creamy-pink Baroque house you now see. The belfry has a clock on each of its four sides, plus a Hebrew one, stuck on the north gable, which, like the Hebrew script, goes "backwards".

Maisel Synagogue (Maiselova synagoga)

MAP p.72, POCKET MAP G11
Maiselova 10.

Like the town hall, the neo-Gothic **Maisel Synagogue** was founded and paid for entirely by Mordecai Maisel. Set back from the neighbouring houses south down Maiselova, the synagogue was, in its day, one of the most ornate in Josefov. Nowadays, its bare, whitewashed interior houses an exhibition on the history of the Czech–Jewish community up until the 1781 Edict of Tolerance. Along with glass cabinets filled with gold and silverwork, Hanukkah candlesticks, Torah scrolls and other religious artefacts, there's also an example of the antiquated ruffs that had to be worn by all unmarried males from the age of twelve, and a copy of Ferdinand I's decree enforcing the wearing of a circular yellow badge.

Klub za starou Prahu

Around 600 houses were demolished in the great Josefov *asanace*, the biggest incursion into the medieval fabric of the Czech capital ever to be permitted by the city authorities. The same fate awaited the Old Town and Malá Strana, the overzealous planners looking to transform medieval Prague into a kind of *fin de siècle* Paris on the Vltava. However, even in the late nineteenth century many Prague dwellers could see the value of their city's heritage and launched a campaign to stop the destruction. This led to the creation of one of Prague's most important civic movements – the **Klub za starou Prahu** (Old Prague Club, ⓦ zastarouprahu.cz), which to this day continues to highlight the excesses of unscrupulous developers and call out corrupt city councillors whose actions threaten the integrity of this most precious city.

Pinkas Synagogue (Pinkasov synagoga)

MAP p.72, POCKET MAP F11
Široká 3.

Built in the 1530s for the powerful Horovitz family, the **Pinkas Synagogue** has undergone countless restorations over the centuries. In 1958, the synagogue was transformed into a chilling memorial to the 77,297 Czech Jews killed during the Holocaust. The memorial was closed shortly after the 1967 Six Day War – due to damp, according to the Communists – and remained so, allegedly due to problems with the masonry, until it was finally, painstakingly restored in the 1990s. All that remains of the synagogue's original decor today is the ornate bimah surrounded by a beautiful wrought-iron grille, supported by barley-sugar columns.

Of all the sights of the Jewish quarter, the **Holocaust memorial** is perhaps the most moving, with every bit of wall space taken up with the carved stone list of victims, stating simply their name, date of birth and date of death or transportation to the camps. It is the longest epitaph in the world, yet it represents a mere fraction of those who died in the Nazi concentration camps. Upstairs in a room beside the women's gallery, there's also a harrowing exhibition of drawings by children from the Jewish ghetto in Terezín, most of whom were killed in the camps.

Old Jewish Cemetery (Starý židovský hřbitov)

MAP p.72, POCKET MAP F11
Široká 3.

At the heart of Josefov is the **Old Jewish Cemetery**, which you enter from the Pinkas Synagogue and leave by the Klausen Synagogue. Established in the fifteenth century, it was in use until 1787, by which time there were an estimated 100,000 people buried here, one

on top of the other, six palms apart, and as many as twelve layers deep. The enormous number of visitors has meant that the graves themselves have been roped off to protect them, but if you get there before the crowds – a difficult task for much of the year – the cemetery can be a poignant reminder of the ghetto, its inhabitants subjected to inhuman overcrowding even in death. The rest of Prague recedes beyond the tall ash trees and cramped perimeter walls, the haphazard headstones and Hebrew inscriptions casting a powerful spell. On many graves you'll see pebbles, some holding down *kvitlech* or small messages of supplication.

Ceremonial Hall (Obřadní síň)

MAP p.72, POCKET MAP F11
U starého hřbitova.

Immediately on your left as you leave the cemetery is the **Ceremonial Hall**, a lugubrious neo-Renaissance house built in 1906 as a ceremonial hall by the Jewish Burial Society. Appropriately enough, it's now devoted to an exhibition on Jewish traditions of burial and death, though it would probably be more useful if you could visit it before heading into the cemetery, rather than after.

Old Jewish Cemetery

Klausen Synagogue (Klausova synagoga)

MAP p.72, POCKET MAP F11
U starého hřbitova 1.

A late seventeenth-century building, the **Klausen Synagogue** was founded in the 1690s by Mordecai Maisel on the site of several small buildings (Klausen), in what was then a notorious red-light district of Josefov. The ornate Baroque interior contains a rich display of religious objects from embroidered *kippah* to Kiddush cups, and explains the very basics of Jewish religious practice, and the chief festivals or High Holidays.

Pařížská

MAP p.72, POCKET MAP F10–G11
Running through the heart of the old ghetto is **Pařížská**, the ultimate bourgeois avenue, lined with buildings covered in a riot of late nineteenth-century sculpturing, spikes and turrets. At odds with the rest of Josefov, its ground-floor premises are home to designer label clothes and accessory shops, jewellery stores and swanky cafés, restaurants and bars.

Rudolfinum

MAP p.72, POCKET MAP F11
Alšovo nábřeží 12. Tues–Sun 10am–6pm.
The **Rudolfinum**, or House of Artists (Dům umělců), is one of the proud civic buildings of the nineteenth-century Czech national revival. Built to house an art gallery, museum and concert hall for the Czech-speaking community, it became the seat of the new Czechoslovak parliament from 1919 until 1941 when it was closed down by the Nazis. Since 1946, the building has returned to its original artistic purpose and it's now one of the capital's main concert venues (home to the Czech Philharmonic) and exhibition spaces.

Pařížská

UPM (Museum of Decorative Arts)

MAP p.72, POCKET MAP F11
17 listopadu 2 ⓦ upm.cz. Closed for refurbishment at the time of writing.
From its foundation in 1885 through to the end of the First Republic, the **Uměleckoprůmyslové muzeum** or **UPM** received the best that the Czech modern movement had to offer – from Art Nouveau to the avant-garde – and its collection is consequently unrivalled. The building itself is richly decorated in mosaics, stained glass and sculptures, and its ground-floor temporary exhibitions are consistently excellent.

In recent years the UPM has undergone a complete rebuild, which has meant the exhibitions have been closed while work is completed. The aim was to more clearly define the curation of its collections after its 2018 re-opening. These collections include textiles and richly embroidered religious vestments from the fifteenth to the eighteenth centuries, lacework from down the ages, costumes spanning three centuries, and impressive glass, ceramic and pottery displays – for many the highlight of the entire UPM. They also cover furniture, jewellery, curios, Czech photography, interwar prints, works by Josef Sudek, avant-garde graphics by Karel Teige, book designs by Josef Váchal and some of Alfons Mucha's famous turn-of-the-twentieth-century Parisian advertising posters.

Spanish Synagogue (Španělská synagoga)

MAP p.72, POCKET MAP G11
Vězeňská 1.

Built in 1868, the **Spanish Synagogue** is by far the most ornate synagogue in Josefov, its stunning, gilded Moorish interior deliberately imitating the Alhambra (hence its name). Every available surface is drowning in a profusion of floral motifs and geometric patterns, in vibrant reds, greens and blues, which are repeated in the synagogue's huge stained-glass windows. The synagogue now houses an interesting exhibition on the history of Prague's Jews from the time of the 1781 Edict of Tolerance to the Holocaust. Lovely, slender, painted cast-iron columns hold up the women's gallery, where the displays include a fascinating set of photos

Spanish Synagogue

depicting the old ghetto at the time of its demolition. There's a section on Prague's German–Jewish writers, including Kafka, and information on the Holocaust. In the upper-floor prayer hall there's an exhibition of silver religious artefacts – a mere fraction of the six thousand pieces collected here, initially for Prague's Jewish Museum (founded in 1906), with more gathered later under the Nazis.

The Golem

Legends concerning the animation of unformed matter (which is what the Hebrew word **golem** means), using the mystical texts of the Kabbala, were around long before Frankenstein started playing around with corpses. The most famous golem was the giant servant made from the mud of the Vltava by **Rabbi Löw**, the sixteenth-century chief rabbi of Prague. It was brought to life when the rabbi placed a *shem*, a tablet with a magic Hebrew inscription, in its mouth.

There are numerous versions of the tale, though none earlier than the nineteenth century. In some, the golem is a figure of fun, flooding the rabbi's kitchen rather in the manner of Disney's *Sorcerer's Apprentice*; others portray him as the guardian of the ghetto, helping Rabbi Löw in his struggle with the anti-Semites at the court of Rudolf II. In almost all versions, however, the golem finally runs amok and Löw has to remove the *shem* once and for all, and hide the creature away in the attic of the Old-New Synagogue (see p.73), where it has supposedly resided ever since – ready to come out again if needed.

Shops

Judaica

MAP p.72, POCKET MAP F11
Široká 7. Mon–Fri & Sun 10am–6pm.
Probably the best stocked of all
the places selling Jewish titles
to tourists, with books and
prints, secondhand and new.

La Bretagne

MAP p.72, POCKET MAP G11
Široká 22. Mon–Sat 9.30am–7.30pm.
There's a wide array of fresh fish
and seafood at this centrally located
fishmonger's, plus takeaway sushi.

Cafés

Mezi řádky

MAP p.72, POCKET MAP F11
Palachovo náměstí 2. Mon–Fri 8am–7pm.
Join Charles University's students
and professors at this no-frills café
deep within the humanities faculty
building. Cheap Czech staples –
meatloaf, salads drowning in mayo,
open sandwiches – plus beer and
wine. To find it, enter the building
and turn immediately right.

Nostress

MAP p.72, POCKET MAP G11
Dušní 10 ☎ 222 317 007, ⓦ nostress.cz.
Mon–Fri 8.30am–midnight, Sat 10am–
midnight, Sun 10am–11pm.

Judaica

Colourful, recently revamped
café with lots of bright cushions
and indoor trees. Claims to have
had Prague's best coffee for two
decades – stress test this alternative
fact between synagogues.

Rudolfinum

MAP p.72, POCKET MAP F11
Alšovo nábřeží 12. Tues–Sun 11am–11pm.
Splendidly grand nineteenth-
century café on the first floor of the
Rudolfinum, serving drinks and
snacks amid potted palms. Worth
seeing, even if you're not thirsty.

Restaurants

Dinitz

MAP p.72, POCKET MAP G11
Bílková 12 ☎ 222 244 000. Mon–Thurs &
Sun 11.30am–10pm, Fri 11.30am–5pm.
Kosher restaurant with Middle
Eastern snacks, sandwiches, pasta,
salads and mains (200–500Kč).

James Dean

MAP p.72, POCKET MAP G11
V Kolkovně 1 ☎ 606 979 797,
ⓦ jamesdean.cz. Mon–Fri 8am–4am,
Sat & Sun 9am–4am.
This retro American diner has an
authentic-looking interior, ceiling
fans, a twangy soundtrack and
serving staff dressed for the part.
Portions of burgers and fries are
Cadillac size. Mains 200–350Kč.

King Solomon

MAP p.72, POCKET MAP F11
Široká 8 ☎ 224 818 752. Mon–Thurs & Sun
noon–11pm. Fri dinner & Sat lunch are
reservation only.
Sophisticated kosher restaurant
serving big helpings of
international dishes and
traditional Jewish specialities. A
three-course set menu (with beer)
is 500–1000Kč.

Kolonial

MAP p.72, POCKET MAP F11
Široká 6 ☎ 224 818 322, ⓦ kolonialpub.cz.
Daily 11am–midnight.

V kolkovně

The first things you'll notice are the penny-farthings in the window, and the old enamel bicycle adverts and saddle bar stools continue the cycling theme inside. The menu is a mixed pannier, ranging from roast pork knee to Caesar salad (mains 200–400Kč).

La Veranda

MAP p.72, POCKET MAP G11
Elišky Krásnohorské 10 ☎ 224 814 733.
Mon–Sat noon–midnight.

Family-run restaurant focused on local ingredients and fresh cooking, with wonderful staff who really add to the experience – take their recommendations when ordering. Mains (around 400Kč) range from tagliatelle with rabbit ragout to brook trout.

Les Moules

MAP p.72, POCKET MAP G11
Pařížská 19 ☎ 222 315 022. Daily
11.30am–midnight.

One of a chain of wood-panelled Belgian brasseries which flies in fresh mussels (333Kč for 900g), serving them with French fries and Belgian beers.

Pizzeria Rugantino

MAP p.72, POCKET MAP G11
Dušní 4 ☎ 222 318 172. Mon–Sat
11am–11pm, Sun noon–11pm.

This pizzeria, just off Dlouhá, is the real deal: an oak-fired oven, thin bases and lots of different toppings (110–225Kč).

U Golema

MAP p.72, POCKET MAP G11
Maiselova 8 ☎ 222 328 165,
ⓦ restaurantugolema.cz. Daily
10am–11.30pm.

Golem himself greets diners at this pleasant restaurant in Josefov's sightseeing zone. The filling, meat-themed menu consists mainly of Czech food, with a few French influences (mains 200–400Kč).

Pubs and bars

Krčma

MAP p.72, POCKET MAP G11
Kostečná 4 ☎ 725 157 262, ⓦ krcma.cz.
Daily 11am–11pm.

If the ghetto of gentrification around Pařížská isn't your style, seek out this cellar tavern for some candlelit, faux-medieval Czech grit. The Urquell is 35Kč a glass, and the old-Bohemian food realistically priced.

Tretter's

MAP p.72, POCKET MAP G11
V kolkovně 3. Daily 7pm–3am.

Wonderfully sophisticated and smart (but not exclusive) American cocktail bar, with very professional staff and a celebrity ambience.

V kolkovně

MAP p.72, POCKET MAP G11
V kolkovně 8. Daily 11am–midnight.

Justifiably popular with passing tourists, this Pilsner Urquell pub has plush decor, excellent pub food and unpasteurized Pilsner on tap.

Venue

Rudolfinum

MAP p.72, POCKET MAP F11
Alšovo nábřeží 12 ☎ 227 059 227,
ⓦ rudolfinum.cz.

A stunning neo-Renaissance concert hall from the late nineteenth century that's home to the Czech Philharmonic.

Wenceslas Square and northern Nové Město

Nové Město – Prague's "New Town" – is the city's main commercial and business district, housing most of its big hotels, cinemas, nightclubs, fast-food outlets and department stores. Architecturally, it comes over as big, bourgeois and predominantly fin de siècle, yet the large market squares and wide streets were actually laid out way back in the fourteenth century by Emperor Charles IV. The obvious starting point in Nové Město is Wenceslas Square (Václavské náměstí), the long, sloping boulevard with its distinctive, interwar shopping malls, which is where Czechs traditionally gather when they have something to protest about and is today at the hub of the modern city.

Wenceslas Square (Václavské náměstí)

MAP p.82, POCKET MAP H13–J13

The natural pivot around which modern Prague revolves, **Wenceslas Square** is more of a wide, gently sloping boulevard than a square as such. It's scarcely a conventional – or even convenient – space in which to

Wenceslas Square

hold mass demonstrations, yet for the past 150 years or more it has been the focus of political protest in Prague. In August 1968 it was the scene of some of the most violent confrontations between the Soviet invaders and the local Czechs. More happily, in late November 1989, more than 250,000 people crammed into the square night after night, often enduring sub-zero temperatures, to demand free elections.

Despite the square's history and its medieval origins, it is now a thoroughly modern, glitzy, slightly seedy boulevard, lined with self-important six- or seven-storey buildings representing every artistic trend of the last hundred years, from neo-Renaissance to Socialist Realism. At the top of the square, in front of the grandiose National Museum, stands the **Wenceslas Monument**, a worthy and heroic, but pretty unexciting, equestrian statue of the country's patron saint. Below the statue, a simple memorial commemorating the victims of Communism is adorned with flowers and photos of Jan Palach and Jan Zajíc, both

Prague Main Train Station

of whom martyred themselves here in 1969 in protest at the Soviet invasion.

Lucerna pasáž

MAP p.82, POCKET MAP H14
Wenceslas Square has an impressive array of old shopping arcades, or *pasáže*, as they're known in Czech, mostly dating from the interwar period. The king of the lot is the lavishly decorated fin-de-siècle **Lucerna pasáž**, stretching all the way from Štěpánská to Vodičkova. Designed in the early part of the twentieth century in Moorish style by, among others, Václav Havel's own grandfather, it boasts an ornate cinema, café and vast concert hall. Suspended from the ceiling in the centre of the arcade is David Černý's parody of the square's equestrian Wenceslas Monument, with the saint astride an upside-down charger.

National Museum (Národní muzeum)

MAP p.82, POCKET MAP J14
Václavské náměstí 68 ⓦ nm.cz. Closed at the time of writing.
Built in 1890, the broad, brooding hulk of the **National Museum** dominates the view up Wenceslas Square like a giant golden eagle with outstretched wings. When it finally reopens after drawn-out

and much delayed renovation work, museum chiefs promise a focus on interactive natural history displays. Be sure to admire the ornate marble entrance hall and splendid monumental staircase leading to the glass-domed Pantheon, with its 48 busts and statues of bewhiskered Czech men (plus a couple of token women and Slovaks). Those with a museum itch might head next door to the **New Building** (Vinohradská 1; daily 10am–6pm; 200Kč), with exhibitions ranging from Czech archeology to scientific and cultural milestones.

Prague Main Train Station (Praha hlavní nádraží)

MAP p.82, POCKET MAP K13
Prague Main Train Station is one of the final architectural glories of the dying Habsburg Empire, designed by **Josef Fanta** and officially opened in 1909 as the Franz-Josefs Bahnhof. Arriving by metro, or buying tickets in the over-polished subterranean modern section, it's easy to miss the station's recently renovated Art Nouveau parts. Upstairs, the original entrance – now blighted by a motorway outside – still exudes imperial confidence, with its wrought-iron canopy and naked figurines clinging to the sides of the towers.

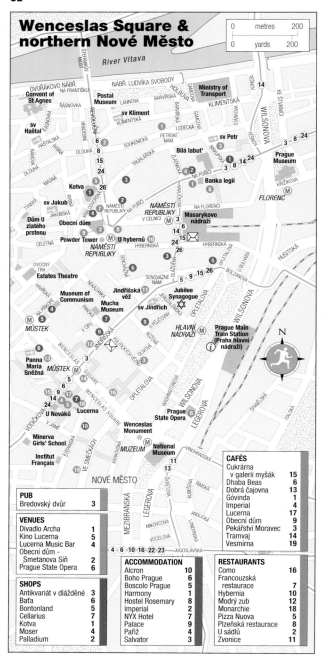

Wenceslas Square & northern Nové Město

	metres		200
0			
	yards		200
0			

Jubilee Synagogue

MAP OPPOSITE, POCKET MAP J12
Jeruzalémská. April–Oct Mon–Fri & Sun
11am–5pm. 80Kč.

Named in honour of the sixtieth
year of the Emperor Franz-Josef
I's reign in 1908, the **Jubilee
Synagogue** was built in an
incredibly colourful Moorish
style similar to that of the
Spanish Synagogue in Josefov,
but with a touch of Art Nouveau.
The Hebrew quote from Malachi
on the facade strikes a note of
liberal optimism: "Do we not
have one father? Were we not
created by the same God?"

Jindříšská věž

MAP OPPOSITE, POCKET MAP J12

This freestanding fifteenth-
century tower is the belfry of
the nearby church of **sv Jindřich**
(St Henry), whose digitally
controlled, high-pitched bells
ring out every fifteen minutes,
and play an entire medley every
four hours. In contrast to every
other surviving tower in Prague,
the **Jindříšská věž** has been
imaginatively and expensively
restored and now contains a
café, restaurant, shop, exhibition
space and, on the top floor, a
small **museum** (daily 10am–7pm;
120Kč) on Prague's hundred-plus
towers, with a good view across
the city's rooftops.

Mucha Museum

MAP OPPOSITE, POCKET MAP H12–H13
Panská 7 Ⓦ mucha.cz. Daily 10am–6pm.
240Kč.

Alfons Mucha (1860–1939) made
his name in turn-of-the-century
Paris, where he shot to fame after
designing Art Nouveau posters
for the actress Sarah Bernhardt.
"Le Style Mucha" became all the
rage, but the artist himself came
to despise this "commercial"
period of his work, and, in
1910, Mucha moved back to his
homeland and threw himself into
the national cause, designing

patriotic stamps, banknotes and
posters for the new republic.
The whole of Mucha's career
is covered in the permanent
exhibition, and an excellent
video (in English) covers the
decade of his life he devoted to
the cycle of nationalist paintings
known as the Slav Epic.

Museum of Communism (Muzeum komunismu)

MAP OPPOSITE, POCKET MAP H12
V Celnice 4 Ⓦ muzeumkomunismu.cz.
Daily 9am–8pm. 190Kč.

Above a casino, on the first
floor of the Savarin Palace,
the **Museum of Communism**
gives a brief rundown of
twentieth-century Czech history,
accompanied by a superb
collection of Communist statues,
film footage and propaganda
posters. The politics are a
bit simplistic – the popular
postwar support for the party
is underplayed – but it's
worth tracking down for the
memorabilia alone.

Jubilee Synagogue

Powder Tower (Prašná brána)

MAP p.82, POCKET MAP H12
Daily: April–Sept 10am–10pm; March & Oct 10am–8pm; Nov–Feb 10am–6pm. 90Kč.

One of the eight medieval gate-towers that once guarded Staré Město, the Powder Tower was begun by King Vladislav Jagiello in 1475, shortly after he'd moved into the royal court, which was situated next door at the time. Work stopped when he retreated to the Hrad to avoid the wrath of his subjects; later on, it was used to store gunpowder – hence the name and the reason for the damage incurred in 1757, when it blew up. Most people, though, ignore the small historical exhibition inside, and climb straight up for the modest view from the top.

Obecní dům (Municipal House)

MAP p.82, POCKET MAP H11–H12
Náměstí Republiky 5 ⓦ obecnidum.cz.
Daily 10am–7pm.

Attached to the Powder Tower, and built on the ruins of the old royal court, the **Obecní dům** is by far the most exciting Art Nouveau building in Prague, one of the few places that still manages to conjure up the atmosphere of Prague's

turn-of-the-twentieth-century café society. Conceived as a cultural centre for the Czech community, it's probably the finest architectural achievement of the Czech national revival, extravagantly decorated inside and out by the leading Czech artists of the day. From the lifts to the cloakrooms, just about all the furnishings remain as they were when the building was completed in 1911.

The simplest way of soaking up the interior – peppered with mosaics and pendulous brass chandeliers – is to have a coffee in the cavernous **café** (see p.87). For a more detailed inspection of the building's spectacular interior, you can sign up for one of the regular **guided tours** at the ground-floor information centre (290Kč).

Banka legií

MAP p.82, POCKET MAP J11
Na poříčí 24. Mon–Fri 9am–5pm. Free.

The **Banka legií** (now a branch of the ČSOB) is one of Prague's most unusual pieces of corporate architecture. A Rondo-Cubist building from the early 1920s, it boasts a striking white marble frieze by Otto Gutfreund, depicting the epic march across Siberia undertaken by the Czechoslovak

Obecní dům

Frieze on the Banka legií

Legion and their embroilment in the Russian Revolution, set into the bold smoky-red moulding of the facade. You're free to wander into the main ground-floor banking hall, which retains its curved glass roof and distinctive red-and-white marble patterning.

Prague Museum

MAP p.82, POCKET MAP K11/F5
Na poříčí 52 ⓦ muzeumprahy.cz.
Tues–Sun 9am–6pm. 120Kč.

Next to Prague's main coach station, a purpose-built neo-Renaissance mansion houses the **Prague Museum**. Inside, there's an ad hoc collection of the city's art, a number of antique bicycles, and usually an intriguing temporary exhibition on some aspect of the city. The museum's prize possession, though, is Antonín Langweil's paper model of Prague which he completed in the 1830s. This is a fascinating insight into early nineteenth-century Prague – predominantly Baroque, with the cathedral incomplete and the Jewish quarter "unsanitized" – and, consequently, has served as one of the most useful records for the city's restorers. The most surprising thing, of course, is that so little has changed.

Postal Museum (poštovní muzeum)

MAP p.82, POCKET MAP J10
Nové mlýny 2 ⓦ postovnimuzeum.cz. Tues–Sun 9am–5pm. 50Kč.

Housed in the **Vávrův dům**, an old mill near one of Prague's many water towers, the **Postal Museum** contains a series of jolly nineteenth-century wall paintings of Romantic Austrian landscapes, and a collection of drawings on postman themes. The real philately is on the ground floor – a vast international collection of stamps arranged in vertical pull-out drawers. The Czechoslovak issues are historically and artistically interesting, as well as of appeal to collectors. Stamps became a useful tool in the propaganda wars of the last century; even such short-lived ventures as the Hungarian-backed Slovak Soviet Republic of 1918–19 and the Slovak National Uprising of autumn 1944 managed to print special issues. Under the First Republic, the country's leading artists, notably Alfons Mucha and Max Švabinský, were commissioned to design stamps, some of which are exceptionally beautiful.

Shops

Antikvariát dlážděná

MAP p.82, POCKET MAP J12
Dlážděná 7. Mon–Fri 9am–6pm, Sat 9am–1pm.

One of the city centre's longest-established and best secondhand bookstores, but it's the prints and original artwork, some by well-known artists, that many come here for.

Baťa

MAP p.82, POCKET MAP H13
Václavské náměstí 6. Mon–Sat 9am–9pm, Sun 10am–9pm.

Functionalist flagship store of Baťa shoe empire, with five floors of fancy footwear located on Wenceslas Square.

Bontonland

MAP p.82, POCKET MAP H13
Václavské náměstí 1. Mon–Fri 9am–8pm, Sat 10am–8pm, Sun 10am–7pm.

In the *pasáž* at the bottom of Wenceslas Square, Prague's biggest record store sells rock, folk, jazz and classical CDs, DVDs and video games.

Cellarius

MAP p.82, POCKET MAP H13
Štěpánská 61. Mon–Fri 9.30am–9pm, Sat 11am–9pm, Sun 3–7pm.

Very well-stocked shop in the Lucerna *pasáž*, where you can taste and take away Czech wines.

Kotva

MAP p.82, POCKET MAP H11
Náměstí Republiky 8. Daily 9am–8pm.

Prague's original 1970s department store has undergone a skin-deep makeover, taking the whole caboodle upmarket – and prices with it.

Moser

MAP p.82, POCKET MAP H12
Na příkopě 12. Daily 10am–8pm.

A high-class emporium selling the most famous glass and crystal from the West Bohemian spa town of Karlovy Vary. Prices are high, but so is quality.

Palladium

MAP p.82, POCKET MAP J11
Náměstí Republiky 1. Daily 7am–11pm.

The apotheosis of Czech consumerism, this is the country's largest shopping mall, occupying spruced-up former barracks opposite the Obecní dům.

Cafés

Dhaba Beas

MAP p.82, POCKET MAP K11
Na poříčí 26. Mon–Fri 11am–9pm, Sat noon–8pm, Sun noon–6pm.

This minimalist Indian vegetarian self-service canteen is a very 21st-century affair in a courtyard at the foot of an office block. The food – all pineapple fritters, chickpeas and basmati rice – costs 20.90Kč per 100g, so the bill can add up faster than you think.

Dobrá čajovna

MAP p.82, POCKET MAP H13
Václavské náměstí 14. Mon–Fri 10am–9.30pm, Sat & Sun 2–9.30pm.

Mellow yet rarefied teahouse, with an astonishing variety of teas

Imperial

(and a few Middle Eastern snacks) served by sandal-wearing waiters.

Góvinda

MAP p.82, POCKET MAP J10
Soukenická 27. Mon–Fri 11am–6pm,
Sat noon–4pm.
Daytime Hare Krishna (Haré Kršna in Czech) restaurant with very basic decor, serving organic Indian veggie dishes for a touch over 100Kč.

Imperial

MAP p.82, POCKET MAP J11
Na poříčí 15. Daily 7am–11pm.
Built in 1914, and featuring the most incredible ceramic friezes on its walls, pillars and ceilings, the *Imperial* is a must for fans of outrageously sumptuous Art Nouveau decor. You can just come for a coffee, but they also serve breakfast, light lunches and main dishes for 300Kč or so.

Lucerna

MAP p.82, POCKET MAP H14
Vodičkova 36. Daily 10am–midnight.
Wonderfully lugubrious fin-de-siècle café-bar on the first floor, en route to the cinema of the same name, with lots of faux marble and windows overlooking the Lucerna *pasáž*.

Myšák

MAP p.82, POCKET MAP H13
Vodičkova 31. Mon–Fri 8am–8pm, Sat & Sun 8.30am–8pm.
Stylish recreation of a famous *cukrárna* that stood on this spot in the interwar years. Expect high-stacked gateaux and tasty ice cream.

Obecní dům

MAP p.82, POCKET MAP H12
Náměstí Republiky 5. Daily 7.30am–11pm.
The vast *kavárna*, with its famous fountain, is a glittering Art Nouveau period piece. Food is nice enough, but most folk come here for a coffee and something from the cake trolley.

Tramvaj

Pekářství moravec

MAP p.82, POCKET MAP K10
Biskupský dvůr 1. Mon–Fri
6.30am–6.30pm, Sat 7am–12.30pm.
Rural Bohemia-style bakery, on a quiet square next to the relatively unvisited Church of sv Petra, selling traditional cakes, pastries, ice cream and coffees. A great spot for an authentically early Czech breakfast.

Tramvaj

MAP p.82, POCKET MAP H13
Václavské náměstí. Mon–Sat 9am–midnight, Sun 10am–midnight.
Two vintage no. 11 trams stranded in the middle of Wenceslas Square (where they used to run) have been converted into a café – a convenient spot for coffee, and easy to locate.

Vesmírna

MAP p.82, POCKET MAP H14
Ve Smečkách 5. Mon–Thurs 11.30am–8pm, Fri 11.30am–3pm.
Used as a training café for people with learning difficulties, *Vesmírna* is a popular, cosy spot serving crepes, sandwiches and Czech cakes.

Restaurants

Como

MAP p.82, POCKET MAP J13
Václavské náměstí 45 ☎ 222 247 240.
Mon–Fri 6.30pm–1am, Sat & Sun
7pm–1am.

High-quality eating on Wenceslas
Square is a rarity, so this place
is to be cherished. There are
sushi sets and Czech food, but
the Mediterranean dishes shine.
Mains around 400Kč.

Francouzská restaurace

MAP p.82, POCKET MAP H11
Obecní dům, Náměstí Republiky 5 ☎ 222
002 770, ⓦ francouzskarestaurace.cz.
Daily noon–11pm.

The Art Nouveau decor in this
cavernous Obecní dům restaurant
is stunning and the French-style
main dishes (600–1000Kč)
are superb.

Hybernia

MAP p.82, POCKET MAP J12
Hybernská 7 ☎ 224 226 004,
ⓦ hybernia.cz. Mon–Fri 8am–midnight,
Sat & Sun 11am–midnight.

Busy restaurant, with a nice
outdoor terrace; specializes in
špízy (needles), aka kebabs, but
also serves good-value Czech food
and pasta dishes (150–300Kč).

Francouzská restaurace

Modrý zub (Blue Tooth)

MAP p.82, POCKET MAP H13
Jindřišská 5 ☎ 222 212 622. Mon–Fri
11am–11pm, Sat noon–11pm, Sun
noon–10pm.

Good-value Thai rice and noodle
dishes (around 200Kč) in a place
that has a modern wine-bar feel
to it – popular with Wenceslas
Square shoppers.

Monarchie

MAP p.82, POCKET MAP H14
Štěpánská 61 ☎ 296 236 513,
ⓦ restaurace-monarchie.cz.
Mon–Fri 11am–11pm.

Imperial coats of arms line the
walls at this interesting restaurant
in the entrance to the Lucerna
pasáž. The Austro-Bohemian
menu includes Wiener schnitzel,
suckling pig, and Pilsen goulash.
Mains 150–350Kč.

Pizza Nuova

MAP p.82, POCKET MAP H11
Revoluční 1 ☎ 221 803 308, ⓦ pizzanuova
.ambi.cz. Daily 11.30am–11.30pm.

Big and stylish, this upstairs pizza
and pasta place (each around
200Kč) affords great views of the
trams wending their way through
Náměstí Republiky.

Plzeňská restaurace

MAP p.82, POCKET MAP H11
Obecní dům, Náměstí Republiky 5 ☎ 222
002 780, ⓦ plzenskarestaurace.cz. Daily
11.30am–11pm.

Located in the cellar of the
Obecní dům, this is the country's
most attractive Art Nouveau
pub-restaurant, with exquisite
tiling, wonderful stained glass
and huge chandeliers. The mains
menu celebrates the best of
Czech meat dishes but is
slightly overpriced, and portions
are miserly.

U sádlů

MAP p.82, POCKET MAP H11
Klimentská 2 ☎ 222 252 411, ⓦ usadlu.
cz. Mon–Thurs 11am–midnight, Fri & Sat
11am–1am, Sun noon–midnight.

Deliberately over-the-top themed medieval banqueting hall offering a hearty Czech menu, with classics such as roast pork knuckle and goulash (around 200Kč), helped down with lashings of frothing Budvar.

Zvonice (Belltower)

MAP p.82, POCKET MAP J12
Jindřišská. Daily 11.30am–midnight.
Atmospheric but rather expensive restaurant crammed into the woodwork on the sixth and seventh floors of a medieval bell tower. Weekday lunch menu under 400Kč; traditional Czech main dishes in the evening from around 750Kč.

Pub

Bredovský dvůr

MAP p.82, POCKET MAP J13
Politických vězňů 12. Mon–Sat 11am–midnight, Sun 11am–11pm.
Popular, brick-vaulted city pub, off Wenceslas Square, serving standard pub food washed down with Pilsner Urquell or Velkopopovický Kozel.

Venues

Divadlo archa

MAP p.82, POCKET MAP J11
Na poříčí 26 ☏ 221 716 333,
ⓦ divadloarcha.cz.
The city's most innovative venue, with two versatile spaces, an art gallery and café. The programme of music, dance and theatre emphasizes new, experimental work, often with English subtitles or translation.

Kino lucerna

MAP p.82, POCKET MAP H14
Vodičkova 36 ☏ 224 216 972,
ⓦ kinolucerna.cz.
Grandiose 1909 cinema that eschews dubbed films and shows English-subtitled Czech films.

Obecní dům

Lucerna Music Bar

MAP p.82, POCKET MAP H14
Vodičkova 36 ☏ 224 217 108, ⓦ musicbar .cz. Daily 9.30am until end of event.
Scruffy basement bar that attracts some great musicians, local and touring, during the week, before descending into pop disco at the weekend. Cover 100Kč and upwards.

Obecní dům – Smetanova síň

MAP p.82, POCKET MAP H12
Náměstí Republiky 5 ☏ 222 002 101,
ⓦ obecnidum.cz.
Fantastically ornate Art Nouveau concert hall which usually kicks off the Prague Spring International Music Festival and is home to the Prague Symphony Orchestra.

Prague State Opera (Státní opera Praha)

MAP p.82, POCKET MAP J14
Wilsonova 4 ☏ 224 227 266,
ⓦ narodni-divadlo.cz.
Sumptuous nineteenth-century opera house, originally built by the German-speaking community. It now holds opera, ballet and drama performances.

Národní třída and southern Nové Město

Off the conventional tourist trail, and boasting only a few minor sights, the network of cobbled streets immediately to the south of Národní is nevertheless great to explore, as it harbours a whole range of interesting cafés, pubs, restaurants and shops that have steadily colonized the area over the past two decades. Southern Nové Město also boasts the city's finest stretch of waterfront, with a couple of leafy islands overlooked by magnificent nineteenth-century mansions that continue almost without interruption south to Vyšehrad.

Jungmannovo náměstí

MAP OPPOSITE, POCKET MAP G13

Jungmannovo náměstí is named for **Josef Jungmann** (1772–1847), a prolific writer, translator and leading light of the Czech national revival, whose pensive, seated statue surveys the small, rather ill-proportioned square. The square itself boasts a couple of Czech architectural curiosities, starting with a unique **Cubist streetlamp** (and seat) from 1912, in the far eastern corner. The most imposing building is the chunky, vigorously sculptured **Palác Adria**, designed in Rondo-

Cubist style in the early 1920s, with extra details added by Otto Gutfreund and a central *Seafaring* group by Jan Štursa. The building's *pasáž* (arcade) still retains its wonderful original portal featuring sculptures depicting the twelve signs of the zodiac. The theatre in the basement was the underground nerve centre of the 1989 Velvet Revolution, where the Civic Forum thrashed out tactics in the dressing rooms and gave daily press conferences in the auditorium against the stage set for Dürenmatt's *Minotaurus*.

The waterfront in southern Nové Město

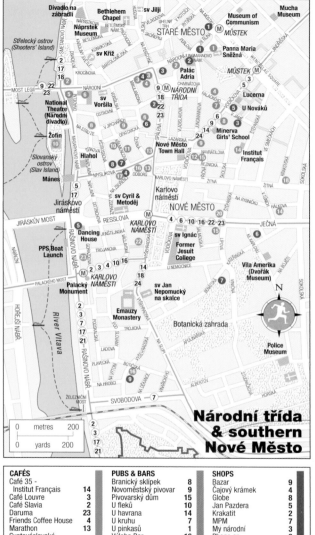

Národní třída & southern Nové Město

CAFÉS	
Café 35 - Institut Français	14
Café Louvre	3
Café Slavia	2
Daruma	23
Friends Coffee House	4
Marathon	13
Svatováclavská cukrárna	22
Velryba	6

PUBS & BARS	
Branický sklípek	8
Novoměstský pivovar	9
Pivovarský dům	15
U fleků	10
U havrana	14
U kruhu	7
U pinkasů	1
Výloha Bar	16

SHOPS	
Bazar	9
Čajový krámek	4
Globe	8
Jan Pazdera	5
Krakatit	2
MPM	7
My národní	3
Phono.cz	6
Pylones	1

RESTAURANTS	
Cicala	18
Dynamo	8
Miss Saigon	16
Pizzeria kmotra	9
Ryby & Chips	17
U Čiriny	15
U Šumavy	20
Žofín Garden	10

CLUBS & VENUES	
Divadlo Minor	12
Evald	2
Laterna magika	6
MAT Studio	13
National Theatre	5
Nebe	11
Reduta	3
Rock Café	4

ACCOMMODATION	
Dancing House Hotel	5
Hotel 16	7
Hotel Jungmann	1
Icon Hotel	3
MadHouse	2
Mánes	4
Miss Sophie's	6

Church of Panna Maria Sněžná

MAP p.91, POCKET MAP H13
Jungmannovo náměstí 18.

Once one of the great landmarks of Wenceslas Square, **Panna Maria Sněžná** (St Mary-of-the-Snows) is now barely visible from the surrounding streets. To reach the church, go through the archway behind the statue of Jungmann, and across the courtyard beyond. Founded in the fourteenth century as a Carmelite monastery by Emperor Charles IV, who envisaged a vast coronation church larger than St Vitus Cathedral, only the chancel was built before the money ran out. The result is curious – a church which is short in length, but equal to the cathedral in height. The 33m-high, prettily painted vaulting is awesome, as is the gargantuan gold and black Baroque main altar which almost touches the ceiling.

Národní třída

MAP p.91, POCKET MAP F14–G13
It was on this busy boulevard, lined with shops, galleries, banks and clubs, that the Velvet Revolution began. On **November 17, 1989**, a 50,000-strong student demonstration worked its way from Vyšehrad to Národní třída, aiming to reach Wenceslas Square in what the authorities deemed

Memorial sculpture on Národní

an illegal march. Halfway down the street their way was barred by the Communist riot police. The students sat down and refused to disperse, some of them handing out flowers. Suddenly, without any warning, the police attacked, and what became known as the *masakr* (massacre) began. In actual fact, no one was killed, though it wasn't for want of trying by the riot police. Under the arches of Národní 16, there's a small symbolic bronze relief of eight hands reaching out for help – candles are lit here every November 17, now a Czech national holiday.

Further down Národní, on the right-hand side, is an eye-catching duo of Art Nouveau buildings. The first, at no. 7, was built for the **Prague Savings Bank (pojišťovna Praha)**, hence the beautiful mosaic lettering above the windows advertising *život* (life insurance) and *kapital* (loans), as well as help with your *důchod* (pension) and *věno* (dowry). Next door, the slightly more ostentatious **Topičův dům**, headquarters of the official state publishers, provides the perfect accompaniment, with a similarly ornate wrought-iron and glass canopy.

Café Slavia

MAP p.91, POCKET MAP F13
Smetanovo nábřeží 2. Mon–Fri 8am–midnight, Sat & Sun 9am–midnight.

The **Café Slavia** (see p.98), opposite the National Theatre at the end of Národní třída, has been a favourite haunt of the city's writers, dissidents, artists and actors since the 1920s when the Czech avant-garde movement, **Devětsil**, used to hold its meetings here, recorded for posterity by Nobel prize-winning poet Jaroslav Seifert. Under the Communists, dissident (and later president) Václav Havel and his pals used to hang out here under the watchful eye of state security agents. The

National Theatre

ambience is not what it once was, and service can be quite gruff, but it still has a great riverside view and Viktor Oliva's classic *Absinthe Drinker* canvas on the wall.

Střelecký ostrov (Shooters' Island)

MAP p.91, POCKET MAP E13–E14
Most Legií (Legion's Bridge).

The **Střelecký ostrov** is where the army held their shooting practice, on and off, from the fifteenth until the nineteenth century. Closer to the other bank, and accessible via **Most Legií** (Legion's Bridge), it became a favourite spot for a Sunday promenade, and is still popular, especially in summer. The first Sokol gymnastics festival was held here in 1882, and the first May Day demonstrations took place on the island in 1890.

National Theatre (Národní divadlo)

MAP p.91, POCKET MAP F14
Národní 2 ⓦ narodni-divadlo.cz.

Overlooking the Vltava is the gold-crested **National Theatre**, one of the proudest symbols of the Czech national revival of the nineteenth century. Refused money from the Habsburg state coffers, Czechs of all classes dug deep into their pockets to raise the funds. After thirteen years of construction, in June 1881, the theatre opened with a premiere of Smetana's *Libuše*. In August of the same year, fire ripped through the building, destroying everything except the outer walls. Within two years the whole thing was rebuilt and even the emperor contributed this time. The grand portal on the north side of the theatre is embellished with suitably triumphant allegorical figures, and, inside, every square centimetre is taken up with paintings and sculptures by leading artists of the Czech national revival. The building has just undergone renovation to restore it to its former glory.

Standing behind the old National Theatre, and in dramatic contrast with it, is the theatre's unattractive extension, the opaque glass box of the **Nová scéna**, completed in 1983. It's one of those buildings most Praguers love to hate (they have an unrepeatable nickname for it), though compared to much of Prague's Communist-era architecture, it's not that bad. Just for the record, the lump of molten rock in the courtyard is a symbolic evocation entitled *My Socialist Country*.

U Nováků on Vodičkova

Vodičkova

MAP p.91, POCKET MAP G14–H13
Vodičkova is probably the most
impressive of the streets that
head south from Wenceslas
Square. Of the handful of
buildings worth checking out
on the way, the most remarkable
is **U Nováků** with its mosaic
of bucolic frolicking and its
delicate, ivy-like wrought
ironwork – look out for the frog-
prince holding up a windowsill.
Further down the street stands
the imposing neo-Renaissance
Minerva girls' school, covered
in bright red sgraffito. Founded
in 1866, it was the first such
institution in Prague, and
notorious for the antics of its
pupils, the "Minervans", who
shocked bourgeois Czech society
by experimenting with fashion,
drugs and sexual freedom.

Karlovo náměstí

MAP p.91, POCKET MAP G15
The impressive proportions of
Karlovo náměstí, once Prague's
biggest square, are no longer so
easy to appreciate, obscured by
trees and cut in two by a busy
thoroughfare. It was created by
Emperor Charles IV as Nové
Město's cattle market and used
by him for the annual public
display of his impressive (and
grisly) collection of saintly relics.
Now it signals the southern limit

of the city's main commercial
district and the beginning of
predominantly residential Nové
Město.

Nové Město Town Hall (Novoměstská radnice)

MAP p.91, POCKET MAP G14
Karlovo náměstí 23 Ⓦ nrpraha.cz.
Mid-April to mid-Oct Tues–Sun 10am–6pm.
60Kč.

Built in the fourteenth century,
the **Nové Město Town Hall**
is one of the finest Gothic
buildings in the city, sporting
three impressive triangular
gables embellished with intricate
blind tracery. It was here that
Prague's **first defenestration** took
place on July 30, 1419, when
the radical Hussite preacher
Jan Želivský and his penniless
religious followers stormed the
building, mobbed the councillors
and burghers, and threw twelve
or thirteen of them (including
the mayor) out of the town
hall windows onto the pikes of
the Hussite mob below, who
clubbed any survivors to death.
Václav IV, on hearing the news,
suffered a stroke and died just
two weeks later. So began the
long and bloody Hussite Wars.
After the amalgamation of
Prague's separate towns in 1784,
the building was used solely as
a criminal court and prison.
Nowadays, you can visit the site

of the defenestration, and climb to the top of the tower for a view over central Prague. The town hall also puts on temporary art exhibitions.

Church of sv Ignác

MAP p.91, POCKET MAP G15
Karlovo náměstí.

Begun in 1665, this former **Jesuit church** is quite remarkable inside, a pink and white confection, with lots of frothy stucco work and an exuberant pulpit dripping with gold drapery, cherubs and saints. The statue of St Ignatius (sv Ignác), which sits above the entrance surrounded by a sunburst, caused controversy at the time, as until then only the Holy Trinity had been depicted in such a way.

Cathedral of sv Cyril and Metoděj (Heydrich Martyrs' Memorial)

MAP p.91, POCKET MAP F15
Corer of Resslova and Na Zderaze
Ⓦ pamatnik-heydrichiady.cz. March–Oct Tues–Sun 9am–5pm; Nov–Feb Tues–Sat 9am–5pm. Free.

Amid all the traffic, it's extremely difficult to imagine the scene outside Prague's **Orthodox cathedral** on June 18, 1942, when seven Czechoslovak secret agents were besieged in the church by hundreds of SS troops. The agents had pulled off the dramatic assassination of Nazi leader **Reinhard Heydrich**, but had been betrayed by one of their own men. The Nazis surrounded the church just after 4am and fought a pitched battle for over six hours, trying explosives, flooding and any other method they could think of to drive the men out of their stronghold in the crypt. Eventually, all seven agents committed suicide rather than give themselves up.

There's a plaque at street level on the south wall to commemorate those who died,

and an exhibition inside – you can also visit the crypt itself, which has been left pretty much as it was at the time.

Slovanský ostrov (Slav Island)

MAP p.91, POCKET MAP E14–F15
Masarykovo nábřeží.

Slovanský ostrov is commonly known as **Žofín**, after the island's very yellow cultural centre, built in 1835 and named for Sophie, the mother of Emperor Franz-Josef I. By the late nineteenth century the island had become one of the city's foremost pleasure gardens. Even today concerts, balls and other social gatherings take place here, and rowing boats can be rented in the summertime. At the island's southern tip stands the onion-domed **Šítek water tower** and, spanning the narrow channel between the island and the embankment, the **Mánes** art gallery, a striking, white functionalist box designed in 1930. At the northern end is a bronze of the best-known Czech female writer, Božena Němcová.

Slovanský ostrov

Dancing House (Tančící Dům)

MAP p.91, POCKET MAP F15
Rašínovo nábřeží 80.

Designed by Frank O. Gehry and Vlado Milunič, this building is known as the **Dancing House** (Tančící dům) or "Fred and Ginger building", after the shape of the building's two towers, which look vaguely like a couple ballroom dancing. The apartment block next door was built at the start of the twentieth century by Václav Havel's grandfather, and was where, until the early 1990s, Havel and his first wife, Olga, lived in the top-floor flat.

Palacký Monument

MAP p.91, POCKET MAP D7
Palackého náměstí.

The **Monument to František Palacký**, the nineteenth-century Czech historian, politician and nationalist, is an energetic and inspirational Art Nouveau sculpture from 1912. Ethereal bronze bodies, representing the world of the imagination, shoot out at all angles, contrasting sharply with the plain stone mass of the plinth, and below, the giant seated figure of Palacký, representing the real world.

Emauzy monastery

MAP p.91, POCKET MAP D8
Vyšehradská 49 ⓦ emauzy.cz. April & Oct Mon–Fri 11am–5pm; May–Sept Mon–Sat 11am–5pm; Nov–March Mon–Fri 11am–2pm. 60Kč.

The intertwined concrete spires of the **Emauzy monastery** are an unusual modern addition to the Prague skyline. The monastery was one of the few important historical buildings to be damaged in World War II, in this case by a stray Anglo-American bomb (the pilot thought he was over Dresden). Founded by Emperor Charles IV, the cloisters contain some very valuable Gothic frescoes.

Dancing House

Shops

Bazar

MAP p.91, POCKET MAP D8
Vyšehradská 8. Opening hours vary.

This junk shop south of the city centre sells a huge range of odds and ends – everything from socialist-era pin badges to 1960s lightshades, and from 1980s Czechoslovak toy cars to German-built wardrobes.

Čajový krámek

MAP p.91, POCKET MAP G13
Národní 20. Mon–Fri 9.30am–7pm, Sat 10am–1pm.

A colourful emporium stocking an amazing range of teas from all over the tea-growing and tea-drinking world, loose in big glass jars as well as bagged and boxed. Czechs don't tend to be big tea drinkers, but the fruit infusions here – of which the range is impressive – are perennially popular.

Globe

MAP p.91, POCKET MAP F15
Pštrossova 6. Mon–Thurs 10am–midnight, Fri–Sun 9.30am–1am.

The expat bookshop *par excellence* – both a social centre and a superbly well-stocked store with friendly staff.

Jan Pazdera

MAP p.91, POCKET MAP H14
Vodičkova 28. Mon–Sat 10am–6pm.

Truly spectacular selection of old and new cameras, microscopes, telescopes, opera glasses and binoculars.

Krakatit

MAP p.91 POCKET MAP G13
Jungmannova 14. Mon–Fri 9.30am–6.30pm, Sat 10am–1pm.

This is big kids' nirvana – a little shop stuffed with fantasy and military literature, plus a good range of science fiction and comics.

Globe

MPM

MAP p.91, POCKET MAP F15
Myslíkova 19. Mon–Fri 9am–6pm, Sat 9am–1pm.

A whole range of kits for making model planes, tanks, trains, ships and cars, and toy soldiers.

My Národní

MAP p.91, POCKET MAP G13
Národní 26. Mon–Sat 8am–9pm, Sun 9am–8pm.

Once Prague's premier downtown department store, with the name a pun on its Communist predecessor (called *Máj*). It's actually owned by British supermarket chain Tesco, as the basement food hall attests.

Phono.cz

MAP p.91, POCKET MAP G14
Patovická 24. Mon–Fri 1–7pm.

Small vinyl shop, excellent for LPs from both western Europe and the former Czechoslovakia. Sells the record players, too.

Pylones

MAP p.91 POCKET MAP H13
28. října 11. Daily 10am–8pm.

More like a museum of the wacky than a shop, filled with colourful gadgets for the office or home.

Cafés

Café 35 – Institut Français

MAP p.91, POCKET MAP H14
Štěpánská 35. Mon–Fri 8.30am–8pm,
Sat 10am–2pm.

Housed as it is in Prague's Institut
Français, you can be sure of
great coffee and fresh pastries –
plus the chance to pose with a
French newspaper.

Café Louvre

MAP p.91, POCKET MAP G13
Národní 22. Mon–Fri 8am–11.30pm,
Sat & Sun 9am–11.30pm.

Swish, turn-of-the-twentieth-
century café with a long pedigree,
still a popular stop for shoppers.
There are high ceilings, inexpensive
food and cakes, a billiard hall and
window seats overlooking Národní.

Café Slavia

MAP p.91, POCKET MAP F13
Smetanovo nábřeží 2. Mon–Fri 8am–
midnight, Sat & Sun 9am–midnight.

This famous 1920s riverside café
pulls in a mixed crowd from
shoppers and tourists to old-timers
and the pre- and post-theatre mob.
Come here for a coffee and the
view, not the food or the service.

Daruma

MAP p.91, POCKET MAP D7
Trojanova 4. Mon–Fri 11am–10pm,
Sat & Sun 2–10pm.

Marathon

Sample around fifty types of tea at
this cellar teahouse with a homely
atmosphere, board games, changing
art on the walls and laid-back staff.

Friends Coffee House

MAP p.91, POCKET MAP H14
Palackého 7. Mon–Fri 9am–9pm, Sat & Sun
noon–8pm.

Big, popular café with great coffee,
fresh sandwiches and other light
snacks – one to linger in.

Marathon

MAP p.91, POCKET MAP G14
Černá 9. Mon–Fri 10am–midnight,
Sat 6pm–midnight.

Self-styled "library café" in the
university's 1920s-style religion
faculty, hidden in the backstreets,
south of Národní třída.

Svatováclavská cukrárna

MAP p.91, POCKET MAP D7
Václavská pasáž, Karlovo náměstí 6.
Daily 8am–7pm.

Join the local pensioner posse for
cheap Turkish coffee and strudel at
this busy *cukrárna* (café-bakery)
within the glass-roofed Václavská
pasáž, an interwar shopping
arcade well off the tourist trail.

Velryba (The Whale)

MAP p.91, POCKET MAP G14
Opatovická 24. Mon–Fri 11am–11pm, Sat &
Sun noon–11pm.

This funky pub-café has been
serving up cheap meals (mains
under 200Kč), beer, coffee and art
exhibitions to a studenty crowd for
over two and a half decades – and
it's still going strong.

Restaurants

Cicala

MAP p.91, POCKET MAP H15
Žitná 43 ☎ 222 210 375. Mon–Sat
11.30am–3pm & 5–10pm.

Very good family-run Italian
basement restaurant specializing
(mid-week) in fresh seafood (from
380Kč). There's also a wide range

of pasta (190–320Kč) and an appetizing antipasto selection.

Dynamo

MAP p.91, POCKET MAP F14
Pštrossova 29 ☏ 224 932 020. Daily 11am–midnight.

Fashionable little spot with eye-catching retro-1960s designer decor. Serves tapas, vegetarian and pasta dishes (150–190Kč), and steaks and Czech dishes for around 250Kč.

Miss Saigon

MAP p.91, POCKET MAP G14
Myslíkova 26 ☏ 222 560 328, Ⓦ miss-saigon.cz. Mon–Fri 10.30am–10.30pm, Sat & Sun 11.30am–11pm.

The Czech Republic has a large Vietnamese population who moved here during the Communist period, but their cuisine is virtually unknown. This simple place tries to put that right. The menu features classic Vietnamese ingredients (bamboo shoots, oyster sauce, cashew nuts, bean curd) and the staple dish – *pho*. Mains 49–250Kč.

Pizzeria kmotra (Godmother)

MAP p.91, POCKET MAP F14
V jirchářích 12 ☏ 224 934 100. Daily 11am–midnight.

This inexpensive, brick-vaulted basement pizza place is popular, and justifiably so – if possible, book a table in advance. Pizzas 135–188Kč.

Ryby & Chips

MAP p.91, POCKET MAP F15
Myslíkova 18 ☏ 222 519 986. Daily 10.30am–9.30pm.

After all that sugary central European starch, just the smell of Prague's best fish 'n' chip shop (it has just the right batter-and-vinegar aroma) will have homesick Brits reaching for the pickled eggs. Only the salad option spoils the sense of authenticity. Cod and chips 109Kč.

Dynamo

U čiriny

MAP p.91, POCKET MAP G14
Navrátilova 6 ☏ 222 231 709. Mon–Sat 11am–11pm.

This little family-run place, with only a handful of tables inside and a summer terrace, offers classic Slovak and Hungarian home cooking with dishes such as *halušky* (gnocchi), goulash and *strapačky* (potato dumplings) coming in at around 200Kč a shot.

U šumavy

MAP p.91, POCKET MAP H15
Štěpánská 3 ☏ 775 555 297, Ⓦ usumavy .cz. Daily 11am–midnight.

Authentically Bohemian restaurant sporting stencilled walls, high ceilings and antique furniture. The menu is a meaty feast of *svíčková* (sirloin in cream sauce), venison, beef goulash and roast pork, all served with fluffy dumplings and tankards of countryside lager. Mains around 200Kč.

Žofín Garden

MAP p.91, POCKET MAP E14
Slovanský ostrov 226 ☏ 774 774 774. Daily 11am–10pm.

On the island nearest the National Theatre, this tranquil place serves beautiful, upmarket Czech food such as venison, pike perch and rabbit (all around 300Kč).

Pubs and bars

Branický sklípek

MAP p.91, POCKET MAP H14
Vodičkova 26. Mon–Fri 9am–11pm,
Sat & Sun 11am–11pm.

Convenient downtown pub (aka *U Purkmistra*) decked out like a pine furniture showroom serving typical Czech dishes and jugs of Prague's Braník beer. The rough-and-ready *Branická formanka* next door opens and closes earlier.

Novoměstský pivovar

MAP p.91, POCKET MAP G14
Vodičkova 20 Ⓦ npivovar.cz. Mon–Fri
10am–11.30pm, Sat 11.30am–11.30pm,
Sun noon–10pm.

Outstanding microbrewery which serves its own 11° home-brew, plus huge portions of Czech food, in twelve sprawling beer halls and rooms, including some underground Gothic affairs.

Pivovarský dům

MAP p.91, POCKET MAP H15
Corner of Lipová/Ječná. Daily
11am–11.30pm.

Busy microbrewery dominated by big, shiny copper vats, serving gorgeous light, mixed and dark unfiltered beer (plus banana,

Pivovarský dům

coffee and wheat varieties), as well as Czech pub dishes.

U fleků

MAP p.91, POCKET MAP F14
Křemencova 11. Daily 10am–11pm.

Famous medieval brewery where the unique dark 13° beer, Flek, has been brewed since 1499. Seats over five hundred at a go, serves short measures (0.4l), charges extra for the music and still you might have to queue. Visit just to sample the beer, which you're best off doing during the day.

U havrana (The Crow)

MAP p.91 POCKET MAP J15
Hálkova 6. Mon–Fri 5pm–5am, Sat
6pm–5am.

The chief virtue of this ordinary and surprisingly respectable Czech pub is that it serves food and Velkopopovický Kozel beer until the wee hours.

U kruhu (The Wheel)

MAP p.91, POCKET MAP H14
Palackého 6. Daily 3–11pm.

Proper Czech pub, serving Plzeň beers and Velkopovický Kozel, with its own garden courtyard out front.

U pinkasů

MAP p.91, POCKET MAP H13
Jungmannovo náměstí 16. Daily
10am–11.30pm.

Famous as the pub where Pilsner Urquell was first served in Prague, it still serves excellent unpasteurized beer and classic Czech pub food.

Výloha Bar

MAP p.91, POCKET MAP D8
Vyšehradská 12 ☏ 606 762 022, Ⓦ www
.vylohabar.cz. Mon–Thurs 5pm–1am, Fri &
Sat 5pm–2am, Sun 5pm–midnight.

At the southern end of the Nové Město, this neighbourhood bar is great for hanging with locals, playing darts and watching the Czechs win at ice hockey. Next door to Prague's Toilet Museum.

Clubs and venues

Divadlo minor

MAP p.91, POCKET MAP G14
Vodičkova 6 ☎ 222 231 351, ⓦ minor.cz.
The former state puppet theatre puts on children's shows most days, plus adult shows on occasional evenings, sometimes with English subtitles.

Evald

MAP p.91, POCKET MAP G13
Národní 28 ☎ 221 105 225, ⓦ evald.cz.
Prague's most centrally located arthouse cinema shows a discerning selection of new releases interspersed with plenty of classics.

Laterna magika (Magic Lantern)

MAP p.91, POCKET MAP G13
Nová scéna, Národní 4 ☎ 224 901 417, ⓦ narodni-divadlo.cz.
The National Theatre's Nová scéna, one of Prague's most modern and versatile stages, is the main base for Laterna magika, founders of multimedia and "black light" theatre in 1958. Their slick productions continue to effortlessly pull in crowds of curious tourists.

MAT Studio

MAP p.91, POCKET MAP G15
Karlovo náměstí 19, entrance on Odborů ☎ 224 915 765, ⓦ mat.cz.
Tiny café and cinema popular with the film crowd, with an eclectic programme of shorts, documentaries and Czech films with English subtitles.

National Theatre (Národní divadlo)

MAP p.91, POCKET MAP F14
Národní 2 ☎ 224 901 448, ⓦ narodni-divadlo.cz.
The living embodiment of the Czech national revival movement, the National Theatre is worth visiting for the decor

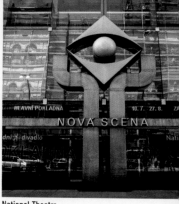

National Theatre

alone (see p.93). Czech plays are core to the repertoire, but there's also ballet and English-subtitled opera.

Nebe (Heaven)

MAP p.91, POCKET MAP F14
Křemecova 10 ⓦ nebepraha.cz. Mon 4pm–3am, Tues–Thurs 4pm–4am, Fri & Sat 4pm–5am, Sun 6pm–3am.
A simple, well-proven formula: a snaking, brick-vaulted cocktail bar with a long ethanol-based menu and DJs that pump out dance music from the last three or four decades. Cover charge 80–150Kč.

Reduta

MAP p.91, POCKET MAP G13
Národní 20 ☎ 224 933 487, ⓦ redutajazzclub.cz. Daily from 9.30pm.
Prague's best-known jazz club – Bill Clinton played his sax here in front of Havel – attracts a touristy crowd, but also some decent acts.

Rock Café

MAP p.91, POCKET MAP G13
Národní 20 ⓦ rockcafe.cz. Mon–Fri 10am–3am, Sat 5pm–3am, Sun 5pm–1am.
Not to be confused with the *Hard Rock Café*, this place is a stalwart of the live music scene; the basement stage showcases mostly new Czech bands. Cover charge 100–150Kč.

Vyšehrad, Vinohrady and Žižkov

South of the city centre, the fortress of Vyšehrad makes for a perfect afternoon escape away from the human congestion of the Old and New towns: its illustrious cemetery shelters the remains of Bohemia's artistic elite; the ramparts afford superb views over the river; and below the fortress there are several interesting examples of Czech Cubist architecture to seek out. The gentrified suburb of Vinohrady, to the east, is a late nineteenth-century residential neighbourhood, dominated by long streets of grandiose apartment blocks, with one or two specific sights to guide your wandering. By contrast, Žižkov, further north, is a grittier working-class district, whose shabby streets contain many pubs and clubs. The highlight here is the National Monument, a must for fans of Eastern European history.

Cubist villas

MAP OPPOSITE, POCKET MAP D8

Even if you harbour only a passing interest in modern architecture, it's worth seeking out the cluster of **Cubist villas** below the fortress in Vyšehrad. The most impressive example is the apartment block at **Neklanova 30**, begun in 1913, which brilliantly exploits its

angular location. Further along Neklanova, at no. 2, there's another Cubist facade, and around the corner is the most ambitious of the lot, the **Kovařovicova vila** (Libušina 49), which uses prism shapes and angular lines to produce the sharp geometric contrasts of light and dark shadows characteristic of Cubist painting.

Kovařovicova vila

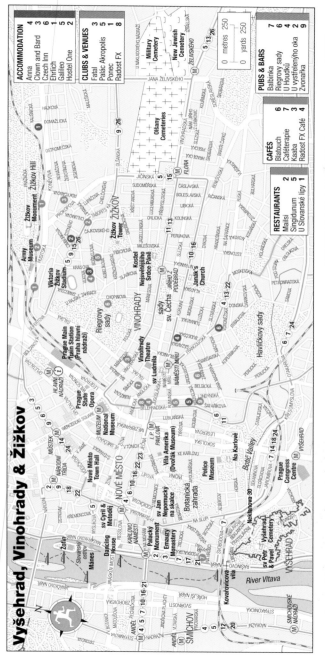

Vyšehrad, Vinohrady & Žižkov

VYŠEHRAD, VINOHRADY AND ŽIŽKOV

ACCOMMODATION	
Anna	4
Clown and Bard	3
Czech Inn	6
Ehrlich	1
Galileo	5
Hostel One	2

CLUBS & VENUES	
Fatal	3
Palác Akropolis	5
Ponec	1
Radost FX	8

PUBS & BARS	
Balbínka	7
Riegrovy sady	6
U Houdků	4
U vystřeleného oka	2
Zvonařka	9

CAFÉS	
Blatouch	6
Cafféterapie	7
Kaaba	3
Radost FX Café	4

RESTAURANTS	
Mailsi	2
Singidunum	5
U Slovanské lipy	1

0 metres 250

0 yards 250

River Vltava

Vyšehrad

MAP p.103, POCKET MAP D9
V pevnosti 5b ⓦ praha-vysehrad.cz.
Open 24hr. Free.

The rocky red-brick fortress of **Vyšehrad** – literally "High Castle" – has more myths attached to it than any other place in Bohemia. According to Czech legend, this is the place where the Slav tribes first settled in Prague and where the "wise and tireless chieftain" Krok built a castle, whence his youngest daughter Libuše went on to found Praha itself. Alas, the archeological evidence doesn't really bear this claim out. What you see now are the remains of a fortified barracks built by the Habsburgs and then turned into a public park.

You can explore the fortress's northern entrance, or **Cihelná brána** (daily: April–Oct 9.30am–6pm; Nov–March 9.30am–5pm; free), and the adjacent **dungeons**, or **kasematy** (same hours; 60Kč). After a short guided tour of a section of the underground passageways underneath the ramparts, you enter a vast storage hall, which shelters several of the original statues from Charles Bridge, and, when the lights are

Cihelná brána, Vyšehrad

Getting to Vyšehrad

To reach Vyšehrad, take tram #2, #3, #7, #14, #17, #18, #21 or #24 to Výtoň, and either wind your way up Vratislavova to the Cihelná brána or take the steep stairway from Rašínovo nábřeží that leads up through the trees. Alternatively, from Vyšehrad metro station, walk west past the ugly Prague Congress Centre, and enter via V pevnosti, where there's an information centre (daily: April–Oct 9.30am–6pm; Nov–March 9.30am–5pm).

switched off, reveals a camera obscura image of a tree.

Over in the southwestern corner of the fortress, in the **Gothic cellar** (same hours; 50Kč), there's also a permanent exhibition on the history of Vyšehrad. The rock's big moment in Czech history was in the eleventh century when Přemysl Vratislav II – the first Bohemian ruler to bear the title "king" – built a royal palace here to get away from his younger brother who was lording it in the Hrad. Within half a century the royals had moved back to Hradčany, into a new palace, and from then on Vyšehrad began to lose its political significance.

Church of sv Petr and Pavel

MAP p.103, POCKET MAP D9
K rotundě 10. Daily 10.30am–5.30pm.
50Kč.

The twin openwork spires of this blackened sandstone church, rebuilt in the 1880s in neo-Gothic style on the site of an eleventh-century basilica, are now the fortress's most familiar landmark. Inside, you can admire the church's **Art Nouveau murals**,

Doors of the Church of sv Petr and Pavel

which cover just about every available surface.

Vyšehrad Cemetery (Vyšehradský hřbitov)

MAP p.103, POCKET MAP D9
ⓦ slavin.cz. Daily: March, April & Oct 8am–6pm; May–Sept 8am–7pm; Nov–Feb 8am–5pm. Free.

Most Czechs come to Vyšehrad to pay a visit to the **cemetery**. It's a measure of the part that artists and intellectuals played in the foundation of the nation, and the regard in which they are still held, that the most prestigious graveyard in the city is given over to them: no soldiers, no politicians – not even the Communists managed to muscle their way in here (except on artistic merit). Sheltered from the wind by its high walls, lined on two sides by delicate arcades, it's a tiny cemetery filled with well-kept graves, many of them designed by the country's leading sculptors.

To the uninitiated only a handful of figures are well known, but for the Czechs the place is alive with great names (there's a useful plan of the most

notable graves at the entrance nearest the church). Ladislav Šaloun's grave for **Dvořák**, situated under the arches, is one of the more showy ones, with a mosaic inscription, studded with gold stones, glistening behind wrought-iron railings. **Smetana**, who died twenty years earlier, is buried in comparatively modest surroundings near the **Slavín monument**, the cemetery's focal point, which is the communal resting place of more than fifty Czech artists, including the painter Alfons Mucha and the opera singer Ema Destinová. The grave of the Romantic poet Karel Hynek Mácha was the assembly point for the demonstration on November 17, 1989, which triggered the Velvet Revolution. This was organized to commemorate the fiftieth anniversary of the Nazi closure of Czech higher education institutions. A 50,000-strong crowd gathered here and attempted to march to Wenceslas Square, getting as far as Národní before being beaten back (see p.92).

Vyšehrad Cemetery

Vila Amerika

Police Museum

MAP p.103, POCKET MAP E8
Ke Karlovu 1, Ⓜ Karlovo náměstí. Tues–Sun
10am–5pm. 50Kč.

The former Augustinian monastery of Karlov houses the **Police Museum**, which concentrates on road and traffic offences, and the force's latest challenges: forgery, drugs and murder. There's a whole section on the old Iron Curtain and espionage, but not a huge amount of information in English. If you've got kids, however, they might enjoy driving round the mini-road layout on one of the museum trikes.

Na Karlově church

MAP p.103, POCKET MAP E8
Ke Karlovu, Ⓜ Karlovo náměstí. Opening
hours vary. Free.

Founded by Emperor Charles IV and designed in imitation of Charlemagne's tomb in Aachen, this octagonal church is quite unlike any other in Prague. If it's open, you should take a look at the dark interior, which was remodelled in the sixteenth century by Bonifaz Wohlmut.

The stellar vault has no central supporting pillars – a remarkable feat of engineering for its time, and one which gave rise to numerous legends about the architect being in league with the Devil.

Vila Amerika (Dvořák Museum)

MAP p.103, POCKET MAP E7
Ke Karlovu 20, Ⓜ I. P. Pavlova. Tues–Sun
10am–1.30pm & 2–5pm. 50Kč.

The russet-coloured **Vila Amerika** was originally named after the local pub, but is now a museum devoted to **Antonín Dvořák** (1841–1904), the most famous of all Czech composers, who lived for a time on nearby Zitná. Even if you've no interest in Dvořák, the villa itself is a delight, built as a Baroque summer house from around 1720. The tasteful period rooms, with the composer's music wafting in and out, and the tiny garden dotted with Baroque sculptures, together go a long way towards compensating for what the display cabinets may lack.

Náměstí Míru

MAP p.103, POCKET MAP F7

If Vinohrady has a centre, it's the leafy square of **Náměstí Míru**, a good introduction to this neighbourhood. The most flamboyant building here is the **Vinohrady Theatre** (Divadlo na Vinohradech), built in 1907, with both Art Nouveau and neo-Baroque elements. Completely dominating the centre of the square is the brick basilica of **sv Ludmila**, designed in the late 1880s in a severe neo-Gothic style by the great neo-Gothicizer Josef Mocker, though the interior has the odd flourish of Art Nouveau. In front a statue commemorates the **Čapek brothers**, writer Karel and painter Josef, local residents who together symbolized the golden era of the interwar republic. Karel died of pneumonia in 1938, while Josef perished in Belsen seven years later.

Kostel Nejsvětějšího Srdce Páně

MAP p.103, POCKET MAP G7
Náměstí Jiřího z Poděbrad, Ⓜ Jiřího z Poděbrad. Opening hours vary. Free.

Prague's most celebrated modern church, **Nejsvětějšího Srdce Páně** (Church of the Most Holy Heart of Our Lord) was built in 1928 by the Slovene architect **Josip Plečnik**. It's a marvellously eclectic work, employing a sophisticated potpourri of architectural styles: a Neoclassical pediment and a great slab of a clock tower with a giant transparent face in imitation of a Gothic rose window, as well as the bricks and mortar of contemporary constructivism. Plečnik also had a sharp eye for detail – look out for the little gold crosses inset into the brickwork like stars, inside and out, and the celestial orbs of light suspended above the congregation.

Žižkov TV Tower (Televizní věž)

MAP p.103, POCKET MAP G6
Mahlerovy sady 1, Ⓜ Jiřího z Poděbrad. Ⓦ www.towerpark.cz. Daily 9am–midnight. 230Kč.

At 216m in height, the **Žižkov TV Tower** is Prague's tallest building. Close up, it's an intimidating futuristic piece of architecture, made all the more disturbing by the giant babies crawling up the sides, courtesy of artist **David Černý**. Begun in the 1970s in a desperate bid to jam West German television transmissions, the tower became fully operational only in the 1990s. In the course of its construction, however, the Communists saw fit to demolish part of a nearby **Jewish cemetery** that had served the community between 1787 and 1891; a small section survives to the northwest of the tower. Following a major **reconstruction**, the tower now features a café, restaurant, bar, observatory and even a one-room hotel.

Žižkov TV Tower

VYŠEHRAD, VINOHRADY AND ŽIŽKOV

Olšany cemeteries (Olšanské hřbitovy)

MAP p.103, POCKET MAP H6–J6
Vinohradská, Ⓜ Flora. Daily dawn–dusk.
Free.

The vast Olšany cemeteries were originally created for the victims of the great plague epidemic of 1680. The perimeter walls are lined with glass cabinets, stacked like shoeboxes, containing funeral urns and mementoes, while the graves themselves are a mixed bag of artistic achievements, reflecting the funereal fashions of the day as much as the character of the deceased. The cemeteries are divided into districts and criss-crossed with cobbled streets; at each gate there's a map and an aged janitor ready to point you in the right direction.

The cemeteries' two most famous incumbents are an ill-fitting couple: **Klement Gottwald**, the country's first Communist president, whose remains were removed from the mausoleum on Žižkov Hill after 1989 and reinterred here; and **Jan Palach**, the philosophy student who set light to himself in January 1969 in protest at the Soviet occupation. More than 750,000 people attended Palach's funeral, and in an attempt to put a stop to the annual vigils at his graveside, the secret police removed his body and reburied him in his home town outside Prague. In 1990, Palach's body was returned to Olšany; you'll find it just to the east of the main entrance.

New Jewish Cemetery (Nový židovský hřbitov)

MAP p.103, POCKET MAP K6
Izraelská 1, Ⓜ Želivského. April–Oct Mon–Thurs & Sun 9am–5pm, Fri 9am–2pm; Nov–March Mon–Thurs & Sun 9am–4pm, Fri 9am–2pm. 50Kč.

Founded in the 1890s, the **New Jewish Cemetery** was designed to last for a century, with room for 100,000 graves. It's a truly melancholy spot, particularly in the east of the cemetery, where large empty allotments wait in vain to be filled by the generation that perished in the Holocaust. Most people come here to visit **Franz Kafka's grave**, which is located 400m east along the south wall and signposted from the entrance. He is buried, along with his mother and father (both of whom outlived him), beneath a plain headstone; the plaque below is dedicated to the memory of his three sisters, who died in the concentration camps.

Gravestone at Olšany

Žižkov monument

Žižkov Hill

MAP p.103, POCKET MAP G5–H5
U památníku, bus #133, #175 or #207 from Ⓜ Florenc.

Žižkov Hill is the thin green wedge of land that separates Žižkov from Karlín, the grid-plan industrial district to the north. From its westernmost point, which juts out almost to the edge of Nové Město, is the definitive panoramic view over the city centre. It was here, on July 14, 1420, that the Hussites enjoyed their first and finest victory at the **Battle of Vítkov**, under the inspired leadership of the one-eyed general, Jan Žižka (hence the name of the district). Outnumbered by ten to one, Žižka and his fanatical troops thoroughly trounced the Bohemian king (and Holy Roman Emperor Sigismund) and his papal forces.

Despite its totalitarian aesthetics, the giant concrete **Žižkov monument**, which graces the crest of the hill, was actually built between the wars as a memorial to the Czechoslovak Legion who fought against the Habsburgs in World War I – the gargantuan statue of the mace-wielding Žižka, which fronts the monument, is reputedly the world's largest equestrian statue. The building was later used by the Nazis as an arsenal, and eventually became a Communist mausoleum. In 1990, the Communists were cremated and quietly reinterred in Olšany. The monument now houses a fascinating **museum** (Ⓦ nm.cz; April–Oct Wed–Sun 10am–6pm; Nov–March Thurs–Sun 10am–6pm; 120Kč) on the country's twentieth-century history; there's also a Communist monument to the fallen of World War II and a café on top, with great views over Prague's suburbs.

Army Museum (Armádní muzeum)

MAP p.103, POCKET MAP G5
U památníku 2, bus #133, #175 or #207 from Ⓜ Florenc Ⓦ vhu.cz. Tues–Sun 10am–6pm. Free.

Guarded by a handful of unmanned tanks, howitzers and armoured vehicles, the **Army Museum** has a permanent exhibition covering the country's military history from 1914 to 1945. A fairly evenly balanced account of both world wars includes coverage of controversial subjects such as the exploits of the Czechoslovak Legion, the Heydrich assassination and the 1945 Prague Uprising.

Cafés

Blatouch

MAP p.103, POCKET MAP F7
Americká 17 ☎ 222 328 643. Mon–Thurs
noon–midnight, Fri noon–1am, Sat
1pm–1am, Sun 1–11pm.
Unpretentious café in the heart of
Vinohrady that predates the flashier
establishments all around. Salads,
toasted sandwiches, pastas and
tortillas, many of them vegetarian,
make up the menu and there's
Ferdinand beer from Benešov.

Caféterapie

MAP p.103, POCKET MAP D8
Na hrobci 3. Mon–Fri 8.30am–10pm,
Sat 9am–10pm, Sun 10am–10pm.
Small, simply furnished café that
serves up healthy Mediterranean-
influenced salads, sandwiches,
toasties and a few hot dishes.

Kaaba

MAP p.103, POCKET MAP K14
Mánesova 20. Mon–Fri 8am–midnight,
Sat 9am–midnight, Sun 10am–midnight.
This stylish ice-cream parlour/
café attracts a young, cool crowd
with its mismatched retro decor.
Serves breakfast, light meals
and sundaes.

Radost FX Café

MAP p.103, POCKET MAP J15
Bělehradská 120. Mon–Sat 11am–11pm,
Sun 11am–3pm.

Radost FX Café

The veggie dishes at this expat
favourite are filling (most under
200Kč), and there's a weekend
brunch, decadent decor and a
dance soundtrack with live DJs at
the weekend. However, it can be a
disappointing culinary experience.

Restaurants

Mailsi

MAP p.103, POCKET MAP G6
Lipanská 1 ☎ 774 972 010, ⓦ mailsi.cz.
Daily noon–3pm & 6–11pm.
Friendly Pakistani place in
Žižkov that's great for a comfort
curry (around 250–500Kč), as
hot as you can handle. There's a
rare subcontinental grocery shop
next door.

Singidunum

MAP p.103, POCKET MAP F7
Bělehradská 92 ☎ 222 544 113,
ⓦ singidunum.cz. Daily 11am–11pm.
Singidunum is the Latin for
Belgrade, and it's the hot-
tempered cuisine of the Balkans
you'll find at this atmospheric
place. There are *čevapčiči* (kebabs),
Adriatic pastas, Croatian *pršut*
(ham) plus Macedonian and
Montenegran wines. Mains
150–500Kč.

U slovanské lípy

MAP p.103, POCKET MAP H5
Tachovské náměstí 6 ☎ 734 743 094,
ⓦ uslovanskelipy.cz. Daily 11am–midnight.
Žižkov's oldest tavern serves
solid, no-nonsense Prague and
Bohemian dishes in a wood-
panelled dining room. Interesting
guest ales on tap. Mains
100–200Kč.

Pubs and bars

Balbinka

MAP p.103, POCKET MAP K15
Balbinova 6. Mon–Fri 3pm–midnight,
Sat & Sun 6pm–midnight.

This small "poet's" pub is cherished by its regulars, and rightly so. With nightly live music ranging from rock to country or folk, part of the charm is never knowing what you might encounter.

Riegrovy sady

MAP p.103, POCKET MAP G6
Riegrovy sady. Daily 11am–11pm.
A real slice of local life, a neighbourhood park café-pub whose beer terrace is perennially popular, especially for big TV sports events.

U houdků

MAP p.103, POCKET MAP G6
Bořivojova 110. Daily 11am–midnight.
Friendly local pub right in the heart of Žižkov, with a beer garden, Kozel on tap and cheap Czech food.

U vystřeleného oka (The Shot-Out Eye)

MAP p.103, POCKET MAP G5
U božích bojovníků 3. Mon–Sat 4.30pm–1am.
Big, loud, heavy-drinking pub with good (sometimes live) indie rock and lashings of Měšťan beer, plus absinthe chasers.

Zvonařka (The Bell)

MAP p.103, POCKET MAP F8
Šafaříkova 1. Mon–Thurs 11.30am–midnight, Fri 11.30am–1am, Sat noon–midnight, Sun noon–11pm.
Not only is this pub smart and modern, but it has an appealing summer terrace with great views over the Nuselské schody and Botič valley.

Clubs and venues

Fatal

MAP p.103, POCKET MAP H5
Rokycanova 29 ⓦ fatalclub.cz.
A young Czech crowd flocks to this club in Žižkov for its winning combination of cheap drinks and unfamiliar acts from

Ponec

around central Europe. Cover charge 50–100Kč.

Palác Akropolis

MAP p.103, POCKET MAP G6
Kubelíkova 27 ⓣ 296 330 913, ⓦ palacakropolis.cz. Mon–Thurs 11am–12.30am, Fri 11am–1.30am, Sat & Sun 3pm–12.30am.
This old Art Deco theatre is Žižkov's most popular club venue – it's also a great place to just have a drink or a bite to eat, as well as checking out the DJ nights or the live gigs. Cover charge 100Kč and upwards for events.

Ponec

MAP p.103, POCKET MAP G5
Husitská 24a ⓣ 222 721 531, ⓦ divadloponec.cz.
Former cinema, now an innovative dance venue and centre for the annual Tanec Praha Dance Festival in June.

Radost FX

MAP p.103, POCKET MAP J15
Bělehradská 120 ⓣ 224 254 776, ⓦ radostfx.cz. Thurs–Sat 10pm–4am.
This spacious club is Prague's longest-running all-round dance venue, with house and techno keeping the expats happy. Up to 250Kč entrance depending on the night.

Holešovice

Tucked into a U-bend in the River Vltava, the late nineteenth-century suburb of Holešovice boasts two huge splodges of green: Letná, overlooking the city centre, and, to the north, Stromovka, Prague's largest public park, bordering the Výstaviště funfair and trade fair grounds. A stroll through the park brings you to the Baroque chateau of Troja and the leafy zoo. Two important art museums are located in Holešovice – the city's main museum of modern art, Veletržní Palace, and the DOX Centre for Contemporary Art. Few tourists make it out here, but it's worth the effort, if only to remind yourself that Prague doesn't begin and end at Charles Bridge.

Letná

MAP OPPOSITE, POCKET MAP D4

A high plateau hovering above the city, the flat green expanse of the **Letná** plain has long been the traditional assembly point for invading and besieging armies. Under the Communists, it was used primarily for the annual May Day parades, during which thousands trudged past the Sparta Prague stadium, where the Communist leaders would salute from their giant red podium. It once boasted the largest **Stalin monument** in

the world: a 30m-high granite sculpture portraying a procession of Czechs and Russians being led to Communism by the Pied Piper figure of Stalin, but popularly dubbed *tlačenice* (the crush) because of its resemblance to a Communist-era bread queue. The monument was unveiled on May 1, 1955, but within a year Khrushchev had denounced Stalin, and the monument was blown up in 1962. On the site of the Stalin statue, overlooking the Vltava, stands a symbolic giant red **metronome** (which is lit up at night).

View from Letná

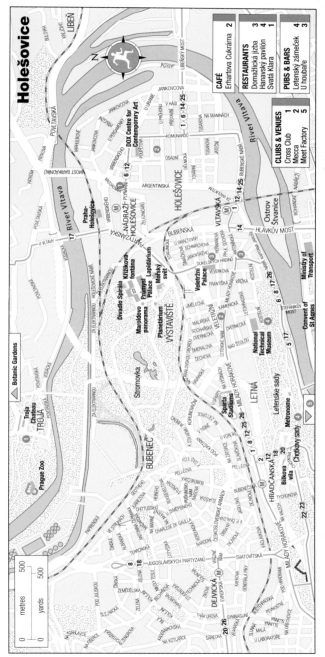

Holešovice

Sculpture by František Bílek, Bílkova vila

Bílkova vila

MAP p.112, POCKET MAP C4
Mieckiewiczova 1 Ⓦ ghmp.cz.
Tues–Sun 10am–6pm. 120Kč.

The **Bílkova vila**, an undervisited branch of the Prague City Gallery, honours one of the most original of all Czech sculptors, **František Bílek** (1872–1941). Built in 1911 to the artist's own design, the house was intended as both a "cathedral of art" and the family's (rather lavish) home. The outside is lined with columns reminiscent of ancient Egypt; inside, Bílek's extravagant religious sculptures line the walls of his "workshop and temple". In addition to his sculptural and relief work in wood and stone, often wildly expressive and spiritually tortured, there are also ceramics, graphics and a few mementoes of Bílek's life. His living quarters have also been restored and have much of the original wooden furniture, designed and carved by Bílek himself, still in place. Check out the dressing table for his wife, shaped like some giant church lectern, and the wardrobe decorated with a border of hearts, a penis, a nose, an ear and an eye plus the sun, stars and moon.

Chotkovy sady

MAP p.112, POCKET MAP C4

Prague's first public park, the **Chotkovy sady**, was founded in 1833 by the ecologically minded city governor, Count Chotek. The atmosphere here is relaxed and you can happily stretch out on the grass and soak up the sun, or head for the south wall, for an unrivalled view of the bridges and islands of the Vltava. At the centre of the park there's a bizarre, melodramatic grotto-like memorial to the nineteenth-century Romantic poet **Julius Zeyer**, an elaborate monument from which life-sized characters from Zeyer's works, carved in white marble, emerge from the blackened rocks.

National Technical Museum (Národní technické muzeum)

MAP p.112, POCKET MAP E4
Kostelní 42 Ⓦ ntm.cz. Tues–Fri
9am–5.30pm, Sat & Sun 10am–6pm.
190Kč.

Despite its dull name, this museum is surprisingly interesting, with a showpiece hangar-like main hall containing an impressive gallery of Czech and foreign motorbikes, plus a wonderful collection of old planes, trains and automobiles from Czechoslovakia's industrial heyday between the wars – when the country's Škoda cars and Tatra soft-top stretch limos were really something to brag about. Other displays trace the development of early photography, while there's an excellent exhibit focusing on Czech architectural feats from the second half of the nineteenth century to the present, and a collection of some of Johannes Kepler and Tycho Brahe's astronomical instruments.

Veletržní palác (Trade Fair Palace)

MAP p.112, POCKET MAP E3
Dukelských hrdinů 45 Ⓦ ngprague.cz.
Tues–Sun 10am–6pm. 250Kč.

The **Veletržní palác** gets nothing like the number of visitors it should. For not only does the building house Prague's best twentieth-century Czech and international art collection, it is also an architectural sight in itself. Built in 1928, the palace is Prague's ultimate functionalist masterpiece, particularly its vast white interior.

The gallery is bewilderingly big and virtually impossible to view in its entirety in a single visit. Temporary exhibitions are housed on the first and fifth floors, while the permanent collection occupies the other three. The popular **French art collection** includes works by Rodin, Renoir, Van Gogh, Matisse and Picasso, while other notable **international** exhibits include cover Surrealist Miró, a couple of Henry Moore sculptures and a perforated Lucio Fontana canvas. There are also a few pieces by Klimt, Kokoschka, Schiele and Munch, whose influence on early twentieth-century Czech art was considerable.

The **Czech art** section starts with Impressionists Preisler and Slavíček, Cubists Čapek, Gutfreund, Filla and Kubišta, and a whole series of works by František Kupka, by far the most important Czech painter of the last century and (possibly) the first artist in the Western world to exhibit abstract paintings. **Socialist Realism** and **performance art** are not neglected either – plan on spending a full day here.

At the time of writing, the most talked-about exhibit was Mucha's Slav Epic (*Slovanská epopej*), a series of twenty oversized canvases painted between 1912 and 1928 following Alfons Mucha's return to his homeland from Paris. Having spent the Communist period in a disused chateau in Moravia, in the early 2000s the city of Prague decided the Slav Epic belonged in the capital and the cycle now hangs in the Veletržní palác as a "temporary exhibition". Where it will go from here, if it ever does, no one knows.

DOX Centre for Contemporary Art

MAP p.112, POCKET MAP G2
Poupětova 1 Ⓦ dox.cz. Mon, Sat & Sun 10am–6pm, Wed & Fri 11am–7pm , Thurs 11am–9pm. 180Kč.

Founded by a private initiative with the goal of making Prague a major European centre for contemporary art, the **DOX Centre** presents mostly group exhibitions that aim to push boundaries and introduce new dialogues. Both Czech and international artists are represented, while the organization's educational programmes, debates and talks make it a pivotal part of the local arts scene. The sprawling building is stunning too, and features a lovely café and good design shop.

Výstaviště (Exhibition Grounds)

MAP p.112, POCKET MAP E2
Dukelských hrdinů Ⓦ vystavistepraha.eu.
Tues–Fri 2–9pm, Sat & Sun 10am–9pm.
50Kč or free.

Since the 1891 Prague Exhibition, **Výstaviště** has served as the city's main trade fair arena and funfair. At the centre of the complex is the flamboyant stained-glass and wrought-iron **Průmysl Palace**, scene of Communist Party rubber-stamp congresses. Several modern structures were built for the 1991 Prague Exhibition, including a circular theatre, **Divadlo Spirála**.

The grounds are busiest at the weekend, particularly in summer, when hordes of Prague families descend to munch hot dogs and drink beer. Apart from the annual trade fairs and special exhibitions, there are a few permanent attractions: the city's **Planetárium** (Ⓦ planetarium.cz; opening hours vary; 50–150Kč), which has static displays and shows films; the **Maroldovo panorama** (April–Oct Tues–Fri 1–5pm, Sat & Sun 10am–5pm; 25Kč), a giant diorama of the 1434 Battle of Lipany; and **Mořský svět** (Ⓦ morsky-svet.cz;

Mon–Fri 8.30am–6pm, Sat & Sun 9am–7pm; 280Kč), an aquarium full of colourful tropical fish, a few rays and some sea turtles. In the long summer evenings, the *Pražon* restaurant shows outdoor films and hosts concerts, and there are hourly evening performances (230Kč) by the dancing **Křižík Fountain**, devised for the 1891 Exhibition by the Czech inventor František Křižík. Call ✆ 220 103 224 or visit Ⓦ krizikovafontana.cz for details.

Lapidárium

MAP p.112, POCKET MAP E2
U Výstaviště Ⓦ www.nm.cz. May–Nov Wed 10am–4pm, Thurs–Sun noon–6pm. 50Kč.

Official depository for the city's sculptures which are under threat either from demolition or from the weather, the **Lapidárium** houses a much overlooked collection, ranging from the eleventh to the nineteenth century. Some of the statues saved from the perils of Prague's polluted atmosphere, such as the bronze equestrian statue of St George, will be familiar if you've visited Prague Castle before; others, such as the figures from the towers of Charles Bridge, were more difficult to

Průmysl Palace, Výstaviště

Getting to Troja and the zoo

To reach Troja and the zoo you can either **walk** from Výstaviště, catch **bus** #112, which runs frequently from metro Nádraží Holešovice, or take a **boat** (⊕ paroplavba.cz; April & Sept Sat & Sun; May–Aug daily; 190Kč) from the PPS landing place on Rašínovo nábřeží, metro Karlovo náměstí.

inspect closely in their original sites. Many of the original statues from the bridge can be seen here, including the ones that were fished out of the Vltava after the flood of 1890.

One outstanding sight is what remains of the **Krocín fountain**, a highly ornate Renaissance work in red marble, which used to grace Staroměstské náměstí (see p.60). Several pompous imperial monuments that were bundled into storage after the demise of the Habsburgs in 1918 round off the museum's collection. By far the most impressive is the bronze statue of Marshal Radecký, scourge of the 1848 revolution, carried aloft on a shield by eight Habsburg soldiers.

Stromovka

MAP p.112, POCKET MAP D2

Originally laid out as hunting grounds for the noble occupants of the castle, **Stromovka** is now Prague's largest and leafiest public park. If you're heading north for Troja and the city zoo, a stroll through the park is by far the most pleasant approach. If you want to explore a little more of it, head west, sticking to the park's southern border, and you'll eventually come to a neo-Gothic former royal hunting chateau, which served as the seat of the Governor of Bohemia until 1918.

Troja chateau (Trojský zámek)

MAP p.112, POCKET MAP C1
U trojského zámku 1 ⊕ ghmp.cz.
April–Oct Tues–Thurs, Sat & Sun
10am–6pm, Fri 1–6pm. 120Kč.

The **Troja** chateau was designed by Jean-Baptiste Mathey for the powerful Šternberg family towards the end of the seventeenth century. The best features of the rust-coloured Baroque facade are the monumental balustrades, where blackened figures of giants and titans battle it out. The star exhibits of the interior are the gushing frescoes depicting the victories of the Habsburg Emperor Leopold I (who reigned from 1657 to 1705) over the Turks, which cover every inch of the walls and ceilings of the grand hall. You also get to wander through the chateau's pristine, trend-setting, French-style formal gardens, the first of their kind in Bohemia.

Troja chateau

HOLEŠOVICE

Prague Zoo (Zoologická zahrada)

MAP p.112, POCKET MAP C1
U trojského zámku 3 Ⓦ zoopraha.cz. Daily:
March 9am–5pm; April, May, Sept & Oct
9am–6pm; June–Aug 9am–9pm; Nov–Feb
9am–4pm. 200Kč.

Founded in 1931 on the site of one of Troja's numerous hillside vineyards, Prague's **zoo** has had a lot of money poured into it and now has some very imaginative enclosures. All the usual animals are on show here – including elephants, hippos, giraffes, zebras, big cats and bears – and kids, at least, will enjoy themselves. A bonus in the summer is the **chairlift** (*lanová dráha*) from the duck pond over the enclosures to the top of the hill, where the prize exhibits – a rare breed of miniature horse known as Przewalski – hang out. Other highlights include the red pandas, the giant tortoises, the Komodo dragons, and the bats that actually fly past your face in the Twilight Zone.

Botanic Gardens (Botanická zahrada)

MAP p.112, POCKET MAP D1
Nádvorní 134 Ⓦ botanicka.cz.
Daily: March & Oct 9am–5pm; April
9am–6pm; May–Aug 9am–8pm; Sept
9am–7pm; Nov–Feb 9am–4pm. 150Kč.

Another reason for coming out to Troja is to visit the city's **Botanic Gardens**, hidden in the woods to the north of the chateau. The botanic gardens feature a vineyard, a Japanese garden, several glasshouses and great views over Prague. Hidden in the woods a little higher up the hill, there's also a spectacular, curvaceous greenhouse, **Fata Morgana** (same hours but closed Mon), with butterflies flitting about amid the desert and tropical plants.

Prague Zoo

Café

Erhartova cukrárna

MAP p.112, POCKET MAP E3
Milady Horákové 56 Ⓦ erhartovacukrarna
.cz. Daily 10am–7pm.

First Republic sweet shop with
delectable cakes and a long queue.
The café's functionalist architecture
is a treat for the eyes as well.

Restaurants

Domažlická jizba

MAP p.112, POCKET MAP E3
Strossmayerovo náměstí 2 Ⓣ 607
556 379, Ⓦ domazlicka-jizba.cz.
Daily 11am–midnight.

Join lunching locals at this wood-
panelled, traditional dining room;
it's been banging down goulash
and chicken schnitzel since 1906.
Mains 150–200Kč, lunch menu
120Kč.

Hanavský pavilón

MAP p.112, POCKET MAP E10
Letenské sady 173 Ⓣ 233 323 641.
Daily 11am–midnight.

Highly ornate wrought-iron Art
Nouveau pleasure pavilion high
above the Vltava, with stunning
views from the terrace; Czech and
international mains 300–500Kč.

Svatá Klara (Saint Clare)

MAP p.112, POCKET MAP C1
U trojského zámku 35 Ⓣ 233 540 173.
Tues–Sat 6pm–1am.

Formal restaurant, opened in 1679,
in a romantic wine cave setting
near the zoo. Specializes in fondues
and game dishes from 600Kč.

Pubs and bars

Fraktal

MAP p.112, POCKET MAP D3
Šmeralova 1. Daily 11am–midnight.

Very popular cellar bar with ad hoc
funky furnishings, exhibitions and
occasional live music, plus a beer
garden and kids' play area outside.

Letenský zámeček

MAP p.112, POCKET MAP E4
Letenské sady. Daily 11am–11.30pm.

The beer garden, with its great
views down the Vltava, is cheap
and popular with locals. The
restaurant is rather upmarket and
less special.

U houbaře (The Mushroom Picker)

MAP p.112, POCKET MAP E3
Dukelských hrdinů 30. Daily 11am–
midnight.

Comfortable local pub, directly
opposite the Veletržní palác,
serving Pilsner Urquell and
inexpensive Czech pub food.

Clubs and venues

Cross Club

MAP p.112, POCKET MAP F2
Plynární 23 Ⓦ www.crossclub.cz. Daily
2pm–2am or later.

Labyrinthine, multi-floor club
decked out in arty industrial decor,
near Nádraží Holešovice. The DJs
on each floor range from techno to
ambient. Entry free–120Kč.

Mecca

MAP p.112, POCKET MAP G2
U Průhonu 3 Ⓦ mecca.cz. Tues–Thurs
7pm–3am, Fri & Sat 7pm–4am.

Despite being out in Prague 7, this
coolly converted factory is one of
the most impressive and popular
clubs in Prague. Entry from 100Kč.

Meet Factory

MAP p.112, POCKET MAP C9
Ke Sklárně 15, Smíchov Ⓣ 251 551 796,
Ⓦ meetfactory.cz. Daily 1pm–late.

Multipurpose venue co-founded
by artist David Černý, with regular
concerts featuring obscure overseas
and Czech acts. It's a way south of
Holešovice, but easy to reach on
tram #12/20 from Chotkovy sady.

ACCOMMODATION

Paříž

Accommodation

Compared to the price of beer, accommodation in Prague is very expensive. If you're looking for a double and can pay around 4000Kč (€150) a night then you'll find plenty of choice. At the other end of the scale, there are numerous hostels charging around 400Kč (€15) for a bed. However, there's a shortage of decent, inexpensive to middle-range places. You can, however, get some very good deals – and undercut the often exorbitant rack rates – by booking online well in advance. Given that Prague can be pretty busy all year round, it's not a bad idea to book ahead in any case. All accommodation prices in this chapter are for the cheapest double room in high season; breakfast is usually included in the price, unless otherwise stated.

Hradčany

DOMUS HENRICI MAP p.34, POCKET MAP B11. Loretánská 11, tram #22 to Pohořelec ☏ 220 511 369, ⓦ domus-henrici.cz. Stylish, discreet hotel in a fabulous location, with just eight rooms/apartments, some with splendid views. Run in conjunction with *Domus Balthasar* on Mostecká, by Charles Bridge. **4300Kč**

QUESTENBERK MAP p.34, POCKET MAP A12. Úvoz 15, tram #22 from ⓜ Malostranská to Pohořelec ☏ 220 407 600, ⓦ questenberk.cz. From the outside, this hotel looks like a Baroque chapel, but inside it's been totally modernized. Rooms are smart but plain, though the views from some are superb. **2750Kč**

SAVOY PRAGUE MAP p.34, POCKET MAP A5. Keplerova 6, tram #22 from ⓜ Malostranská to Pohořelec ☏ 224 302 430, ⓦ hotelsavoyprague.com. Dated, charming luxury hotel on Hradčany's western edge, still sporting its original Art Nouveau facade. Popular for its marble bathrooms and free minibar, there's also a lovely lounge area. Breakfast extra. **4300Kč**

U KRÁLE KARLA (KING CHARLES) MAP p.34, POCKET MAP B11. Úvoz 4, tram #22 to Pohořelec ☏ 257 531 211, ⓦ ukralekarla.cz. Possibly the most tastefully exquisite of all the small luxury hotels in the castle district, with beautiful antique furnishings and stained-glass windows. Situated at the top of Nerudova, it's a steep walk from the nearest tram stop, however. **3500Kč**

U RAKA (THE CRAYFISH) MAP p.34, POCKET MAP A10. Černínská 10, tram #22 from ⓜ Malostranská to Brusnice ☏ 220 511 100, ⓦ hoteluraka.cz. The perfect hideaway, six double rooms in a little half-timbered, eighteenth-century cottage in Nový Svět. No children under 12 or dogs, and advance reservation a must. **4400Kč**

Malá Strana

ALCHYMIST GRAND HOTEL MAP p.42, POCKET MAP C12. Tržiště 19, tram #12, #20 or #22 to Malostranské náměstí ☏ 257 286 011, ⓦ alchymisthotel .com. Total decadent luxury abounds in this sixteenth-century palace, which has been tastefully converted into a secluded spa hotel, complete with Indonesian masseuses and an indoor pool. **6000Kč**

ARIA MAP p.42, POCKET MAP C12. Tržiště 9, tram #12, #20 or #22 to Malostranské náměstí ☏ 225 334 111,

Ⓦ ariahotel.net. A popular hotel with musically themed rooms and a special music library. Guests can enjoy the stunning roof terrace and private access to one of Prague Castle's gardens. **5500Kč**

DIENTZENHOFER MAP p.42, POCKET MAP D12. Nosticova 2, tram #12, #20 or #22 to Hellichova ☎ 257 311 319, Ⓦ dientzenhofer.cz. Birthplace of the eponymous architect Kilian Ignác Dientzenhofer and a very popular and unpretentious pension, as it's one of the few reasonably priced places (anywhere in Prague) to have wheelchair access. **2150Kč**

DŮM U VELKÉ BOTY (THE BIG SHOE) MAP p.42, POCKET MAP B12. Vlašská 30, tram #12, #20 or #22 to Malostranské náměstí ☎ 257 532 088, Ⓦ dumuvelkeboty.cz. The sheer discreetness of this pension, in a lovely old building in the quiet backstreets, is one of its main draws. Run by a very friendly couple, who speak good English, it has a series of cosy rooms, complete with genuine antiques, some en suite, some not. Breakfast is extra, but worth it. **3000Kč**

LOKAL INN MAP p.42, POCKET MAP D12. Míšenská 12, tram #12, #20 or #22 to Malostranské náměstí ☎ 257 014 800, Ⓦ lokalinn.cz. Top-drawer boutique hotel where the original features of the Baroque building have been preserved to provide a backdrop for the interesting design features. There is also a superb contemporary restaurant downstairs. **2800Kč**

NERUDA MAP p.42, POCKET MAP B11. Nerudova 44, tram #12, #20 or #22 to Malostranské náměstí ☎ 257 535 557, Ⓦ designhotelneruda.com. This stylish hotel is a fair walk up Nerudova, but it has a funky, glass-roofed foyer, uses lots of cool natural stone, and boasts smart, minimalist modern decor in the rooms. **3000Kč**

NOSTICOVA MAP p.42, POCKET MAP D12. Nosticova 1, tram #12, #20 or #22 to Hellichova ☎ 257 312 513, Ⓦ nosticova.com. Baroque house with ten beautifully restored rooms replete with antique furnishings, sumptuous bathrooms and some with kitchens, on a tranquil square not far from Charles Bridge. **6300Kč**

POD VĚŽÍ MAP p.42, POCKET MAP D12. Mostecká 2, tram #12, #20 or #22 to Malostranské náměstí ☎ 257 532 041, Ⓦ podvezi.com. One of Prague's best small hotels, a few steps from Charles Bridge with understated but luxurious rooms. Restaurant and crêperie on the premises. **4500Kč**

SAX MAP p.42, POCKET MAP C12. Janský vršek 3, tram #12, #20 or #22 to Malostranské náměstí ☎ 257 531 268, Ⓦ hotelsax.cz. Perfectly located in the backstreets off Nerudova, this hotel has gone for a remarkably convincing groovy retro 1960s look, but it's also a very well-run, well-equipped place with a DVD library. **2400Kč**

U KARLOVA MOSTU MAP p.42, POCKET MAP E12. Na Kampě 15, tram #12, #20 or #22 to Malostranské náměstí ☎ 234 652 808, Ⓦ archibald.cz. Situated on a lovely tree-lined square, just off Charles Bridge, the rooms in this former brewery (now a pub-restaurant) have real character, despite the slick, urban furniture. **3900Kč**

U PÁVA (THE PEACOCK) MAP p.42, POCKET MAP E11. U lužického semináře 32 Ⓜ Malostranská ☎ 257 533 573, Ⓦ hotel-upava.cz. Tucked away in the quiet backstreets, *U páva* boasts some impressively over-the-top Baroque fittings – real and repro. Some rooms have views over to the castle, and service is good. **2850Kč**

U ZLATÉ STUDNĚ (THE GOLDEN WELL) MAP p.42, POCKET MAP D11. U zlaté studně 4, tram #12, #20 or #22 to Malostranské náměstí ☎ 257 011 213, Ⓦ goldenwell.cz. A special location: tucked into the terraces below Prague Castle, next to the terraced gardens, with incredible views across the rooftops. The rooms feature lots of original ceilings, and there's a good restaurant with a wonderful summer terrace. **6600Kč**

U ZLATÝCH NŮŽEK (THE GOLDEN SCISSORS) MAP p.42, POCKET MAP E12. Na Kampě 6, tram #12, #20 or #22 to Malostranské náměstí ☎ 257 530 473, ⓦ uzlatychnuzek.cz. Ten rooms with parquet flooring, the odd beam and simple modern furnishings. On Kampa island, close to Charles Bridge. 3200Kč

WILLIAM MAP p.42, POCKET MAP D13. Hellichova 5, tram #12, #20 or #22 to Hellichova ☎ 257 320 242, ⓦ sivekhotels .com. The 42 well-maintained, mostly spacious, but somewhat unexciting rooms here are a good deal, and breakfast is better than average. Helpful staff. 2000Kč

Staré Město

ČERNÝ SLON (BLACK ELEPHANT) MAP p.56, POCKET MAP G11. Týnská 1 Ⓜ Náměstí Republiky ☎ 222 321 521, ⓦ hotelcernyslon.cz. Another ancient building tucked away off Old Town Square by the north portal of the Týn church, now tastefully converted into a very comfortable small hotel. 3450Kč

CLOISTER INN MAP p.56, POCKET MAP F13. Konviktská 14 Ⓜ Národní třída ☎ 224 211 020, ⓦ hotel-cloister.com. Pleasant, well-equipped hotel housed in a nunnery in one of the backstreets; the rooms are simply furnished with modern fittings, and the location is good. 2700Kč

GRAND HOTEL BOHEMIA MAP p.56, POCKET MAP H12. Kralodvorská 4 Ⓜ Náměstí Republiky ☎ 234 608 111, ⓦ grandhotelbohemia.cz. Probably the most elegant luxury hotel in the Old Town, just behind the Obecní dům, with some very tasty Art Nouveau decor and all the amenities you'd expect from an Austrian outfit. 5800Kč

GRAND HOTEL PRAHA MAP p.56, POCKET MAP G12. Staroměstské náměstí 22 Ⓜ Můstek ☎ 221 632 556, ⓦ grandhotelpraha.cz. If you want a room overlooking the astronomical clock on Old Town Square, then book in here, well in advance. There are beautiful antique furnishings, big oak ceilings, but only a very few rooms, including a single, as well an attic suite for four. 6700Kč

HAŠTAL MAP p.56, POCKET MAP H11. Haštalská 16 Ⓜ Náměstí Republiky

☎ 222 314 335, ⓦ hotelhastalprague. com. Opposite the sv Haštala church on peaceful Haštalské náměstí, this established hotel offers good value for money. Rooms sport dark-wood furniture and Prague-themed artwork, and the restaurant is an authentic piece of Art Nouveau. 3500Kč

HOTEL U ČERVENÉ ŽIDLE MAP p.56, POCKET MAP F12. Liliová 4, tram #17 or #18 to Karlovy lázně ☎ 296 180 018, ⓦ redchairhotel.com. Unassuming hotel on a pretty Old Town lane, offering thirteen rooms with green-stained timber furniture and high ceilings. There's a car park in the courtyard for anyone brave enough to drive into the Old Town's maze of streets. 3800Kč

JOSEF MAP p.56, POCKET MAP H11. Rybná 20 Ⓜ Náměstí Republiky ☎ 221 700 111, ⓦ hoteljosef.com. Prague's top design hotel exudes hipsterish professionalism; the lobby is a symphony in off-white efficiency and the rooms continue the crisply maintained minimalist theme with limestone showers and sharply pressed linens. 3400Kč

LIPPERT HOTEL MAP p.56, POCKET MAP G12. Mikulášská 2 Ⓜ Staroměstská ☎ 224 232 250, ⓦ lipperthotel.cz. So central it's ridiculous, yet with friendly and helpful staff; well-appointed rooms, hand-painted ceilings and some with incredible views onto Old Town Square, and quieter ones at the back. 2950Kč

RESIDENCE ŘETĚZOVÁ MAP p.56, POCKET MAP F12. Řetězová 9 Ⓜ Staroměstská ☎ 222 221 800, ⓦ retezova.com. Attractive apartments of all sizes, with kitchenettes, wooden or stone floors, Gothic vaulting or wooden beams and repro furnishings throughout. Apartments from 3500Kč

RITCHIE'S HOSTEL MAP p.56, POCKET MAP F12. Karlova 9 and 13 Ⓜ Staroměstská ☎ 222 221 229, ⓦ ritchieshostel.cz. In the midst of the human river that is Karlova, this Old Town hostel is clean, with accommodation ranging from en-suite doubles to twelve-bed dorms; no in-house laundry or cooking facilities. Dorms 380Kč, doubles 1850Kč

SAVIC MAP p.56, POCKET MAP G12. Jilská 7 Ⓜ Národní třída ☎ 224 248 555, Ⓦ savic.eu. This hotel, in the heart of the Old Town, has retained plenty of period features: painted ceilings, vaulting, exposed beams and the like. Staff are as helpful as can be, and the buffet breakfast is superb. **3900Kč**

SMETANA HOTEL MAP p.56, POCKET MAP F12. Karoliny Světlé 20 Ⓜ Národní třída ☎ 234 705 111, Ⓦ smetanahotel. com. Former Baroque palace, now luxury hotel, in the heart of the Old Town, with charming and efficient staff, rooms and suites decked in a blend of antique and repro furniture. **6950Kč**

TRAVELLERS HOSTEL MAP p.56, POCKET MAP H11. Dlouhá 33 Ⓜ Náměstí Republiky ☎ 777 738 608, Ⓦ travellers. cz. This very central party hostel situated above the *Roxy* nightclub has been around for years. It's the main booking office for a network of hostels – if there's not enough room here, staff will find you a bed in one of their other central branches. **Dorms 540Kč, doubles 1600Kč**

TÝN MAP p.56, POCKET MAP H11. Týnská 19 Ⓜ Náměstí Republiky ☎ 224 808 301, Ⓦ hostelpraguetyn.com. Prague's most central hostel is a funky but basic affair, located in a quiet courtyard within staggering distance of the Old Town Square. **Dorms 375Kč, doubles 1300Kč**

U MEDVÍDKŮ (THE LITTLE BEARS) MAP p.56, POCKET MAP G13. Na Perštýně 7 Ⓜ Národní třída ☎ 224 211 916, Ⓦ umedvidku.cz. The rooms above this famous Prague pub are plainly furnished, quiet considering the locale, and therefore something of an Old Town bargain; booking ahead essential. **2200Kč**

UNITAS MAP p.56, POCKET MAP F13. Bartolomějská 9 Ⓜ Národní třída ☎ 224 230 533, Ⓦ unitas.cz. Set in a Franciscan convent, the *Unitas* offers simple and spacious double and twin rooms – though they are slightly overpriced. **4800Kč**

U TŘÍ BUBNŮ (THE THREE DRUMS) MAP p.56, POCKET MAP G12. U radnice 8–10 Ⓜ Staroměstská ☎ 224 214 855, Ⓦ utribubnu.cz. Small hotel just off Old Town Square with five tastefully furnished rooms, either with original fifteenth-century wooden ceilings or lots of exposed beams. No lift but plenty of stairs. **2800Kč**

VENTANA MAP p.56, POCKET MAP G12. Celetná 7 Ⓜ Náměstí Republiky ☎ 221 776 600, Ⓦ ventana-hotel.net. Guests who stay at this super-central luxury boutique hotel rave about the spacious rooms, excellent breakfast and impeccably regimented staff. Add to this Prague's most stylish hotel lobby, gleaming marble-and-tile bathrooms and a library illuminated with crystal chandeliers and the *Ventana* shapes up as one of Prague's top places to unpack your suitcase. **4800Kč**

Wenceslas Square and northern Nové Město

ALCRON MAP p.82, POCKET MAP H14. Štěpánská 40 Ⓜ Můstek or Muzeum ☎ 222 820 000, Ⓦ radissonblu.com/ en/hotel-prague. Giant 1930s luxury hotel, located just off Wenceslas Square, superbly restored to its former Art Deco glory by the Radisson chain. Double rooms here are without doubt the most luxurious and tasteful you'll find in Nové Město. **4450Kč**

BOHO PRAGUE MAP p.82, POCKET MAP J12. Senovážná 4 Ⓜ Hlavní nádraží ☎ 234 622 600, Ⓦ hotelbohoprague. com. Go boho in Bohemia at one of Prague's most stylish hotels, where rooms sport shades of grey you never knew existed. There's an in-house restaurant, plus leisure facilities. **8000Kč**

Our Picks

Budget choice: *Czech Inn* p.127
Central hotel: *Grand Hotel Praha* p.124
Boutique: *Lokal Inn* p.123
Room with a view: *Dancing House Hotel* p.126
Romance: *Domus Henrici* p.122
Luxury: *Paříž* p.126

BOSCOLO PRAGUE MAP p.82, POCKET MAP K12. Senovážné náměstí 13 Ⓜ Hlavní nádraží ☏ 224 593 111, Ⓦ prague.boscolohotels.com. Occupying one of Prague's grandest city-centre palaces, this five-star establishment has some incomparably swish public areas, a remarkable spa, rooms done out with Italian flair and lots of facilities such as a fitness centre and a pool. **8800Kč**

HARMONY MAP p.82, POCKET MAP K11. Na Poříčí 31 Ⓜ Florenc ☏ 272 114 444, Ⓦ hotelharmony.cz. For those on a budget, this is a very sound low-cost option. As an added advantage, it's only a dumpling's throw from the main sights. Good for those who want to sleep, shower and breakfast – for medieval grandeur go elsewhere. **2200Kč**

HOSTEL ROSEMARY MAP p.82, POCKET MAP J13. Růžová 5 Ⓜ Můstek or Hlavní nádraží ☏ 222 211 124, Ⓦ praguecityhostel.cz. Clean, modern hostel just a short walk from the main train station, Praha hlavní nádraží. There are three- to twelve-bed mixed dorms, plus double rooms with or without en-suite and kitchen facilities. There's a communal kitchen and free internet, but breakfast isn't included. **Dorms 350Kč, doubles 1200Kč**

IMPERIAL MAP p.82, POCKET MAP J11. Na poříčí 15 Ⓜ Náměstí Republiky ☏ 246 011 600, Ⓦ hotel-imperial.cz. Despite describing itself as Art Deco, this place is actually more of an Art Nouveau masterpiece. Built in 1914, the public rooms are simply dripping with period ceramic friezes; the rest of the hotel is standard twenty first-century luxury. **4100Kč**

NYX HOTEL MAP p.82, POCKET MAP H13. Panská 9 Ⓜ Můstek ☏ 226 222 800, Ⓦ nyx-hotels.com/prague. One of the capital's most striking but affordable hotels, just a schnitzel's throw from Wenceslas Square. The bold interiors and artwork choices combined create a memorable, design-led hotel experience. **3000Kč**

PALACE MAP p.82, POCKET MAP H13. Panská 12 Ⓜ Můstek ☏ 224 093 111, Ⓦ palacehotel.cz. This luxury five-star hotel, just off Wenceslas Square, is renowned for its excellent service and facilities. All the rooms are kept spotless, and the buffet breakfast is top-class. **4300Kč**

PAŘÍŽ MAP p.82, POCKET MAP H11. U Obecního domu 1 Ⓜ Náměstí Republiky ☏ 222 195 195, Ⓦ hotel-paris.cz. This is a good top-notch hotel with plenty of fin-de-siècle atmosphere still intact – it was used as the setting for Bohumil Hrabal's *I Served the King of England*. **6700Kč**

SALVATOR MAP p.82, POCKET MAP J11. Truhlářská 10 Ⓜ Náměstí Republiky ☏ 222 312 234, Ⓦ salvator.cz. The *Salvator* boasts a very good location for the price, just a minute's walk from náměstí Republiky. The small but clean rooms – the cheaper of which have shared facilities – are all set around a courtyard. The buffet breakfast is delicious, and the staff are friendly and helpful. **2300Kč**

Národní třída and southern Nové Město

DANCING HOUSE HOTEL MAP p.91, POCKET MAP F15. Jiráskovo náměstí 6 Ⓜ Karlovo náměstí ☏ 720 983 172, Ⓦ dancinghousehotel.com. Love or hate the Dancing House, few can fail to be impressed by what former Czech footballer Vladimír Šmicer has done with the building to turn it into one of Prague's more interesting twenty first-century hotels. The Fred Royal and Ginger Royal suites in the building's towers, with truly awesome views of Prague Castle, are two of the most desirable rooms in the capital. **3900Kč**

HOTEL 16 MAP p.91, POCKET MAP E7. Kateřinská 16 Ⓜ Karlovo náměstí ☏ 224 920 636, Ⓦ hotel16.cz. Really friendly, family-run hotel offering small, plain but clean en-suite rooms. There's a little terraced garden at the back where you can relax, as well as botanic gardens nearby. **3500Kč**

HOTEL JUNGMANN MAP p.91, POCKET MAP G13. Jungmannovo náměstí 2 Ⓜ Můstek ☏ 224 219 501, Ⓦ antikhotels.com. Small hotel in a very tall, narrow building – with no lift – just a step away from the bottom of Wenceslas Square. The rooms are spacious – especially the suites – and decked out with tasteful modern decor and furnishings. **4300Kč**

ICON HOTEL MAP p.91, POCKET MAP H14. V jámě 6 Ⓜ Můstek ☎ 221 634 100, Ⓦ iconhotel.eu. Modern designer hotel, whose sleek, white-walled rooms are equipped with large, handmade Hästens beds. The all-day, a la carte breakfast is delicious, and a great perk for late risers. **3500Kč**

MADHOUSE MAP p.91, POCKET MAP G14. Spálená 39 Ⓜ Můstek ☎ 222 240 009, Ⓦ themadhouseprague.com. The name rather gives the game away at this New Town hostel, with its funky, wall-spanning hand-painted murals, group dinners, colourful TV lounge and well-equipped kitchen. If party hostels are not your thing, go elsewhere. **Dorms 610Kč**

MÁNES MAP p.91, POCKET MAP F15. Myslíkova 20 Ⓜ Karlovo náměstí ☎ 221 516 388, Ⓦ hotelmanes.cz. Star ratings mean little in the Czech Republic, but the *Mánes*, named after the nineteenth-century Czech artist, deserves every one of its four twinklers. The fifty rooms are finished with contemporary panache, the bathrooms are spacious and stylish, and the location near Karlovo náměstí puts you near enough to the main sights. **2400Kč**

MISS SOPHIE'S MAP p.91, POCKET MAP E7. Melounová 3 Ⓜ I.P. Pavlova ☎ 246 032 620, Ⓦ miss-sophies.com. A central, slick designer hostel offering everything from cheap dorm beds to fully equipped self-catering apartments. It's certainly not the right place for anyone seeking rough-and-ready backpacker digs (though it still won't break the bank). The all-you-can-eat breakfast is 150Kč extra. **Dorms 610Kč, doubles 2300Kč**

Vyšehrad, Vinohrady and Žižkov

ANNA MAP p.103, POCKET MAP F7. Budečská 17 Ⓜ Náměstí Míru ☎ 222 513 111, Ⓦ hotelanna.cz. Plain but smartly appointed rooms, warm friendly staff and a decent location make this a popular choice in Vinohrady, with trams and the metro close by. **2100Kč**

CLOWN AND BARD MAP p.103, POCKET MAP G6. Bořivojova 102, tram #5, #9, #26 or #29 to Husinecká ☎ 222 716 453, Ⓦ clownandbard.com. Žižkov hostel that attracts backpackers who like to party. Still, it's clean and undeniably cheap, stages events and has laundry facilities. Breakfast costs extra (vegetarian option available). **Dorms 350Kč, doubles 1200Kč**

CZECH INN MAP p.103, POCKET MAP G8. Francouzská 76, tram #4 or #22 to Krymská ☎ 267 267 612, Ⓦ czech-inn. com. Upbeat, designer hostel that feels and looks like a hotel, with friendly and helpful staff. The 36-bed cellar dorm is the biggest in the Czech Republic. **Dorms 385Kč, doubles 2000Kč**

EHRLICH MAP p.103, POCKET MAP H5. Koněvova 79, tram #9, #10, #11 or #16 to Biskupcova ☎ 236 040 555, Ⓦ hotelehrlich.cz. Few tourists would actually choose to stay in Žižkov, but perhaps if they saw this spacious, well-maintained hotel on the district's main thoroughfare they might consider it as an option. Some rooms have baths and air conditioning and there's a decent café in the building. **1900Kč**

GALILEO MAP p.103, POCKET MAP F7. Bruselská 3, tram #6 or #11 to Bruselská ☎ 222 500 222, Ⓦ hotelgalileoprague.com. Chic, modern hotel furnished with style, offering apartments as well as en-suite double rooms. **4550Kč**

HOSTEL ONE MAP p.103, POCKET MAP G6. Cimburkova 8 Ⓜ Hlavní nádraží ☎ 222 221 423, Ⓦ districthostel1.com. Part of a European chain, this great chill-out hostel recently moved to a location in Žižkov. Good facilities and a party vibe. **Dorms 390Kč, doubles 1300Kč**

ESSENTIALS

Malostranská metro station

Arrival

Prague is one of Europe's smaller capital cities. The airport lies just over 10km northwest of the city centre, with only a bus link or taxi to get you into town. Both the international train stations and the main bus terminal are linked to the centre by the fast and efficient metro system.

By plane

Prague's **Václav Havel airport** (☎ 220 111 888, ⊛ prg.aero) is connected to the city by minibus, bus and taxi. **Prague Airport Shuttle** (⊛ praguetransport.com) will take you into town for 600Kč for up to four passengers.

The cheapest way to get into town is on local **bus #119** (daily 5am–midnight; every 15–20min; journey time 25min), which stops frequently and ends its journey outside Nádraží Veleslavín metro station. You can buy your ticket from the public transport (DP) information desk in arrivals (daily 7am–9pm), or from the nearby machines. If you're going to use public transport while in Prague, you might as well buy a pass straight away (see opposite). If you arrive between midnight and 5am, you can catch the hourly **night bus** #910 to Divoká Šárka, the terminus for night tram #91, which will take you on to Národní in the centre of town. Another cheap alternative is **Linka AE** (Airport Express), which connects to Dejvická metro (60Kč) and the

main train station, Praha hlavní nádraží (daily 5.45am–10.05pm; every 30min; 60Kč).

If you're thinking of taking a **taxi** from the airport, make sure you choose the official airport taxi companies Taxi Praha (☎ 220 414 414, ⊛ taxi14007.cz) and Fix Taxi (☎ 220 113 892, ⊛ airportcars.cz), as Prague taxi drivers still have a reputation for wild overcharging. Both companies have desks at arrivals and the journey to the city centre should cost around 400–500Kč.

By train

International trains arrive either at Praha hlavní nádraží, on the edge of Nové Město and Vinohrady, or at Praha-Holešovice, which lies north of the city centre. At both stations you'll find exchange outlets, 24hr left-luggage offices (*úschovna zavazadel*) and accommodation agencies (plus a tourist office at Hlavní nádraží). Both stations are on metro lines, and Hlavní nádraží is only a five-minute walk from Václavské náměstí (Wenceslas Square).

By bus

Prague's **main bus terminal** is Praha-Florenc (Ⓜ Florenc), on the eastern edge of Nové Město, where virtually all long-distance international and domestic services terminate. There's a tourist office here, as well as a left-luggage office and a computer for checking bus times.

Getting around

The centre of Prague is reasonably small and best explored on foot. At some point, however, particularly to reach some of the more widely dispersed attractions, you'll need to use the city's cheap and efficient public transport system (*dopravní podnik* or DP; Ⓦ dpp.cz), which comprises the metro and a network of trams and buses. You can get free maps, tickets and passes from the DP **information offices** (☏ 296 191 817) at both airport terminals (daily 7am–9pm), or from Nádraží Veleslavín metro (Mon–Fri 6am–8pm, Sat 9.30am–5pm), Můstek metro (daily 7am–9pm), Andel metro (daily 7am–9pm), Hradčanská metro (Mon–Fri 6am–8pm, Sat 9.30am–5pm) and the main railway station, Praha hlavní nádraží (Mon–Fri 6am–10pm, Sat & Sun 7am–9pm).

Tickets and passes

Most Praguers buy annual passes, and to avoid having to understand the complexities of the single ticket system, you too are best off buying a **travel pass** (*jízdenka*) for either 24 hours (*1 den*; 110Kč) or three days (*3 dny*; 310Kč); no photos or ID are needed, though you must punch it to validate when you first use it. All the passes are available from DP outlets and ticket machines.

Despite the multitude of buttons on the **ticket machines** – found inside all metro stations and at some bus and tram stops – there are just two basic choices. The 24Kč version (*krátkodobá*) allows you to travel for 30 minutes on the trams or buses, or up to five stops on the metro; it's also known as a *nepřestupní jízdenka*, or "no change ticket", although you can in fact change metro lines (but not buses or trams). The 32Kč version (*základní*) is valid for 90 minutes, during which you may change trams, buses or metro lines as many times as you like, hence its alternative name, *přestupní jízdenka*, or "changing ticket". A full-price ticket is called *plnocenná*; discounted tickets (*zvýhodněna*) are available for children aged 6–15; under-6s travel free.

To buy a ticket from one of the machines, press the appropriate button followed by the *výdej*/enter button, then put your money in. The machines do give change, but another option if you don't have enough coins is to buy your ticket from a tobacconist (*tabák*), street kiosk, newsagent, PIS (Prague Information Service) office or any other place that displays the yellow DP sticker. When you enter the metro, or board a tram or bus, validate your ticket in one of the machines to hand.

There are no barriers, but plain-clothes inspectors (*revizoři*) make random checks and will issue an on-the-spot fine of 800Kč to anyone caught without a valid ticket or pass; controllers should show you their ID (a small metal disc) and give you a receipt (*paragon*).

Metro

Prague's futuristic, Soviet-built **metro** is fast, smooth and ultra-clean, running daily 5am till midnight with trains every two minutes during peak hours, slowing down to every four to ten minutes by late evening. Its three lines intersect at various points in the city centre.

The stations are fairly discreetly marked above ground with the metro logo, in green (line A), yellow (line B) or red (line C). Inside the metro, *výstup* means exit and *přestup* will lead you to one of the connecting lines. The digital clock at the end of the platform tells you what time it is and how long it was since the last train.

Trams

The electric tram (*tramvaj*) system negotiates Prague's hills and cobbles with remarkable dexterity. Modern rolling stock is gradually being introduced, but most of Prague's trams (traditionally red and cream) date back to the Communist era. After the metro, trams are the fastest and most efficient way of getting around, running every six to eight minutes at peak times, and every five to fifteen minutes at other times – check the timetables posted at every stop (*zastávka*), which list the departure times from that stop. Note that it is the custom for younger folk to vacate their seat when an older person enters the carriage.

Tram #22, which runs from Vinohrady to Hradčany via the centre of town and Malá Strana, is a good, cheap way of sightseeing, though you should beware of pickpockets. **Night trams** (*noční tramvaje*; #91–99; every 30–40min; roughly midnight–4.30am) run on different routes from the daytime ones, though at some point all night trams pass along Lazarská in Nové Město.

Buses

You're unlikely to need to get on a **bus** (*autobus*) in Prague, since most of them keep well out of the centre. If you're intent upon visiting the zoo, staying in one of the city's more obscure suburbs, or taking the cheap option to the airport, you will need to use them: their hours of operation are similar to those of the trams (though generally less frequent). **Night buses** (*noční autobusy*) run once an hour midnight–5am.

Ferries and boats

Though few would regard them as a part of the public transport system, a handful of small summer **ferry services** (*přívoz*) operate on the Vltava between the islands and the riverbanks (April–Oct daily 6am–10pm, every 30min). In the summer months there are also regular boat trips on the River Vltava run by the PPS (Pražská paroplavební společnost; ☎ 224 930 017, ⓦ paroplavba.cz) from just south of Jiráskův, most on Rašínovo nábřeží. Three boats a day in summer run to Troja (see p.117) in the northern suburbs (April & Sept Sat & Sun; May–Aug daily; 160Kč one-way).

The PPS also offers boat trips around Prague (May–Sept daily every 1–2hr; 220–290Kč) on board a 1930s paddle steamer.

Taxis

Taxis are, theoretically at least, relatively cheap. However, many Prague taxi drivers will attempt to overcharge, particularly at taxi ranks close to the tourist sights. Officially, the initial fare on the meter should be around 40Kč plus around 20Kč/km within Prague and 4–6Kč/min waiting time. The best advice is to have your hotel or pension call you one – you then qualify for a cheaper rate – rather than hail one or pick one up at the taxi ranks. The cab company with the best reputation is AAA Taxi (☎ 14014, ⓦ aaataxi.cz), which has metered taxis all over Prague.

Directory A–Z

Addresses

The street name is always written before the building number in Prague addresses. The city is divided into numbered postal districts: of the areas covered in the Guide, central Prague is Prague 1; southern Nové Město and half of Vinohrady is Prague 2; the rest of Vinohrady and Žižkov is Prague 3; Holešovice is Prague 7.

Bike rental

City Bike, Králodvorská 5. April–Oct daily 9am–7pm; ☎ 776 180 284, ⓦ citybike-prague.com; Ⓜ Náměstí Republiky.

Children

Despite a friendly attitude to kids and babies in general, you'll see very few children in museums and galleries, or in pubs, restaurants or cafés. Apart from the zoo and the mirror maze, there aren't very many attractions specifically aimed at kids. The castle and the Petřín funicular usually go down well, as does a ride on a tram.

Cinema

Cinema tickets still cost less than 250Kč. Most films are shown in the original language with subtitles (*titulky* or *české titulky*); some blockbusters are dubbed (*dabing* or *česká verze*). Occasionally you can get to see a Czech film with English subtitles (*anglický titulky*).

Crime

There are two main types of police: the **Policie** are the national force, with white shirts, navy blue jackets and grey trousers, while the **Městská** policie, run by the Prague city authorities, are distinguishable by their all-black uniforms. The main central police station is at Bartolomějská 6, Staré Město.

Cultural institutes

American Center, Tržiště13 ⓦ americkecentrum.cz; **Austrian Cultural Institute**, Jungmannovo náměstí 18 ⓦ oekfprag.at; **Instituto Cervantes**, Na rybníčku 6 ⓦ praga.cervantes.es; **Goethe Institut**, Masarykovo nábřeží 32 ⓦ goethe.de/prag; **Institut Français**, Štěpánská 35 ⓦ ifp.cz; **Instituto Italiano di Cultura**, Šporkova 14 ⓦ iicpraga.esteri.it.

Disabilities

The *Accessible Prague/Přístupná Praha* guidebook is available from the Prague Wheelchair Association (Pražská organizace vozíčkářů), Benediktská 6 ☎ 224 827 210, ⓦ pov.cz.

Electricity

The standard continental 220 volts AC. Most European appliances should work as long as you have an adaptor for continental-style two-pin round plugs. North Americans will need this plus a transformer.

Embassies

Australia, Klimentská 10, Nové Město (☎ 221 729 260); Ⓜ Náměstí Republiky); **Canada**, Ve Struhách 2, Dejvic (☎ 272 101 800, ⓦ canada.cz; Ⓜ Hradčanská); **Ireland**, Tržiště 13, Malá Strana (☎ 257 011 280, ⓦ embassyofireland.cz; Ⓜ Malostranská); **New Zealand**, Václavské náměstí 11, Nové Město (☎ 234 784 777; Ⓜ Můstek); **South Africa**, Ruská 65, Vršovice (☎ 267 311 114, ⓦ saprague.cz; Ⓜ Flora); **UK**, Thunovská 14, Malá Strana (☎ 257 402 111, ⓦ gov.uk/government/world/organisations/british-embassy-prague; Ⓜ Malostranská); **US**, Tržiště 15, Malá Strana (☎ 257 022 000, ⓦ usembassy.cz; Ⓜ Malostranská).

Emergencies

All services ☎ 112; Ambulance ☎ 155; Police ☎ 158; Fire ☎ 150.

Health

For an English-speaking doctor, go to Nemocnice na Homolce, Roentgenova 2, Motol (☎ 257 271 111). If it's an emergency, dial ☎ 155 for an ambulance. For an emergency dentist, head for Spálená 12, Nové Město (☎ 222 924 268; Ⓜ Národní třída). For a 24hr chemist, try Palackého 5 (☎ 224 946 962) or Belgická 37 (☎ 222 513 396).

Internet

Internet cafés are a thing of the past in Prague. The vast majority of hotels and cafés have free wi-fi and there's free access at the airport and the coach station.

Left luggage

Prague's main bus and train stations each have lockers and/or a 24hr left-luggage office, with instructions in English.

LGBT+ Prague

There's a friendly and well-established gay and lesbian scene with its spiritual heart in the leafy suburbs of Vinohrady and the more run-down neighbourhood of Žižkov. Up-to-date listings are available from Ⓦ prague.gayguide.net.

Lost property

The main train stations have lost property offices – look for the sign *ztráty a nálezy* – and there's a central municipal one at Karoliny Světlé 5 (Mon & Wed 8am–5.30pm, Tues & Thurs 8am–4pm, Fri 8am–2pm; ☎ 224 235 085). If you've lost your passport, then get in touch with your embassy (see p.133).

Money

The currency is the Czech crown or *koruna česká* (abbreviated to Kč or CZK). At the time of going to press there were roughly 30Kč to the pound sterling, 26Kč to the euro and around 23Kč to the US dollar. For up-to-date exchange rates, consult Ⓦ oanda. com or Ⓦ xe.com. Notes come in 100Kč, 200Kč, 500Kč, 1000Kč and 2000Kč (and less frequently 5000Kč) denominations; coins as 1Kč, 2Kč, 5Kč, 10Kč, 20Kč and 50Kč. Banking hours are Monday–Friday 8am–5pm, often with a break at lunchtime. ATMs can be found across the city.

Newspapers

You can get most foreign dailies and magazines at the kiosks at the bottom of Wenceslas Square, outside metro Můstek.

Opening hours

Shops in Prague are generally open Monday–Friday 9am–5pm, though most tourist shops stay open until 6pm or later. Some shops close by noon or 1pm on Saturday and close all day Sunday, but there's no law against opening on Sundays and many shops in the centre do (including both main supermarkets/department stores). Museums and galleries are generally open Tuesday–Sunday 10am–6pm.

Phones

Most public phones take only phone cards (*telefonní karty*), available from post offices, tobacconists and some shops (prices vary). The best-value ones are prepaid phone cards that give you a phone number and a code to enter. There are instructions in English, and if you press the appropriate button the language on the digital readout will change to English. If you have any problems, ring ☎ 1181 to get through to international information. Phone numbers in Prague consist of nine digits. There are no separate city/area codes in the Czech Republic. Mobile phones from the EU can now be used in the Czech Republic as at home with no roaming charges.

Post

The main 24hr post office (*pošta*) is at Jindřišská 14, Nové Město ☎ 840 111 244; take a ticket and wait for your number to come up. A more tourist-friendly branch exists in the third courtyard of Prague Castle.

Prague Card

The Prague Card (ⓦ praguecard.com) is valid for two, three or four days and gives free entry into over fifty sights for 1550/1810/2080Kč (though not including the sights of the former Ghetto of Josefov). All in all, the card will save you a lot of hassle, but not necessarily that much money. The card is available from all travel information and Prague City Tourism offices.

Smoking

In 2017 the Czech Republic finally introduced a complete smoking ban in public places. At cafés and restaurants you can no longer light up indoors, but this has simply moved smokers out onto terraces and street seating.

Time

The Czech Republic is on Central European Time (CET), one hour ahead of Britain and six hours ahead of EST, with the clocks going forward in spring and back again some time in autumn – the exact date changes from year to year. Generally speaking, Czechs use the 24-hour clock.

Tipping

Tipping is normal practice in cafés, bars, restaurants and taxis, usually done simply by rounding up the total. For example, if the waiter tots≈up the bill and asks you for 138Kč, you should give him 150Kč and tell him to keep the change. Automatic service charges that appear on the bill are not standard Czech practice.

Toilets

Apart from the automatic ones in central Prague, public toilets (*záchody*, *toalety* or WC) are few and far between. In some, you have to buy toilet paper (by the sheet) from the attendant, whom you will also have to pay as you enter. Standards of hygiene can be low. Gentlemen should head for *muži* or *páni*; ladies should head for *ženy* or *dámy*.

Tourist information

The tourist office is **Prague City Tourism**, whose main branch is within the **Staroměstská radnice** on Staroměstské náměstí (daily 9am–7pm; ⓦ praguecitytourism. cz). There are additional offices at **Rytířská 12** (daily 9am–7pm), **Staré Město** (daily 9am–7pm; ⓜ Můstek), in **Wenceslas Square** (daily 10am–6pm), plus an office in the **airport** (daily 9am–7pm). The staff speak English, but their helpfulness varies enormously; however, they can usually answer most enquiries, and can organize accommodation, and sell maps, guides and theatre tickets.

The best **website** for finding your way around the capital is ⓦ mapy.cz, which will help you locate any hotel, restaurant, pub, shop or street in Prague. A more general, informative site is Radio Prague's ⓦ radio.cz/ english, which includes the latest news. For information on what's happening in Prague as well as other suggestions for things to see and do, check the website ⓦ expats.cz.

Festivals and events

Epiphany (tří králové)

January 6
The letters K + M + B followed by the date of the new year are chalked on doorways across the capital to celebrate the "Day of the Three Kings" when the Magi came to worship Christ.

Masopust or Carnevale

Shrove Tuesday
The approach of Masopust (the Czech version of Mardi Gras) is celebrated locally in the Žižkov district of Prague, where there's a five-day programme of parties, concerts and parades; a more mainstream series of events takes place under the umbrella of Carnevale, in the city centre.

Easter (Velikonoce)

The age-old sexist ritual of whipping girls' calves with braided birch twigs tied together with ribbons (*pomlázky*) is still practised outside of Prague. To prevent such a fate, the girls are supposed to offer the boys a coloured Easter egg and pour a bucket of cold water over them. You'll see *pomlázky* and Easter eggs on sale, but precious little whipping.

Days of European Film (Dny evropského filmu)

April ⓦ eurofilmfest.cz
This is the nearest Prague comes to hosting a film festival: a fortnight of arty European films shown at various screens across the capital.

"Burning of the Witches" (Pálení čarodějnic)

April 30
Halloween comes early to the Czech Republic when bonfires are lit across the country, and old brooms thrown out and burned, as everyone celebrates the end of the long winter.

Prague International Marathon

Early May ⓦ runczech.com
Runners from over fifty countries come to race through the city's cobbled streets and over Charles Bridge.

Prague Spring Festival (Pražské jaro)

May 12–June 2 Box office at Obecní dům, Náměstí Republiky 5, ☎ 257 312 547, ⓦ festival.cz
By far the biggest annual arts event and the country's most prestigious international music festival. Established in 1946, it traditionally begins on May 12, the anniversary of Smetana's death, with a procession from his grave in Vyšehrad to the Obecní dům where the composer's *Má vlast* (My Country) is performed in the presence of the president, finishing on June 2 with a rendition of Beethoven's *Ninth Symphony*. Tickets for the festival sell out fast – they are typically made available online in December.

World Roma Festival (Khamoro)

Late May ⓦ khamoro.cz
International Roma festival of music, dance and film, plus seminars and workshops.

Prague Fringe Festival

Late May/early June ⓦ praguefringe.com
Your best chance to see English-language theatre in Prague, and good stuff at that. Organizers pack in the shows, and venues are all conveniently located in Malá Strana.

Dance Prague (Tanec Praha)

Four weeks in late May–late June
Ⓦ tanecpraha.cz
An established highlight of Prague's cultural calendar, this international festival of modern dance takes place at venues throughout the city.

Respect Festival

June Ⓦ rachot.cz/respect-festival
This world music weekend is held at various venues across the city in June, including the Akropolis and Štvanice island.

Burčák

September
For a couple of weeks, stalls on street corners sell the year's partially fermented new wine, known as *burčák*, a misty, heady brew.

Strings of Autumn

Late September–early November
Ⓦ strunypodzimu.cz
Excellent line-up of local and international orchestras and musicians from a wide range of genres. Tickets for this creative festival held in interesting venues go fast.

Christmas markets

December
Markets selling gifts, food and mulled wine (*svářák*) are set up at several places around the city in December: the biggest ones are in Wenceslas Square and the Old Town Square. Temporary ice rinks are also constructed at various locations.

Public holidays

January 1 New Year's Day; **Easter Monday**; **May 1** May Day; **May 8** VE Day; **July 5** SS Cyril and Methodius Day; **July 6** Jan Hus Day; **September 28** St Wenceslas Day; **October 28** Foundation of the Republic; **November 17** Battle for Freedom and Democracy Day; **December 24** Christmas Eve; **December 25** Christmas Day; **December 26** St Stephen's Day

Eve of St Nicholas

December 5
On the evening of December 5, numerous trios, dressed up as St Nicholas (svatý Mikuláš), an angel and a devil, tour the streets. The angel hands out sweets and fruit to children who've been good, while the devil dishes out coal and potatoes to those who've been naughty. The Czech St Nick has white hair and beard, and dresses not in red but in a white priest's outfit, with a bishop's mitre.

Christmas Eve (Štědrý večer)

December 24
Traditionally a day of fasting, broken only when the evening star appears, signalling the beginning of the Christmas feast of carp, potato salad, schnitzel and sweetbreads. Only after the meal are the children allowed to open their presents, which miraculously appear beneath the tree, thanks not to Santa Claus, but to baby Jesus (Ježíšek).

Chronology

895 First recorded Přemyslid duke and first Christian ruler of Prague, Bořivoj, baptized by saints Cyril and Methodius.

929 Prince Václav ("Good King Wenceslas") is martyred by his pagan brother Boleslav the Cruel.

973 Under Boleslav the Pious, Prague becomes a bishopric.

1212 Otakar I secures a royal title for himself and his descendants, who thereafter become kings of Bohemia.

1305 Václav II dies heirless, ending the Přemyslid dynasty.

1346–78 During the reign of Holy Roman Emperor Charles IV, Prague enjoys its first Golden Age as the city is transformed by building projects into a fitting imperial capital.

1389 Three thousand Jews slaughtered in the worst pogrom of the medieval period.

1415 Czech religious reformer Jan Hus is found guilty of heresy and burnt at the stake in Konstanz (Constance).

1419 Prague's first defenestration. Hus's followers, known as the Hussites, throw several councillors to their deaths from the windows of Prague's Nové Město's town hall.

1420 Battle of Vítkov (a hill in Prague). Jan Žižka leads the Hussites to victory over papal forces.

1434 Battle of Lipany. The radical Hussites are defeated by an army of moderates and Catholics.

1526 Habsburg rule in Prague begins, as Emperor Ferdinand I is elected King of Bohemia.

1576–1611 Emperor Rudolf II establishes Prague as the royal seat of power, and ushers in the city's second Golden Age, summoning artists, astronomers and alchemists from all of Europe.

1618 Prague's second defenestration. Two Catholic governors are thrown from the windows of Prague Castle by Bohemian Protestants. The Thirty Years' War begins.

1620 Battle of the White Mountain, just outside Prague. The Protestants, under the "Winter King" Frederick of the Palatinate, are defeated by the Catholic forces; 27 Protestant nobles are executed on the Old Town Square.

1648 The (Protestant) Swedes are defeated on Charles Bridge by Prague's Jewish and student populations. The Thirty Years' War ends.

1713 Plague kills 13,000.

1757 During the Seven Years' War, Prague is besieged and bombarded by the Prussians.

1781 Edict of Tolerance issued by Emperor Joseph II, allowing a large degree of freedom of worship for the first time in 150 years.

1848 Uprising in Prague eventually put down by Habsburg commander Alfred Prince Windischgätz. The ensuing reforms allow Jews to settle outside the ghetto for the first time.

1918 The Habsburg Empire collapses due to defeat in World War I. Czechoslovakia founded.

1920 Tomáš Masaryk elected as first president of Czechoslovakia.

1935 Edvard Beneš elected as the second president of Czechoslovakia.

1938 According to the Munich Agreement drawn up by Britain, France, Fascist Italy and Nazi Germany, the Czechs are forced to secede the border regions of the Sudetenland to Hitler.

1939 In March, the Germans invade and occupy the rest of the Czech Lands. Slovakia declares independence.

1941 Prague's Jews deported to Terezín (Theresienstadt) before being sent to the concentration camps.

1942 Nazi leader Reinhard Heydrich assassinated in Prague. The villages of Lidice and Ležáky are annihilated in retaliation.

1945 On May 5, the Prague Uprising against the Nazis begins. On May 9, the Russians liberate the city. The city's ethnic German population is brutally expelled.

1946 Communist Party wins up to forty percent of the vote in the first postwar general election. Beneš formally re-elected as president.

1948 The Communist Party seizes power in a bloodless coup in February. Thousands flee the country. Jan Masaryk, Foreign Minister and son of the former president, dies in mysterious circumstances. Beneš resigns as president, replaced by Communist leader, Klement Gottwald.

1952 Twelve leading Party members (eleven of them Jewish) sentenced to death as traitors in Prague's infamous show trials.

1953 Gottwald dies five days after Stalin.

1968 During the "Prague Spring", reformers within the Party abolish censorship. Soviet troops invade and stop the reform movement. Thousands go into exile.

1977 243 Czechs and Slovaks, including playwright Václav Havel, sign the Charter 77 manifesto, reigniting the dissident movement.

1989 After two weeks of popular protest, known as the Velvet Revolution, the Communist government resigns. Havel is elected as president.

1993 Czechoslovakia splits into the Czech Republic and Slovakia. Havel is elected as Czech president.

1999 The Czech Republic joins NATO.

2002 In August, Prague is devastated by the worst floods in 200 years.

2003 Václav Klaus, former Finance Minister and Prime Minister, is elected as the second Czech president.

2004 The Czech Republic enters the European Union, along with nine other accession countries, including Slovakia.

2011 Václav Havel dies, at the age of 75.

2013 Czechs elect Miloš Zeman in the country's first direct presidential election.

2017/18 The Czechs hold key elections which dictate the future direction the country will take.

Czech

A modicum of English is spoken in Prague's central restaurants and hotels, and among the city's younger generation. Any attempt to speak Czech will be heartily appreciated, though don't be discouraged if people seem not to understand, as most will be unaccustomed to hearing foreigners stumble through their language. Unfortunately, Czech (**český**) is a highly complex western Slav tongue, into which you're unlikely to make much headway during a short stay.

Pronunciation

English-speakers often find Czech impossibly difficult to pronounce: just try the Czech tongue-twister, strč prst skrz krk (stick your finger down your neck). The good news is that, apart from a few special letters, each letter and syllable is pronounced as it's written – the trick is to always stress the first syllable of a word, no matter what its length; otherwise you'll render it unintelligible.

Short and long vowels

Czech has both short and long vowels (the latter being denoted by a variety of accents):

a like the u in c**u**p
á as in f**a**ther
e as in p**e**t
é as in f**ai**r
ě like the ye in **ye**s

i or y as in p**i**t
í or ý as in s**ea**t
o as in n**o**t
ó as in d**oo**r
u like the oo in b**oo**k
ů or ú like the oo in f**oo**l

Vowel combinations and diphthongs

There are very few diphthongs in Czech, so any combinations of vowels other than those below should be pronounced as two separate syllables.

au like the ou in f**ou**l
ou like the oe in f**oe**

Consonants and accents

There are no silent consonants, but it's worth remembering that r and l can form a half-syllable if standing between two other consonants or at the end of a word, as in Brno (Br-no) or Vltava (Vl-ta-va). The consonants listed below are those which differ substantially from the English. Accents look daunting, particularly the háček, which appears above c, d, n, r, s, t and z, but the only one which causes a lot of problems is ř, probably the most difficult letter to say in the entire language – even Czech toddlers have to be taught how to say it.

c like the **ts** in boats
č like the **ch** in chicken
ch like the **ch** in the Scottish loch
ď like the **d** in duped
g always as in goat, never as in general
h always as in have, but more energetic
j like the **y** in yoke

The alphabet

In the Czech alphabet, letters which feature a **háček** (as in the č of the word itself) are considered separate letters and appear in Czech indexes immediately after their more familiar cousins. More confusingly, the consonant combination ch is also considered as a separate letter and appears in Czech indexes after the letter h.

kd pronounced as **gd**

mě pronounced as **mnye**

ň like the **n** in nuance

p softer than the English **p**

r as in rip, but often rolled

ř approximately like the sound of **r** and **ž** combined

š like the **sh** in shop

t' like the **t** in tutor

ž like the **s** in pleasure; but at the end of a word like the **sh** in shop

Words and phrases

Basics

Yes	ano
No	ne
Please/excuse me	prosím vás
Don't mention it	není zač
Sorry	pardon
Thank you	děkuju
Bon appétit	dobrou chuť
Bon voyage	šťastnou cestu
Hello/goodbye (informal)	ahoj
Hello (formal)	dobrý den
Goodbye (formal)	na shledanou
Good morning	dobré ráno
Good evening	dobrý večer
Good night (when leaving)	dobrou noc
How are you?	jak se máte?
I'm English	ja jsem angličan(ka)
/Irish	/ir(ka)
/Scottish	/skot(ka)
/Welsh	/velšan(ka)
/American	/američan(ka)
Do you speak English?	mluvíte anglicky?
I don't speak Czech	nemluvím česky
I don't speak German	nemluvím německy
I don't understand	nerozumím
I understand	rozumím
I don't know	nevím
Speak slowly	mluvte pomalu
How do you say that in Czech?	jak se to řekne česky?
Could you write it down for me?	mužete mi to napsat?
Today	dnes
Yesterday	včera
Tomorrow	zítra
The day after tomorrow	pozítří
Now	hned
Later	později
Wait a minute!	moment!
Leave me alone!	dej mi pokoj!
Go away!	jdi pryč!
Help!	pomoc!
This one	toto
A little	trochu
Another one	ještě jedno
Large/small	velký/malý
More/less	více/méně
Good/bad	dobrý/špatný
Cheap/expensive	levný/drahý
Hot/cold	horký/studený
With/without	s/bez
The bill please	zaplatím prosím
Do you have ...?	máte ...?
We don't have	nemáme
We do have	máme

Questions

What?	co?
Where?	kde?
When?	kdy?
Why?	proč?
Which one?	který/která/které?
This one?	tento/tato/toto?
How many?	kolik?
What time does it open?	kdy máte otevřeno?
What time does it close?	kdy zavíráte?

Getting around

Over here	tady
Over there	tam
Left	nalevo
Right	napravo
Straight on	rovně
Where is ...?	kde je ...?
How do I get to Prague?	jak se dostanu do Prahy?
How do I get to the...?	jak se dostanu k...?
By bus	autobusem
By train	vlakem
By car	autem

CZECH

On foot	pěšky
By taxi	taxíkem
Stop here, please	zastavte tady, prosím
Ticket	jízdenka/lístek
Return ticket	zpáteční
Train station	nádraží
Bus station	autobusové nádraží
Bus stop	autobusová zastávka
When's the next train to Prague?	kdy jede další vlak do Prahy?
Is it going to Prague?	jede to do Prahy?
Do I have to change?	musím přestupovat?
Do I need a reservation?	musím mít místenku?
Is this seat free?	je tu volno?
May we (sit down)?	můžeme (se sednout)?

Accommodation

Are there any rooms available?	máte volné pokoje?
Do you have a double room?	máte jeden dvoulůžkový pokoj?
For one night	na jednu noc
With shower	se sprchou
With bath	s koupelnou
How much is it?	kolík to stojí?
With breakfast?	se snídaní?

Some signs

Entrance	vchod
Exit	východ
Toilets	záchody/toalety
Men	muži
Women	ženy
Ladies	dámy
Gentlemen	pánové
Open	otevřeno
Closed	zavřeno
Pull/Push	sem/tam
Danger!	pozor!
Hospital	nemocnice
No smoking	kouření zakázáno
No entry	vstup zakázán
Arrival	příjezd
Departure	odjezd

Days of the week

Monday	pondělí
Tuesday	úterý
Wednesday	středa
Thursday	čtvrtek
Friday	pátek
Saturday	sobota
Sunday	neděle
Day	den
Week	týden
Month	měsíc
Year	rok

Months of the year

Many Slav languages have their own highly individual systems in which the words for the names of the months are descriptive nouns, sometimes beautifully apt for the month in question.

January	leden (ice)
February	únor (hibernation)
March	březen (birch)
April	duben (oak)
May	květen (blossom)
June	červen (red)
July	červenec (red)
August	srpen (sickle)
September	září (blazing)
October	říjen (rutting)
November	listopad (leaves falling)
December	prosinec (millet porridge)

Numbers

1	jeden
2	dva
3	tři
4	čtyři
5	pět
6	šest
7	sedm
8	osm
9	devět
10	deset
11	jedenáct
12	dvanáct
13	třináct
14	čtrnáct
15	patnáct
16	šestnáct

17	sedmnáct
18	osmnáct
19	devatenáct
20	dvacet
21	dvacetjedna
30	třicet
40	čtyřicet
50	padesát
60	šedesát
70	sedmdesát
80	osmdesát
90	devadesát
100	sto
101	sto jedna
155	sto padesát pět
200	dvě stě
300	tři sta
400	čtyři sta
500	pět set
600	šest set
700	sedm set
800	osm set
900	devět set
1000	tisíc

Food and drink terms

Basics

chléb	bread
chlebíček	(open) sandwich
cukr	sugar
hořčice	mustard
houska	round roll
knedlíky	dumplings
křen	horseradish
lžíce	spoon
maso	meat
máslo	butter
med	honey
mléko	milk
moučník	dessert
nápoje	drinks
na zdraví!	cheers!
nůž	knife
oběd	lunch
obloha	garnish
ocet	vinegar
ovoce	fruit
pečivo	rolls
pepř	pepper
polévka	soup

předkrmy	starters
přílohy	side dishes
rohlík	finger roll
ryby	fish
rýže	rice
sklenice	glass
snídaně	breakfast
sůl	salt
šálek	cup
talíř	plate
tartarská omáčka	tartare sauce
večeře	supper/dinner
vejce	eggs
vidlička	fork
volské oko	fried egg
zeleniny	vegetables

Common terms

čerstvý	fresh
domácí	home-made
dušený	stew/casserole
grilovaný	roast on the spit
kyselý	sour
na kmíně	with caraway seeds
na roštu	grilled
nadívaný	stuffed
nakládaný	pickled
(za)pečený	baked/roast
plněný	stuffed
s máslem	with butter
sladký	sweet
slaný	salted
smažený	fried in breadcrumbs
studený	cold
syrový	raw
sýrový	with cheese
teplý	hot
uzený	smoked
vařený	boiled

Soups

boršč	beetroot soup
bramborová	potato soup
čočková	lentil soup
fazolová	bean soup
hovězí vývar	beef broth
hrachová	pea soup
kuřecí	thin chicken soup
rajská	tomato soup
zeleninová	vegetable soup

CZECH

Fish

kapr	carp
losos	salmon
makrela	mackerel
platys	flounder
pstruh	trout
rybí filé	fillet of fish
sardinka	sardine
štika	pike
treska	cod
zavináč	herring/rollmop

Meat dishes

bažant	pheasant
biftek	beef steak
čevapčiči	spicy meatballs
dršťky	tripe
drůbež	poultry
guláš	goulash
hovězí	beef
husa	goose
játra	liver
jazyk	tongue
kachna	duck
klobásy	sausages
kotleta	cutlet
kuře	chicken
kýta	leg
ledvinky	kidneys
řízek	steak
roštěná	sirloin
salám	salami
sekaná	meat loaf
skopové maso	mutton
slanina	bacon
svíčková	fillet of beef
šunka	ham
telecí	veal
vepřový	pork
vepřový řízek	breaded pork cutlet or schnitzel
zajíc	hare
žebírko	ribs

Vegetables

brambory	potatoes
brokolice	broccoli
celer	celery
cibule	onion
červená řepa	beetroot
česnek	garlic
chřest	asparagus
čočka	lentils
fazole	beans
houby	mushrooms
hranolky	chips, French fries
hrášek	peas
květák	cauliflower
kyselá okurka	pickled gherkin
kyselé zelí	sauerkraut
lečo	ratatouille
lilek	aubergine
mrkev	carrot
okurka	cucumber
pórek	leek
rajče	tomato
ředkev	radish
špenát	spinach
zelí	cabbage
žampiony	mushrooms

Fruit, cheese and nuts

arašídy	peanuts
banán	banana
borůvky	blueberries
broskev	peach
brusinky	cranberries
bryndza	goat's cheese in brine
citrón	lemon
grep	grapefruit
hermelín	Czech brie
hrozny	grapes
hruška	pear
jablko	apple
jahody	strawberries
kompot	stewed fruit
maliny	raspberries
mandle	almonds
meruňka	apricot
niva	semi-soft, crumbly, blue cheese
ostružiny	blackberries
oštěpek	heavily smoked, curd cheese
pivní sýr	cheese flavoured with beer
pomeranč	orange
rozinky	raisins
švestky	plums
třešně	cherries

tvaroh	fresh curd cheese
uzený sýr	smoked cheese
vlašské ořechy	walnuts

Drinks

čaj	tea
destiláty	spirits
káva	coffee
koňak	brandy
láhev	bottle
minerální (voda)	mineral (water)
mléko	milk
pivo	beer
presso	espresso
s ledem	with ice
soda	soda
suché víno	dry wine
šumivý	fizzy
svařené víno /svařak	mulled wine
tonic	tonic
vinný střik	white wine with soda
víno	wine

A glossary of Czech terms

brána	gate
český	Bohemian
chrám	cathedral
divadlo	theatre
dům	house
hora	mountain
hospoda/hostinec	pub
hrad	castle
hřbitov	cemetery
kaple	chapel

katedrála	cathedral
kavárna	coffee house
klášter	monastery/convent
kostel	church
koupaliště	swimming pool
Labe	River Elbe
lanovka	funicular/cable car
les	forest
město	town
most	bridge
muzeum	museum
nábřeží	embankment
nádraží	train station
náměstí	square
ostrov	island
palác	palace
památník	memorial or monument
pasáž	interior shopping arcade
pivnice	pub
radnice	town hall
restaurace	restaurant
sad	park
sál	room/hall
schody	steps
svatý/svatá	saint; often abbreviated to sv
třída	avenue
ulice	street
věž	tower
vinárna	wine bar/cellar
Vltava	River Moldau
vrchy	hills
výstava	exhibition
zahrada	garden
zámek	chateau

Publishing information

This fourth edition published March 2018 by **Rough Guides Ltd**

80 Strand, London WC2R 0RL

11, Community Centre, Panchsheel Park, New Delhi 110017, India

Distributed by Penguin Random House

Penguin Books Ltd, 80 Strand, London WC2R 0RL

Penguin Group (USA) 345 Hudson Street, NY 10014, USA

Penguin Group (Australia) 250 Camberwell Road, Camberwell, Victoria 3124, Australia

Penguin Group (NZ) 67 Apollo Drive, Mairangi Bay, Auckland 1310, New Zealand

Penguin Group (South Africa) Block D, Rosebank Office Park, 181 Jan Smuts Avenue,

Parktown North, Gauteng, South Africa 2193

Rough Guides is represented in Canada by

DK Canada 320 Front Street West, Suite 1400, Toronto, Ontario M5V 3B6

Typeset in Minion and Din to an original design by Henry Iles and Dan May.

Printed and bound in China

© Rough Guides 2018

Maps © Rough Guides

152pp includes index

A catalogue record for this book is available from the British Library

ISBN 978-0-24130-635-2

1 3 5 7 9 8 6 4 2

Rough Guides credits

Editor: Rebecca Hallett

Layout: Pradeep Thapliyal

Cartography: Richard Marchi

Picture editor: Michelle Bhatia

Photographers: Natascha Sturny, Dan Bannister and Eddie Gerald

Proofreader: Emma Beatson

Managing editor: Monica Woods

Production: Jimmy Lao

Cover photo research: Chloe Roberts

Editorial assistant: Aimee White

Senior DTP coordinator: Dan May

Publishing director: Georgina Dee

Author: Marc Di Duca has been a full-time travel guide author for over a decade, covering destinations as diverse as Madeira and Siberia for most major travel publishers. An expat living in the Czech Republic, Marc first arrived in Prague in the early 1990s and speaks fluent Czech. As well as penning guides he also works as a translator for CzechTourism, Czech Airlines, COT Media and various other travel- and tourism-related companies and organizations.

Help us update

We've gone to a lot of effort to ensure that the fourth edition of the **Pocket Rough Guide Prague** is accurate and up-to-date. However, things change – places get "discovered", opening hours are notoriously fickle, restaurants and rooms raise prices or lower standards. If you feel we've got it wrong or left something out, we'd like to know, and if you can remember the address, the price, the hours, the phone number, so much the better.

Please send your comments with the subject line "**Pocket Rough Guide Prague Update**" to mail@uk.roughguides.com. We'll credit all contributions and send a copy of the next edition (or any other Rough Guide if you prefer) for the very best emails.

Browse all our latest guides, read inspirational features and book your trip at roughguides.com.

Photo credits

All photos © Rough Guides except the following:
(Key: t-top; c-centre; b-bottom; l-left; r-right)

1 AWL Images: Nordic Photos
2 4Corners: Pietro Canali / SIME (bl).
Alamy Stock Photo: imageBROKER / Martin Moxter (cr). **Dreamstime.com:** Lindrik (tl)
6 Naše maso
11 4Corners: Pietro Canali / SIME (t).
Dreamstime.com: Darellian (b)
12 iStockphoto.com: Kavalenkava Volha
13 Alamy Stock Photo: Jan Fidler (b)
14–15 Robert Harding Picture Library: Jason Langley (t)
15 Alamy Stock Photo: Alpineguide (br)
16–17 Getty Images: Frank Chmura (t)
17 Alamy Stock Photo: GoneWithTheWind (b)
19 Ambiente (b)
20 Alamy Stock Photo: Ian Dagnall Commercial Collection (b)
21 Alamy Stock Photo: Profimedia. CZ a.s. (b). **Getty Images:** Dennis Macdonald (c)
22 Alamy Stock Photo: Marek Stepan (c). **Dreamstime.com:** Baarka (b).
Getty Images: Elena Pejchinova (t)
23 Alamy Stock Photo: Karel Tupy (c).
Getty Images: Miguel Sotomayor (t)
31 Alamy Stock Photo: Profimedia. CZ a.s.

40 Alamy Stock Photo
55 Dreamstime.com: Vitaly Titov & Maria Sidelnikova
63 SuperStock: Peter Erik Forsberg
65 Naprstek museum
79 Alamy Stock Photo: Yadid Levy
80 Dreamstime.com: Singhsomendra
81 Dreamstime.com: Tomas Pisek
88 Francouzská restaurace: Martin Siebert
95 Alamy Stock Photo: Peter Erik Forsberg
98 Alamy Stock Photo: Profimedia. CZ a.s.
99 Dynamo
101 Alamy Stock Photo: Frank Sanchez
103 Alamy Stock Photo: AA World Travel Library
109 Alamy Stock Photo: Profimedia. CZ a.s.
111 Alamy Stock Photo: CTK
112 Dreamstime.com: Mirekdeml
118 Zoo Praha: Tomáš Adamec
120–121 Hotel Paris: Filip Obr
128–129 Dreamstime.com: David Pereiras Villagrá
Cover: *Old Town Square, Týn Church*
4Corners: Pietro Canali

Index

Maps are marked in **bold**

CONTENTS

INTRODUCTION

Reading is one of the most satisfying of all human skills. We can survive – people do survive – perfectly well without it, and yet many would list it high among the things which make life worth living. Even such eager readers, however, can be daunted by the sheer number of books on offer. Libraries and bookshops are stuffed with treasures; like explorers in some vast, land-markless new continent, we hardly know where to turn.

The *Bloomsbury Good Reading Guide* seeks to answer two main questions: 'Where shall I start?' and 'Where shall I go next?' The bulk of the text is articles on some 300 authors, describing the kind of books they wrote, listing titles and suggesting books, by the same authors and by others, which might make interesting follow-ups.

There are also, scattered throughout the *Guide*, 19 'skeins' and over 70 'menus' of suggested reading. The menus, listed alphabetically alongside the author-articles, are straightforward lists of about seven or eight books of a similar kind, ranging from **Action Thrillers** (see page 2) to **Weepies** (see page 255). The skeins, on the other hand, range wider; each one starts with a specific book and suggests follow-ups both predictable and unexpected, a haul of reading as varied as fish in a net—E.M. Forster's *A Passage to India*, for example, leads to both Paul Theroux's *Fong and the Indians* and John Le Carré's *The Perfect Spy*. Also included as a menu is a list of all Booker Prize short-listed authors and titles as well as each year's winner (see page 25). These are generally considered to be the best books of their year and so act as reliable pointers to good reading.

The *Guide* deals with prose fiction only. There is no literary criticism: I wanted to describe books, not to be clever at their expense. In particular, I tried to avoid ranking authors by 'literary merit', on assessments of whether their work is 'great' or 'light'. The length of each entry depends solely on how much needed to be said. If this had been a travel guide, New York (say) might have had more space than the commuter village up the line – but that would have had no bearing on where one might choose to live.

Throughout the text, ▷ before someone's name means that that person has a main entry of his or her own. All books mentioned in the *Guide* were written in English or are widely available in translation. We have tried to cover as wide a range of writers of English as possible and have included authors from Australia, Canada, New Zealand, the Republic of Ireland, South Africa and the USA as well as the UK. Some books may be published under different titles in the USA. If this is the case the UK title is given first, followed by the US title:

Daphne Du Maurier: *The Apple Tree/Kiss Me Again Stranger*

Books originally written in a foreign language are listed by their English titles. Original titles follow in brackets where they may be familiar to readers or where they may be used for some English editions.

Emile Zola: *The Boozer* (L'assommoir)
Andre Gide: *The Pastoral Symphony* (La symphonie pastorale)

Main author entries are listed alphabetically by surname. Each author-article contains some or all of four different strands of information:

1 a paragraph about the author's work and style in general
2 description of a particular book, a good example of the author's work
3 list of main books by the author
4 suggestions of follow-ups
   by the same author   ●
   by other authors   ▶

The cut-off date for inclusion in this edition was October 1987. We hope to update the *Guide* regularly, and to include good new books as they come along. We welcome ideas, comments and suggestions, especially for follow-ups and skeins.

Throughout the *Guide*, the final choice of books and authors, the comments and the text were my responsibility: I take the blame. But many people helped, and the *Guide* has benefited from suggestions and comments from Lucy Banister, Sian Facer, Sheila Hardy, Pamela Henderson, Simon McLeish, Kathy Rooney and Stella Yates. I warmly thank them all. As always, my greatest debt is to my wife, Valerie McLeish: her inspiration and encouragement were essential to every page.

Kenneth McLeish,
October 1987

A

ACHEBE, Chinua • *(born 1930)*
Nigerian novelist.

Things Fall Apart (1958), Achebe's best-known novel, is a story of the people of Umuofia on the river Niger, and especially of Okonkwo, a rich and headstrong elder. To British readers the period seems early Victorian; to the men and women of Umuofia it would have no date, it would be part of the gentle continuum of existence. Their lives depend on the harmony between human beings and spirits, and that is preserved by a precise set of rituals and beliefs, established by precedent, explained by folk-tale and so familiar that instead of constricting the soul they liberate it. White people are as mythical as the tortoise in the story who learned to fly: they live far away, snatch slaves, laugh at the gods; no one believes in them. Okonkwo wins respect among his people by a magnificent wrestling-throw when he is 18, and keeps it by his hard work as a farmer, his love for the land. Then, by accident, he kills a relative, and is forced by custom to live out of the village for seven years. While he is away Christian missionaries come; they speak through interpreters, understand nothing of the people's beliefs and are followed by white commissioners whose laws destroy the society they were devised to 'civilise'. Achebe's points are blunt, and (for ex-colonialists) shamingly unanswerable. But his novel's main fascination is not political but social. External observers, however sophisticated their cameras or meticulous their anthropological methods, can only describe the surface of timeless, tribal societies: they report and explain events. Achebe, by contrast, uses a series of direct, uncomplicated scenes, reverberant as poetry, to reveal his people's souls.

Achebe's other novels are No Longer at Ease, Arrow of

> **READ ON** ▷

▶ Amos Tutuola, *My Life in the Bush of Ghosts* (making a denser, more Homeric use of Nigerian folk-styles).
▷ I.B. Singer, *Satan in Goray*. Janet Lewis, *The Trial of Sören Kvist*.

God, A Man of the People (*a satirical farce about what happens when the white imperialists leave and black politicians set up a 'western' state) and* Anthills of the Savannah. Chike and the River *is a children's book, sweet as a folk-tale.*

ACTION THRILLERS

▷Richard Condon, *The Manchurian Candidate*
Clive Cussler, *Cyclops*
▷Ken Follett, *Lie Down With Lions*
▷Frederick Forsyth, *The Day of the Jackal*
Martin Cruz Smith, *Stallion Gate*
Scott Turow, *Presumed Innocent*
Walter Wager, *Telefon*

Agents and Double Agents (p 3); High Adventure (p 117); Historical Adventure (p 120); Terrorists/Freedom Fighters (p 234)

ADAMS, Douglas • *(born 1952)*
British novelist.

In *The Hitchhiker's Guide to the Galaxy* (1979), the first of Adams' genial SF spoofs, Earthman Arthur Dent is informed that his planet is about to be vaporised to make room for a hyper-space bypass, and escapes by stowing away on an alien space-craft. This is the beginning of a wild journey through time and space, in the course of which he meets the super-cool President of the Galaxy, Zaphod Beeblebrox, discusses the coastline of Norway with Slartibartfast (who won prizes for designing it), watches the apocalyptic floor-show in the Restaurant at the End of the Universe, and discovers the answer to the 'ultimate question about life, the universe and everything'. Adams himself is on a spree, spray-painting the stuffiest corners of the genre. There are three Hitchhiker sequels (*The Restaurant at the End of the Universe*; *Life, the Universe and Everything*; *So Long, and Thanks for All the Fish*); *Dirk Gently's Holistic Detective Agency* (1987), whose title suggests the plot, is a cascade of equally loony fantasy, ▷Chandler and ▷Vonnegut swapping one-liners on an intergalactic roller-coaster ride.

> **READ ON**

▶ **SF spoofs in similarly lunatic vein:** Terry Pratchett, *The Colour of Magic*; ▷Harry Harrison, *The Stainless Steel Rat*; ▷Kurt Vonnegut, *The Sirens of Titan*.
▶ **Non-SF books featuring bewildered heroes at the centre of chaos:** Patrick Dennis, *Auntie Mame*; Charles Webb, *The Graduate*; William Boyd, *Stars and Bars*; ▷Evelyn Waugh, *Decline and Fall*.

ADOLESCENCE

▷Maeve Binchy, *Echoes*
▷Colette, *The Ripening Seed*
▷Miles Franklin, *My Brilliant Career*
　Jane Gardam, *Bilgewater*
　Rumer Godden, *The Greengage Summer*
　Harper Lee, *To Kill a Mocking Bird*
　Sue Townsend, *The Secret Diary of Adrian Mole,
　aged 13¾*
▷Antonia White, *Frost in May*

Children (p 42); Families: Eccentric (p 72); Growing
Up: Teenagers (p 101); Parents and Children (p 187);
Schools (p 215)

AGAINST THE STREAM
(people at odds with the society around them)

▷James Baldwin, *Go Tell it on the Mountain*
▷Charles Dickens, *Oliver Twist*
▷Maxim Gorky, *Foma Gordeev*
▷Nathaniel Hawthorne, *The Scarlet Letter*
▷Somerset Maugham, *Liza of Lambeth*
▷John Steinbeck, *The Grapes of Wrath*
▷Émile Zola, *Nana*

'Only Connect' (p 183); Perplexed by Life (p 190);
Revisiting One's Past (p 203)

AGENTS AND DOUBLE AGENTS

▷Ted Allbeury, *The Secret Whispers*
▷Joseph Conrad, *The Secret Agent*
▷Frederick Forsyth, *The Fourth Protocol*
　John Kruse, *The Hour of the Lily*
▷John Le Carré, *The Perfect Spy*
▷Ruth Rendell, *Talking to Strange Men*
　Hardiman Scott and Becky Allan, *Bait of Lies*

Action Thrillers (p 2); High Adventure (p 117)

ALDISS, Brian • *(born 1925)*
British novelist.

For the last 30 years Aldiss has been a major propagandist for British SF, editing anthologies, speaking at conventions and writing several non-fiction books including *Billion Year Spree* (revised version: *Trillion Year Spree*), a critical history of the genre. His own SF covers the whole range from space opera (eg *Non-stop*) to future-catastrophe (eg *Hot-house*, about the 'greenhouse effect' when the Earth's air-temperature rises uncontrollably), from philosophical fantasy (eg *Frankenstein Unbound* and *Moreau's Other Island*, extensions of themes from earlier SF masterpieces) to stories of alternative worlds (eg the Helliconia trilogy: see below). He is also known for non-SF novels. These range from a comic trilogy about the oversexed 1950s adolescent Horatio Stubbs (*A Hand-reared Boy*; *A Soldier Erect*; *A Rude Awakening*) to *Life in the West*, a ▷Bellow-like book about the plight of a man who has made his reputation preaching science and technology as the salvation of humanity, and is now forced, by the disintegration of his own emotional life, to give his views more intimate analysis.

THE HELLICONIA TRILOGY • *(1982–5)*
Helliconia is one of four planets which revolve round Batalix, itself a satellite of the giant star Freyr. Helliconia seasons last not for months but for hundreds of Earth years, and the planet is inhabited by two separate and incompatible races, one adapted to winter life, the other to summer. The three novels (*Helliconia Spring*, *Helliconia Summer*, *Helliconia Winter*) explore the effects of Helliconia's enormous seasons, each long enough for whole civilisations to rise, flourish and die. Colonial wars, racism, ecology, the clash between religion, science and the arts, are underlying themes – and all the time, Helliconia is observed: watching it provides entertainment, a blend of travel-documentary and soap-opera, for the bored inhabitants of Earth.

Aldiss' other SF books include Earthworks, The Saliva Tree, Barefoot in the Head, Enemies of the System, *and a dozen short-story collections including* Starswarm, Cosmic Inferno *and* New Arrivals, Old Encounters. *His non-SF novels include* The Brightfount Diaries, The Primal Urge, The Male Response *and* The Malacia Tapestry.

READ ON ▷

● *The Dark Light Years*.
▶ **To the Helliconia books:** ▷Ursula Le Guin, *The Left Hand of Darkness*.
▶ **To Aldiss' SF in general:** Ray Bradbury, *The Golden Apples of the Sun*; ▷Isaac Asimov, *The Foundation Trilogy*.
▶ **To the Horatio Stubbs books:** Leslie Thomas, *The Virgin Soldiers*.
▶ **To *Life in the West*:** ▷John Fowles, *Daniel Martin*; David Lodge, *Small World*.

ALLBEURY, Ted • *(born 1917)*
British novelist.

Allbeury writes packed, fast spy thrillers, usually with cold-war settings. His titles include *A Choice of Enemies*, *Moscow Quadrille*, *The Man With the President's Mind*, *The Lantern Network*, *The Alpha List*, *The Crossing*, *Children of Tender Years* and *The Secret Whispers* (about a double agent attempting to escape from East Germany). He also uses the pseudonym Richard Butler (*Where All the Girls Are Sweeter*; *Italian Assets*).

> **READ ON** ⟩
>
> ▶ Duff Hart-Davis, *The Heights of Rimring*. Ted Willis, *The Churchill Commando*. ▷Richard Condon, *The Manchurian Candidate*. ▷John Le Carré, *The Spy Who Came in from the Cold*.

ALLENDE, Isabel • *(born 1942)*
Peruvian novelist.

The House of the Spirits, Allende's first novel, was a glowing family tapestry in the manner of ▷Márquez' *One Hundred Years of Solitude*, spanning five generations and thronged with larger-than-life characters and supernatural events. Her second book, *Of Love and Shadows*, takes a narrower, more political focus, to devastating effect. Irene Beltrán, a journalist, and her photographer-lover Francisco Leal are investigating the disappearance of a disturbed, possibly saintly adolescent. In the jackbooted dictatorship in which they live, however, the child is not simply missing but 'disappeared', one of thousands snatched by the authorities who will never be seen again. Allende surrounds the four main characters – the fourth is Lieutenant Ramirez, the child's abductor – with a web of fantastic personal history in true magic-realist style. But the further the investigators thread their way through the sadism and ruthlessness of a labyrinthine fascist state, the more fact begins to swallow fairy tale. The investigators themselves begin to lose reality – their love-affair becomes a swooning parody of romantic fiction – but what they discover grows more and more uncomfortably like real South American life, like nightmare fleshed.

> **READ ON** ⟩
>
> ▶ Carlos Fuentes, *A Change of Skin*. ▷Günter Grass, *The Tin Drum*. ▷Richard Condon, *Winter Kills*. ▷Mario Vargas Llosa, *Captain Pantoja and the Special Service* gives a more farcical view of Allende's terrifying haunted world.

ALLINGHAM, Margery • *(1905–66)*
British novelist.

Allingham wrote 'crime fiction' only in the senses that each of her books contains the step-by-step solution of a crime, and that their hero, Albert Campion, is an amateur detective whose amiable manner conceals laser intelligence and iron moral integrity. But instead of confining Campion by the boundaries of the detective-story genre,

> **READ ON** ⟩
>
> ● *Death of a Ghost* (set in London's eccentric art-community and involving – what else? – forged paintings); *Hide My Eyes*.

Allingham put him in whatever kind of novel she felt like writing. Some of her books (*More Work for the Undertaker*; *The Beckoning Lady*) are wild, ▷Wodehousian farce, others (*Sweet Danger*; *Traitor's Purse*) are ▷Buchanish, ▷Amblerish thrillers. Her best books are those of the 1940s and 1950s, and especially two set in an atmospheric, cobble-stones-and-alleyways London filled with low-life characters as vivid as any in ▷Dickens, *The Tiger in the Smoke* and *Hide My Eyes*.

FLOWERS FOR THE JUDGE • *(1936)*

Strange things are happening at the old-established publishing firm of Barnabas and Company. First the junior partner turns a street-corner in Streatham and vanishes into thin air, then there is skullduggery over a priceless but obscene manuscript, and soon afterwards the firm's stuffy senior partner is murdered and Mr Campion has three intertwined mysteries on his hands.

Allingham's other Campion books include Coroner's Pidgin, Police at the Funeral, Look to the Lady *and the short-story collections* Mr Campion and Others *and* Take Two at Bedtime. *After Allingham's death, her husband* P. Youngman Carter *wrote two further Campion novels, one of which,* Mr Campion's Farthing, *is up to his wife's most sparkling standard.*

ALL THE WORLD'S A STAGE
(books about theatre)

Richard Bissell, *Say, Darling*
Caryl Brahms and S.J. Simon, *A Bullet in the Ballet*
Bamber Gascoigne, *The Heyday*
H.R.F. Keating, *Death of a Fat God*
▷Thomas Keneally, *The Playmaker*
▷J.B. Priestley, *The Good Companions*
▷Mary Renault, *The Mask of Apollo*

ALTHER, Lisa • *(born 1944)*
US novelist.

Kinflicks (1976) is the 'autobiography' of Ginny Babcock, a 'typical' US adolescent in the late 1960s and early 1970s. The book sends up every cliché of the genre and of the period: Ginny spends her high school years jerking off a muscle-brained football star, discovers lesbian love at

▶ ▷Michael Innes, *The Daffodil Affair*. Edmund Crispin, *The Case of the Gilded Fly*. H.R.F. Keating, *A Rush on the Ultimate*. ▷P.D. James, *An Unsuitable Job for a Woman*. Joan Smith, *Masculine Ending* is a tongue-in-cheek whodunnit starring a feminist sleuth.

> READ ON ⟩

▶ **To *Kinflicks*:** ▷John Irving, *The World According to Garp*; ▷Philip Roth, *Portnoy's Complaint*;

university, joins protest marches, takes up macrobiotic diets, zen and LSD, marries, has a child and divorces – and treats each experience as if she were the first person in the world ever to discover it, as if she were hypnotized by her own adventurousness. Alther intersperses Ginny's first-person narrative with chapters set ten years further on, when Ginny visits her dying mother in hospital, trying to come to terms with her feelings about herself, her family and her future. These sections give the book a harsher, more elegiac tone: the young Ginny symbolises a whole adolescent generation, as rebellious and zestful as any other but engulfed by the age they live in. Alther's second novel, *Original Sins* (1980), similarly blends satire, slapstick and irony. A 1980s equivalent to ▷Mary McCarthy's *The Group*, it traces the experience of five childhood friends as they grow to adulthood, discovering in the process civil rights, the women's movement and the pleasures and preposterousnesses of the sexual revolution. *Other Women* (1985), a less larky exploration of women's experience in the last generation, counterpoints the lives of two utterly different people, a 'flower-child' depressed at the first wiltings of middle age and the prickings of lesbianism, and her English psychiatrist.

AMBLER, Eric • *(born 1909)*
British novelist and screenwriter.

The deadpan style of Ambler's thrillers lets him move easily from violence to farce, and he either sets his books in exotic places (the Levant, the Far East, tropical Africa), or else makes familiar European locations seem exotic as the scene of sinister and unlikely goings-on. His central characters are minor crooks, conmen, or innocent bystanders trapped by circumstances or curiosity into a chain of bizarre and dangerous events. His supporting casts are crammed with improbable, unsavoury specimens, very few of whom are quite what they seem to be. Films and TV series have made this kind of thriller endlessly familiar. But Ambler was one of the first to write it, and he is still among the best.

THE LIGHT OF DAY • *(1962)*
Arthur Simpson, a middle-aged, scruffy conman (played in the film version, *Topkapi*, by Peter Ustinov), is blackmailed into driving a car across the border from Greece into Turkey – and is promptly arrested and forced by the police to spy on the car's owners. They are a dangerous gang of – what? Terrorists? Drug-smugglers? Criminals? Simpson spends the whole book trying to find

Letting Go; Marge Piercy, *The High Cost of Living*.
► **To *Original Sins*:** ▷Mary McCarthy, *The Group*; Rona Jaffé, *Class Reunion*.
► **To *Other Women*:** ▷Alison Lurie, *Foreign Affairs*.

READ ON ▷

● Ambler continued Simpson's sleazy career in the appropriately-named *Dirty Story*. His more serious thrillers include *The Mask of Dimitrios/ Coffin for Dimitrios*, in which a bored writer sets out to track down an elusive Levantine criminal, and *The Levanter*, a story of terrorists in Palestine.
► **To *The Light of Day*:** David Dodge, *Bullets for the Bridegroom*; ▷Graham Greene, *Our Man in Havana*; Donald Westlake, *The Busy Body*.
► **To Ambler's less larky thrillers:** ▷Len

out, and at the same time to save his own sweaty dignity and to make as much profit as he can.

Ambler's other thrillers include Cause for Alarm, Dr Frigo, Epitaph for a Spy, Passage of Arms, The Schirmer Inheritance *and* To Catch a Spy. *He also wrote thrillers (eg* The Maras Affair; Charter to Danger*) in collaboration with* Charles Rodda, *published under the name* Eliot Reed. *They are more straightforward, but no less gripping, than his solo books.*

AMIS, Kingsley • *(born 1922)*
British writer of novels, poems and non-fiction.

In the 1950s, when Amis' writing career began, the end of post-second-world-war austerity had led to an upsurge of optimistic egalitarianism in Britain. Since this mood was not reflected by actual British society, which remained class-ridden, snobbish and élitist, writers of all kinds – the 'angry young men' – began shouting in plays, films and novels about the inequity of life. Whingeing became an artistic form – and Amis' novels showed its funny side. The working-class hero of *Lucky Jim*, a yuppie 30 years before the word was invented, tries to conform with his madrigal-singing, right-newspaper-reading, wine-savouring university colleagues, and in the process shows them up for the pretentious fools they are. The central character of *That Uncertain Feeling*, a small-town librarian, thinks that devastating sexual charm will carry him to the pinnacle of local society; the results are farcical. The hero of *Take a Girl Like You* finds it hard to persuade anyone else in his circle that 'free love' and 'the swinging sixties' are the good things glossy magazines crack them up to be. In the 1960s and 1970s Amis' farcical fires burned low. He began to affect a ponderous, self-consciously right-wing fuddy-duddiness, and abandoned satire for books of other kinds (a ghost story, a James Bond spy thriller and several science fiction books). In the 1980s, however, he returned to the satirical muttering which he always did better than any of his imitators – and his most recent books (eg *Jake's Thing*, about a middle-aged man trying to recapture the sexual energy of youth, and *The Old Devils*: see below) are among his funniest.

THE OLD DEVILS • *(1986)*
A group of old men, acquaintances for over 40 years, meet daily in a Welsh bar to grumble. They are obsessed by failure, their own and the world's. Nothing has ever gone right, and nothing now is as good even as it used to be (which wasn't much). They are especially vitriolic

Deighton, *Horse Under Water*; ▷Richard Condon, *The Manchurian Candidate.*

> READ ON

● *Jake's Thing*; *Stanley and the Women.*
▶ ▷Malcolm Bradbury, *Eating People is Wrong.* A.N. Wilson, *Love Unknown.* ▷Tom Sharpe, *Porterhouse Blue.* William Boyd, *A Good Man in Africa.* Howard Jacobson, *Peeping Tom.* William Cooper, *Scenes from Provincial Life.*

about other people's success – and their discomfort with the world is brought to a peak when one of their 'friends', a famous TV Welshman and an expert on a Dylan-Thomasish poet, comes to settle in the town.

Amis has published several books of light verse, and numerous works on literary matters (eg New Maps of Hell, a history of SF). The best of his comic novels not mentioned above are One Fat Englishman and Ending Up; the best of his serious novels are The Anti-Death League, about a top-secret army unit whose aim is to abolish death, and which is therefore in direct conflict with God, and The Alteration, set in a fantasy contemporary Britain in which modern science and modern religion have never happened, so that we are still organising our lives in medieval ways.

ANCIENT GREECE

▷Robert Graves, *The Golden Fleece/Hercules My Shipmate*
Peter Green, *Achilles His Armour*
▷Homer, *Odyssey*
Naomi Mitchison, *The Corn King and the Spring Queen*
▷Mary Renault, *The King Must Die*
Rosemary Sutcliffe, *Flowers for Adonis*
Henry Treece, *Electra*

Ancient Rome (p 9); Bible: New Testament (p 22); Bible: Old Testament (p 23); Other Peoples, Other Times (p 186)

ANCIENT ROME

Edward Bulwer-Lytton, *The Last Days of Pompeii*
▷Robert Graves, *I Claudius; Count Belisarius*
Peter Vansittart, *Three Six Seven*
▷Gore Vidal, *Julian*
▷Thornton Wilder, *The Ides of March*
Marguerite Yourcenar, *Memoirs of Hadrian*

Ancient Greece (p 9); Bible: New Testament (p 22); The Middle Ages (p 170); Renaissance Europe (p 201)

ANDREWS, Virginia • *(born 1933)*
US novelist.

Andrews writes domestic chillers: claustrophobic stories of tense relationships in 'ordinary' US families. Her books include a quartet about the unhappy Dollenganger family: it begins with *Flowers in the Attic* (about a brother and sister kept prisoners in an attic until an inheritance is claimed), and continues with *Petal on the Wind*, *If There be Thorns* and *Seeds of Yesterday*.

READ ON ▷

► ▷Patricia Highsmith, *The People Who Knock on the Door*. Elizabeth Peters, *The Love Talker*. Celia Fremlin, *The Trouble Makers*. Josephine Tey, *The Franchise Affair*.

THE ANIMAL KINGDOM

Richard Adams, *Watership Down*
Rowena Farre, *Seal Morning*
Paul Gallico, *The Snow Goose*
▷Ernest Hemingway, *Fiesta/The Sun Also Rises*
▷Jack London, *White Fang*
Tony Weeks-Pearson, *Dodo*
Henry Williamson, *Tarka the Otter*

ANTHONY, Evelyn • *(born 1928)*
British novelist.

Anthony's early books were historical romances: they include *Imperial Highness/Rebel Princess*, *Curse Not the King/Royal Intrigue*, *The Heiress/The French Bride* and *Anne of Austria/The Cardinal and the Queen*. In the 1970s she made a second name as writer of romantic thrillers and 20th-century espionage stories. These include *The Tamarind Seed*, *Stranger at the Gates/The Occupying Power*, *The Persian Ransom/The Persian Prince* and *Voices on the Wind* (in which an ex-resistance worker relives her second-world-war fight against the nazis, her love-affairs and a betrayal).

READ ON ▷

► **To the historical romances:** ▷Jean Plaidy, *Perdita's Prince*; ▷Dorothy Dunnett, *Queen's Play*.

► **To the thrillers:** Helen MacInnes, *The Snare of the Hunted*; ▷Mary Stewart, *Airs Above the Ground*.

ANTHONY, Piers • *(born 1934)*
US novelist.

With R. Fuentes, Anthony has written half a dozen martial arts thrillers, including *Bamboo Bloodbath* and *Ninja's Revenge*. On his own he is a prolific SF writer whose novels range from the 5-volume 'autobiography' of a fu-

READ ON ▷

● *On a Pale Horse.*
► Alan Dean Foster, *Spellsinger*. Terry Brookes, *The Sword of*

ture tyrant of Jupiter to the adventures of Death. In his best-known books, instead of winning through by sword and sorcery, his heroes and heroines have to use their wits: in *A Spell for Chameleon* (1977), for example (the first of a series set in the country of Xanth), everyone except Bink (the hero) has a magic talent, and Bink's quest is to find some quality in himself which will prevent him being exiled for ordinariness.

ARCHER, Jeffrey • *(born 1940)*
British novelist.

Archer writes incident-packed stories of intrigue in high and low places. His books include *Not a Penny More Not a Penny Less*, *A Matter of Honour* and the 1970s trilogy *Kane and Abel*, *The Prodigal Daughter* and *Shall We Tell the President?* (which begins with the separate but interlocking careers of two rivals in the worlds of business and politics, and continues with the daughter of one of them, who becomes the first woman president of the USA).

ART FOR WHOSE SAKE?
(painters; fakers; patrons; art-enthusiasts)

▷Marjorie Allingham, *Death of a Ghost*
 Michael Ayrton, *The Mazemaker*
 Joyce Cary, *The Horse's Mouth*
 Mary Flanagan, *Trust*
▷Wyndham Lewis, *Tarr*
▷Somerset Maugham, *The Moon and Sixpence*
 Irwin Shaw, *The Agony and the Ecstasy*

ASIMOV, Isaac • *(born 1920)*
US writer of novels, short stories and non-fiction.

Since the age of 19, when Asimov published his first story, he has written over 300 books, ranging from Bible guides and history text-books to the SF novels and stories for which he is best-known. Unlike many SF writers, he never puts ingenious ideas above character, plot or literary quality. His books are carefully, even tortuously plotted and his characters have depth; he adds scientific detail as the final flourish and the more extraordinary his ideas, the more deadpan their presentation. All this gives his fiction intellectual as well as literary appeal. Flattered that we

---

Shannara. ▷Anne McCaffrey, *Dragonsong.*

> READ ON

▶ ▷Frederick Forsyth, *The Fourth Protocol.* Jon Cleary, *Spearfield's Daughter.* ▷Dick Francis, *Risk.*

> READ ON

● **The best Asimov follow-ups are his robot books:** the short stories in *The Complete Robot* and the novels *The Caves of Steel* and *The Naked Sun.*
▶ **To Asimov's short stories:** ▷Italo

know more science than we thought we did, we feel that we are sharing in the wonders Asimov reveals rather than (as with most SF writers) merely gaping in astonishment.

THE FOUNDATION SAGA • *(1951 to present day)*

The first three books, a self-contained trilogy, appeared in the 1950s; Asimov began adding new novels 30 years later, and three have so far appeared. The Saga is 'space opera' (SF soap opera) on a huge scale, an account of political manoeuvrings among nations and civilisations of the far future. Hari Seldon, a professor of psychohistory (statistical and psychological prediction of the future) foresees a disastrous era of war in the galactic empire, and establishes two Foundations on the galaxy's edge, dedicated to safeguarding civilised knowledge until it is again required. The saga describes the nature and work of each Foundation, their uniting to defeat external threat (from an alien intelligence, 'the Mule') and their subsequent internecine struggles. For, like all human constructs, they are themselves prey to emotion and irrationality, to a bias which can lead towards dark as well as light.

Asimov's SF novels include Pebble in the Sky, The Stars Like Dust *and* The Currents of Space *(all on themes related to the Foundation Saga). His short SF stories are gathered in* The Early Asimov *Volumes 1-3.* Opus *is a useful anthology, an excellent sampler from his dazzling list of works.*

ATWOOD, Margaret • *(born 1939)*

Canadian writer of novels, short stories and poems.

Atwood is a poet as well as a novelist, and her gifts of precise observation and exact description illuminate all her work. She is fascinated by the balance of power between person and person, and by the way our apparently coherent actions and words actually float on a sea of turbulent unseen emotion. Her books often follow the progress of relationships, or of one person's self-discovery. The heroine of *Life Before Man*, for example, is caught up in a sexual quadrilateral (one of whose members, her lover, has just committed suicide), and our interest is as much in seeing how she copes with her own chaotic feelings as in the progress of the affair itself. Many writers have tackled similar themes, but Atwood's books give a unique impression that each moment, each feeling, is being looked at through a microscope, as if the swirling, nagging 'real' world has been momentarily put aside for something more urgent which may just – her characters consistently put

Calvino, *Cosmicomics.*

▶ **To the Foundation saga:** ▷Frank Herbert, *Dune*; Gordon Dickinson, *Tactics of Mistake.* ▷Tom De Haan, *A Mirror for Princes* uses SF techniques to describe a mesmeric society not of the future but of the past. For anyone who finds Asimov's ideas too poker-faced, they are magnificently sent up in ▷Douglas Adams, *The Hitchhiker's Guide to the Galaxy.*

$$\boxed{\text{READ ON}\rangle}$$

● *Surfacing* (about a woman trying to discover the truth about her relationship with her father, by re-examining her childhood in the Canadian wilderness).

▶ **To *The Handmaid's Tale:*** ▷George Orwell, *1984.*

▶ **To Surfacing:** Lynne Reid Banks, *Children at the Gate*; ▷Alison Lurie, *Imaginary Friends.*

▶ **To Atwood's work in general:** ▷Doris

hope above experience – make sense of it.

THE HANDMAID'S TALE • *(1985)*

In the 21st-century Republic of Gilead, fundamentalist Christianity rules and the laws are those of Genesis. Women are chattels: they have no identity, no privacy and no happiness except what men permit them. Offred, for example, is a Handmaid, and her life is devoted to one duty only: breeding. Public prayers and hangings are the norm; individuality – even looking openly into a man's face or reading a woman's magazine – is punished by mutilation, banishment or death. The book shows Offred's struggle to keep her sanity and her identity in such a situation, and her equivocal relationship with the feminist Underground which may be Gilead's only hope.

Atwood's other novels include The Edible Woman *and* Bodily Harm. Dancing Girls *and* Bluebeard's Egg *contain short stories.* The Journals of Susannah Moodie *and* True Stories *are poetry collections, and her* Selected Poems *are also available.*

AUSTEN, Jane • *(1775–1817)*
British novelist.

Austen loved the theatre, and the nearest equivalents to her novels, for pace and verve, are the social comedies of such writers as Sheridan or Goldsmith. The kind of novels popular at the time were epic panoramas (like those of ▷Sir Walter Scott), showing the human race strutting and swaggering amid stormy weather in vast, romantic landscapes. Austen preferred a narrower focus, concentrating on a handful of people busy about their own domestic concerns. Her books are about the bonds which draw families together and the ambitions and feelings (usually caused by grown-up children seeking marriage-partners) which divide them. Her plots fall into 'acts', like plays, and her dialogue is as precise and witty as in any comedy of the time. But she offers a delight available to no playwright: that of the author's own voice, setting the scene, commenting on and shaping events. She is like a bright-eyed, sharp-tongued relative sitting in a corner of the room watching the rest of the family bustle.

PRIDE AND PREJUDICE • *(1813)*
Genteel Mr and Mrs Bennet and their five grown-up daughters are thrown into confusion when two rich, marriageable young men come to live in the neighbourhood. The comedy of the story comes from Mrs Bennet's mother-hen-like attempts at matchmaking, and the way

Lessing, *Martha Quest*; ▷Nadine Gordimer, *A Sport of Nature.*

> **READ ON** ▷

● *Emma* (about a young woman so eager to manage other people's lives that she fails, for a long time, to realise where her own true happiness lies); *Mansfield Park* (a darker comedy about a girl brought up by a rich, charming family who is at first dazzled by their easy brilliance, then comes to see that they are selfish and foolish, and finally, by unassuming persistence, wins through to the happiness we have always hoped for her).
▶ The 'taming' aspect of Austen's plots has inspired a library-ful of lighter fiction by others, of which the best by

Jane AUSTEN

PRIDE AND PREJUDICE *(social comedy in Regency England: choosing marriage-partners)*

William THACKERAY, VANITY FAIR
(social comedy; girls conforming with or rebelling against society)

Edith WHARTON, THE CUSTOM OF THE COUNTRY
(social comedy, New York 1910s: young people prey on foolish elders)

Miles FRANKLIN, MY BRILLIANT CAREER
(young Australian, 1910s, preys on follies of European bourgeoisie)

'TAMING' OR 'BEING TAMED'

Georgette HEYER, REGENCY BUCK
(England, 1810s: will he tame her or will she tame him?)

Baroness ORCZY, THE SCARLET PIMPERNEL
(languid English milord is really romantic hero of French revolution)

ROMANCE

Catherine COOKSON, THE PARSON'S DAUGHTER
(spirited girl 'tames' philandering husband in 19th-century English town)

Colleen MCCULLOUGH, THE THORN BIRDS
(Australian outback: will hero put priestly vocation before earthly love?)

Anthony TROLLOPE, BARCHESTER TOWERS
(marriage and career-machinations in 19th-century English cathedral city)

H.G. WELLS, KIPPS
(personable young man makes his way in 1910s London society)

P.G. WODEHOUSE, THE CODE OF THE WOOSTERS
(problems in idyllic 1920s English country house? Ring for Jeeves . . .)

COMEDY OF MANNERS

Mary MCCARTHY, BIRDS OF AMERICA
(likeable 1960s young American dismayed by Europe)

Mrs GASKELL, CRANFORD
(gossip and intrigue in small 1830s English town)

Barbara PYM, A GLASS OF BLESSINGS
(gossip and foolishness in 1950s London high Anglican parish)

STYLISH, BEADY-EYED SATIRE

Robertson DAVIES, A MIXTURE OF FRAILTIES
(intrigue and the arts in small 1950s Canadian town)

Alison LURIE, FOREIGN AFFAIRS
(Americans in 1970s England cling to each other for comfort and affection)

fate and the young people's own inclinations make things turn out entirely differently from her plans. The more serious sections of the novel show the developing relationship between Elizabeth Bennet, the second daughter, and cold, proud Mr Darcy. She tries to 'tame' him, to show him the effects of his character on others – and in the process she both falls in love with him and is 'tamed' herself. Although secondary characters (henpecked Mr Bennet, snobbish Lady Catherine de Bourgh, Elizabeth's romantic younger sister Lydia, the dashing army officer Wickham and the conceited bore Mr Collins) steal the limelight whenever they appear, the book hinges on half a dozen magnificent set-piece scenes between Elizabeth and Darcy, the two headstrong young people we yearn to see realising their love for one another and falling into one another's arms.

Apart from a number of unfinished works (eg The Watsons; Sanditon), Austen's output consists of six novels: Northanger Abbey *(a spoof of romantic melodrama, unlike any of her other books),* Sense and Sensibility, Pride and Prejudice, Mansfield Park, Emma *and* Persuasion.

▶ far are the Regency novels of ▷Georgette Heyer.

▶ Of more serious writings, the ones which most nearly share Austen's ironical, satirical insight into human character and behaviour are ▷Mrs Gaskell, *Wives and Daughters,* ▷William Thackeray, *Vanity Fair,* ▷E.M. Forster, *A Room With a View,* ▷Alison Lurie, *Only Children,* and the short stories of ▷Anton Chekhov and ▷Katherine Mansfield.

▶ Joan Aiken, *Mansfield Revisited* is a lively sequel to *Mansfield Park,* the best of many authors' attempts to follow in Austen's steps.

AUTOBIOGRAPHIES AND MEMOIRS

(GHOSTED!)

Alan Brien, *Lenin: the Novel*
Margaret George, *The Autobiography of Henry VIII*
▷Robert Graves, *I Claudius*
▷Joseph Heller, *God Knows* (King David of Israel)
Stephen Marlowe, *The Memoirs of Christopher Columbus*
▷Robert Nye, *Falstaff*
Augusto Roa Bastos, *I, The Supreme* (Francia, dictator of Paraguay)

B

BAGLEY, Desmond • *(1923–83)*
British novelist.

Many of Bagley's tense thrillers are set in Africa, and involve groups of people forced together by circumstance and battling not just outsiders and the environment but each other. In *Juggernaut* (1985), for example, an English adventurer leads a convoy through the war-torn state of Nyala. At the convoy's heart is a huge truck carrying the transformer for an oil-rig, and as it trundles across the countryside it becomes a mobile hospital, a battle-wagon and a symbol of hope for streams of refugees who flock round it like pilgrims, making their way to a new home somewhere beyond the war.

Bagley's other thrillers include The Golden Keel, High Citadel, Landslide, The Spoilers, The Freedom Trap, Flyaway, Windfall *and* Night of Error.

READ ON ▷

● *Running Blind*.
▶ James Graham, *The Khufra Run*. Lionel Davidson, *The Rose of Tibet*. ▷C.S. Forester, *The Gun*.

BALDWIN, James • *(1924–87)*
US writer of novels, plays and non-fiction.

In a series of non-fiction books (*Notes of a Native Son*; *The Fire Next Time*; *No Name in the Street*), Baldwin described the fury and despair of alienated US blacks, urging revolution as the only way to maintain racial identity in a hostile environment. His plays and novels tackle the same theme, but add two more, equally passionate: the way fundamentalist Christianity is a destructive force, and the quest for sexual identity in an amoral world. *Go Tell it on the Mountain* (1953) is a novel about a poor Harlem family torn apart by the pressures of born-again Christianity. *Another Country* (1962) shows people living lives of increasing desperation in a corrupt, all-engulfing and

READ ON ▷

▶ In Ralph Ellison, *Invisible Man* a rootless black American travels the USA in search of identity, and finally — as the book becomes increasingly surreal — continues his quest in hell.
▶ A surrealist Harlem, a fantasy-land of crime, jazz, drugs and

terrifying New York. *Giovanni's Room* (1956) is about an American in Paris, having to choose between his mistress and his (male) lover.

Baldwin's other novels are Tell Me How Long the Train's Been Gone, If Beale Street Could Talk *and* Evidence of Things Not Seen; *his short stories are in* Going to Meet the Man. *His plays include* The Amen Corner *and* Blues for Mr Charlie, *and his other non-fiction books are* Nobody Knows My Name, Nothing Personal *(with photos by Richard Avedon) and* A Rap on Race *(written with Margaret Mead).*

graveyard humour, is the location for Chester Himes' detective novels (eg *Cotton Comes to Harlem*): crime plots apart, they are as unsparing and compulsive as Baldwin's books. Maya Angelou's autobiographical sequence, beginning with *I Know Why the Caged Bird Sings*, give sunnier reactions to equally abrasive Southern US black experience. Books as bleak as Baldwin's about the conjunction of sex, violence and despair are Jean Genet, *Querelle of Brest*, John Rechy, *The City of Night* and John Edgar Wideman, *A Glance Away*.

BALLARD, J.G. (James Graham) •
(born 1930)
British novelist.

Ballard's SF is pessimistic and satirical about the human race: each of his novels takes an aspect of the way we treat the planet and each other and extends it towards catastrophe. In some books (eg *The Drowned World*, about the melting of the polar ice-caps, or *The Burning World*, about the coming of permanent drought) our actions trigger natural disaster. In others (eg *Concrete Island*, which imagines the Earth engulfed by motorways, and *High Rise*, about the effects on human nature of living in ever-higher tower-blocks) we laboriously reconstruct the world as a single, megalopolitan prison-cell. His most savage, most dazzling SF novel is *The Unlimited Dream Company* (1979), a fable about human credulity. A youth who has never flown before steals a plane and crashes in the London suburbs. The people take him for a wonder-worker, even a messiah – and their credulity spirals into a religious cult involving orgiastic sex, telepathy and levitation. The story is told by the bewildered boy himself. At

READ ON >

● *The Day of Creation.*
▶ ▷George Turner, *The Sea and Summer.*
▷Robert Silverberg, *Master of Life and Death.* ▷Gore Vidal, *Kalki.*

first disgusted and appalled, he gradually comes to believe in his own magic powers, and slowly but surely metamorphoses into the ultimate being, the god-figure everyone takes him for. Apart from SF, Ballard is best-known for *Empire of the Sun* (1984), a powerful autobiographical novel about a young teenager in a second-world-war Japanese internment camp.

Ballard's other books include The Atrocity Exhibition/ Love and Napalm: Export USA, The Four-Dimensional Nightmare *and* The Vermilion Sands. The Voices of Time *and* Low-flying Aircraft *are collections of short stories.*

BALZAC, Honoré de • *(1799–1850)*
French novelist.

Photography was invented during Balzac's lifetime, and there was talk of using it to produce an encyclopedia of human types, catching each trade, profession and character in a suitable setting and at a particularly revealing moment. Balzac determined to do much the same thing in prose: to write a set of novels which would include people of every possible kind, described so minutely that the reader could envisage them as clearly as if they had been photographed. He called the project *The Human Comedy*, and although he died before completing it, it still runs to some 90 pieces of fiction – which can be read separately – and includes over 2000 different characters.

OLD GORIOT (Père Goriot) • *(1834)*
Goriot is a lonely old man obsessed by love for his two married daughters. He lives in a seedy Parisian boarding-house (whose contents and inhabitants Balzac meticulously describes), and gradually sells all his possessions, and even cuts down on food, to try to buy his daughters' love with presents. They treat him with a contempt he never notices – in fact everyone despises him except Rastignac, a student living in the same house. Goriot's death-bed scene, when he clutches Rastignac's hands thinking that his daughters have come to visit him at last, is one of Balzac's most moving passages, a deliberate reminiscence of King Lear's death-scene in Shakespeare's play.

The best-known novels from The Human Comedy *are* César Birotteau *(about a shopkeeper destroyed by ambition),* Eugénie Grandet *(a love story, one of Balzac's few books with a happy ending), and* Cousin Bette *(about a man whose obsessive philandering tears his family apart).* Droll Tales *is a set of farcical short stories, similar to*

> **READ ON**

● *The Curé of Tours* (a similarly detailed, and almost equally moving, study of desolate old age).
▶ **To Balzac's power and emotional bleakness:** ▷Émile Zola, *Nana*; ▷François Mauriac, *The Woman of the Pharisees*; Theodore Dreiser, *An American Tragedy*; ▷Carson McCullers, *The Ballad of the Sad Café*; Hugh Walpole, *The Old Ladies*.
▶ **To his evocation of city life:** ▷Somerset Maugham, *Liza of Lambeth*; ▷Saul Bellow, *Mr Sammler's Planet*.
▶ **To his vision of the 'ant-hill of human aspiration', the senseless, self-destructive bustle of affairs:** ▷Charles Dickens, *Dombey and Son*; George Gissing, *New Grub Street*.

those in Giovanni Boccaccio's Decameron *or* The Arabian Nights.

BARBER, Noel • *(1911–88)*
British novelist.

Barber wrote romantic thrillers, usually set in the Middle East. His books include *The Other Side of Paradise*, *Farewell to France* and *A Woman of Cairo* (1984), in which two lovers are drawn together and pushed apart by the pressure of events in war-torn Egypt.

READ ON ▷

● *Tanamera.*
▶ Valerie Fitzgerald, *Zemindar.* M.M. Kaye, *Shadow Moon.* ▷J.G. Farrell, *The Singapore Grip.* ▷Olivia Manning, *Fortunes of War.*

BARNES, Djuna • *(1892–1982)*
US novelist and short-story writer.

Nightwood (1936), Barnes' best-known novel, is a dark tale of lesbianism, adultery and madness among US exiles in Paris in the 1930s. T.S. Eliot compared it, for 'horror and doom', to Elizabethan tragedy; it is also like ▷Sartre's play *Huis Clos*, a glimpse of damned souls in an ultra-modern hell. The characters – a transvestite doctor, a womanising German baron, a frail young girl and the bisexual publicist for a travelling circus – spend their time alternately betraying one another emotionally or spending maudlin, boozy nights discussing their own and each other's erotic preferences. Barnes' style is a poetic version of the stream-of-consciousness monologues of Freud's patients, halfway between ▷Proust and Molly Bloom's soliloquy in ▷Joyce's *Ulysses*. *Nightwood* is no easy read, but it is compulsive and unforgettable.

Barnes' other fiction consists of the novel Ryder *and the story-collections* The Book of Repulsive Women, Spillway *(originally published with poems and plays, as* A Book *and* A Night Among the Horses*) and* Vagaries Malicieux. *She is also known for her plays, especially* The Antiphon.

READ ON ▷

▶ ▷Jean Rhys, *Good Morning, Midnight.* ▷Angela Carter, *The Infernal Desire Machines of Doctor Hoffman.* Desmond Hogan, *A New Shirt.*

BEERBOHM, Max • *(1876–1956)*
British artist and writer.

A caricaturist and satirist, Beerbohm published cartoons, parodies, essays and articles ridiculing literary and social figures of the day. His only novel, *Zuleika Dobson* (1911) is a send-up of the university-set romantic novels of Ouida

READ ON ▷

● *Seven Men* (short stories).
▶ Nancy Mitford, *Don't Tell Alfred.* Angela

(in which gels' hearts thud as they watch their heroes' rippling muscles in the rowing or boxing teams). Beerbohm turns Ouida's conventions on their heads. His Oxford undergraduates, whether gentlemen (world-weary and overbred) or scholars (weedy and obsessive) think of nothing but themselves, until Zuleika, the beautiful grand-daughter of the Warden of Judas College, sweeps into the university and every male in the place (even the statues on their pedestals) starts swooning for love of her. There are arguments, duels and suicide-pacts, and Zuleika is blind to them all. Her quarry is the Duke of Dorset, the handsomest, best-connected man in England, and her head will not rest easy, blessing the pillow it lies on, until she makes him her slave. But what, dear reader, if she should fall for *him* …?

BELLOW, Saul • *(born 1915)*
US novelist and playwright.

In Bellow's view, one of the most unexpected aspects of life in the modern world, and particularly in the post-Christian west, is that many people have lost all sense of psychological and philosophical identity. All Bellow's leading characters feel alienated from society. Some are content to suffer; others try to assert themselves, to invent an identity and live up to it – an attempt which is usually both bizarre and doomed. The hero of *The Adventures of Augie March* (1953), trying to model himself on one of ▷Hemingway's laconic men of action, takes his sophisticated girl-friend lizard-hunting in Mexico with a tame eagle, and is amazed when she leaves him. The hero of *Henderson the Rain King* (1959) goes on safari to darkest Africa, only to be taken prisoner by a remote people who think him a god-king and mark him for sacrifice. Devices like these warm Bellow's books, adding life and energy to what is already philosophically intriguing. His novels are compelling intellectual entertainments, thrillers of the mind.

HUMBOLDT'S GIFT • *(1975)*
The book's hero, Charlie Citrine, is a wise-cracking, street-wise failure. He is a writer whose inspiration has run out, a husband whose wife is divorcing him and whose mistress despises him, an educated man terrified of brainwork. Unexpectedly, a legacy from a dead friend, a drunken, bawdy poet, turns out not to be the worthless pile of paper everyone imagines but a scenario which forms the basis for a hugely successful film. Wealth is now added to Citrine's problems, and he is battened on by

Thirkell, *August Folly.*
▷Jerome K. Jerome, *Three Men in a Boat.*
Noel Langley, *Cage Me a Peacock.* Oscar Wilde, *The Portrait of Dorian Gray* takes a darker view of similarly self-obsessed characters.

| READ ON ▷ |

● *Herzog* (about a panic-stricken intellectual who revisits the scenes of his past life trying to find clues to his psychological identity: cue for a magnificent travelogue through the city of Chicago, Bellow's consistent inspiration and this book's other central 'character').
▶ **To Bellow's theme of people searching for identity:** ▷Albert Camus, *The Fall*; ▷William Golding, *The Paper Men*; Max Frisch, *I'm Not Stiller*; ▷Jean Rhys, *Good Morning, Midnight*; Bernard Malamud, *A New Life*; ▷Margaret Atwood, *Surfacing.*
▶ **To his vision of the city (in his case, Chicago) as a metaphor for the turbulence of the soul:** James Plunkett,

tax officials, accountants, salesmen and an unsuccessful crook who tries to extort from him first money and then friendship. As the novel proceeds, Citrine keeps nerving himself to make the decision – any decision – that will focus his life, and is hampered each time by ludicrous circumstances and by the contrast between his own inadequacy and the memory of his larger-than-life, dead friend.

Bellow's other full-length novels are Mr Sammler's Planet, Herzog, The Dean's December *and* More Die of Heartbreak. Dangling Man, The Victim *and* Seize the Day *are mid-length novellas, and his short stories are collected in* Mosby's Memoirs *and* Him With the Foot in his Mouth. *He has also written plays and a fascinating political memoir about a visit to Israel,* To Jerusalem and Back.

BENNETT, Arnold • *(1867–1931)*
British novelist and non-fiction writer.

Bennett wrote hundreds of thousands of words each year, and much of his output was pot-boiling. But his best novels and stories, set in the English Midlands (the area he called 'the Five Towns', now Stoke-on-Trent), are masterpieces. They deal in a realistic way with the lives and aspirations of ordinary people (factory hands, shop assistants, housewives), but are full of disarming optimism and fantasy. Bennett's characters have ambitions; they travel, they read, they dream. Apart from the Five Towns novels his best-known works are two books originally written as magazine-serials: *The Card* (about a bouncy young man whose japes outrage provincial society but who ends up as mayor) and *The Grand Babylon Hotel*, a set of linked stories about the guests and staff in a luxury hotel.

THE OLD WIVES' TALE • *(1908)*
The lives of two sisters are contrasted: vivacious Sophia and steady Constance. Sophia feels constricted by life in the Five Towns, falls for a handsome wastrel and elopes with him to Paris, where he deserts her. Constance meanwhile marries a clerk in her father's shop, and settles to a life of bored domesticity. The novel charts the sisters' lives, and includes memorable scenes of the 1870 siege of Paris in the Franco-Prussian War. Its concluding section unites the sisters, now elderly, and shows, as their lives draw to a close, that those lives were all they had, that neither achieved anything or made any impact on the world.

The Five Towns novels are Anna of the Five Towns,

Strumpet City (set in pre-1914 Dublin); ▷Christina Stead, *The Beauties and Furies* (set in 1930s Paris); Colin MacInnes, *City of Spades* (set in racially divided 1950s London).

> **READ ON**

● *Clayhanger*; *Riceyman Steps*.
▶ ▷D.H. Lawrence, *The Rainbow*. ▷H.G. Wells, *Ann Veronica*. Theodore Dreiser, *Sister Carrie*. ▷Somerset Maugham, *Of Human Bondage*. ▷J.B. Priestley, *Angel Pavement*. Sherwood Anderson, *Winesburg, Ohio* is a set of stories echoing the feelings and lives of Bennett's characters in a small-town US setting.

The Old Wives' Tale, Clayhanger, Hilda Lessways, These Twain *and* The Roll Call. Riceyman Steps, *set in London, is grimmer and more Zolaesque.* Mr Prohack *is an entertainment, a good follow-up to* The Card. *Of Bennett's many other writings, particularly fascinating are his* Journals, *discussing such matters as his love of France, the meals he ate, the plays and novels he enjoyed, and above all his phenomenal day-to-day productivity.*

BENSON, E.F. (Edward Frederic) •
(1867–1940)
British novelist and non-fiction writer.

Although Benson wrote books of many kinds, he is best-known today for acid social comedies, and particularly for the 'Mapp and Lucia' series, televised with enormous success in the mid-1980s. His characters are well-to-do, middle-class Edwardians, whose chief interest in life is social one-upmanship. One's bridge-party, one's garden, one's paintings or one's recipes must simply outclass everyone else's, and if there is the slightest risk of failure, devious means must be employed.

MAPP AND LUCIA • *(1935)*
In previous books in the series, we have already met Lucia, the social queen of Riseholme, and Miss Mapp, who holds the same position in Tilling. Now Lucia moves to Tilling for the summer with her friend Georgie Pillson, rents Mapp's beloved house Mallards, and proceeds to upstage Mapp socially at every moment and in every way. The war between the ladies is fought at garden parties, poetry evenings, dinner-parties (at which Lucia's recipe Lobster à la Riseholme is a major weapon), and finally reaches its climax – one of Benson's most preposterous inventions – on an upturned table in the English Channel.

Benson's books include school stories, biographies, reminiscences, ghost stories (collected as Spook Stories *and* More Spook Stories*), and a shoal of comic novels, similar in themes and wit to the 'Lucia' books, including the 'Dodo' series and the (slightly) more serious* Mrs Ames *and* Secret Lives.

READ ON ⟩

● *Queen Lucia*; *Paying Guests*.
▶ Tom Holt, *Lucia in Wartime* and *Lucia Triumphant* (sequels, as good as Benson at his best). Gabriel Chevalier, *Clochemerle*. Nancy Mitford, *Love in a Cold Climate*. Angela Thirkell, *Before Lunch*.

BIBLE: NEW TESTAMENT

▷ Anthony Burgess, *The Kingdom of the Wicked*
 Severia Huré, *I, Mary, Daughter of Israel*

Pär Lagerkvist, *Barabbas*
George Moore, *The Brook Kerith*
▷Michèle Roberts, *The Wild Girl*
Henryk Sienkiewycz, *Quo Vadis?*
Frank Slaughter, *The Shoes of the Fisherman*

Ancient Rome (p 9); Bible: Old Testament (p 23)

BIBLE: OLD TESTAMENT

▷Joseph Heller, *God Knows*
▷Thomas Mann, *Joseph and his Brothers*
Jeanette Winterson, *Boating for Beginners*

Bible: New Testament (p 22); Other Peoples, Other Times (p 186)

BINCHY, Maeve
Irish novelist.

Binchy's books are affectionate tapestries of the lives of ordinary people, often in small Irish towns in the earlier years of this century. 'Great' events happen offstage; the spotlight is on birth, friendship, marriage, death and the engrossing bustle of everyday life. Her style is gently satirical – village gossip turned into art – and her dialogue is warm with the cadences of Irish speech. Her novels include *Light a Penny Candle*, *Dublin Four*, *Firefly Summer* and *Echoes* (1986), about a group of 1950s teenagers growing up in a quiet seaside resort. *The Lilac Bus* (1986) is a set of linked short stories about the passengers who travel regularly on a small country bus.

READ ON ▷

▶ Edna O'Brien, *The Country Girls*. Elizabeth North, *Worldly Goods*. Rony Robinson, *The Beano*. Laurie Lee, *Cider With Rosie* (nostalgic memoirs of childhood in a 1930s Gloucestershire village, of the English countryside as it used to be). Laura Ingalls Wilder, *The Little House on the Prairie* (much less schmaltzy than the TV series). ▷Eudora Welty, *Delta Wedding*.

BLISH, James • *(1921–75)*
US novelist.

Blish used space-opera to discuss complex philosophical and religious ideas. *A Case of Conscience* (1959), for example, sets born-again Christian Earth-scientists on a vast

READ ON ▷

▶ ▷Frank Herbert, *Dune*. ▷Isaac Asimov, *Foundation*. ▷J.G.

unexplored planet wondering whether the fact that they are human beings, God's supreme creation, gives them the right to exploit the planet's mineral wealth at the expense of the alien inhabitants, a lower order of existence; the book is part of the 'After Such Knowledge' tetralogy (the other volumes are *Black Easter*, *Doctor Mirabilis* and *The Day After Judgement*) in which Blish tried to work out a compromise between alchemy, black magic, religion and modern science. His best-known books are the 'Cities in Flight' novels, in which a mechanism is devised to spin whole sections of the Earth's surface into space, where their inhabitants eagerly or apprehensively set about reinventing their own lives. The series' protagonist is not a person but an entire community: Manhattan.

The 'Cities in Flight' novels are They Shall Have Stars, A Life for the Stars, Earthman Come Home *and* A Clash of Cymbals. *Blish's other books include* And All the Stars a Stage, Jack of Eagles *and* Midsummer Century. Anywhen *is a collection of short stories.*

Ballard, *The Burning World*. ▷Brian Aldiss, *The Helliconia Trilogy*.

BÖLL, Heinrich • *(1917–85)*
German novelist and non-fiction writer.

For decades after the second world war and the 'economic miracle' which followed it, German novelists hovered over their country like doctors examining a particularly interesting patient. How could any nation be so outwardly flourishing and seem so dead inside? Were such things as student riots in the 1960s or the urban terrorism of the 1970s isolated phenomena or symptoms of a deeper-rooted sickness? Böll, a Roman Catholic, linked the malaise of society with another kind of moral disintegration, the collapse of faith – but instead of preaching or hectoring he tried to alert his readers with bitter, saturnine irony. He is at his most savage in short stories and medium-length novels: *The Safety Net* (about terrorism), *The Lost Honour of Katherina Blum* (satirising the gutter press), *The Unguarded House* (scathing about miracles, economic or religious). Böll's longer books spread his rage more widely – and paradoxically, although this makes them more relaxed, as pacy and witty as ▷Bellow's, the urbane tone makes their messages even more unsettling.

GROUP PORTRAIT WITH LADY (Gruppenbild mit Dame) • *(1971)*
Böll takes a 'typical' German citizen of the post-war years – an inoffensive, dull woman in her 60s – and tries to find out more about her by questioning her family, friends, neighbours, work-mates and old school-fellows. A jigsaw

READ ON ⟩

● *Billiards at Half-past Nine* (a panoramic view of the last 50 years of German society, focussed on a single family); *The Clown* (a bleak study of one person's attempt to retain dignity and moral integrity, to say nothing of religious faith, in a society where such qualities are no longer valued).
▶ Robert Musil, *Young Törless*. Siegfried Lenz, *The Heritage*. ▷Saul Bellow, *Mr Sammler's Planet*. Nathalie Sarraute, *Portrait of an Unknown Man*. J.P. Marquand, *The Late George Apley*. Janet Hitchman, *Meeting for Burial*.

puzzle of interlocking interviews, assembled to make a single picture. But two pictures in fact emerge: one of the woman herself and one of the teeming German society of which she is part. The book's style is brisk, witty and apparently uncontroversial, so that it is not till the end that we realise just what Böll is saying about Germany's moral plight.

Böll's other novels are And Where Were You, Adam?, Acquainted with the Night *and* Billiards at Half-past Nine. *His short stories are in* Absent Without Leave, Traveller, if you Come to Spa *and* Children are Civilians Too. What's To Become of the Boy? *is a brief, savage memoir of adolescence under the nazis;* Irish Journal *describes his stay in Ireland in the 1960s.*

THE BOOKER PRIZE

In 1968 Booker International set up an annual prize for fiction by British and Commonwealth authors, intending it to be of major status, equal to such awards as the Prix Goncourt in France. Although the prize-money (currently £15,000) has long been overtaken by other British awards, the Booker competition still attracts more publicity than any other. Publishers submit promising titles each year, and a panel of judges makes a short list in September and selects a winner in October. The following list shows all the short-listed authors and titles so far, with winners' names in bold.

1969
  Barry England, *Figures in a Landscape*
  N. Mosley, *The Impossible Object*
▷Iris Murdoch, *The Nice and the Good*
▷**P.H. Newby, Something to Answer For**
▷Muriel Spark, *The Public Image*
  G.M. Williams, *From Scenes Like These*

1970
  A.L. Barker, *John Brown's Body*
▷Elizabeth Bowen, *Eva Trout*
▷Iris Murdoch, *Bruno's Dream*
▷**Bernice Rubens, The Elected Member**
  William Trevor, *Mrs Eckdorff in O'Neill's Hotel*
  T. Wheeler, *The Conjunction*

1971
  Thomas Kilroy, *The Big Chapel*
▷Doris Lessing, *Briefing for a Descent into Hell*
▷**V.S. Naipaul, In a Free State**
▷Mordecai Richler, *St Urbain's Horseman*
  Derek Robinson, *Goshawk Squadron*
▷Elizabeth Taylor, *Mrs Palfrey at the Claremont*

1972
  John Berger, G
▷Susan Hill, *Bird of Night*

▷Thomas Keneally, *The Chant of Jimmie Blacksmith*
David Storey, *Passmore*

1973
Beryl Bainbridge, *The Dressmaker*
▷**J.G. Farrell, *The Siege of Krishnapur***
Elizabeth Mavor, *The Green Equinox*

1974
▷Kingsley Amis, *Ending Up*
Beryl Bainbridge, *The Bottle Factory Outing*
▷**Nadine Gordimer, *The Conservationist***
Stanley Middleton, *Holiday*
▷C.P. Snow, *In Their Wisdom*

1975
▷**Ruth Prawer Jhabvala, *Heat and Dust***
▷Thomas Keneally, *Gossip from the Forest*

1976
André Brink, *An Instant in the Wind*
R.C. Hutchinson, *Rising*
Brian Moore, *The Doctor's Wife*
Julian Rathbone, *King Fisher Lives*
David Storey, *Saville*
William Trevor, *The Children of Dynmouth*

1977
Paul Bailey, *Peter Smart's Confessions*
Caroline Blackwood, *Great Granny Webster*
Jennifer Johnston, *Shadows on our Skin*
Penelope Lively, *The Road to Lichfield*
▷Barbara Pym, *Quartet in Autumn*
Paul Scott, *Staying On*

1978
▷Kingsley Amis, *Jake's Thing*
André Brink, *Rumours of Rain*
Penelope Fitzgerald, *The Bookshop*
Jane Gardam, *God on the Rocks*
▷**Iris Murdoch, *The Sea, The Sea***
▷Bernice Rubens, *A Five-year Sentence*

1979
Penelope Fitzgerald, *Offshore*
▷Thomas Keneally, *Confederates*
▷V.S. Naipaul, *A Bend in the River*
Julian Rathbone, *Joseph*
▷Fay Weldon, *Praxis*

1980
▷Anthony Burgess, *Earthly Powers*
Anita Desai, *Clear Light of Day*
▷**William Golding, *Rites of Passage***
▷Alice Munro, *The Beggar Maid*
Julia O'Faolain, *No Country for Young Men*
Barry Unsworth, *Pascali's Island*
J.L. Carr, *A Month in the Country*

1981
Molly Keane, *Good Behaviour*
▷Doris Lessing, *The Sirian Experiments*

Ian McEwan, *The Comfort of Strangers*
▷**Salman Rushdie, *Midnight's Children***
Anne Schlee, *Rhine Journey*
▷Muriel Spark, *Loitering with Intent*
D.M. Thomas, *The White Hotel*

1982
John Arden, *Silence Among the Weapons*
William Boyd, *An Ice-cream War*
▷Lawrence Durrell, *Constance or Solitary Practices*
▷**Thomas Keneally, *Schindler's Ark***
Alice Thomas Ellis, *The 27th Kingdom*
Timothy Mo, *Sour Sweet*

1983
▷Malcolm Bradbury, *Rates of Exchange*
J.M. Coetzee, *Life & Times of Michael K*
John Fuller, *Flying to Nowhere*
Anita Mason, *The Illusionist*
▷Salman Rushdie, *Shame*
▷Graham Swift, *Waterland*

1984
▷J.G. Ballard, *Empire of the Sun*
Julian Barnes, *Flaubert's Parrot*
▷**Anita Brookner, *Hôtel du Lac***
Anita Desai, *In Custody*
Penelope Lively, *According to Mark*
David Lodge, *Small World*

1985
Peter Carey, *Illywhacker*
J.L. Carr, *The Battle of Pollocks Crossing*
▷**Keri Hulme, *The Bone People***
▷Doris Lessing, *The Good Terrorist*
Jan Morris, *Last Letters from Hav*
▷Iris Murdoch, *The Good Apprentice*

1986
▷**Kingsley Amis, *The Old Devils***
▷Margaret Atwood, *The Handmaid's Tale*
Paul Bailey, *Gabriel's Lament*
▷Robertson Davies, *What's Bred in the Bone*
▷Kazuo Ishiguro, *An Artist of the Floating World*
Timothy Mo, *An Insular Possession*

1987
▷Chinua Achebe, *Anthills of the Savannah*
Peter Ackroyd, *Chatterton*
Nina Bawden, *Circles of Deceit*
Penelope Lively, *Moon Tiger*
Brian Moore, *The Colour of Blood*
▷Iris Murdoch, *The Book and the Brotherhood*

1988
Peter Carey, *Oscar and Lucinda*
Bruce Chatwin, *Utz*
Penelope Fitzgerald, *The Beginning of Spring*
David Lodge, *Nice Work*
▷Salman Rushdie, *The Satanic Verses*

▷Marina Warner, *The Lost Father*

BORGES, Jorge Luis • *(1899–1987)*
Argentinian short-story writer and poet.

Until the 1950s Borges worked as a librarian and was an admired poet – though, because his verse seems flat in translation, he was hardly known outside Spanish-speaking countries. But in the 1950s his 'fictions' began to appear in other languages, and his reputation spread worldwide. A 'fiction' is a short prose piece, ranging in length from a paragraph to a half a dozen pages. Some are short stories, in the manner of ▷Kipling, ▷Hemingway or ▷Kafka (whom Borges translated into Spanish). Others are tiny surrealist meditations, zen-like philosophical riddles or prose-poetry. A 20th-century writer produces a version of *Don Quixote* for modern times – and it is identical, word for word, to the original. (But is it any less real for all that?) A man meets a mysterious stranger by a riverside, and finds that the stranger is himself. A man writes about the terrifying prison which traps him – and only at the end reveals its name: the world.

Borges' stories and fictions are in Labyrinths, A Universal History of Infamy, Fictions, The Aleph, Dreamtigers, The Book of Sand *and* Doctor Brodie's Report. *His Selected Poems were published in English translation in 1972.*

BOWEN, Elizabeth • *(1899–1973)*
Irish novelist and short-story writer.

Although Bowen's themes were emotional – loneliness; longing for love; lack of communication – she wrote in a brisk and faintly eccentric style (italicising the most unlikely words, *for* example) which gives her stories an exhilarating feeling of detachment from the events and reactions they describe. She was especially skilful at evoking atmosphere in houses or locales: London streets and tube-stations during the second-world-war blitz become places of eerie fantasy rather than reality. Her concern, despite her characters' craving to preserve the social niceties, was to show 'life with the lid off' – and this, coupled with the unpredictability of her writing style, constantly edges her plots from actuality through dream to nightmare.

THE DEATH OF THE HEART • *(1938)*
Portia, a naive 16-year-old orphan (in a more modern

READ ON ▷

● *The Book of Imaginary Beings* (descriptions of 120 fanciful creatures from the weirder recesses of the world's imagination.
▶ ▷Gabriel García Márquez, *The Innocent Erendira*. Robert Coover, *Pricksongs and Descants*. Samuel Beckett, *More Pricks than Kicks*. ▷Italo Calvino, *Invisible Cities*. Michael Ayrton, *Fabrications*.
▶ **An unexpected parallel to Borges at his most surreal – so close at times that it seems like a send-up:** Woody Allen, *Without Feathers*.

READ ON ▷

● *The Heat of the Day; Eva Trout*.
▶ **To Bowen's novels:** ▷Henry James, *The Wings of the Dove*; ▷Angus Wilson, *The Middle Age of Mrs Eliot*; ▷Iris Murdoch, *The Sandcastle*. Peter Taylor, *A Summons to Memphis* sets scenes of similar emotional ambiguity in the US mid-west.
▶ **To Bowen's short stories:** ▷Elizabeth Taylor, *A Dedicated*

book she might be 12 or 13) goes to live with her stuffy half-brother and his brittle, insecure wife in fashionable 1930s London. Her innocence is in marked contrast to their world-weary sophistication, and they are as exasperated with her as she is with them. Then she falls in what she imagines to be love, and all parties are launched on an ever-bumpier emotional ride.

Bowen's other novels include The House in Paris, A World of Love *and* Eva Trout. *Her short stories are published in* Encounters, Ann Lee's, Joining Charles, The Cat Jumps *and the second-world-war collections* Look at All Those Roses *and* The Demon Lover.

BOYD, Martin • *(1893–1969)*
Australian novelist.

One of a large artistic family, Boyd originally trained as an architect, only taking up full-time writing in his 30s. He also spent much time in Europe, and writes in his autobiography of the pull between the cultural traditions of the Old World and the openness and opportunity of Australia. He turned all these themes and feelings into fiction. His principal characters are artistically sensitive people growing up in Australia, balancing the claims of family life against the need they feel to experience European art, culture and religion for themselves. He writes with malicious, ironical glee of large middle-class families, keeping up their pretensions and the façade of polite manners in what they feel is an exciting but barbarian environment. His best-known books are the 'Langton' tetralogy (1952–62): the 'biography' of Guy Langton and his extended family in the 80 years preceding the first world war. It centres on Guy's artistic and spiritual restlessness, but a major subsidiary theme is the gradual disintegration of a once tight-knit family as social opportunities in Australia increase and ties with the Old World grow less. The Langtons understand the past but have no sense of future opportunity; as Australia waxes, all they can do is wane.

The books in the Langton tetralogy are The Cardboard Crown, A Difficult Young Man, Outbreak of Love *and* When Blackbirds Sing. *Boyd's other novels include* Lucinda Brayford, Such Pleasure *and* The Montfords *(originally published under the pseudonym Martin Mills). His autobiographies* A Single Flame *and* Day of My Delights, *and the travel-book* Much Else in Italy, *interestingly reflect the main themes of his fiction.*

Man; ▷John Fowles, *The Ebony Tower.*

READ ON ▷

● *The Montfords.*
▶ **To the theme of the disintegrating family:** ▷Thomas Mann, *Buddenbrooks.*
▶ **To the Australian theme:** ▷Miles Franklin, *My Brilliant Career;* ▷H.H. Richardson, *The Fortunes of Richard Mahony.*
▶ **To the theme of young people uneasy with their cultural background:** ▷Ford Madox Ford, *Parade's End;* ▷Willa Cather, *My Antonia;* ▷J.D. Salinger, *The Catcher in the Rye.*

BRADBURY, Malcolm • *(born 1932)*
British novelist and screenwriter.

A university professor, Bradbury writes sharp satires on academic life. The form and style of his first two novels were straightforward, but from *The History Man* onwards he began using experimental methods: fragmenting the plots into short scenes like those of TV plays, writing in the present tense, incorporating footnotes, commentaries and asides. The feeling is that each book is a game, meant to amuse the author as well as the reader – a feature which sets Bradbury apart from all other 'campus' novelists.

THE HISTORY MAN • *(1975)*
The book – far funnier than the TV series it inspired – is set in a ghastly British 'new' university, all bare concrete and graffiti. Its hero is an equally abrasive 'new' academic, the sociologist Howard Kirk. Kirk thinks that sociology is the only study relevant to the modern world, and that it should be a vehicle for radical change. He also believes in sleeping with as many female staff and students as he can entice to bed. He preaches left-wing politics in his seminars, humiliates anyone he suspects of right-wing opinions (for example young men who wear ties and call him 'Sir'), organises sit-ins and strikes, and strides happily through the destabilised, quivering society he creates all round him.

Bradbury's other novels are Eating People is Wrong, Stepping Westward, *and (the most experimental)* Rates of Exchange. Cuts *is a long short story,* Mensonge *a send-up of current French lit-crit pretentiousness and* No, Not Bloomsbury *a collection of essays, articles and reviews. He has also written TV adaptations of his own and other people's books.*

BRADFORD, Barbara Taylor
British novelist.

Bradford's books – many set in the north of England – are stories of characterful young women who rise in the worlds of business and society despite all obstacles. Her best-known books are *A Woman of Substance* and *Hold the Dream*.

READ ON >

● *Stepping Westward* (about a naive English lecturer on an exchange visit to a liberal western US campus).
▶ To *The History Man*: ▷Mary McCarthy, *The Groves of Academe*; ▷Vladimir Nabokov, *Pnin*; ▷Randall Jarrell, *Pictures from an Institution*; John Barth, *The End of the Road*.
▶ To *Stepping Westward*: David Lodge, *Changing Places*. Michael Frayn, *Towards the End of the Morning* and Colin Douglas, *The Houseman's Tale* are 'campus' novels of a different kind, set not in universities but, respectively, in a newspaper office and a hospital.
▶ Tom Sharpe, *Wilt* and its glorious, tasteless sequels are campus farce rather than comedy, entertainment for its own gross sake without a whiff of satire.

READ ON >

● *Act of Will*.
▶ Nicola Thorne, *Where the Rivers Meet*. Audrey Howard, *Ambitions*. Pamela Oldfield, *The Gooding Girl*. ▷Judith Krantz, *Princess Daisy*.

BRENT OF BIN BIN: see FRANKLIN, Miles

BRONTË, Charlotte • *(1816–55)*
BRONTË, Emily • *(1818–48)*
British novelists.

Much has been made of the Brontës' claustrophobic life in the parsonage at Haworth in Yorkshire, and of the way they compensated for a restricted and stuffy daily routine by inventing wildly romantic stories. Their Haworth life was first described by a novelist (▷Gaskell), and is as evocative as any fiction of the time. In some ways it colours our opinion of their work: for example, if the third sister, Anne, had not been a Brontë, few people would nowadays remember her novels, which are pale shadows of her sisters' books. But Charlotte and Emily need no biographical boosting. They were geniuses, with a (remarkably similar) fantastical imagination, a robust, melodramatic view of what a 'good story' ought to be, and a pre-Freudian understanding of the dark places of the soul. Their brooding landscapes and old, dark houses may have been drawn from life, but what they made of them was an original, elaborate and self-consistent world, as turbulent as dreams.

JANE EYRE • *(by Charlotte Brontë, 1847)*
The plot is a romantic extravaganza about a poor governess who falls in love with her employer Mr Rochester, is prevented from marrying him by the dark secret which shadows him, and only finds happiness on the last page, after a sequence of melodramatic and unlikely coincidences. The book's power is in its counterpointing of real and psychological events. We read about storms, fires, wild-eyed creatures gibbering in attics and branches tapping at the windows – but what we are really being shown is the turmoil in Jane's own soul, the maturing of a personality. This emotional progress, magnificently described, unifies the book and transmutes even its silliest events to gold.

WUTHERING HEIGHTS • *(by Emily Brontë, 1847)*
The story begins in the 1770s, when a rich Yorkshire landowner, Earnshaw, brings home a half-wild, sullen foundling he names Heathcliff. Heathcliff grows up alongside Earnshaw's own children, and falls in love with Cathy, the daughter. But he overhears her saying that she will never marry him because she is socially above him – and the rest of the novel deals with his elaborate revenge

| READ ON ⟩ |

▶ **To Jane Eyre:**
Wuthering Heights.
▶ **To Wuthering Heights:** *Jane Eyre.*
▶ **To Jane Eyre:**
▷Daphne Du Maurier, *Rebecca*; ▷Jean Rhys, *Wide Sargasso Sea*; ▷Margaret Mitchell, *Gone With the Wind*; George Douglas Brown, *The House With the Green Shutters*.
▶ **To Wuthering Heights:** R.D. Blackmore, *Lorna Doone*; ▷Thomas Hardy, *Tess of the d'Urbervilles*; ▷Iris Murdoch, *The Unicorn* (about the turbulent passions of a more modern heroine).

on her whole family and the way the emotional poison is eventually neutralised. As in *Jane Eyre*, desolate moorland and lonely, rain-lashed houses are used as symbols of the passions in the characters' hearts. Heathcliff, in particular, is depicted as if he were a genuine 'child of nature', the offspring not of human beings but of the monstrous mating of darkness, stone and storm.

All three sisters wrote Wordsworthy, nature-haunted poetry. Emily's only completed novel˙*was* Wuthering Heights; *Charlotte's were* Jane Eyre, The Professor *and* Villette; *Anne's were* Agnes Grey *and* The Tenant of Wildfell Hall.

BROOKNER, Anita • *(born 1928)*
British novelist.

Brookner's novels are written in trim, witty prose, style for its own sake, a civilised delight. This exactly suits the characters of the people in her stories. They are middle-aged, upper-middle-class women (professors, librarians, novelists): well-off, well-tailored, well-organised and desperately lonely. Something has blighted their emotional lives, leaving them to order their comfortable, bleak existences as best they can, to fill their days. The books show us what brought them to their condition – usually the actions of others, husbands, parents or friends – and sometimes tell us how the problem is resolved. In 'well-made' stage and film dramas of the 1930s, women were always blinking back tears and bravely facing the future. Brookner's heroines, except that they have lost even the power to cry, try to do the same.

LOOK AT ME • *(1983)*
Frances Hinton, librarian at a medical research institute, lives a disciplined, unvarying existence which she compares wistfully with what she imagines to be the exuberant, exciting lives of the research workers and others who use the books. She is 'taken up' by one of the most brilliant men, dazzling as a comet, and by his emotionally extrovert wife. She falls in love, and imagines that she is loved in return. But what looks like being a sentimental education in fact teaches her only that all human beings are islands, and that unless we hoard our inner lives and treasure our privacy, we will lose even what peace of mind we have.

Brookner's other novels are A Start in Life, Providence, Hôtel du Lac, Family and Friends, A Misalliance *and* A

READ ON ⟩

● *Hôtel du Lac.*
▶ Elizabeth Jane Howard, *Something in Disguise.* Edward Candy, *Scene Changing.* A.S. Byatt, *The Virgin in the Garden.* Jenny Diski, *Rainforest.* Susan Fromberg Shaeffer, *The Injured Party.*

Friend from England. *She is an expert on fine art, and has published books about the painters Watteau, Greuze and David.*

BUCHAN, John • *(1875–1940)*
British novelist.

Buchan's thrillers play virtuoso variations on the same basic plot. A stiff-upper-lipped hero (often Richard Hannay) discovers a conspiracy to End Civilisation as We Know It, and sets out single-handed, or with the help of a few trusted friends, to frustrate it. He is chased (often by the police as well as by the criminals), and wins through only by a combination of physical courage and absolute moral certainty. The pleasure of Buchan's novels is enhanced by the magnificently-described wild countryside he sets them in (usually the Scottish highlands or the plains of southern Africa), and by their splendid gallery of minor characters, the shopkeepers, tramps, local bobbies and landladies who help his heroes, often at enormous (if shrugged-off) personal risk.

THE THIRTY-NINE STEPS • *(1915)*
Richard Hannay, returning from South Africa, is told by a chance American acquaintance of a plot to invade England. Soon afterwards the American is killed and Hannay is framed for his murder. To escape two manhunts, one by the conspirators and the other by the police, he takes to the hills, and only after 300 pages of breathtaking peril and hair's-breadth escapes does he succeed in saving his country and clearing his name.

Buchan's other thrillers include Huntingtower, John MacNab *and* Witchwood *(all set in Scotland), and the Hannay books* Greenmantle, Mr Standfast *and* The Three Hostages. *He also wrote lively biographies (of ▷Scott, the emperor Augustus and Oliver Cromwell), and an autobiography,* Memory-Hold-the-Door.

BURGESS, Anthony • *(born 1917)*
British novelist and non- fiction writer.

Originally a composer, Burgess began writing books in his mid-30s, and since then has poured out literary works of every kind, from introductions to ▷Joyce (*Here Comes Everybody/Re Joyce*) to filmscripts, from opera libretti to book-reviews. Above all he has written novels, of a diversity few other 20th-century writers have ever equalled.

READ ON ▷

● *Greenmantle*; *Mr Standfast*; *Prester John* (an African adventure as exciting and bizarre as anything by ▷H. Rider Haggard, whose *She* makes an excellent follow-up).
▶ Erskine Childers, *The Riddle of the Sands*. ▷Geoffrey Household, *Rogue Male*. ▷Ken Follett, *Storm Island/ The Key To Rebecca*. ▷Helen MacInnes, *The Snare of the Hunted*. Craig Thomas, *Firefox*. ▷Robert Ludlum, *The Gemini Contenders*.

READ ON ▷

● *Earthly Powers* (a blockbuster embracing every kind of 20th-century 'evil', from homosexual betrayal to genocide, and the

They range from fictionalised biographies of Shakespeare (*Nothing Like the Sun*) and the early Christian missionaries (*The Kingdom of the Wicked*) to farce (the four Enderby stories, of which *Inside Mr Enderby* is the first and *Enderby's Dark Lady* is the funniest), from experimental novels (*The Napoleon Symphony*, about Napoleon, borrows its form from Beethoven's Eroica Symphony) to semi-autobiographical stories about expatriate Britons in the Far East (*The Malaysian Trilogy*). The literary demands of Burgess' books vary as widely as their contents: the way he finds a form and style to suit each new inspiration is one of the most brilliant features of his work.

A CLOCKWORK ORANGE • *(1962)*

In a grim future Britain, society is divided into the haves, who live in security-screened mansions in leafy countryside, and the have-nots, who swagger in gangs through the decaying cities, gorging themselves on violence. The book is narrated by the leader of one such gang, and is written in a private language, a mixture of standard English, cockney slang and Russian. (Burgess provides a glossary, but after a few pages the language is easy enough to follow, and its strangeness adds to the feeling of alienation which pervades the book.) The young man has committed a horrific crime, breaking into a house, beating up its owner and raping his wife, and the police are 'rehabilitating' him. His true 'crime', however, was not action but thought – he aspired to a way of life, of culture, from which his class and lack of money should have barred him – and Burgess leaves us wondering whether his 'cure' will work, since he is not a brute beast (as the authorities claim) but rather the individuality in human beings which society has chosen to repress.

Burgess' other novels include a reflection on what he sees as the death-throes of modern western civilisation, 1985, and a gentler, ▷Priestleyish book about provincial English life earlier this century, The Piano-players. Little Wilson and Big God *is autobiography, and* Urgent Copy *and* Homage to Qwert Yuiop *are collections of reviews and literary articles.*

Church's reluctance or inability to stand aside from it).

▶ **To *A Clockwork Orange*:** ▷Aldous Huxley, *Brave New World*; ▷Margaret Atwood, *The Handmaid's Tale*; ▷Russell Hoban, *Riddley Walker*.

▶ **To Burgess' historical novels:** John Hersey, *The Wall*; ▷Michèle Roberts, *The Wild Girl*.

▶ **To *The Malaysian Trilogy*:** ▷Paul Theroux, *Jungle Lovers*.

▶ **To the Enderby comedies:** David Lodge, *Small World*; ▷Peter De Vries, *Reuben, Reuben*.

C

CALVINO, Italo • (1923–85)
Italian novelist and short-story writer.

Calvino's first works followed the grim neo-realist tradition of the late 1940s, treating contemporary subjects in an unsparing, documentary way. But in the 1950s he decided to change his style, to write (as he put it) the kind of stories he himself might want to read. These were fantastic, surrealist tales, drawing on medieval legend, fairy stories, SF and the work of such 20th-century experimental writers as ▷Kafka and ▷Borges. The style is lucid and poetic; the events, however bizarre their starting-point, follow each other logically and persuasively; the overall effect is magical. In *Cosmicomics* huge space-beings play marbles with sub-atomic particles and take tea with one another as decorously as any Italian bourgeois family. The people in *The Castle of Crossed Destinies* are struck magically dumb, and have to tell each other stories using nothing but tarot cards. In *Invisible Cities* Marco Polo invents fantasy-cities to tickle the imagination of Kubla Khan. Calvino's wide-eyed, bizarre fantasy has been imitated but never surpassed; he is one of the most entrancing writers of the century.

OUR ANCESTORS • (1951–9)
This book contains a full-length novel (*The Baron in the Trees*) and two long stories. In *The Baron in the Trees* a boy abandons the ground for the treetops and – in one of Calvino's most sustained and lyrical tours-de-force – lives an entire, fulfilled life without ever coming down to earth. In *The Cloven Viscount* a medieval knight is split in two on the battlefield – and each half goes on living independently, one good, one bad, deprived of the link which made them a whole human being and gave them moral identity. In *The Non-Existent Knight* an empty suit of ar-

READ ON ⟩

● *Invisible Cities*; *Cosmicomics*.
▶ John Gardner, *Vlemk the Box-painter* (a long medieval allegory, in the collection *The Art of Living and Other Stories*, which otherwise contains modern tales). ▷Thomas Mann, *The Holy Sinner*. T.H. White, *The Sword in the Stone*. Milan Kundera, *The Unbearable Lightness of Being*.
▶ **Good short-story follow-ups:** ▷Jorge Luis Borges, *Fictions*; Martin Amis, *Einstein's Monsters*; Angela Carter, *The Bloody Chamber* (extraordinary post-Freudian, feminist reworkings of fairy tales).

mour takes on its own identity, fighting, discussing tactics, brawling – and forever yearning after the reality of life, the psychological and emotional fullness which it/he can never know.

Calvino's neo-realist books are The Path to the Nest of Spiders *(a novel) and* Adam, One Afternoon *(short stories). His fantasies are collected in* T Zero, Cosmicomics, Invisible Cities, Our Ancestors, The Castle of Crossed Destinies, Mr Palomar *and* The Watcher and Other Stories. Italian Folk-Tales *reworks traditional material in a similar, uniquely personal way.*

CAMUS, Albert • *(1913–60)*
French novelist and non-fiction writer.

Throughout his life, in newspaper articles, plays, essays and novels, Camus explored the position of what he called *l'homme revolté*, the rebel or misfit who feels out of tune with the spirit of the times. His characters recoil from the values of society. They believe that our innermost being is compromised by conformity, and that we can only liberate our true selves if we choose our own attitude to life, our day-to-day philosophy. Camus compared the human condition to that of Sisyphus in Greek myth, forever rolling a stone up a hill only to have it crash back down every time it reached the top – and said that the way to cope with this situation was to abandon ambition and concentrate on the here and now. But despite his uncompromising philosophy, his books are anything but difficult. His descriptions of sun-saturated Algeria (in *The Outsider*), rainy Amsterdam (in *The Fall*) or disease-ridden, rotting Oran (in *The Plague*) are fast-moving and evocative, and he shows the way inner desolation racks his heroes with such intensity that we sympathise with every instant of their predicament and long, like them, for them to break through into acceptance, into happiness.

THE PLAGUE • *(1947)*
Plague ravages the Algerian town of Oran. Quarantined from the outside world, the citizens cope with their tragedy as best they can, either clinging to the outward forms of social life (petty city ordinances; the formalities of religion) or pathetically, helplessly suffering. (For Camus' original readers, the novel was an allegory of France under wartime nazi occupation.) At the heart of the story are Dr Rieux (the story-teller) and a group of other intellectuals. Each has different feelings about death, and for each of them the plague is not only a daily reality, an

READ ON

● *The Fall.*
▶ ▷Saul Bellow, *The Victim.* ▷Hermann Hesse, *Rosshalde.* ▷William Golding, *The Spire.* Carlo Gébler, *Work and Play.* Simone de Beauvoir, *The Mandarins.* Paul Bowles, *The Sheltering Sky.*
▶ **More extrovert books, cloaking the philosophy in action and comedy respectively:** ▷Graham Greene, *A Burnt-out Case*; ▷Joseph Heller, *Something Happened.*

external event which has to be endured, but a philosophical catalyst, forcing them to decide what they think about the world and their place in it.

As well as in novels, Camus set out his philosophy in two substantial essays, The Rebel (L'homme revolté) *and* The Myth of Sisyphus. *His plays are* Caligula, Cross Purpose, The Just Assassins *and* State of Siege *(a stage version of* The Plague*).* Exile and the Kingdom *collects short stories.*

CARR, Philippa • *(born 1906)*
British novelist.

'Philippa Carr' is one of the pseudonyms of ▷Eleanor Hibbert. She writes historical romances, showing the effect of great events on ordinary people's lives. Her best-known books are the *'Daughters of England' series*; other titles include *The Witch from the Sea*, *Sara Band of Two Sisters* and *Lament for a Lost Lover*.

READ ON ▷

▶ Jane Aiken Hodge, *Judas Flowering*. Juliette Benzoni, *'Catherine' series*. Pamela Bennetts, *A Dragon for Edward*.

CARTER, Angela • *(born 1940)*
British novelist and non-fiction writer.

Carter's inspiration includes fairy tales, Jung's theory of the collective unconscious, horror movies and the fantasies of such writers as ▷Poe and ▷Shelley. Above all, she is concerned with female sexuality and with men's sexual predations on women. Her books range from Gothic reworkings of fairy tales (*The Bloody Chamber*) to such surrealist nightmares as *The Passion of New Eve* (see below). The novels begin with dream-images, and spiral quickly into fantasy. In the opening chapter of *The Magic Toyshop* (1967), for example, 15-year-old Melanie walks in a garden at night in her mother's wedding dress –a common, if none too reassuring dream. Soon afterwards, however, Melanie's parents die, she is fostered by a mad toymaker-uncle, and the book climaxes when she is forced to re-enact the myth of Leda and the Swan with a life-sized puppet-swan. At first sight such stories seem little more than an upmarket literary equivalent of the occult, sex-and-sadism shockers of ▷James Herbert or Stephen ▷King. But Carter's books are less titillating than psycho-political. They are nightmare-visions, designed to induce self-examination and to lead to change.

READ ON ▷

● *Heroes and Villains*.
▶ D.M. Thomas, *The White Hotel*. ▷Margaret Atwood, *The Handmaid's Tale*. Joanna Russ, *The Female Man*. Kathy Acker, *Blood and Guts in High School*. ▷Gore Vidal, *Myra Breckinridge*.

THE PASSION OF NEW EVE • *(1977)*
In a near-future USA where armies of blacks, feminists

and pubescent children are waging guerrilla war, the young man Evelyn hides in the California desert, only to be kidnapped by devotees of the multi-breasted, all-engulfing Earth Mother. She rapes him, castrates him and remakes him as a woman, Eve; the intention is to impregnate him/her with his own spilled sperm, to make her/him the parent of a second human race. But Eve escapes, trembling with fury at the outrage to her/his sexuality, and it is only after a series of even more nightmarish adventures that she is able at last to accept herself for what she is, to open herself to destiny.

Carter's other novels are Shadow Dance, Several Perceptions, Nights at the Circus, Heroes and Villains, Love *and* The Infernal Desire Machines of Dr Hoffman. *The* Sadeian Woman *is non-fiction, a study of the social and sexual potential of women.* Fireworks *collects short stories (among her most disturbing works), and* Nothing Sacred *collects essays and journalism.*

CATHER, Willa • *(1876–1947)*
US novelist.

Most of Cather's books are set in the south-western USA, and are about settlers (often European immigrants) coming to terms with the wilderness. But there is no Hollywood melodrama: her interests are in the contrast between civilised feelings and the wild natural environment, in psychological growth and change. In two characteristic books, *My Antonia* and *A Lost Lady*, the central female characters (the ones who change) are described by men who have watched them, and loved them, from a distance since childhood – a device which allowed Cather the objective, emotional distance from her characters which she preferred. This objectivity, and the elegance of her style, are two of the most enjoyable features of her books. Her sentences seem placid and unhurried: every event, every description seems to be given the same measured treatment. But nothing is extra. Every phrase has emotional or philosophical resonance, and after a few pages the reader is drawn into the narrative, hypnotised by nuance.

DEATH COMES FOR THE ARCHBISHOP • *(1927)*
Based on true events, and on diaries and letters by real people, this novel tells of two French Catholic missionaries to New Mexico in the second half of the 19th century. The book is partly about landscape, and contains magnificent descriptions of the desert. But it is mainly concerned with relationships: between the two priests, friends for

READ ON ⟩

● *Shadows on the Rock* (a similarly quiet book about the impact of the American wilderness on Europeans, this time 17th-century explorers in Quebec).
▶ Janet Lewis, *The Trial of Sören Kvist*.
▷ Hermann Hesse, *Rosshalde*. George Moore, *The Brook Kerith* (about Joseph of Arimathea).
▷ Patrick White, *A Fringe of Leaves*. Neil M. Gunn, *The Well at the World's End*.

many years, between the humans and their animals (who have to carry them on long, lonely desert journeys from one Christian settlement to another), and between the missionaries' ancient European culture and the stripped-to-essentials, 'primitive' habits of life and mind of their New Mexican flock. The book's title is not a promise of high drama. It refers to a Holbein painting, and suggested to Cather the feeling of frozen movement, of life arrested at the instant of recording, which she found in paintings and tried to recapture in her prose.

Two of Cather's novels, The Song of the Lark *and* Lucy Gayheart, *are about young women torn between the claims of family life and an artistic, musical career.* O Pioneers!, *like* My Antonia, *is about foreign immigrants settling in the wilderness. The main character of* The Professor's House *is a successful academic who suddenly feels that he has failed, that lack of danger (emotional, intellectual or physical) has blighted his life. Other novels are* One of Ours *and* My Mortal Enemy. Obscure Destinies *is a collection of short stories.*

CHANDLER, Raymond • *(1888–1959)*
US novelist.

In the 1930s Chandler (an ex-businessman and journalist) began writing gangster-stories for magazines, treating violence, prostitution and betrayal in the cynical, hard-boiled style popular in films of the time. His ambition was to replace the kind of detective novels then fashionable (stories of bizarre crimes solved by wildly eccentric detectives, distantly modelled on Sherlock Holmes: see ▷Christie; ▷Sayers) with books about realistic crimes, investigated in a plausible way by a detective who would be ordinary, with recognisable human hopes, fears and reactions. Philip Marlowe (Chandler's private-eye hero) is an honest, conscientious man who sweats, cowers and lusts just like anyone else. He narrates the stories himself, in a wisecracking, deadpan style – 'The next morning was bright, clear and sunny. I woke up with a motorman's glove in my mouth, drank two cups of coffee and went through the morning papers' – which has made two generations of literary critics fawn over Chandler, claiming him, somewhat snobbishly, as one of the few 'true novelists' in US crime fiction.

FAREWELL, MY LOVELY • *(1940)*
Marlowe, as often, is drifting with nothing particular to do when he is picked up (literally, by the scruff of the neck)

READ ON ▷

● *The Big Sleep*; *The Lady in the Lake.*
▶ ▷Dashiell Hammett, *The Maltese Falcon.* ▷Ernest Hemingway, *To Have and Have Not.* Ross MacDonald, *The Drowning Pool.* John Milne, *Shadow Play* (set in the London underworld). James Hadley Chase, *No Orchids for Miss Blandish* is a sombre, bleak book, Chandler without the wisecracks. Greg MacDonald, *Fletch* is the first of a series starring a pleasingly farcical private eye, a would-be Marlowe who succeeds only in being himself.

by a muscle-bound ex-convict called Moose Malloy. From this simple event, as ripples spread on a pond, the story grows to take in a priceless necklace, kidnapping, blackmail and murder – and at its heart, like the still centre of a whirlwind, Marlowe slouches from clue to clue, a martyr to his own curiosity, pushing open every door and investigating each alleyway even though he knows, from long experience, that painful or nasty surprises are all he'll find.

Chandler's Marlowe novels are The Big Sleep, Farewell My Lovely, The High Window, The Lady in the Lake, The Little Sister, The Long Goodbye *and* Playback. Killer in the Rain *is a collection of short stories.*

CHEEVER, John • *(1912–82)*
US novelist and short-story writer.

Most of Cheever's stories appeared in the New Yorker between 1945 and 1975. The majority of his characters are prosperous New England commuters. They have beautiful houses in tidy neighbourhoods, their children go to good schools, and they can afford European holidays (often in Italy). But they are walking wounded: their emotions may be intact, but their hearts and consciences have been sliced away. They lacerate one another with sexual affairs, rows, petty-minded gossip and dispiriting, single-minded malice. The reason is that they believe that they are living in the American Dream – and by the day, by the minute, they find that it is a mirage. Cheever narrates their empty lives in sleek, ironic prose: his dialogue is particularly good at suggesting overtones of menace or longing in commonplace remarks.

THE STORIES • *(1978)*
This book of 61 stories contains all but a few teenage pieces. Most of the stories are set in commuter villages – fine examples are 'The Country Husband' or 'The Trouble of Marcie Flint' – but a few place their characters' wasted, tragic lives in lakeside summer homes (eg 'The Day the Pig Fell into the Well') or in a favourite Cheever location, Italy, where his people gape at the culture and civilisation they miss in their own drab lives. (Good examples are 'The Bella Lingua' and 'A Woman Without a Country'.)

Cheever's novels are The Wapshot Chronicle, The Wapshot Scandal, Bullet Park, Oh What A Paradise it Seems *and* Falconer *(on an uncharacteristic subject: the rehabili-*

READ ON

● Cheever's two Wapshot novels are set in the same world and among the same kind of bewildered characters as his stories. The Wapshot family, however, contains wonderful eccentrics, and the novels consequently spill into slapstick farce.
▶ **To Cheever's novels:** ▷John Updike, *The Centaur;* ▷Peter De Vries, *The Tunnel of Love.*
▶ **To the stories:** Peter Taylor, *Happy Families Are All Alike;* ▷Katherine Mansfield, *Bliss;* ▷L.P. Hartley, *The Killing Bottle.*

tation of a murderer in a 'correctional facility'). His story-collections are The Way Some People Live; The Enormous Radio; The Housebreaker of Shady Hill; Some People, Places and Things that will not Appear in my Next Novel; The Brigadier and the Golf Widow *and* The World of Apples.

CHEKHOV, Anton • *(1860–1904)*
Russian short-story writer and playwright.

Chekhov paid his way through medical school by writing short comic articles for magazines; in his mid-twenties he began publishing more elaborate pieces, and by the time he was 40 (and turning from stories to plays) he was considered one of the finest of all Russian prose-writers. Many of his stories are first-person monologues – he said that he was inspired by the sort of things people tell doctors during consultations, or penitents murmur at confession – and, like such monologues, they often reveal far more than the speaker intends. We hear symptoms, as it were, and from them diagnose a whole sick life. In other stories it is as if Chekhov were sitting beside us, drawing our attention to people moving about in the distance, and commenting in a quiet, compassionate way on their motives and feelings. Sympathetic detachment is the essence of his art: reading his stories (like watching his plays) is like looking through a window into other people's lives.

LADY WITH THE LITTLE DOG • *(1899)*
Chekhov's best-known story – perhaps because it seems exactly to match the ironical, tragi-comic mood of his plays – tells of two people who begin a casual holiday love-affair, find that they can't live without each other, and are then forced to do just that.

Chekhov's stories are published (by Oxford University Press) in a fine translation by Ronald Hingley, who catches every nuance of the original graceful style.

CHILDREN

▷David Cook, *Sunrising*
▷William Golding, *Lord of the Flies*
▷L.P. Hartley, *Eustace and Hilda*
   Richard Hughes, *A High Wind in Jamaica*
   Nancy Mitford, *The Blessing*
▷Marcel Proust, *Swann's Way* (part 1 of *Remembrance of Things Past*)

> **READ ON**

● Of Chekhov's plays, the nearest in mood to his stories are *Uncle Vanya* and *The Seagull*. (Michael Frayn's translations are recommended.)
▶ ▷Ivan Turgenev, *Sportsman's Sketches*. Guy De Maupassant, *Miss Harriet*.
▷Katherine Mansfield, *In a German Pension*. Seán O'Faoláin, *Foreign Affairs*.
▷Katherine Anne Porter, *The Leaning Tower*.

▷Mark Twain, *The Adventures of Tom Sawyer*

Adolescence (p 3)

CHRISTIE, Agatha • *(1890–1976)*
British novelist.

Ingenuity is the essence of Christie's detective stories. She confined herself largely to two detectives, pompous Poirot and elderly, inquisitive Miss Marple. Nowadays, as well as her plots, it is the period detail of her books which fascinates: her English villages, spa hotels, 1930s cruise-ships and above all country houses are caught (as Poirot might put it) like ze flies in ze amber. She chronicles a vanished pre-second-world-war, upper-middle-class Brit-ain with an accuracy which is enhanced rather than dimin-ished by the staginess of her characters and plots.

MURDER AT THE VICARAGE • *(1930)*
This typical Miss Marple story is set in a picture-postcard English village riven by gossip and inhabited by as un-likely a collection of eccentrics as even Christie ever threw together. Everyone could be guilty of murder, and Miss Marple's investigation is so gently persistent, so self-effacingly officious, that one trembles in case she ends up as victim rather than as sleuth.

MURDER IN MESOPOTAMIA • *(1936)*
A nurse goes to look after the neurotic wife of an archae-ologist on a dig, and is thrown into the middle of intrigue, suspicion, rancorous insult and finally, inevitably, mur-der. At the end of it all Poirot applies his 'little grey cells' to unearthing means, motive and opportunity as painstak-ingly as an archaeologist trowelling treasure.

Among the best-known of Christie's 83 detective novels are The Murder of Roger Ackroyd, Ten Little Niggers/ Ten Little Indians/Then There Were None, Murder on the Orient Express *and* The Crooked House. *She also wrote stage plays (including* The Mousetrap), *an excellent sec-ond-world-war espionage thriller (*N or M), *and six ro-mantic novels under the pseudonym Mary Westmacott.*

READ ON ⟩

▶ To *Murder at the Vicarage*: A Murder is Announced;
▶ To *Murder in Mesopotamia*: Death on the Nile.
▶ Patricia Wentworth, *Miss Silver Investigates*. Gladys Mitchell, *Come Away, Death*. Dorothy Simpson, *The Night She Died*. Cyril Hare, *An Ill Wind*. The detective stories of Erle Stanley Gardner (eg *The Case of the Howling Dog*) and ▷Georges Simenon (eg *Maigret's Pipe*) describe a similar mixture of patient sleuthing and brilliant deduction; their settings (California and Paris) are as much part of their appeal as Christie's English villages and creepy country mansions are of hers.

CITIES: NEW WORLD

▷Saul Bellow, *Herzog* (Chicago)
Paul Gallico, *Mrs Harris in New York*
▷Mordecai Richler, *The Apprenticeship of Duddy Kravitz* (Montreal)
▷George Turner, *The Sea and Summer* (Melbourne, 1990)
▷Jerome Weidman, *Fourth Street East* (New York, 1920s)
Donald Westlake, *Gangway* (San Francisco)
▷Edith Wharton, *The Age of Innocence* (New York, 1880s)

CITIES: OLD WORLD

▷Marjorie Allingham, *The Tiger in the Smoke* (London)
▷Lawrence Durrell, *The Alexandria Quartet*
▷Mrs Gaskell, *Amos Barton* (Manchester)
▷Victor Hugo, *Notre Dame de Paris*
▷Christopher Isherwood, *Goodbye to Berlin*
John Lear, *Death in Leningrad*

CLARKE, Arthur C. (Arthur Charles) •
(born 1917)
British writer of novels, short stories and non-fiction.

Apart from ▷Asimov, Clarke is the best 'real' scientist among SF writers. His subject is space travel, and his 1940s and 1950s non-fiction books and articles predicted, in accurate detail, many things which have since happened, such as the invention of communications satellites, the first moon-landing and the development of laser space-weaponry. Like ▷Verne, he begins a fictional story with existing scientific fact or theory, and then extends it logically; even his wildest fantasies thus seem rooted in the possible. His main themes are the colonisation from Earth of other planets and visits to Earth by explorers from distant galaxies. His stories bustle with the detail of space-travel and setting up home in alien environments, and he is particularly interested in the psychological stress on people faced with the unknown, and with the relationship between human beings and high technology. These ideas outweigh sometimes wooden character-drawing and creaky plots: Clarke's stories are less interesting than his lively attitude to space and to the attempts of human beings to master it.

READ ON >

● *Rendezvous with Rama* (as so often with Clarke, the straightforward development of a stunningly simple idea: that human beings land on and explore a planet which is a living, sentient being. A good, and psychologically more elaborate, follow-up to this is ▷Stanislaw Lem, *Solaris*.)
▶ ▷Jules Verne, *The First Men in the Moon*. ▷H.G. Wells, *The War of the Worlds*. ▷Robert Heinlein, *Have Space-suit, Will Travel*.
▷James Blish,

Julian **SYMONS, THE END OF SOLOMON GRUNDY**
(murder, obsession and madness in the English suburbs)

Friedrich **DÜRRENMATT, THE PLEDGE**
(maniacal child-killer stalks — and is stalked — across idyllic Swiss countryside)

PSYCHOLOGICAL CRIME

Patricia **HIGHSMITH, STRANGERS ON A TRAIN**
*(two men agree to commit 'perfect murder' for each other — and
everything goes wrong)*

H.R.F. **KEATING, FILMI, FILMI, INSPECTOR GHOTE**
(mild Bombay police inspector; murder at the film studio)

POLICE PROCEDURAL

Lesley **EGAN, CRIME AT CHRISTMAS**
(no holiday for the men of Glendale Police Department, Los Angeles)

Nicholas **FREELING, CASTANG'S CITY**
(who gunned down Deputy Mayor of small French town?)

Rex **STOUT, WHERE THERE'S A WILL**
(orchid-loving, gourmet recluse; murderous family)

Dorothy L. **SAYERS, THE NINE TAILORS**
(lordly super-sleuth; death in a remote church tower)

DETECTIVES OF CHARACTER

Gladys **MITCHELL, TWELVE HORSES AND THE
HANGMAN'S NOOSE**
(elderly, lizard-like Dame; death at the riding stables)

(one murderer, nine potential victims, all cooped up together — who is who?)

CRIME PUZZLES

Josephine **TEY, DAUGHTER OF TIME**
(hospitalised woman investigates 'crimes' of English King Richard III)

Carter **DICKSON, THE RED WIDOW MURDERS**
(locked-room mystery in old, dark house)

Freeman Wills **CROFTS, DEATH OF A TRAIN**
(railway timetables; cast-iron alibis; Inspector French investigates)

Delano **AMES, CORPSE DIPLOMATIQUE**
(blackmail and murder in Brown's Hotel in Nice)

Cyril **HARE, WHEN THE WIND BLOWS**
*(murder in the Markshire Orchestral Society, where 'harmony' is
a word unknown)*

Pamela **BRANCH, MURDER'S LITTLE SISTER**
(who is trying to murder the bitchiest agony aunt in London?)

MURDER — WHERE?

A. Conan **DOYLE, THE HOUND OF THE BASKERVILLES**
(Sherlock Holmes and the fiend that stalks the moor)

Edmund **CRISPIN, THE MOVING TOYSHOP**
(Oxford poetry professor; death at a vanishing toyshop)

Harry **KEMELMAN, THURSDAY THE RABBI WALKED
OUT** *(Rabbi Small; murder of anti-semitic millionaire in Barnard's
Crossing, Massachusetts)*

PRIVATE SLEUTHING

THE SANDS OF MARS · *(1951)*

Martin Gibson, a world-famous writer of SF and on space-travel, is invited to make his first-ever real space journey, to report on a project for 'greening' Mars, making it fit for human habitation. The book is a straightforward account of Gibson's reactions to what he sees, and to the relationship between reality and his own writings. One might imagine that events since 1951 would have superceded Clarke's imaginings – but although some of the detail now seems old hat (for example Gibson's reactions to weightlessness), the meticulousness of other descriptions, especially of the way humans cope with daily life on Mars, still fascinates.

Clarke's short stories are admired: one, 'The Sentinel', *is regularly claimed to be the finest SF story ever written. (It was the basis of the film* 2001.*) A splendid selection is* The Nine Billion Names of God. *His novels include* Childhood's End, A Fall of Moondust *and* Imperial Earth.

Earthman Come Home (first of the 'Cities in Flight' series).

CLASSIC DETECTION

G.K. Chesterton, *The Innocence of Father Brown*
▷Michael Innes, *Stop Press*
▷P.D. James, *The Skull Beneath the Skin*
Harry Kemelman, *Tuesday the Rabbi saw Red*
Emma Lathen, *Banking on Death*
▷Ngaio Marsh, *Surfeit of Lampreys*
Gladys Mitchell, *Laurels are Poison*

Great Detectives (p 100); Murder Most Mind-Boggling (p 174); Police Procedural (p 192); Private Eyes (p 196)

COLETTE (Sidonie Gabrielle) · *(1873–1954)*
French novelist.

In the 1900s Colette's works were condemned as pornographic; in the 1970s she was claimed by the women's movement as one of the founders of feminism. The reason in each case is the same. Her themes are the awakening of sensual feelings in adolescence, the way in which young women first discover their sexual power, and the attempts by middle-aged people (of both sexes) to rejuvenate themselves by preying on innocence. Her stories are not explic-

READ ON ▷

● *A Lesson in Love* (La naissance du jour).
▶ Françoise Sagan, *Bonjour Tristesse.*
Edna O'Brien, *The Country Girls* (and its sequels *The Lonely Girl* and the magnificent *Girls in*

itly sexual, but she writes in an impressionistic style in which sun, flowers, insects, animals and the textures of skin, grass and clothes blur into a kind of drowsy, erotic reverie, a counterpart to the awakening feelings of her characters. Adult experience is always just ahead – and few of her young people notice, as the reader does, that every adult in Colette's books is a tragic figure, ineffectual or cynical. Youth, in the end, is the only worthwhile possession in life, and it is daily, hourly, squandered for experience.

THE RIPENING SEED (Le Blé en herbe) · *(1923)*

Colette's own favourite among her books, this tells of the relationship between two teenagers, Philippe and Vinca. They have been friends from childhood, and their families have spent the summer months every year together at the seaside. Now, in Vinca's sixteenth and Philippe's seventeenth year, the young people feel a new tension in their relationship –an anxiety about each other, and about themselves, which is not helped when Philippe is seduced by another, older summer visitor.

The most substantial of Colette's works is the 'Claudine' series of novels, about a young girl growing up in the early years of this century. Another pair of books, Chéri *and* The Last of Chéri, *is on a favourite theme, the corrupting effects of a young man's first sexual experience. Her other books, many based on her own experience and family, include* Sido, My Apprenticeship *and* The Tendrils of the Vine. *Her collected short stories were published in English in 1984.*

Their Married Bliss). David Garnett, *Aspects of Love.* ▷Vladimir Nabokov, *Ada* and ▷André Gide, *The Immoralist,* though their purposes and plot-development are very different, catch the same sensual and poetic mood as Colette. ▷Carson McCullers, *The Member of the Wedding* is a harsher view of the awakening of a young girl to adult feelings. Charles Webb, *The Graduate* is a riotous send-up of the young man/older woman theme.

COMEDY THRILLERS

Delano Ames, *Murder, Maestro, Please*
▷Eric Ambler, *The Light of Day*
Pamela Branch, *The Wooden Overcoat*
▷Richard Condon, *Prizzi's Honour*
Greg MacDonald, *Fletch*
Jean Potts, *Go, Lovely Rose*
Andrew Taylor, *Caroline Type*
Donald Westlake, *A New York Dance*

COMPTON-BURNETT, Ivy · *(1884–1969)*
British novelist.

After a single false start (*Dolores,* an imitation of George ▷Eliot, later disowned), Compton-Burnett produced 19

READ ON ▷

▶ The uniqueness of Compton-Burnett's

comic novels in a uniquely bizarre, uncompromising style. Each book is set in a large late-Victorian or early-Edwardian household, ruled by a tyrant (one of the parents or some elderly, inflexible relative). Isolated by wealth from the outside world, the family members – often grown-up, middle-aged children – bicker, snub and plot against one another, powerless and embittered. There are family secrets to be revealed – incest, murder, insanity – and no member of the household, neither family nor servants, is a 'normal', unwarped human being. The books are written largely in dialogue, spectacularly wooden and artificial. Compton-Burnett's detractors find her novels unreadable; her fans think them hilarious.

Compton-Burnett's novels are Pastors and Masters, Brothers and Sisters, Men and Wives, More Women than Men, A House and its Head, Daughters and Sons, A Family and a Fortune, Parents and Children, Elders and Betters, Manservant and Maidservant, Two Worlds and their Ways, Darkness and Day, The Present and the Past, Mother and Son, A Father and his Fate, A Heritage and its History, The Mighty and their Fall, A God and his Gifts *and* The Last and the First.

CONDON, Richard • *(born 1915)*
US novelist.

Condon's black comedies treat horrifying matters – insanity, kidnapping, assassination – in a deadpan way, as if part of everyday experience. His characters live each moment with unflustered obsession, shopping, for example, for hand-grenades with the same matter-of-fact orderliness as for peaches or toothpaste. Condon is fascinated by wealth and power, and his books are set among politicians, financiers, mafia godfathers, generals and film-studio executives. It is a world in which power always corrupts, money never brings happiness and the devil always, delightfully, wins every trick.

ANY GOD WILL DO • *(1966)*
The hero, Francis Vollmer, is a bank executive in pre-1914 New York – and a maniac. Convinced that he is the unacknowledged son of a European aristocrat, he embezzles a fortune, learns French (and, in the process, the skills of cooking and acrobatic sex), changes his identity and sets out to find and claim his inheritance. Despite a wonderfully boring literal mind – he talks like an encyclopedia-entry on any subject, given only a trigger-word such as 'wine' or 'symphony' – he is irresistible to women, and his quest for identity is intertwined with a love-affair

style means that no other writers' works are truly similar. Stories of claustrophobic families, however, in artificial 'high styles' of their own and equally compulsive, are: Samuel Butler, *The Way of All Flesh* (a book which influenced Compton-Burnett herself); ▷Edith Wharton, *The Age of Innocence*; Jean Cocteau, *The Children of the Game* (Les enfants terribles); Molly Keane, *Good Behaviour;* ▷Mervyn Peake, *Titus Groan.*

READ ON ▷

● *Prizzi's Honour*; *Prizzi's Family* (comedies about an upwardly-mobile mafia hit-man, a murderer with cultural aspirations).
▶ ▷Jerome Weidman, *Other People's Money.* ▷Thomas Mann, *Confessions of Felix Krull, Confidence Man.* ▷John Irving, *The Hotel New Hampshire.*

which might have brought him happiness if he had not, underneath all his suaveness, been as crazy as the man in every lunatic asylum who thinks himself Napoleon.

Condon's novels include The Whisper of the Axe, Arigato, The Vertical Smile, Mile High, The Manchurian Candidate *and* The Oldest Confession.

CONRAD, Joseph • *(1857–1924)*
Polish/British novelist.

Born in Poland, Conrad ran away to sea at 17 and ended up a captain in the merchant navy and a naturalised British subject. He retired from the sea at 37 and spent the rest of his life as a writer. There was at the time (1890s–1910s) a strong tradition of sea-stories, using the dangers and tensions of long voyages and the wonders of the worlds sailors visited as metaphors for human life. Most of this writing was straightforward adventure, with little subtlety; Conrad used its conventions for deeper literary ends. He was interested in 'driven' individuals, people whose psychology or circumstances force them to extreme behaviour, and the sea-story form exactly suited this idea. His books often begin as 'yarns', set in exotic locations and among the mixed (and mixed-up) human types who crew ocean-going ships. But before long psychology takes over, and the plot loses its straightforwardness and becomes an exploration of compulsion, obsession and neurosis.

HEART OF DARKNESS • *(from Youth, 1902)*
This 120-page story begins as a 'yarn': Marlow, a sea-captain, tells of a journey he once made up the Congo river to bring down a stranded steamer. He became fascinated by stories of an ivory-merchant, a white man called Kurtz who lived deep in the jungle and was said to have supernatural powers. Marlow set out to find Kurtz, and the journey took him deeper and deeper into the heart not only of the 'Dark Continent', but into the darkness of the human soul. (Francis Ford Coppola's 1970s film *Apocalypse Now* updated this story to the Vietnam War, making points about US colonialism as savage as Conrad's denunciation of the ivory-trade.)

Conrad's major novels are Lord Jim, The Nigger of the Narcissus, Nostromo, The Secret Agent *and* Under Western Eyes. *His short-story collections (an excellent introduction to his work) are* Tales of Unrest, Youth, Ty-

> **READ ON**

● *Typhoon* (which deals with corruption and exploitation of a different kind, this time using as its metaphor a passenger steamer caught in a typhoon in the China Sea); *The Secret Agent* (about the conflict between innocence and corruption among a group of terrorists in 1900s London).
▶ ▷Herman Melville, *Billy Budd, Foretopman*. ▷Graham Greene, *The Comedians*. Lionel Davidson, *Making Good Again*. B. Traven, *The Treasure of the Sierra Madre*. ▷Paul Theroux, *The Mosquito Coast*. John Kruse, *The Hour of the Lily*. ▷J.G. Ballard, *The Drowned World* is an SF novel of Conradian intensity.

phoon, A Set of Six, 'Twixt Land and Sea, Within the Tides *and* Tales of Hearsay.

COOK, David • *(born 1940)*
British novelist.

Cook's 1970s books were compassionate stories about the kind of people usually shunned by society (and by novelists): a depressive widow and a catamite in *Happy Endings*, a child molester in *Albert's Memorial*, a Downs Syndrome sufferer in *Walter*. The combination of clinical descriptions of awful events and warm-heartedness allowed him to take even greater risks in his next novels, *Winter Doves* (in which two inhabitants of a mental home, Walter and a would-be suicide, fall in love and run away to seek happiness together), and *Sunrising* (see below). Although Cook's early books seemed to place him with such British fictional horror novelists as Martin Amis, Ian McEwan or Iain Banks, the humanity and optimism of his work soon carried him far beyond the range of such contemporaries.

SUNRISING • *(1984)*
This book steps aside from the late-20th-century inadequates of Cook's other novels. It is set in the 1830s, and tells of three orphaned children who befriend each other and travel in search of a home. The descriptions of rural England, of the Oxford Goose Fair and especially of the London slums are as gripping as anything in ▷Dickens (but far less wordy), and the story is radiant with humanity. Despite the miseries and deprivation the children suffer, they find help and friendship, ordinary human decency, at every turn.

COOKSON, Catherine • *(born 1906)*
British novelist.

Cookson's romances are warm-hearted stories of 'ordinary people'. She sets most of them in the north-east of England (Tyneside) where she was born, and shows how her characters cope with the harsh conditions of 19th-century life in the area. Apart from her style, which is matter-of-fact, not moralising – it has learned lessons from 20th-century documentary – her books are in the unsentimental tradition of such great 'social' novels as those of ▷Mrs Gaskell or ▷George Eliot. She grouped many of her stories in series, in particular the 'Mary-Ann' books (beginning with *A Grand Man*) and the Mallen trilogy (*The Mal-*

READ ON ▷

● *Missing Persons* (an equally warm-hearted comedy about two elderly ladies who refuse to give in to old age. One sets up as a private detective, the other goes to find a lover and a new home in Tuscany).
▶ **To *Sunrising*:** ▷Charles Dickens, *Oliver Twist*; Richard Hughes, *A High Wind in Jamaica*; ▷J.G. Ballard, *Empire of the Sun*.
▶ **To *Missing Persons*:** Julian Barnes, *Staring at the Sun*.
▶ **To Cook's other books:** ▷Susan Hill, *I'm the King of the Castle*; Paul Bailey, *At the Jerusalem*; *Gabriel's Lament*.

READ ON ▷

▶ Catherine Gaskin, *Sarah Dane*. Marie Joseph, *Gemini Girls*, Danielle Steele, *The Promises*. ▷George Eliot, *The Mill on the Floss*. ▷Mrs Gaskell, *North and South*.

len Girl, *The Mallen Litter* and *The Mallen Streak*). The heroine of *Tilly Trotter*, *Tilly Trotter Wed* and *Tilly Trotter Widowed* (a characteristic series, written in the 1960s) is a poor but spirited girl in 1830s County Durham who becomes the mistress of the owner of the 'big house', emigrates to America when he dies, and returns in middle age to find happiness at last in her beloved native county.

COUNTRY HOUSES

Mazo de la Roche, *Jalna*
▷E.M. Forster, *Howards End*
▷Hermann Hesse, *Rosshalde*
▷Eudora Welty, *Delta Wedding*
▷Michael Innes, *Old Hall, New Hall*
▷Evelyn Waugh, *Brideshead Revisited*
▷P.G. Wodehouse, *Summer Lightning*

Old Dark Houses (p 183)

THE COUNTRYSIDE
(the implacability of nature)

Stella Gibbons, *Cold Comfort Farm*
▷Thomas Hardy, *The Woodlanders*
▷Geoffrey Household, *Rogue Male*
▷Paul Theroux, *The Black House*
Mary Webb, *Precious Bane*
▷Fay Weldon, *The Heart of England*
▷Edith Wharton, *Ethan Frome*

The Rhythm of Nature (p 204)

COX, Richard • *(born 1931)*
British novelist.

Cox was a defence correspondent, and is an expert on aerial warfare. His best-known thrillers (eg *The Time It Takes*, about mercenaries in central Africa) have a flying background, but everything he writes is enriched by his knowledge of modern weapons-systems and global politics.

READ ON ▷

▶ Ernest K. Gann, *The Aviator*. Spencer S. Dunmore, *The Sound of Wings*. ▷Frederick Forsyth, *The Dogs of War*.

CULTURE-CLASH
▷Chinua Achebe, *Things Fall Apart*
▷E.M. Forster, *A Passage to India*
 Brian Glanville, *Along the Arno*
▷William Golding, *The Inheritors*
▷Henry James, *The Europeans*
 Joseph Olshan, *A Warmer Season*
▷Evelyn Waugh, *The Loved One*
▷H.G. Wells, *Kipps*

D

DARK, Eleanor • *(born 1901)*
Australian novelist.

Dark's novels are psychological meditations like those of Virginia ▷Woolf, showing the movement of their characters' minds as they react to apparently ordinary events. The theme of *Prelude to Christopher* (1934) is that we are the prisoners of our past, that we carry the burden of previous actions and understandings – as Dark put it – the way snails carry their shells. *Sun Across the Sky* and *Waterway* each focus on a single day, during which a group of characters reaches a moment of self-realisation and psychological crisis which results in violent, tragic action. *Return to Coolami* (1936) is about the relationship of four people on a 300-mile drive through New South Wales; although the book is marvellously evocative of the Australian landscape (a recurring pleasure in Dark's work), the exploration is really of character not countryside and physical travelling is a metaphor for the journey of the soul. In the 1940s Dark applied similar techniques of psychological investigation to a historical subject, writing a novel-trilogy (*The Timeless Land*; *Storm of Time*; *No Barrier*) about the first European settlements in Australia. The counterpoint of lyrical descriptions of what (to the whites) was a virgin, beautiful land with analyses of the soul's turbulence caused by their amputation from their European culture and families gives these books extraordinary power; only ▷William Golding and ▷Patrick White so strikingly combine the epic and the intimate.

Dark's other novels are Slow Dawning, The Little Company *and the lighter* Lantana Lane, *the anecdotal story of a farming family in Queensland.*

READ ON ▷

▶ **To Dark's psychological novels:** ▷Virginia Woolf, *The Waves*; ▷Nadine Gordimer, *The Conservationist*; ▷Anita Brookner, *A Misalliance*.
▶ **To the historical trilogy:** ▷William Golding, *Darkness Visible*; ▷Thomas Keneally, *The Playmaker*; ▷Patrick White, *Voss*; ▷William Faulkner, *Sartoris*.
▶ **To *Lantana Lane*:** ▷Miles Franklin (writing as 'Brent of Bin Bin'), *Up the Country*.

DAVIES, Robertson • *(born 1913)*
Canadian novelist, journalist and playwright.

The deceptively gentle, expansive tone of Davies' satires belies their extraordinary subject-matter: it is as if ▷Jane Austen had reworked ▷Rabelais. Davies' books are comedies of manners, many set in small university towns riven with gossip and pretension. *Tempest-tost* (1951) is about an amateur production of Shakespeare's *The Tempest* all but sabotaged by the unexpected, lacerating love of the middle-aged leading man for the girl who plays his daughter. *A Mixture of Frailties* (1958) describes the chain of bizarre events after a woman leaves money to educate a girl in the arts, unless and until the woman's son sires a male heir. In each novel of the 'Deptford trilogy' (1970–75) a different narrator tries to explain the circumstances leading up to the death of a man killed by a stone wrapped in a snowball. What each man does, however, is reveal his own tangled life-history and his bizarre enthusiasms (which range from medieval saints to Houdini, from the history of vaudeville to experiments into 'the collective unconscious').

THE REBEL ANGELS • *(1982)*
Alternate chapters of this story are told by Father Darcourt, a professor of Biblical Greek at a small Canadian university, and Ms Maria Magdalene Theotoky, a research student. The university is a quiet place, dedicated to placid scholarship and barbed common-room gossip. Ms Theotoky is researching Rabelais, and the plot suddenly erupts with priceless manuscripts, bizarre lusts and unsavoury accusations, devil-worship, scatology, and a storm of passion and deceit against which no grove of academe could stand unbowed. Davies is asking whether traditionalists (symbolised by the university Fathers) or 'rebel angels' (symbolised by a riotous gipsy family) are true guardians of the human soul. But he surrounds serious philosophical enquiry with a circus-parade of jokes, lists, parodies and slapstick. If Jane Austen rules his earlier books, in this one Rabelais is firmly, fruitily in charge.

The books in the 'Deptford trilogy' are Fifth Business, The Manticore *and* World of Wonders. *Davies's other novels include* Leaven of Malice *and* What's Bred in the Bone. *His humorous journalism is collected in* The Diary of Samuel Marchbanks, The Table Talk of Samuel Marchbanks *and* Marchbanks' Almanac, *and his plays include* A Jig for the Gipsy, Hunting Stuart *and the political satire* Question Time.

READ ON ▷

● *What's Bred in the Bone* (about a man who makes a fortune as an international conman, anti-nazi spy and art-forger, and about the horror of his stuffy, middle-class Canadian family when they discover the source of his – and their – riches, after his will is read).

▶ **To *Rebel Angels*:** ▷Randall Jarrell, *Pictures from an Institution*; ▷Anthony Burgess, *Enderby's Dark Lady*; Andrew Davies, *A Very Peculiar Practice*.

▶ **To *What's Bred in the Bone*:** ▷Laurence Sterne, *Tristram Shandy*; ▷Thomas Mann, *The Confessions of Felix Krull, Confidence Man*.

▶ **To Davies' work in general:** ▷John Irving, *The Hotel New Hampshire*; ▷Barbara Pym, *Quartet in Autumn*; Howard Jacobson, *Peeping Tom*.

DEEP SOUTH, USA

  Harper Lee, *To Kill a Mocking Bird*
▷ Carson McCullers, *The Ballad of the Sad Café*
▷ Margaret Mitchell, *Gone With the Wind*
▷ Mark Twain, *The Adventures of Huckleberry Finn*
▷ Alice Walker, *The Color Purple*
▷ Eudora Welty, *Delta Wedding*
▷ Thomas Wolfe, *Look Homeward, Angel*

Places (p 191): US Small Town Life (p 246)

DEFOE, Daniel • *(1660–1731)*
British novelist and non-fiction writer.

A journalist, Defoe wrote over 500 essays, poems, political satires and other works, including a history of England, a handbook of good manners and a guide-book to Britain. In his 60s he began writing what he called 'romances': books which purported to be the autobiographies of people who had led unusual or adventurous lives (pirates, whores, treasure-hunters) but which were really fiction and among the earliest English novels. Apart from his characters' proneness to theological and philosophical reflection (eminently skippable), his books lack the ponderousness of later 18th-century fiction. His fast-moving, simple prose and his journalist's talent for description give his work a freshness which belies its age.

ROBINSON CRUSOE • *(1719)*
The germ of this story came from the autobiography of a real-life sailor, Alexander Selkirk, who was marooned on a desert island in 1704. As often in his works, Defoe was fascinated by the idea of the confrontation between civilisation and barbarism, in this case by how a 'modern' European, filled with the knowledge and aspirations of the Age of Reason, might cope if all the trappings of civilisation were stripped from him. Crusoe is allowed nothing but a few tools and other possessions saved from the shipwreck, and the resources of his own ingenuity. Later, after Crusoe has lived alone for 26 years, Defoe provides him with a companion, the 'savage' Friday, and so lets us see 'civilised' humanity through innocent, unsophisticated eyes.

Defoe's 'romances' include The Life and Adventures of Mr Duncan Campbell *(whose hero is a deaf-and-dumb conjurer),* Captain Singleton *(whose hero is a pirate),* Memoirs of a Cavalier *and* Memoirs of Captain George

READ ON ▷

● *The Farther Adventures of Robinson Crusoe.* Moll Flanders is a 'romance' of a similar kind, using the story of a woman forced by circumstances into crime to give a vivid picture of the thieves, prostitutes and highwaymen of the 18th-century English underworld, and of life in the convict settlements of Virginia.
▶ ▷Henry Fielding, *Tom Jones.* ▷William Golding, *Pincher Martin*; *Rites of Passage.* ▷Patrick White, *Tarr.* Michel Tournier, *The Other Friday* and Jane Gardam, *Crusoe's Daughter* play fascinating games with *Robinson Crusoe*'s themes and plot, Tournier by retelling the story from Friday's point of view, and Gardam by focussing on a reclusive girl

Carleton *(whose heroes are swashbuckling soldiers-of-fortune), and – more serious –* A Journal of the Plague Year, *a day-by-day, first-person account of life during the Great Plague of London in 1664.*

fixated on *Robinson Crusoe* who makes it her chief emotional resource. C.S. Lewis, *Out of the Silent Planet* is a similar novel of survival, set on the planet Mars, and J.M. Coetzee, *Foe* gives an alternative account of how *Robinson Crusoe* came to be written, and of the 'real' events which might have inspired it – Friday and Crusoe are the sole survivors from a wrecked slave-ship.

DE HAAN, Tom • *(born 1964)*
British novelist.

At one level, De Haan's *A Mirror for Princes* (1987) is a swaggering medieval tale, as crammed as a Breughel painting. Its setting is a glittering, barbarous feudal court. Its pages jostle with tyranny, intrigue, incest and delight in the earthier human pleasures. Its dialogue wastes no words, and the central element of its plot – the relationship between the poetry-loving third son of a tyrant and his hard-fighting, hard-wenching brothers while they wait for the old king to die – is hardly unfamiliar. But the book's title gives the game away: appearances are deceptive. *A Mirror for Princes* is set not in reality but in an imagined, timeless world of De Haan's own invention. The medieval detail, however fascinating, is no more important than the wimples and hautboys in religious paintings of the period. The book is a sustained meditation on power and love, a moral and philosophical allegory in the manner of ▷Hesse's *The Glass Bead Game*. The combination of this and red-blooded action is magnificently handled; *A Mirror for Princes*, De Haan's first novel, is a masterpiece.

> **READ ON** ⟩

▶ Pär Lagerkvist, *The Dwarf*. Helen Waddell, *Héloïse and Abelard*. ▷Thomas Mann, *The Holy Sinner*.

DEIGHTON, Len • *(born 1929)*
British novelist.

In the 1960s, fired by dislike of snobbish spy fantasies of the James Bond school, Deighton produced a series of books (beginning with *The IPCRESS File*) showing spies as ordinary human beings, functionaries of a ridiculous and

> **READ ON** ⟩

● *Goodbye Mickey Mouse* (a detailed, convincing – and, in its

outdated bureaucracy in which requisitions for paper-clips could take precedence over analyses of the danger of nuclear war. He devised for them a documentary, 'dossier' technique, flooding the text with lists, letters, memoranda, meeting-transcripts, diary-entries and technical notes – and went on to use it in a series of devastatingly authentic-seeming novels on non-spy subjects. Although his material is fictional, it reads like fact, like the transcript of a TV documentary which shows us people's thoughts and feelings as meticulously as what they do and say.

BOMBER · *(1970)*

In direct contrast to the stiff-upper-lip, jolly-good-show British war-films of the 1950s, Deighton gives a blunt, detailed idea of what it was probably like to prepare for and make an RAF bombing-raid in 1943. He is particularly interested in the tensions between service and civilian personnel, the class-divisions between officers and other ranks and the bumbling and paper-chasing which contrasted with, and sometimes jeopardised, the bravery of actual combat.

Deighton's spy-books include Funeral in Berlin, Horse Under Water, Spy Story *and the trilogy* Berlin Game, Moscow Set, London Match. Close-up *is a black satire on the film business. Only* When I Larf *is a comedy about confidence-tricksters. His 'dossier' novels include* SS-GB, *a nightmarish vision of what might have happened if Britain had lost the second world war and were now under nazi rule.*

implications for Western defence, horrifying – novel about USAF personnel manning a nuclear-weapons airfield in the UK).

▶ **To the spy-stories:** ▷John Le Carré, *The Spy Who Came in from the Cold*; Adam Hall, *The Quiller Memorandum*. (Hall also writes Deightonish war-stories under the name Elleston Trevor).

▶ **To Deighton's flying-stories:** Gavin Lyall, *Midnight Plus One*; Peter George, *Red Alert* (about the accidental triggering of the nuclear holocaust).

DEPRESSION AND PSYCHIATRY

▷Lisa Alther, *Other Women*
Paul Bailey, *Peter Smart's Confessions*
Roy Brown, *The Siblings*
Jonathan Kellerman, *Shrunken Heads*
▷Doris Lessing, *The Golden Notebook*
▷H.H. Richardson, *Maurice Guest*
▷J.D. Salinger, *Franny and Zooey*
▷Antonia White, *Beyond the Glass*

Madness (p 159); On the Edge of Sanity (p 183)

DE VRIES, Peter • *(born 1910)*
US novelist and journalist.

De Vries worked for the *New Yorker*, and his novels sa-
tirise a favourite target of that magazine, the upwardly-
mobile suburbanites he himself called 'globules of metro-
politan life'. His characters live in trim stockbroker villages on Long Island or in Connecticut. The husbands
commute into New York to work; the wives stay at home
to mind their beautiful houses, tend their lawn-sprinklers,
go to coffee mornings and PTA meetings and bore each
other to death. Evenings and weekends are given up to
self-improving parties (at which people read modern poetry and make bitchy remarks about each other's clothes)
and to furtive, desperate love-affairs. Most of De Vries'
books are first-person novels, and his narrators enliven
them with aphorisms, wisecracks, puns and parodies of
everything from TV commercials to the *Reader's Digest*.
It is an empty, panic-stricken society, pathetically narcissistic – but instead of merely sending it up, as many other
New Yorker writers and cartoonists do, De Vries shows it
with compassion as well as wit. His books may be slapstick, but they end in tears.

THE TUNNEL OF LOVE • *(1954)*
The story is told by Dick, the cartoons editor of a New
York magazine called *The Townsman*. He is happy in his
work and his marriage, but affects to be bored, constantly
making world-weary jokes which no one else appreciates,
and fantasising about a Maine hideaway called Moot Point
at which he woos beautiful women in the manner of Cary
Grant, Clark Gable or George Sanders. He and his wife
are asked to sponsor their neighbours as a suitable couple
to adopt a child – and the more Dick finds out about the
husband, a womanising cartoonist, the more he himself is
tangled in lust, deceit and sexual compromise.

De Vries' comic novels include Comfort Me with Apples,
Through the Fields of Clover, Reuben Reuben, Mrs Wal-
lop, I Hear America Swinging, Into Your Tent I'll Creep,
Sauce for the Goose, Madder Music *and* The Prick of
Noon. The Blood of the Lamb *is serious, about the death
of a child.*

DICKENS, Charles • *(1812–70)*
British novelist.

In his early 20s Dickens worked as a journalist, writing
reports of law court proceedings and Parliamentary de-

READ ON

● *The Mackerel Plaza;
Let Me Count the
Ways.*
▶ ▷John Updike, *The
Witches of Eastwick.*
▷Iris Murdoch, *A
Severed Head.*
▷Kingsley Amis, *That
Uncertain Feeling.*
Martin Amis, *The
Rachel Papers.*
George Axelrod,
*Where Am I Now –
and Do I Need Me?*

READ ON

● *Nicholas Nickleby;
Oliver Twist.*

bates, and short essays on the life and manners of the time (later collected as *Sketches by Boz*). It was not until the success of his first novel *Pickwick Papers*, when he was 25, that he made writing a full-time career. He composed large parts of his novels in dialogue, and was proud of his gift for showing character through speech alone; he also gave his minor characters (pot-boys, shop-customers, carters, oystermen, toddlers) turns of speech or physical eccentricities to make them instantly memorable – another theatrical technique. This character-vividness is matched by a sustained commentary on human nature and society: Dickens consistently savaged the humbug and petty-mindedness of the middle classes who bought his books, and said that human happiness comes not from law, religion, politics or social structures but from gratuitous, individual acts of kindness. In his later books, notably *Great Expectations* and *Our Mutual Friend*, savagery predominated over sentimentality to an extent rivalled only in ▷Zola.

DAVID COPPERFIELD • *(1849–50)*

Dickens' own favourite among his novels, this tells the story (in the first person, as if an autobiography) of a boy growing up: his unhappy childhood and adolescence, his first jobs and first love-affair, and the way he finally transmutes his experience into fiction and becomes a writer. As often in Dickens' books, subsidiary characters seem to steal the show: the grim Murdstones, the optimistic Micawbers, salt-of-the-earth Peggotty, feckless Steerforth and above all the viperish hypocrite Uriah Heep. But the book's chief interest is the developing character of Copperfield himself: apparently passive, at other people's mercy, he learns and grows by each experience, maturing before our eyes.

Dickens' novels, in order of publication, are Pickwick Papers, Oliver Twist, Nicholas Nickleby, The Old Curiosity Shop, Barnaby Rudge, Martin Chuzzlewit, Dombey and Son, David Copperfield, Bleak House, Hard Times, Little Dorrit, A Tale of Two Cities, Great Expectations, Our Mutual Friend *and* Edwin Drood. *His shorter works include* A Christmas Carol, A Child's History of England *and three collections of articles,* Sketches by Boz, American Notes *and* The Uncommercial Traveller.

DICKINSON, Peter • *(born 1927)*

British novelist and children's writer.

Although Dickinson's crime novels contain their quota of murders and clues, they centre on the unravelling of mysteries of a different kind. Each is set in a self-contained,

▶ Novels of 'growing up', using a biographical framework to give a picture (documentary, satirical or both at once) of society: ▷Henry Fielding, *Tom Jones*; ▷Somerset Maugham, *Of Human Bondage*; ▷Mark Twain, *Huckleberry Finn*; ▷James Joyce, *Portrait of the Artist as a Young Man*.

▶ **To Dickens' more savage social novels:** ▷Mrs Gaskell, *North and South*; ▷John Steinbeck, *The Grapes of Wrath*; ▷Patrick White, *Riders in the Chariot*.

▶ **To his more relaxed tableaux of human life:** ▷H.G. Wells, *Kipps*; ▷Angus Wilson, *Anglo-Saxon Attitudes*.

READ ON ⟩

● *The Lively Dead.*
▶ To Dickinson's crime-

Victor **HUGO, LES MISÉRABLES**
(1820s France: honest man convicted to galleys escapes and rebuilds his life)

Anthony **TROLLOPE, THE LAST CHRONICLE OF BARSET**
(1860s England: honest man wrongly accused of theft; student making his way in London)

Edith **WHARTON, THE HOUSE OF MIRTH**
(1880s New York heiress rejects ways of society to 'be herself')

J.B. **PRIESTLEY, ANGEL PAVEMENT**
(1920s London firm taken over, developed and ruined by confidence-trickster)

John **O'HARA, THE LOCKWOOD CONCERN**
(1930s Pennsylvania family becomes wealthy by violence, destroys itself)

James **BALDWIN, GO, TELL IT ON THE MOUNTAIN**
(1950s Harlem: son of slum family learns about sex, racism and born-again Christian love)

'DICKENSIAN' NOVELS:
BLEAK SIDE OF LIFE

'DICKENSIAN' NOVELS:
CHEERFUL SIDE OF LIFE

David **COOK, SUNRISING**
(1830s England: three children rescued from degradation in rural and urban slums)

Mark **TWAIN, THE ADVENTURES OF HUCKLEBERRY FINN** *(1860s Mississippi: boy's adolescence on river and in riverside communities)*

H.G. **WELLS, THE HISTORY OF MR POLLY**
(1890s England: middle-aged 'drop-out' has many adventures, finds happiness)

Thomas **MANN, THE CONFESSIONS OF FELIX KRULL, CONFIDENCE MAN** *(1900s Europe: confidence-man's cheerful, amoral adventures among the bourgeoisie)*

Angus **WILSON, THE MIDDLE AGE OF MRS ELIOT**
(1950s widow travels world in search of happiness)

Saul **BELLOW, THE ADVENTURES OF AUGIE MARCH**
(1930s Chicago: zestful account of slum boy using his wits to make his way)

(dark childhood, miserable growing-up and eventual happiness in 19th-century London)

LEARNING HOW TO BE GROWN-UP

William **THACKERAY, PENDENNIS**
(1840s London: after many escapades, young man finds literary success)

W. Somerset **MAUGHAM, OF HUMAN BONDAGE**
(1890s London school days, Paris student life and eventual happiness of lonely young man)

Johann Wolfgang von **GOETHE, THE APPRENTICESHIP OF WILHELM MEISTER**
(1790s Europe: young man runs away to be an actor, experiences real life, 'finds' himself)

André **GIDE, THE COUNTERFEITERS**
(1920s Paris: young people growing up, initiated into life and love)

Mordecai **RICHLER, THE APPRENTICESHIP OF DUDDY KRAVITZ**
(1930s Montreal: young man moves from rags to riches, loses his soul)

Lisa **ALTHER, KINFLICKS**
(1960s USA: young woman learns about sex, love, feminism, protest-politics and 'dropping out')

bizarre society about which we long to learn more – and the further his detective investigates the crime, the deeper we are drawn into the surrounding atmosphere. *Sleep and His Brother* is set in a community of brain-damaged, psychically sensitive children, and the only being who knows the identity of the murderer is a 'talking' chimpanzee. *The Seals* is about a crazy religious community waiting for the apocalypse on a remote Scottish island. In *King and Joker* someone commits murder in a Buckingham Palace inhabited by an egalitarian, trendy-left royal family whose dark secrets give the book its fun. In later novels, Dickinson abandoned the crime format to explore wider themes, especially of identity. The mysteries in *A Summer in the Twenties*, *The Last House-Party* and *Hindsight*, for example, are not murders but long-forgotten love-affairs, betrayals and family secrets whose effects stain the lives of the present generation.

SKIN DEEP • *(1968)*

A tribe of people from Papua New Guinea lives in a terraced house in London, carrying out stone-age rituals in the attics. Their chief is murdered, and the community begins to fall apart. Superintendent Pibble must not only find the murderer, but reassure the tribespeople – and to do that he must try to enter their minds and understand their culture.

Dickinson's adult novels include A Pride of Heroes, The Lizard in the Cup, The Poison Oracle, The Lively Dead *and* One Foot in the Grave. *He has also written children's books:* Tulku, Annerton Pit *and an SF trilogy,* The Changes.

DONALDSON, Stephen • *(born 1947)*
US novelist.

Donaldson's major work, the 2600-page Thomas Covenant series (1977–84), is adventure-fantasy inspired by – and as good as – ▷Tolkien's *The Lord of the Rings*. Thomas Covenant, a leper, is transported to a distant country in the grip of the evil Lord Foul. He finds that his wedding-ring is a powerful magic talisman, but is at first reluctant to use it because he believes himself psychologically tainted by his illness – in fact he wonders if the Land and its plight are not fantasies of his own sick mind. The novels chart his spiritual agonising, his recruitment of a band of helpers and followers, and his epic battles against Lord Foul.

novels: ▷Michael Innes, *The Daffodil Affair*; H.R.F. Keating, *Death and the Visiting Firemen*; Gladys Mitchell, *The Twenty-third Man*.
▶ **To his non-crime books:** Macdonald Harris, *The Balloonist*; Bamber Gascoigne, *The Heyday*; ▷John Irving, *The World According to Garp*.

> **READ ON**

▶ ▷David Eddings, *Pawn of Prophecy* (first of the Belgariad quintet). Jack Vance, *Lyonesse*. R.A. MacAvoy, *Damiano*.

The Thomas Covenant books are Lord Foul's Bane, The Illearth War, The Power That Preserves, The Wounded Land, The One Tree, White Gold Wielder *and the brief* Gildenfire.

DONLEAVY, J.P. (James Patrick) •
(born 1926)
Irish novelist.

Beginning with *The Ginger Man* (1955), Donleavy has written a series of bawdy, boozy 'biographies', like shaggy-dog stories reworked by ▷Joyce. Nothing much happens to his heroes: they wander amiably through life, spending much time in bed and even more in pubs, and endlessly, riotously reflecting on the meaning of life and love. His other novels include *A Singular Man*, *The Beastly Beatitudes of Balthazar B*, *The Destinies of Darcy Dancer, Gentleman*, and *Are You Listening, Rabbi Löw?*.

> READ ON ⟩

▶ Flann O'Brien, *At Swim-Two-Birds*. ▷John Kennedy Toole, *A Confederacy of Dunces*. Robert Coover, *Pricksongs and Descants* (short stories).

DOSTOEVSKI, Fyodor • *(1821–81)*
Russian novelist.

Dostoevski admired ▷Balzac and ▷Dickens, and set out to describe Russian characters and society in a similar way, creating atmosphere by a series of vivid evocations (verbal snapshots) of everything from people's skin and clothes to the texture of furniture or the gleam of rain on cobble-stones. His characters are a gallery of 'types', particularly strong on the destitute, the suffering and the inadequate. He was fascinated by people driven to extreme behaviour by despair or lack of external moral guidance, such as the teaching of his own Christian faith. Raskolnikov, the central character of *Crime and Punishment*, makes himself a moral outsider by committing murder. Myshkin in *The Idiot* is so tormented by the thought of his own inadequacy that he becomes the imbecile he thinks he is. Every member of the Karamazov family (in *The Brothers Karamazov*) is morally tainted, and only the youngest, a novice monk, is able to wrestle with his own evil nature and win. If Dostoevski had been a 20th-century writer, his pessimistic view of human existence might have led him to surrealist black comedy (see ▷Kafka); as it was, the psychological intensity of his books is closer to stage tragedy (*King Lear* or *Medea*, say) than to prose fiction, and has a similar all-engulfing power.

> READ ON ⟩

● *The Idiot*; *The Brothers Karamazov*.
▶ ▷Victor Hugo, *Les misérables*. ▷Nathaniel Hawthorne, *The Scarlet Letter*. ▷Joseph Conrad, *Under Western Eyes*. ▷Albert Camus, *The Fall* (La chute). ▷Vladimir Nabokov, *Despair*. ▷Georges Simenon, *Act of Passion*. ▷François Mauriac, *The Nest of Vipers* (Le nœud de vipères). Paul Bailey, *A Distant Likeness* reverses one of the themes of *Crime and Punishment*: obsession with a crime triggers self-condemnation and madness not in the criminal but in the investigating officer.

CRIME AND PUNISHMENT • *(1866)*
Raskolnikov, a student, driven to neurotic frenzy by his

powerlessness to change the injustice of the world, decides to demonstrate the freedom of his soul by a single
gratuitous act: murder. Instead of being liberated, however, he is enslaved by his own guilt-feelings, and the
book describes, in a remorseless and clinical way, the disintegration of his personality. The part of his 'conscience'
is embodied in Inspector Petrovich, who harries him like a
Fury from ancient myth, goading and cajoling him to admit his guilt and so to purge his soul.

Dostoevski's other books include Notes From the House
of the Dead *(based on his own prison-camp experiences:
he was a political dissident),* Winter Notes on Summer
Experiences *(a horrified account of the degenerate Europe
he found while visiting the London World Exhibition of
1862), and the novels* Notes from Underground, The
Gambler *and* The Possessed.

DOYLE, Arthur Conan • *(1859–1930)*
British writer of novels, short stories and non-fiction.

A doctor with very few patients, Doyle began writing to
improve his income. His main interest was military history, and he regarded his historical novels (eg *The White
Company*, the story of a band of 14th-century knight-er-
rants, or the Brigadier Gerard books, set during the Napoleonic Wars) as his best work. His Sherlock Holmes stories were meant as potboilers, and throughout his life he
claimed (while still going on writing them) to be embarrassed by their success. The Holmes stories were published by *Strand Magazine* in the UK and by *Harper's* in
the USA; these papers also serialised Doyle's Professor
Challenger novels (beginning with *The Lost World*), about
a flamboyant scientific genius and explorer, a blend of the
heroes of ▷Verne and ▷Rider Haggard.

THE MEMOIRS OF SHERLOCK HOLMES • *(1893)*
In each of the 11 stories in this collection, Holmes is pre-
sented with a problem which seems insoluble – at least so
far as his friend and chronicler Dr Watson can see – and
solves it by a mixture of dazzling deductive reasoning and
melodramatic adventure. He is a master of disguise, an
expert shot and boxer, a drug-taker, a neurotic introvert, a
plausible liar who uses every trick to trap his suspects –
and Doyle's style has a single-mindedness, an obsessive-
ness, which perfectly suits both Holmes' character and the
mysteries he is set to solve.

Doyle's Holmes books are the novels A Study in Scarlet,

> **READ ON**

● *The Case Book of
  Sherlock Holmes.*
▶ Nicholas Meyer, *The
  Seven-per-cent
  Solution* (one of the
  most convincing of
  many Holmes stories
  by others since Doyle
  went out of copyright).
  G.K. Chesterton, *The
  Father Brown Stories.*
  Gladys Mitchell,
  *Twelve Horses and the
  Hangman's Noose.*
  John Dickson Carr,
  *The Emperor's Snuff
  Box.*

The Sign of Four, The Hound of the Baskervilles *and* The Valley of Fear, *and the short-story collections* Adventures of Sherlock Holmes, The Return of Sherlock Holmes, His Last Bow *and* The Case Book of Sherlock Holmes. *The Challenger books include* The Poison Belt *and* The Land of Mist, *and Doyle's historical novels, apart from those mentioned, include* Micah Clarke *(set during the Monmouth Rebellion of 1685 and its bloody aftermath).*

DRABBLE, Margaret • *(born 1939)*
British novelist and non- fiction writer.

An admirer of ▷Eliot and ▷Bennett, Drabble has updated their fictional ideas to the present day. Her books are crammed with the detail of everyday lives – fetching children from school, making gravy, taking inter-city trains, washing tights – and are about 'ordinary' people: housewives, librarians, teachers, midwives. But Drabble, like Eliot and Bennett, is also interested in intellectual ideas, in describing the spirit of the times as well as their domestic detail. Without being feminist, her books centre on women's experience. They tell us how middle-class girls of the late 1950s felt about their lives, how they went on in the 1960s to balance marriage, motherhood and careers, and how they coped in the 1970s and 1980s with teenage children and rocky marriages. It is fiction so honest that it seems almost like autobiography: every one of Drabble's women shares an outlook, a tone of voice, which sounds (rightly or wrongly) like the author's own.

THE RADIANT WAY • *(1987)*
The lives of three women of similar age (late 40s) and background (educated middle-class) are contrasted, in a brilliantly-evoked mid-1980s Britain. All were born in the north of England; Liz has moved south and made a career as a Harley Street psychiatrist; her sister has stayed at home to look after their senile mother; Alix and her husband, failing to make a success in London, are returning north to regenerate their lives. The characters' contrasting experience, and their middle-aged views of the way their younger ambitions have worked out, match the political and social feelings Drabble sees as typical of Britain in the 1980s, when the young adults of the flower-power generation are just beginning to feel that life has passed them by.

Drabble's novels are The Garrick Year, The Millstone, Jerusalem the Golden, The Waterfall, The Realms of

READ ON ▷

● *The Garrick Year* (a moving study, set in the 1960s, of a woman trying to manage both marriage, to a rising actor, and the claims of her own career).
▷ Penelope Mortimer, *The Pumpkin Eater.*
Deborah Moggach, *Close to Home.*
▷Margaret Atwood, *The Edible Woman.*
Joan Didion, *A Book of Common Prayer.*
Mary Flanagan, *Trust.*
▷ **Earlier books foreshadowing Drabble's concerns:**
▷George Eliot, *Middlemarch;* ▷Arnold Bennett, *Hilda Lessways;* ▷Virginia Woolf, *Mrs Dalloway.*

Gold, The Ice Age *and* The Radiant Way. *She has also written biographies of Wordsworth and Bennett.*

DREAMING SPIRES
(books set in Cambridge and Oxford Universities)

▷Max Beerbohm, *Zuleika Dobson*
  Glyn Daniel, *The Cambridge Murders*
  Alan Judd, *The Noonday Devil*
▷Barbara Pym, *Crampton Hodnett*
▷Dorothy L. Sayers, *Gaudy Night*
▷Tom Sharpe, *Porterhouse Blue*
▷C.P. Snow, *The Affair*

Higher (?) Education (p 118)

DUMAS, Alexandre • *(1802–70)*
French writer of novels, plays short stories and non-fiction.

In his 20s Dumas worked as a civil service clerk; it was not until he was 29 that he was able to take up writing full-time. From then till his death, working with a team of assistants, he poured out over 250 plays, novels, essays, books on history, travel and cooking and no less than 22 volumes of memoirs. He was one of the most popular authors of his century, and the genre he specialised in, swashbuckling historical romance, was a favourite for 120 years, a forerunner of both modern spy stories and fantasy.

THE THREE MUSKETEERS • *(1844–5)*
At the beginning of the 17th century d'Artagnan, a young country squire, goes to Paris to seek adventure. He makes friends with three of the King's musketeers (by the unusual method of challenging each of them to a duel on the same day) and the four become inseparable. D'Artagnan is accepted for royal service, and the musketeers throw themselves into the political intrigues centring on weak king Louis, his unhappy queen and her arch-enemies Cardinal Richelieu and the seductive, treacherous Milady. The story involves stolen jewels, masquerades, bluff and double bluff, and the musketeers gallop the length and breadth of France, duelling, drinking, wenching and making a thousand skin-of-the-teeth escapes. Although the book's style is old-fashioned, its breathless plot, its good humour and above all the wisecracking, bantering friendship between the four central characters, give it irresistible

READ ON ▷

● Dumas continued the Musketeers' adventures in *Twenty Years After*, *The Vicomte of Bragelonne* and *The Man in the Iron Mask*.
▶ **Swashbuckling stories:** Rafael Sabatini, *Captain Blood*; Jeffery Farnol, *The Broad Highway*; Stanley J. Weyman, *Gentleman of France*; Baroness Orczy, *The Scarlet Pimpernel*.
▶ **The idea of buddies united against the world is repeated, in a similar tongue-in-cheek way, in** ▷Len Deighton, *Only When I Larf* (about 1960s conmen) and Donald Westlake, *Gangway!* (about 1860s San Francisco crooks).

gusto. After a few dozen pages of acclimatisation, it may prove hard to put it down.

Although Dumas was best-known – and is now best-remembered – for his Musketeers adventures, he wrote fine novels set in other periods, notably The Queen's Necklace *and* The Countess of Charny (*both of which take place during the French Revolution) and* The Count of Monte Cristo, *about a man falsely imprisoned for helping the defeated Napoleon, who escapes, discovers hidden treasure and proceeds to hunt down the people who betrayed him.*

DU MAURIER, Daphne • *(born 1907)*
British novelist and non-fiction writer.

Although Du Maurier wrote novels and stories of many kinds, she is best known for a series of atmospheric romances set in the English West Country (Cornwall, Devon and Somerset) and drawing on the moorland landscape and seafaring associations of the area. In her best-loved book, *Rebecca* (1938), a girl marries an enigmatic young widower and goes to be mistress of his large country house Manderley, only to find it haunted by the mystery of his first wife's death. Solving that mystery (against the wishes of the sinister housekeeper Mrs Danvers) is the only way to bring happiness to the young girl (who is unnamed) and peace to her tormented husband – and the search leads her into a psychological labyrinth as threatening as the corridors of the dark old house itself.

Du Maurier's romances include Jamaica Inn, Frenchman's Creek, My Cousin Rachel *and* Mary Anne. *Her other novels include* The King's General, The Parasites, The Glassblowers *and* The House on the Strand. *The Apple Tree/Kiss Me Again Stranger,* The Breaking Point *and* Early Stories *are collections of short stories. She also wrote plays, biographies (of her family, Branwell Brontë and Francis Drake) and an autobiography,* The Shaping of a Writer/Myself When Young.

DUNNETT, Dorothy • *(born 1923)*
British novelist.

Dunnett is best-known for two enormous historical sagas, swashbuckling romances set in the 15th and 16th centuries. The hero of the 'Lymond' books is a Scottish soldier of fortune whose adventures take him as far as Malta, the Ottoman Empire and Russia (where he serves in the army

READ ON >

▶ Jane Gardam, *Crusoe's Daughter.* ▷Charlotte Brontë, *Jane Eyre.* Susan Howatch, *Penmarric.* ▷Frank Yerby, *A Woman Called Fancy.* Catherine Darby, *Rowan Garth.*

READ ON >

▶ Reay Tannahill, *The World, the Flesh and the Devil.* ▷Tom De Haan, *A Mirror for Princes.* ▷Jean Plaidy,

of Ivan the Terrible). Back home, he becomes the protector of the infant Mary Queen of Scots and is embroiled in the religious and political intrigues of the English Tudor court. A second series (beginning with *Niccolò Rising* and continuing with *The Spring of the Ram*) is in progress. It is the story of an equally charming adventurer, this time set in Renaissance Italy (Florence at the time of the Medicis and Savonarola) and Germany (during the religious wars triggered by Martin Luther's condemnation of the Roman Catholic Church). Dunnett's other books include *King Hereafter*, a novel about the historical Macbeth, King of Scotland, and a series of romantic thrillers set in the present day, all of whose titles − at least in the UK editions − include the name 'Dolly'. (These were originally published under the pseudonym Dorothy Halliday.)

The Lymond books, in order, are The Game of Kings, Queen's Play, The Disorderly Knights, Pawn in Frankincense, The Ringed Castle *and* Checkmate. *The 'Dolly' books are* Dolly and the Singing Bird/The Photogenic Soprano, Dolly and the Cookie Bird/Murder in the Round, Dolly and the Doctor Bird/Match for a Murderer, Dolly and the Starry Bird/Murder in Focus *and* Dolly and the Nanny Bird.

DURRELL, Lawrence • *(born 1912)*
British writer of novels, poems and non-fiction.

Durrell has lived most of his life out of Britain, in Greece, Egypt and France. As well as fiction, he has written poetry and half a dozen non-fiction books about Greek islands: they are among his most enjoyable work, allowing scope for the impressionistic descriptions of landscape and character and the ruminations on love and life which sometimes clog his novels. In his fiction, he uses experimental forms, constantly varying each story's structure and standpoint; this sets up a dialogue between writer and reader, a feeling of collaboration, which is one of the most exhilarating aspects of his work.

THE ALEXANDRIA QUARTET • *(1957–60)*
Each book in the quartet, *Justine, Balthazar, Mountolive* and *Clea*, tells us part of the story: they give different viewpoints of the same events, and it is not till the end that every motive, every action, every twist of character becomes clear. The people are a group of friends and lovers, English, Greek and Egyptian, living in the turmoil of late-1930s Alexandria. At the centre is Darley, a teacher

The Plantagenet Prelude and its sequels: the Plantagenet Saga. Frans Bengtsson, *The Long Ships* (set in Viking times). ▷R.L. Stevenson, *Kidnapped* and its sequels (set in 18th-century Scotland, during the Jacobite uprisings).

> READ ON

● *Tunc* and *Numquam* (a pair of Siamese-twin novels) are similarly dreamlike, setting bizarre events and characters in a blur of countries and climaxing magnificently, if unexpectedly, under the dome of St Paul's Cathedral, London.
▶ Stuart Evans, *Centres of Ritual* (and its sequels: the 'Windmill Hill' sequence).
▷Nathanael West, *The Dream Life of Balso Snell*. D.M. Thomas, *Birthstone*. ▷Olivia Manning, *The Balkan*

and would-be writer who observes events, partakes, but cannot explain. A main 'character' is the city of Alexandria itself. Durrell/Darley pretends to be giving accurate pictures of its souks, bars, palaces, brothels and crumbling embassies, but it is a dream-city, a fantasy-land where reality is subjective and events are only what you make of them.

As well as The Alexandria Quartet, *Durrell's novels include* The Black Book, The Dark Labyrinth/Cefalù *and the five-novel 'Avignon quincunx',* Monsieur, Livia, Constance, Sebastian *and* Quinx. *His* Collected Poems *are published, and* Antrobus Complete *is a collection of satirical stort stories about diplomats, like TV sitcom frozen on the page. His island books include* Prospero's Cell *(about Corfu, also the subject of his brother Gerald's* My Family and Other Animals*),* Reflections on a Marine Venus *(about Rhodes) and* Bitter Lemons *(about Cyprus).*

Trilogy (set in Bucharest and Athens during the second world war); *The Levant Trilogy* (set in Cairo).

E

EDDINGS, David • *(born 1931)*
US novelist.

After one modern adventure story, *High Hunt*, Eddings concentrated on fantasy. His best-known work is the 'Belgariad quintet' (1982–4), a ▷Tolkien-influenced saga of good and evil, magic and mysticism – but laced, unlike *The Lord of the Rings*, with a strong sense of the absurd. The books in the series are *Pawn of Prophecy*, *Queen of Sorcery*, *Magician's Gambit*, *Castle of Wizardry* and *Enchanter's Endgame*. Eddings is currently writing a second series, further adventures of his hero Garion, who begins as a scullion, graduates to be sorcerer's apprentice and ends up a fully-fledged wizard.

> **READ ON**
>
> ▶ Alan Dean Foster, *Spellsinger*. ▷Piers Anthony, *A Spell for Chameleon*. T.H. White, *The Once and Future King*. ▷J.R.R. Tolkien, *Lord of the Rings*.

ELIOT, George • *(1819–80)*
British novelist.

'George Eliot' was the pen-name of Marian Evans, a farm-manager's daughter. She grew up in the stifling provincial pieties of middle-class Victorian England, but after her father's death became an atheist and freethinker, travelled abroad and set up home in London. She was at the heart of the liberal intellectual circles of her time: a supporter of Darwin, an admirer of ▷William Morris and other early socialists. A similar receptivity to new ideas and disdain for convention mark her novels. They deal with the kind of moral issues (such as whether a 'good life' can be lived without religion, or if sexual happiness is essential to a successful marriage) which were rarely discussed in polite Victorian company and were even less common in literature. At the same time her books teem with realistic detail of provincial society, minutely observed. The combination of exact documentation of beha-

> **READ ON**
>
> ● *The Mill on the Floss* (about a brother and sister who are idyllically happy together as children, grow apart in adult life, and are finally, tragically reunited).
> ▶ **Matching Eliot's concern for the individual stifled by society:** ▷Gustave Flaubert, *Madame Bovary*; ▷Mrs Gaskell, *North and South*; ▷Thomas Hardy, *Jude the Obscure*; Benjamin

viour and character with unashamed discussion of ideas normally left unspoken was a heady one: she was one of the most widely read authors of her day.

MIDDLEMARCH · (1871–2)

Two people try to break free from the petty-minded boredom of the English provincial town of Middlemarch. Dorothea Brooke marries because of intellectual infatuation, only to find that her husband (an elderly scholar) is a domestic tyrant. Tertius Lydgate, a doctor struggling to introduce new medical ideas in a society which is deeply suspicious of them, marries for love, only to find that his wife's brainless following of fashion destroys his bank-balance, his self-confidence and his social position.

Apart from Romola, *set in 15th-century Florence, all Eliot's novels have 19th-century English locations and characters. Her first book,* Scenes from Clerical Life, *contains three mid-length stories; it and the short novel* Silas Marner *(about a freethinking country weaver tormented for his beliefs and for a crime he did not commit) are the most accessible of all her works. Her full-length novels are* Adam Bede, The Mill on the Floss, Felix Holt, Middlemarch *and* Daniel Deronda.

Disraeli, *Sybil*.
► **To *Daniel Deronda*:**
▷Henry James, *Portrait of a Lady*; Janet Lewis, *The Trial of Sören Kvist*.
► **Contemporary books combining social observation with 'issues' in an Eliotish way, though their styles are entirely different:** ▷Margaret Drabble, *The Millstone*; ▷Katharine Anne Porter, *Pale Horse, Pale Rider*; Winifred Holtby, *South Riding*; Simone De Beauvoir, *The Mandarins*.

F

FAMILIES: ALL-ENGULFING

▷Anita Brookner, *Family and Friends*
▷Angela Carter, *The Magic Toyshop*
▷William Faulkner, *The Sound and the Fury*
▷John Galsworthy, *The Forsyte Saga*
  Irene Handl, *The Sioux*
▷François Mauriac, *The Nest of Vipers*
▷Christina Stead, *The Man Who Loved Children*

Families: Eccentric (p 72); Families: Many Generations (p 72)

FAMILIES: ECCENTRIC

  H.E. Bates, *The Darling Buds of May*
▷Ivy Compton-Burnett, *A House and its Head*
▷John Irving, *The Hotel New Hampshire*
  Nancy Mitford, *The Pursuit of Love*
▷Vladimir Nabokov, *Ada*
  Peter Tinniswood, *A Touch of Daniel*
▷Virginia Woolf, *To the Lighthouse*

Families: All-engulfing (p 72); Families: Many Generations (p 72); Parents and Children (p 187)

FAMILIES: MANY GENERATIONS

▷Isabel Allende, *The House of the Spirits*

▷Gabriel García Márquez, *One Hundred Years of Solitude*
▷Winston Graham, *Poldark*
▷Thomas Mann, *Buddenbrooks*
▷Maisie Mosco, *Almonds and Raisins*
  Richard Peck, *This Company of Women*
▷I.B. Singer, *The Family Moskat*
  Nicola Thorne, *A Place in the Sun*
  Jan Webster, *Collier's Row*

Families: All-engulfing (p 72); Families: Eccentric (p 72)

FANTASY ADVENTURE

▷Stephen Donaldson, *'Thomas Covenant' series*
▷A. Conan Doyle, *The Lost World*
▷David Eddings, *'Belgariad' quintet*
  C.S. Lewis, *Out of the Silent Planet*
  Terry Pratchett, *The Colour of Magic*
▷J.R.R. Tolkien, *Lord of the Rings*
▷Jules Verne, *Journey to the Centre of the Earth*
  Patricia Wrightson, *The Ice is Coming*

Fantasy Societies (p 73); High Adventure (p 117)

FANTASY SOCIETIES

▷Tom De Haan, *A Mirror for Princes*
  Michael Frayn, *Sweet Dreams*
▷Ursula Le Guin, *Malafrena*
▷Anne McCaffrey, *Dragonflight*
▷Robert Silverberg, *Lord Valentine's Castle*
▷Jonathan Swift, *Gulliver's Travels*
▷H.G. Wells, *The Time Machine*
  T.H. White, *The Once and Future King*

Future Societies (p 86)

FARMER, Philip José • *(born 1918)*
US novelist.

Each of Farmer's SF novels is the exploration of a single, brilliantly surreal initial idea: in *Dayworld*, for example, that the world's overpopulation leads to each human being

READ ON

● *Jesus on Mars*.
▶ ▷Michael Moorcock, *Warlord of the Air*.

being allowed one day per week of 'life' and having to spend the other six in cold storage. His best-known work is the 'Riverworld' series (1972–80; the individual titles are *To Your Scattered Bodies Go*; *The Fabulous Riverboat*; *The Dark Design*; *The Magic Labyrinth*; *Gods of Riverworld*.) Riverworld is a planet on which every human being ever born, from the dawn of history to beyond the present day, has been reborn in the far future as part of a psychological experiment. The series tells how three people, Samuel Clemens (alias ▷Mark Twain), Richard Burton (translator of the *Kama Sutra*) and Alice Hargreaves (née Liddell: the inspiration for *Alice In Wonderland*) explore Riverworld and try to discover the nature and purpose of the experiment of which they – to say nothing of King John of England, plotting a political coup – are part.

▷Frank Herbert, *The Dosadi Experiment*.
▷Isaac Asimov, *Foundation*.

FARRELL, J.G. (James Gordon) •
(1935–79)
British novelist.

READ ON ⟩

After three contemporary novels, including *The Lung* (1965, based on his own experience), about the onset of polio, Farrell took all his themes from history. *Troubles* (1970), set in Ireland after the first world war, is a barbed account of the Irish freedom-struggle against the English, and draws uncomfortable parallels with the present-day situation in Northern Ireland. *The Siege of Krishnapur* (1973), equally vitriolic and farcical – its tone is close at times to ▷Heller's *Catch-22* – is set in 1850s India, during the so-called 'Mutiny'. *The Singapore Grip* (1978) is a blockbuster about the Japanese capture of Malaysia in the second world war – for Farrell, the beginning of Britain's eclipse as a global power. Taken together, the three books are an indictment of Britain's attitude towards its empire: not so much thuggishness as boneheaded indifference, the unconcern of those who never imagine that others might resent their rule.

▶ **To *Troubles*:** Liam O'Flaherty: *The Informer*; Bernard MacLaverty, *Cal*.
▶ **To *The Siege of Krishnapur*:** ▷John Masters, *Nightrunners of Bengal*; Idries Shah, *Kara Kush*.
▶ **To *The Singapore Grip*:** ▷J.G. Ballard, *Empire of the Sun*; Timothy Mo, *An Insular Possession*.

FAULKNER, William • *(1897–1962)*
US novelist and short-story writer.

READ ON ⟩

Faulkner's work deals obsessively with a single theme: the moral degeneracy of the US Deep South. His characters are the descendants of the cotton barons of the time before the Civil War, and of the slaves who worked for them. The whites live in crumbling mansions, dress in finery handed down from previous generations and bolster their sagging self-esteem with snobbery, racism and drink. The

● *Sartoris* (about the family of a Southern Civil War general coming to terms with defeat); *Intruder in the Dust* (a comparatively sunny book about an

blacks either fawn, as if slavery had never been abolished, or seethe in decaying slums on the edge of town. The air itself seems tainted: despair, lust, introversion and murder clog people's minds. It is a society without hope or comfort, and Faulkner describes it in a series of moral horror stories, compulsive and merciless.

THE SOUND AND THE FURY · *(1929)*

The novel's theme is how moral decadence overwhelms two generations of the white Compson family. We see a brother and sister, Caddy and Quentin, growing up as bright, happy adolescents, full of hope for the future, only to fall victims to the family taint and spiral into incest, nymphomania and suicide. One of their brothers, Jason, a morose bully, succeeds his father as head of the family and becomes a miser and a tyrant; their other brother Benjy has a mental age of two. In the second half of the book we see the corruption threatening to engulf Caddy's and Quentin's incestuous daughter, and her attempts to break free from the family curse. Large sections of the book are told as first-person narratives, by Caddy, Jason, Quentin and – eerily, a tour de force of writing, demanding concentration in the reader –the idiot Benjy. A final strand of claustrophobia is added by the Compsons' negro servants: watching, always-present, like the chorus of a particularly fraught Greek tragedy.

Faulkner's short stories are in two fat volumes, Collected Stories *and* Uncollected Stories. *His main Southern novels, a series set in the imaginary Yoknapatawpha County, Mississippi, are* Sartoris, Absalom, Absalom!, The Unvanquished *and the trilogy* The Hamlet, The Town *and* The Mansion. *His other books include* Intruder in the Dust, The Sound and the Fury, Light in August, The Rievers *and two books in experimental styles,* As I Lay Dying *and* Requiem for a Nun.

FIELDING, Henry · *(1707–54)*
British novelist and playwright.

Fielding's first successes were with satirical stage comedies: *Rape upon Rape* (a farce) and *The Tragedy of Tom Thumb* (a parody of melodramatic tragedy). But his plays were too political for the authorities, who closed them down. He turned to fiction, announcing that he meant to write an English equivalent of *Don Quixote*. His books are life-stories, involving charming young people in a series of escapades as they journey from country-house to inn, from farmyard to theatre-box, from law-court to bedroom,

adolescent awakening to adulthood).

▶ **Good Deep South follow-ups:** ▷Carson McCullers, *The Ballad of the Sad Café*; William Styron, *Lie Down in Darkness*; Harper Lee, *To Kill a Mocking Bird*; Tenessee Williams, *Short Stories*.

▶ **More cheerful:** ▷Eudora Welty, *Delta Wedding*; Calder Willingham, *Eternal Fire*.

▶ **Good follow-ups on the theme of the degenerate, collapsing family:** ▷Thomas Mann, *Buddenbrooks*; Giuseppi Tomaso di Lampedusa, *The Leopard*; ▷Ivy Compton-Burnett, *Mothers and Sons*.

▶ **Good stylistic follow-ups:** ▷James Joyce, *Ulysses*; ▷Virginia Woolf, *To the Lighthouse*.

READ ON ▷

● *Joseph Andrews* (a parody of the heroine-in-moral-danger novels of ▷Samuel Richardson, the story of a young man so beautiful that every woman he meets longs to entice him into bed, and so innocent that

gathering experience and outwitting would-be predators at every step. Fielding's novels are long and leisurely: it is as if he is taking a stroll through English society, high and low, and everything he sees or hears reminds him of an anecdote, genial, unhurried and preposterous.

TOM JONES • *(1749)*

Tom Jones is a foundling brought up by kindly Squire Allworthy. He is a personable, amorous young man, and his immorality finally makes Allworthy send him into the world to seek his fortune. The novel tells Tom's adventures, in and out of bed, as he wanders through England enjoying life as it comes, torn by the thought of his true-love Sophia Western, but still ready to be seduced by every pretty girl he meets. The story is told in short chapters, like extended anecdotes, and Fielding keeps breaking off to address the reader directly, telling jokes, pointing morals and commenting on the life and manners of the time.

Fielding's other novels are Joseph Andrews *and* Amelia. A Journey from This World to the Next *and* The Life and Death of Jonathan Wild the Great *are short, savage satires: the second, for example, treats a notorious, real-life highwayman as if he were an epic hero.* Journal of a Voyage to Lisbon *is a fascinating travel-diary about crossing the Bay of Biscay in a leaky, storm-tossed ship.*

he notices neither this nor the more dangerous pitfalls of his path through life).
▶ Bob Coleman, *The Later Adventures of Tom Jones* (a 1986 sequel to *Tom Jones*, taking Tom to colonial America, where he is embroiled not only in love-affairs but in the War of Independence). Apuleius, *The Golden Ass* (in the ▷Robert Graves translation). Miguel de Cervantes Saavedra, *Don Quixote*. ▷Daniel Defoe, *Moll Flanders*. ▷Laurence Sterne, *Tristram Shandy*.
▶ **Later books in a similarly relaxed, satirical and biographical vein:** ▷H.G. Wells, *Kipps*; ▷Thomas Mann, *Confessions of Felix Krull*; ▷Mary McCarthy, *Birds of America*; ▷Saul Bellow, *The Adventures of Augie March*.

THE FILM BUSINESS

Dirk Bogarde, *West of Sunset*
▷Len Deighton, *Close-up*
▷Peter De Vries, *The Prick of Noon*
H.R.F. Keating, *Filmi, Filmi, Inspector Ghote*
▷Frederic Raphael, *California Time*
Terry Southern, *Blue Movie*
▷Nathanael West, *The Day of the Locust*
Donald Westlake, *Who Stole Sassi Manoon?*

FITZGERALD, F. Scott (Francis Scott) •
(1896–1940)
US novelist and short-story writer.

In the USA of the 1920s the earnestness which had been needed to win the first world war was replaced by giddy exhilaration. Jazz, bootleg liquor, drugs and sex seemed to be not merely pleasures, but symbols of a new, liberated age – and the fact that that age was clearly doomed, that the dancing would end in tears, gave every party, every spending-spree, an edge of extra excitement, as if people were roller-skating on the brink of the abyss. Fitzgerald, rich, handsome, athletic and talented, not only wrote about this doomed high society, but was one of its leaders. In the 1930s, when the inevitable reckoning came – the Great Depression was parallelled in Fitzgerald's life by his wife's madness and his own alcoholism and bankruptcy – his books not unnaturally turned sour and sad. But his 1920s stories and novels told the legend of the 'jazz age' with such glittering force that it is easy, now, to believe that all America, and not just a few thousand sophisticates, lived like that.

THE GREAT GATSBY • *(1925)*
In a millionaire community on Long Island, the enigmatic bachelor Gatsby gives huge all-night parties at his mansion, orgies of dancing, drugs and sex, the season's most fashionable events. His fascinated neighbour, the book's narrator Nick Carraway, makes friends with him and begins unravelling the secrets of his personality. Carraway's intervention triggers revelations about Gatsby's criminal past, and a love-affair between Gatsby and the wife of a wealthy oaf, Tom Buchanan; these in turn lead to further tragedy. At the end of the book Carraway sits alone outside Gatsby's deserted house, reflecting on the emptiness of the lives he has just described.

Fitzgerald's 1920s novels are This Side of Paradise, The Beautiful and Damned *and* The Great Gatsby. Tender is the Night, *bitterly autobiographical, describes the life of an alcoholic writer and his insane wife on the French Riviera, and the unfinished* The Last Tycoon *is a satire on the Hollywood for which he wrote rubbish to earn money in his last desperate months of life.* Tales of the Jazz Age *and* Taps at Reveille *are collections of short stories.*

READ ON ▷

● *The Beautiful and Damned* (about the doomed marriage of two bright young things, leaders of jazz-age society: a book given ferocious ironical point for today's readers by what we know of the decay to come in Fitzgerald's own marriage).
▶ ▷Evelyn Waugh, *Vile Bodies*. ▷Anthony Powell, *Afternoon Men*. Anita Loos, *Gentlemen Prefer Blondes*. Ronald Firbank, *Valmouth*. Vita Sackville West, *The Edwardians*. Andrew Sinclair, *The Breaking of Bumbo*. Martin Amis, *Success* applies Fitzgerald's tone of hopeless, cynical black farce to a much later 'doomed' generation: our own, and ▷William Thackeray, *Vanity Fair* takes a similar view of 19th-century English middle-class society.

FLAUBERT, Gustave • *(1821–80)*
French novelist.

Many of Flaubert's contemporary writers – even such 'realists' as ▷Balzac and ▷Dickens – believed that 'fiction' involved larger-than-life characters, events or emotions. Flaubert's ambition, by contrast, was to hold up a mirror to ordinary people in humdrum situations, to take the boring events of commonplace lives and make them interesting. He also avoided heightened language, wit, irony and the other devices novelists used to enliven their narrative. He worked to make his prose evenly-paced and unobtrusive, taking its tensions and climaxes from the flow of events themselves. In modern times, similar techniques have been used in 'fly-on-the-wall' TV documentaries, where a camera-crew records unscripted scenes from daily life.

MADAME BOVARY • *(1857)*
Emma, a romantic and foolish young woman, dreams of being swept away on clouds of ecstasy, either by a handsome lover or into the arms of the Church. She marries a small-town doctor, and finds the routine of provincial life stifling and unfulfilling. She tries to bring excitement into her life by flirting, and is gradually trapped in pathetic and grubby love-affairs, stealing from her husband to pay for her ever more eccentric whims. In the end, destroyed by her inability to live up to her own dreams, she kills herself – and everyone else's life goes on as if she had never existed.

Flaubert's novels of ordinary French life are Madame Bovary, Sentimental Education *(L'Éducation sentimentale) and the unfinished* Bouvard and Pécuchet. Salammbô *applies the same techniques to a story of the Carthage of Hannibal's time, to bizarre effect, as if an archaeological treatise had been jumbled up with the script for a Hollywood epic film.* The Temptation of St Anthony *seeks to describe all the temptations, of flesh, spirit and will, which might assail a devout Catholic believer;* Three Stories *contains 'A Simple Heart', one of the most moving of all Flaubert's works.*

FLEMING, Ian • *(1908–64)*
British novelist.

Fleming's James Bond books are like comic strips for adults: Bond is a super-hero who saves the world from spectacularly nasty, psychopathic master-criminals. Bond

---

READ ON ▷

● *Sentimental Education* (about a young man who tries, like Emma Bovary, to spice his boring life with grand passions, and fails. A secondary strand in the book is the political situation leading up to the 1848 revolution – something as busy and sterile, in Flaubert's opinion, as his hero's attempts to find meaning in existence).
▶ ▷Italo Svevo, *A Life.* ▷Arnold Bennett, *Hilda Lessways.* ▷Joseph Heller, *Something Happened.* ▷Elizabeth Taylor, *A Wreath of Roses.* ▷Iris Murdoch, *Under the Net.* ▷R.K. Narayan, *The English Teacher,* though set in a society (provincial India) and a period (the 1950s) remote from *Madame Bovary,* and less than a quarter as long, magnificently matches Flaubert's insight into the way that the joys and sorrows of small lives, no less than large, can tear the heart.

READ ON ▷

● *From Russia With Love.*
▶ In the 1960s, until

wins through by a mixture of supreme physical prowess and bizarre, Batmanish technology which turns every fountain-pen into a two-way radio and every watch or shoe-lace into an arsenal of deadly weapons. Adult tastes are catered for less by psychological insight or intellectual depth than by frequent sex-scenes (Bond, as well as everything else, is a super-stud) and by laconic, hardboiled wit. In everything but plot – over-the-top technology, larky dialogue, high-gloss violence – the Bond films give the exact flavour of Fleming's books.

GOLDFINGER • (1959)
Auric Goldfinger has two obsessions: gold and power. He plans to smash the vaults of Fort Knox with a nuclear missile and use the stolen gold to finance world domination. Only Bond can stop him – and the book shows in deadpan, second-by-second detail how he does it.

Other Bond novels include Moonraker, Thunderball, From Russia With Love, Diamonds are Forever, Dr No, On Her Majesty's Secret Service, You Only Live Twice *and* The Man With the Golden Gun. Octopussy *is a collection of short stories.*

FOLLETT, Ken • (born 1949)
British novelist.

Follett's novels are fast-action thrillers, many with industrial-espionage or wartime themes. His books include *The Bear Raid* (about stock-market espionage), *Storm Island/ The Key to Rebecca* (a fight for survival on an uninhabited island during the second world war) and *The Man from St Petersburg* (about the secret negotiations between the powers before the first world war, and moving, with biting social relevance, from scenes set in the London slums to the whispers and backstabbings of an opulent Imperial court).

FORD, Ford Madox • (1873–1939)
British novelist and non-fiction writer.

Although Ford produced books of all kinds, from biographies to historical novels (*The Fifth Queen*, a Tudor trilogy), he is best remembered for *Parade's End* and *The Good Soldier*. *The Good Soldier* (1915) is a ▷Jamesian story about two couples who meet in a German hotel and become emotionally and sexually entwined, with devastating results for both themselves and the innocent young ward of one of them. The four novels of *Parade's End*

▷Deighton and ▷Le Carré took the spy-story in a different direction, there were a million Bond imitations and spoofs, of which some of the jolliest are by John Gardner, Fleming's official successor as chronicler of Bond. Leslie Charteris, *The Saint Goes On,* and his other 1930s Saint books, share Fleming's blend of fast action and affable wit.
► **More recent follow-ups:** ▷Robert Ludlum, *The Matarese Circle*; Joe Poyer, *The Chinese Agenda.*

READ ON ▷

► Palma Harcourt, *A Matter of Conscience.* Clive Egleton, *Troika.* George Markstein, *Soul Hunters.*

READ ON ▷

► Vita Sackville-West, *The Edwardians.* Isabel Colegate, *The Shooting Party.* ▷C.P. Snow, *Strangers and Brothers.* ▷Kazuo Ishiguro, *An Artist of The Floating World*

(1924–8) tell how a country landowner, a young man rooted in the social and moral attitudes of the past, is forced by experience (as an officer in the first world war and as a reluctant participant in the freer sexual atmosphere of the post-war years) to slough off the skin of Victorian morality and come to terms, a dozen years later than everyone else, with 20th-century values.

(setting the 'coming-to-terms' theme in post-war Japan). Lynne Reid Banks, *Casualties* (set in present-day Holland, among survivors of wartime nazi persecution). Richard Aldington, *The Hero*. Frank Swinnerton *(Nocturne; Young Felix; Harvest Comedy)* and Elizabeth M. Roberts *(The Time of Man; My Heart and My Flesh)* are novelists much like Ford, and almost equally neglected.

FORESTER, C.S. (Cecil Scott) •
(1899–1966)
British novelist.

Forester is best-known for his 'Hornblower' novels, about a career officer in the British navy of Nelson's time. The books are rich in the detail of life on wooden fighting ships, and the historical background is meticulous; Forester however gives Hornblower 20th-century sensibilities (he is for example sickened by floggings and horrified by the brutality of war) which both flesh him out as a character and draw the reader into the story. The Hornblower series has overshadowed Forester's other books, which include two superb novels set during the Napoleonic Wars (*Death to the French*; *The Gun*), the psychological crime stories *Payment Deferred* and *Plain Murder*, and the comedy-thriller *The African Queen*, memorably filmed in the 1950s with Katharine Hepburn and Humphrey Bogart.

BROWN ON RESOLUTION • *(1929)*
This tense thriller is about a man captured by an enemy ship during the first world war and taken to the remote island of Resolution, where he escapes and tries, single-handed, to hinder the refitting of the warship before he himself can be tracked down and killed.

The core of the Hornblower series is a trilogy of books (The Happy Return, Flying Colours, Ship of the Line) *often published together as* Captain Horatio Hornblower. *Other books in the series fill in details of Hornblower's*

> READ ON

● *The African Queen* (about a prissy missionary and a rough-diamond ship's captain who take a leaky old boat full of dynamite downriver in second-world-war Africa to blow up an enemy convoy – and fall in love on the way).
▶ **To Forester's thrillers:** ▷Geoffrey Household, *Watcher in the Shadows*; ▷Graham Greene, *A Gun for Sale/This Gun for Hire.*
▶ **To the Hornblower books:** Bernard Cornwell, *Sharpe's Honour* (one of a series about an army officer at the time of the Peninsular War); Alexander Kent, *Richard Bolitho,*

career, tracing his adventures over a quarter of a century.
Typical titles are Mr Midshipman Hornblower, Hornblower and the Atropos, Hornblower in the West Indies
and Lord Hornblower.

FORSTER, E.M. (Edward Morgan) •
(1879–1970)
British novelist.

All Forster's novels were written in the 1900s (though *A
Passage to India* was not published until 1924), and all are
concerned with the crippling emotional reticence he considered typical of the Edwardian age. Outwardly extrovert and
competent, the Edwardians (Forster thought) were afraid of
intimacy. They replaced it with 'manners', and often even
members of the same family, even husbands and wives,
were inhibited from showing towards each other the kind of
genuine feelings they revealed towards God, the flag or
their pampered pets. Forster's plots all turn on the disastrous results of emotional inexperience, of people blunder-
ing about in each other's sensibilities. In *Where Angels
Fear to Tread* an Edwardian family's inability to believe
that an Italian can have true paternal feelings for his baby
leads to a doomed expedition to Italy to kidnap the child. In
Howards End a note from one friend to another, confessing
love (in fact one snatched kiss in a garden) leads to a hurri-
cane of emotional misunderstanding and disapproval which
involves a dozen people and three generations. The central
character in *The Longest Journey* tries to 'connect' emotionally with his newly-discovered, no-good step-brother,
and in the process destroys first his marriage and then himself. Forster, himself an emotional introvert (a self-depre-
cating homosexual), offers no solutions. But few writers
have better described the problem: his intuition for emotional nuance and his compelling characterisation (especially of women), give his books fascination despite their
narrow focus.

Midshipman (Kent also
writes modern naval
adventures under his
real name, Douglas
Reeman: a good
example is *Winged
Escort).* George
Macdonald Fraser,
Flashman and its
sequels turn the whole
idea splendidly upside-
down, telling us the
outrageous grown-up
career of the caddish
bully from *Tom
Brown's Schooldays.*

> **READ ON**

● *A Room With a View*
(about the emotional
awakening of a
snobbish English girl
visiting Italy for the first
time and realising that
there is a real world
beyond Edwardian
English convention).

▶ **To *A Passage to
India*:** ▷Ruth Prawer
Jhabvala, *Heat and
Dust*; Paul Scott, *The
Raj Quartet*; M.M.
Kaye, *The Far
Pavilions.*

▶ **To Forster's work in
general:** ▷Henry
James, *The Wings of
the Dove*; ▷Marcel
Proust, *Within a
Budding Grove* (the
second part of
*Remembrance of
Things Past*); ▷L.P.
Hartley, *The Go-
Between*; ▷Somerset
Maugham, *East and
West.*

E.M. FORSTER

A PASSAGE TO INDIA *(1910s English girl confused by experience of the Raj)*

Rudyard **KIPLING, KIM**
(adventures of Anglo-Indian boy in heyday of Raj)

Timothy **MO, AN INSULAR POSSESSION**
(Blockbusting novel about English imperialism in Hong Kong)

James **BLISH, A CASE OF CONSCIENCE**
(should mineral-rich planet be exploited at expense of native inhabitants' life and culture?)

Kingsley **AMIS, RUSSIAN HIDE AND SEEK**
(life in Orwellian Britain, part of Russian 'evil empire')

IMPERIALISM, GOOD AND BAD

R.K. **NARAYAN, THE VENDOR OF SWEETS**
(devout Hindu in rural India dismayed by son's 'progressive' ways)

V.S. **NAIPAUL, A HOUSE FOR MR BISWAS**
(Indian Hindu in Jamaica caught between dependence on his wife's all-engulfing family and his longing to lead his own life)

L.P. **HARTLEY, THE GO-BETWEEN**
(small boy in 1910s England carries love-messages, emotions he only dimly understands)

Willa **CATHER, MY ANTONIA**
(daughter of 19th-century Bohemian immigrants growing up in rural Nebraska)

Paul **THEROUX, FONG AND THE INDIANS**
(Indian shopkeeper struggling to survive in rural, tribal Africa)

CONFUSED EMOTIONS

Ruth Prawer **JHABVALA, HEAT AND DUST**
(Englishwoman contrasts modern India with her aunt's 1920s experience)

Henry **JAMES, THE AMBASSADORS**
(Rich 1900s Americans take 'culture' to Europe, find it more civilised than they expected)

John **LE CARRÉ, THE PERFECT SPY**
(memoirs of elderly double agent, trying to discover where his loyalty lies)

James **CLAVELL, SHŌGUN**
(American becomes samurai in 17th-century Japan)

BETWEEN TWO WORLDS

Paul **SCOTT, STAYING ON**
(plight of English in India after independence)

Peter **VANSITTART, THREE SIX SEVEN**
(Romanised Britons watching advance of barbarism after 4th century collapse of Roman power)

P.H. **NEWBY, THE PICNIC AT SAKKARA**
(English teacher in 1950s Egypt confused by collapse of British Empire)

Morris **WEST, THE AMBASSADOR**
(US ambassador in Vietnam, appalled by his country's actions there)

Gerald **SEYMOUR, FIELD OF BLOOD**
(undercover SAS officer hunts IRA suspect in present-day Belfast)

TWILIGHT OF EMPIRE

A PASSAGE TO INDIA · (1924)

Adela Quested leaves for India to get to know her fiancé Ronny before she marries him. Her openness of manner, and especially the way she treats Indians as equals, offends the stuffy British community. For her part, she is overwhelmed by India, and her stupefaction leads her to a moment of mental confusion during which she accuses an Indian friend, Dr Aziz, of molesting her on a visit to the Malabar Caves. In court, oppressed by the certainty of the English that Aziz must be guilty, she reruns the events at Malabar in her mind, and suddenly recants. Her behaviour has, however, made apparent the unbridgeable gulf between Indians and English under the Raj, not to mention the lack of communication between 'free spirits' such as herself and her more hidebound contemporaries.

Forster's other fiction includes the novel Maurice *(about a homosexual friendship; written in the 1910s but not published until the 1970s) and three collections of short stories,* Celestial Omnibus, The Eternal Moment *and* The Life to Come.

▶ **Fascinating books showing culture-clash going the other way** (people used to 'abroad' being discomforted by contemporary Britain): ▷Paul Theroux, *The Black House*; ▷P.H. Newby, *Leaning in the Wind*.

FORSYTH, Frederick · *(born 1938)*
British novelist.

Forsyth worked as a BBC reporter and a war correspondent, and his thrillers are as immediate and waffle-free as good news-stories. They often include real people and events; only the hair-trigger tension of his plots makes actuality look tame. In *The Odessa File* (1972), for example, a journalist covering the hunt for a war-criminal uncovers a nazi arms-smuggling conspiracy to help Arab terrorists in Israel. The details are fiction, but the story is as fresh as this morning's news.

Forsyth's novels are The Day of the Jackal, The Devil's Alternative, The Fourth Protocol *and* The Dogs of War. The Shepherd *is a short novel;* No Comebacks *collects short stories.*

READ ON ▷

▶ Walter Wager, *Telefon*. ▷Ted Allbeury, *The Crossing*. Daniel Easterman, *The Seventh Sanctuary*.

FOWLES, John · *(born 1926)*
British novelist.

Obsession and delusion are Fowles' main themes. The deranged hero of *The Collector* 'collects' a pretty girl as one might a butterfly. The heroes of *Daniel Martin* and *Mantissa* are authors deserted by the Muse, one a screenwriter corrupted by success, the other a novelist undergoing crea-

READ ON ▷

● *The Magus* (revised version): about a man trying obsessively to find out if what he thinks he experiences

tive therapy at the hands (and other parts) of a seductive, feminist goddess. *A Maggot*, set in the 18th century, re-works a real-life murder investigation to take in erotic obsession, witchcraft, religious mania and flying saucers. Fowles further blurs the boundary between 'truth' and 'fiction' by using experimental techniques. He shifts between past and present, makes authorial asides and comments, and gives us two, three or half a dozen alternative versions of the same events. As with ▷Durrell, this experimentalism is coupled with ornate prose (sometimes in brilliant imitation of 18th and 19th century styles); few modern best-selling writers offer such a packed experience.

THE FRENCH LIEUTENANT'S WOMAN • *(1969)*

The book's heart is a straightforward 19th-century story about the obsessive love-affair between a rich man and an outcast, the 'French Lieutenant's Woman' of the title. They meet in the seaside town of Lyme Regis; their affair scandalises society; she runs away; he pursues her. Fowles' prose, likewise, is for much of the time straightforward and solid in the 19th-century manner. But he also plays games with the reader. He keeps interrupting the story to tell us things about Lyme Regis (home of Mary Anning the fossil-collector), Darwin, Freudian psychology and the social customs of Victorian London. He claims that he has no idea what will happen next, that this is the characters' story, not his. He supplies alternative endings, so that we can choose our own. These devices give the book an unexpectedness in marked contrast to its sober 19th-century heart – it is as if someone reading us ▷Eliot or ▷Thackeray kept breaking off to perform conjuring tricks.

Apart from novels, Fowles has published a story-collection, The Ebony Tower, *and* The Aristos, *a set of philosophical meditations.*

FRANCIS, Dick • *(born 1920)*
British novelist.

Francis writes brilliantly-paced, characterful thrillers, most of them about blackmail, fraud and revenge among jockeys, owners, trainers, bookies and others involved in the racing business. In *Break In* (1986), for example, champion steeplechaser Kit Fielding sets out to discover why someone is trying to ruin his brother-in-law, the trainer Bobby Allardeck – and at once himself becomes the target of newspaper smears, bribery, entrapment and attempted murder.

is real or fantasy. Much of it involves magic, and takes place on a mysterious Greek island – or seems to, for our perception of 'truth' and 'fiction' is as shifting as the character's.

▶ **To *The French Lieutenant's Woman*:** John Barth, *The Sotweed Factor*; John Berger, *G*; ▷William Golding, *Rites of Passage*; Thornton Wilder, *The Bridge of San Luis Rey*.

▶ **To *The Magus*:** ▷Lawrence Durrell, *The Dark Labyrinth/ Cefalù*; D.M. Thomas, *The White Hotel*.

> **READ ON**

▶ Grant Adamson, *Wild Justice*. ▷Jeffrey Archer, *A Matter of Honour*. Nicholas Freeling, *The Dresden Green*.

Francis' novels include Dead Cert, Blood Sport, Forfeit, Bonecrack, Slay-Ride, Risk, Whip Hand *and* Proof. The Sport of Queens *is autobiography, fascinating about his own racing days.*

FRANKLIN, Miles • *(1879–1954)*
Australian novelist.

'Miles Franklin' was one of the pseudonyms of Stella Miles Franklin. She wrote optimistic tales of pioneer farming life in Australia, in a cheerful, bustling style; her novels are like literary patchwork quilts. Under the name Miles Franklin she is best-known for *My Brilliant Career* (1901), its sequel *My Career Goes Bung* (1946) – the story of a breathlessly enthusiastic adolescent, Sybylla Melvyn, as she learns about life, the arts and love on outback farms and in the big city – and *All That Swagger* (1936), a more serious panorama of outback life. Under a second pseudonym, 'Brent of Bin Bin', Franklin published six lighter novels on the same lines, 'snapshots of ordinary life' modelled on the writings of ▷Mark Twain. Their titles are *Up the Country, Ten Creeks Run, Back to Bool Bool, Cockatoos, Prelude to Waking*, and *Gentlemen at Gyang Gyang*. One editor (Carmen Callil) called her an 'unsophisticated genius', prone to 'ebullient outpourings'; the description is exact.

Franklin's other books under her own name include the novels Some Everyday Folk and Dawn, Old Blastus of Bandicoot *and* Bring the Monkey *and the autobiographical memoir* Childhood at Brindabella. *Under the pseudonym 'Mrs Ogniblat l'Artsau' she published one novel,* The Net of Circumstance.

FREEMANTLE, Brian • *(born 1936)*
British novelist.

As well as his own name, Freemantle uses the pseudonyms Richard Gant and Leslie Street. His books include thrillers (*Goodbye to an Old Friend; Face Me When You Walk Away*) and a series of spoof spy-stories (eg *Clap Hands, Here Comes Charlie*) featuring the amiable down-and-out Charlie Muffin, whose past life and whose character are as fascinating as the missions he undertakes.

| READ ON ⟩ |

▶ ▷Mark Twain, *The Adventures of Tom Sawyer*. H.E. Bates, *The Darling Buds of May*. Betty MacDonald, *The Egg and I*. Laura Ingalls Wilder, *The Little House on the Prairie*.

▶ **Exactly matching Franklin's bouncy, happy style, though its theme and location are entirely different:** ▷Jerome K. Jerome, *Three Men in a Boat*.

| READ ON ⟩ |

▶ ▷Len Deighton, *Horse Under Water*. Roy Lewis, *A Certain Blindness*. Sara Woods, *Cry Guilty*. John Wainwright, *All On a Summer's Day*.

FRIENDS (?) AND NEIGHBOURS
(gossip; bitchiness; one-up-manship)
▷E.F. Benson, *Mapp and Lucia*
▷Peter De Vries, *The Mackerel Plaza*
▷Mrs Gaskell, *Cranford*
▷Sinclair Lewis, *Main Street*
▷Barbara Pym, *A Glass of Blessings*
▷John Updike, *Couples*

The Human Comedy (p 124)

FUTURE SOCIETIES

▷Margaret Atwood, *The Handmaid's Tale*
▷Angela Carter, *The Passion of New Eve*
▷Robert Graves, *Seven Days in New Crete*
▷Aldous Huxley, *Brave New World*
▷Walter M. Miller, *A Canticle for Leibowitz*
▷William Morris, *News from Nowhere*
▷George Orwell, *1984*
▷George Turner, *The Sea and Summer*
▷John Wyndham, *The Chrysalids*

Fantasy Societies (p 73)

G

GALSWORTHY, John • *(1867–1933)*
British novelist and playwright.

In the 1960s an adaptation of Galsworthy's *The Forsyte Saga* was the most popular British TV series ever shown till then. It spawned a thousand imitations – series and books about rich families quarrelling over multi-million pound businesses and living wretched private lives have become a genre in themselves. Some critics say that this is unfair to Galsworthy, who was regarded as a heavyweight writer in his day (of plays as well as novels). But although he intended his first Forsyte book (*The Man of Property*) as a serious novel, as soon as the Forsytes became popular he quite happily extended it into a saga, adding another dozen novels and short stories.

THE FORSYTE SAGA • *(1922)*
This contains three novels and two short stories. Its subject is the way money-making and commercial endeavour atrophy the emotions. Three generations of Forsytes are morally tainted by their family's business success, in particular Soames and his unhappy wife Irene. Every boardroom victory is balanced by a bedroom defeat; children inherit not only wealth, but the poisoned character which goes with it. There is more than a whiff of Victorian moralising about it all: in Galsworthy the bad always end unhappily (and so do the good). But unlike many later family-business sagas, his books offer three-dimensional characters, and he is particularly good at showing the ebb and flow of relationships between the sexes. *To Let*, the third volume of the saga, a Romeo and Juliet story with a devastating final twist, is a fine example of this, one of Galsworthy's most satisfying books.

Apart from the Forsyte books (two trilogies – The Forsyte

READ ON

● *A Modern Comedy.*
▶ ▷Anthony Trollope, *Can You Forgive Her?* (and its sequels: the 'Palliser' family saga). ▷Thomas Mann, *Buddenbrooks* (an equally withering, but jollier, account of the decline of a powerful mercantile family). ▷C.P. Snow, *The Conscience of the Rich* (a moving study of the son of a family dynasty at odds with his parents). ▷Henry James, *The Spoils of Poynton* (a study of property as 'the middle-class deity'). ▷Christina Stead, *House of All Nations.*
▶ **Of the dozens of family-business blockbusters which followed the TV success of *The Forsyte Saga*, the juiciest are** Harold Robbins, *The Adventurers*; ▷Judith Krantz, *Princess Daisy*

Saga; A Modern Comedy – *and the short-story collections* Four Forsyte Stories *and* On Forsyte Change*), Galsworthy's novels include* The Island Pharisee, Fraternity *and the trilogy* End of the Chapter, *a saga about the Charwell family (cousins of the Forsytes).*

GASKELL, Mrs (Elizabeth Cleghorn) •
(1810–65)
British novelist.

For a century after her death, Gaskell was chiefly remembered for a biography of her friend ▷Charlotte Brontë, and for *Cranford*, a gently malicious book about middle-class life in a provincial town. (It reads like a collaboration between ▷Austen and ▷Trollope, without being quite as good as either.) But she was actually a novelist of a far tougher kind. She was a friend of ▷Dickens and ▷Eliot, and shared their interest in social themes, particularly the way men treat women and the plight of the urban poor. She lived in Manchester, and wrote pungently about life among the 'dark Satanic mills' (as Blake had called them) which her southern readers had till then imagined were figments of the revolutionary imagination. Her novels were discussed in Parliament and led to social reform, a result which greatly pleased her. They survive today less as social documents than as powerful stories of people struggling against their environment or the indifference of others.

MARY BARTON • *(1848)*
Mary's father is a mill-hand employed by the unfeeling Henry Carson. He is also a staunch fighter for workers' rights. When the mill-owners ignore their workers' requests for better treatment, the men decide to murder Carson as a warning to his class, and nominate Barton to fire the gun. Mary's beloved Jem Wilson is arrested for the crime, and Mary has to face the agony of proving his innocence by incriminating her father.

Gaskell's novels Ruth, Cousin Phyllis *and* Wives and Daughters *concern the relationship between the sexes.* Sylvia's Lovers, *an unsmiling tale set in 18th-century Whitby, is about a man snatched by the press gang.* Mary Barton *and* North and South *are about class war.* Lois the Witch, *a long short story, is set during the Salem witch-hunts of the 17th century.*

and ▷Barbara Taylor Bradford, *A Woman of Substance.*

> **READ ON** ⟩

● *North and South* (in which a southern minister goes to preach God's word in a northern mill-town, and his wife and daughter become involved in the class-struggle – a concern greatly complicated when the daughter falls in love with a mill-owner's son).

▶ ▷Charlotte Brontë, *Shirley.* ▷Charles Dickens, *Hard Times.* ▷Émile Zola, *Germinal.* ▷Arnold Bennett, *Clayhanger.* ▷D.H. Lawrence, *Sons and Lovers.* ▷Jack London, *The People of the Abyss* (about slum life), David Storey, *Radcliffe* and Upton Sinclair, *The Jungle* carry Gaskell's themes into the 20th century.

▶ Lewis Grassic Gibbon, *A Scots Quair* (partly in Scots dialect, but comprehensible) is a saga of three generations coping with harsh conditions, on West highland crofts and in industrial Glasgow during the 1920s General Strike.

GIDE, André • *(1861–1951)*
French novelist, poet and non-fiction writer.

In Plato's dialogues, Socrates tries to reach the core of a philosophical argument by elimination: each wrong assumption, each false trail is considered and rejected until what is left is 'truth'. Gide admired Plato – his favourite among his own works was *Corydon*, a set of four Platonic dialogues discussing homosexuality – and he used Socrates' methods in his fiction. His heroes seek the truth about themselves, the core of their being, and they do it by considering and rejecting all religious, social, sexual and intellectual conventions. Sometimes a quest results in the happiness of self-knowledge, but often the young men – Gide was not over-interested in young women – find, when they reach the core of themselves, that there is nothing there at all. Gide's contemporaries found his moral stripteases shocking, and condemned him as a pornographer; nowadays the most striking thing about his books is their spare, limpid style, which makes even more startling the things they say.

THE IMMORALIST • *(1902)*
Michel, a young intellectual, nearly dies of tuberculosis, and his brush with death changes his character. He rejects his former convention-ridden life in favour of living each moment for itself, of doing exactly what he pleases. As his personality flowers, that of his beloved wife begins to wither, leaving him to agonise over whether his actions have led to psychic liberation or to a surrender to selfishness.

Gide's other fiction includes Strait is the Gate *(La porte étroite),* The Vatican Cellars, Isabelle, The Pastoral Symphony *(La Symphonie pastorale) and* The Counterfeiters. *His non-fiction works on similar themes include* If it Die *(Si le grain ne meurt),* Et nunc manet in te/Madeleine *and* Journals.

READ ON

● *Strait is the Gate; The Pastoral Symphony. The Vatican Cellars* is a more extrovert, ironic romp involving murder, the kidnapping of the Pope and a frantic chase across Europe. *The Counterfeiters* is about a group of secondary schoolboys in Paris, their adolescent friendships and the adults who initiate them into grown-up life.
▶ **To Gide's short, philosophical books:** ▷Hermann Hesse, *Peter Camenzind*; Joris-Karl Huysmans, *Against Nature*; Frederick Rolfe, *The Desire and Pursuit of the Whole*; ▷Aldous Huxley, *Eyeless in Gaza*.
▶ **To *The Counterfeiters*:** ▷Colette, *A Lesson in Love*; ▷Marcel Proust, *Cities of the Plain* (the fourth part of *Remembrance of Things Past*).
▶ **More modern books on Gidean themes:** ▷Iris Murdoch, *The Flight from the Enchanter*; Ian McEwan, *The Comfort of Strangers*.

GOETHE, Johann Wolfgang von •
(1749–1832)
German writer of novels, poems, plays and non-fiction.

Goethe's genius expressed itself in restless intellectual en-

READ ON

● *The Travels of Wilhelm Meister* takes Meister

ergy: he never heard an idea without wanting to develop it. He took the nearest convenient form – Shakespearean or Greek tragedy, letters, biography – and crammed it with philosophical and political reflections, discussions and suggestions. During his lifetime he was regarded as an innovator, forming European thought; by hindsight he seems rather to have caught ideas in the air – humanism, romanticism, political libertarianism – expanded them and given them wide circulation. Like Shakespeare, he distilled the spirit of his age – and this feeling, the sense that in reading him we are communing with the 18th and early 19th centuries at their sanest and most stimulating, is one of the main pleasures of his work.

THE APPRENTICESHIP OF WILHELM MEISTER ·
(1796)

This enormously long, leisurely novel is the spiritual and moral 'biography' of Wilhelm Meister. As a young man, fascinated by the stage (and by Marianne, an actress), he gives up his business career and runs away to join an acting company. He takes part enthusiastically in their lives, and observes both their sorrows (symbolised by the brutal treatment of Mignon by her trapeze-artist 'protector') and their triumphs (symbolised by a production of Hamlet in which he takes part). He decides that this life – 'the world' – is not for him, and leaves. In the castle of Lothario he experiences both earthly pleasures ('the flesh') and religious conversion ('the spirit') and rejects them. Finally, matured by all his experiences, he decides to devote his life to education, to passing on all he knows, 'the balance that makes a human being', to his young son.

Goethe is best-known for his poetry, and for such plays as Egmont, Iphigenie in Tauris, Götz von Berlichingen/Ironhand *and* Faust. *Apart from* Wilhelm Meister, *his novels are* The Sorrows of Young Werther *and* Elective Affinities.

and his son on a ramble through Europe. They sample every kind of human society, and their experiences make this book a reflection on 'manners' and politics, just as *The Apprenticeship of Wilhelm Meister* dealt with individual human personality. *The Sorrows of Young Werther*, in letter-form, tells the story of a young man tormented by love for his friend's fiancée. *Elective Affinities* is a heartless, amoral book (anticipating ▷Gide) about a married couple each of whom has a love-affair.

► **To Wilhelm Meister:** ▷Miguel de Cervantes Saavedra: *Don Quixote*. ▷Thomas Mann, *The Magic Mountain*.

► **To *Elective Affinities*:** ▷George Eliot, *Daniel Deronda*; ▷Christina Stead, *The Man Who Loved Children*.

► **To *The Sorrows of Young Werther*:** ▷Hermann Hesse, *Gertrud*. Thomas Love Peacock, *Nightmare Abbey* sends up the 'Werther syndrome', the idea that the only way to be a true romantic hero, or a creative artist, is to tell the world every detail of the anguish in your soul.

GOGOL, Nikolai Vasilevich • *(1809–52)*
Russian writer of novels, short stories and plays.

The despair which seems to hover over much Russian fiction was replaced in Gogol by hilarity: he was a 20th-century surrealist ahead of his time, a forerunner of ▷Kafka and Ionesco. His best-known work, the stage-farce *The Government Inspector*, is about a confidence trickster mistaken for a high official by a village of pompous fools. In one of his stories a nose takes on a malign, satirical life independent of its owner's will; in another a man saves for years to buy a new coat, only to be mugged and robbed the first time he wears it. Gogol's preferred form was the short story: he was terrified of writer's block. He struggled for a dozen years to finish his one long book, *Dead Souls*, and in 1852, convinced by a religious adviser that the second (unpublished) half of the book was 'sinful' and that if he went on writing he would go to hell, he burned the manuscript and fasted until he died.

DEAD SOULS • *(1842)*
In 19th-century Russia landowners estimated their wealth not only by the acres they owned, but also by the number of their serfs, or slaves. Chichikov, a confidence-trickster, realises that serfs who die between official censuses are not legally dead until the next census, and so still count as property. He travels the length and breadth of Russia, buying 'dead souls' from landowners, and becomes – on paper at least – one of the wealthiest men in the country. Gogol uses this simple story as the basis for a set of farcical character-studies: he saw the book as a portrait-gallery of contemporary Russia, and filled it with short, self-contained comic episodes. He also wrote, with ironical pointedness, that Chichikov's journey stands for the journey of every human being through life: we move on, never sure of what is coming next, relieved each time that whatever it was we did, we got away with it.

Gogol's most surreal short stories are 'Diary of a Madman', 'Nevski Prospekt', 'The Portrait', 'The Nose' *and* 'The Overcoat'. *His collections* Evenings on a Farm, Mirgorod *and* Arabesques *are more farce than surrealism, short sketches about tongue-tied suitors, credulous peasants and feather-headed, pretty girls.*

GOLDING, William • *(born 1911)*
British novelist.

From his first novel (*Lord of the Flies*, 1954, about choir-

> **READ ON**

▶ Gogol's sinister brilliance is matched in the short stories of ▷Kafka, Saki and Roald Dahl; his gentler comic stories are like ▷Chekhov's.
▶ **Good follow-ups to Dead Souls:** Ivan Goncharov, *Oblomov* (about a man so alienated from the world that he decides to spend the rest of his life in bed); ▷Franz Kafka, *America*; ▷Jaroslav Hašek, *The Good Soldier Švejk*; Bernard Malamud, *The Fixer*; Miguel de Cervantes Saavedra, *Don Quixote*.

> **READ ON**

● *The Inheritors* (a

LORD OF THE FLIES (*choirboys lost on desert island revert to satanic evil, humanity's dark side*)

Daniel **DEFOE, ROBINSON CRUSOE**
(*18th-century shipwrecked sailor builds new life on desert island*)

Jonathan **SWIFT, GULLIVER'S TRAVELS**
(*18th-century sailor tries to teach European 'culture' in fantasy lands he visits*)

SURVIVING

James Vance **MARSHALL, WALKABOUT**
(*English children marooned in Australian outback, taught survival by Aboriginal boy*)

Susan **HILL, I'M THE KING OF THE CASTLE**
(*devil-child, jealous of rival, torments the life from him*)

Stephen **KING, CARRIE**
(*bullied girl in junior high school uses Devil's power to take revenge*)

EVIL AND CHILDREN

John **WYNDHAM, THE MIDWICH CUCKOOS**
(*alien race seeks to capture England by breeding race of hyper-intelligent, soulless children*)

Henry **JAMES, THE TURN OF THE SCREW**
(*neurotic governess tries to protect two innocent charges against half-sensed, wholly evil ghosts*)

Fay **WELDON, THE HEART OF ENGLAND**
(*evil forces in Glastonbury countryside interfere with yuppie lives*)

John **UPDIKE, THE WITCHES OF EASTWICK**
(*bored Connecticut housewives play with witchcraft – and raise the Devil*)

THE DEVIL

James **BLISH, BLACK EASTER**
(*nuclear scientist enlists Devil's help in bringing about Armageddon*)

Patrick **WHITE, VOSS**
(*half-crazy explorer leads doomed 19th-century expedition into heart of Australia*)

Joseph **CONRAD, HEART OF DARKNESS**
(*African jungle used as metaphor for the evil in humanity*)

THE WILDERNESS

C.S. **LEWIS, PERELANDRA**
(*battle for survival – and against unrelenting evil – on the empty planet Venus*)

Brian **MOORE, THE BLACK ROBE**
(*17th-century Jesuit among 17th-century Indians: bloody, hopeless culture-clash*)

boys reverting to savagery after being marooned on a desert island) onwards, Golding has explored the dark side of human nature. He believes that homo sapiens is corrupt, that we destroy more than we create, that we are devilish without redemption. But instead of baldly stating this philosophy, he dresses it in allegories of the most unusual and fantastical kind. He pictures the devil engulfing not only choirboys on an island, but also (in other novels) a drowning sailor, a tribe of neanderthal people, the dean of a medieval cathedral, a boy growing up in 1960s Britain, and a group of 18th-century people sailing towards Australia. He evokes these situations with absolute conviction: few writers are better at suggesting the feel, taste, smell and sound of things, the texture of experience.

THE SPIRE · (1964)

Inspired by a vision, medieval Dean Jocelin commissions for his cathedral a 400-foot spire. He intends it as proof of human aspiration towards God; his enemies see it as a symbol of vanity, the devil's work; the master-builder points out that as the cathedral's foundations are inadequate, the tower will bring the whole building crashing down. Jocelin over-rides all objections, the work proceeds – Golding gives fascinating, vertigo-inducing detail of medieval building techniques – and the higher the spire rises the more people are destroyed. In the end the struggle between God and the devil takes over Jocelin's own self. In truly medieval manner, his brain and body become a battleground, and the issue moves from the tower to questions of his own moral integrity and saintliness.

Golding's novels are Lord of the Flies, Pincher Martin, Free Fall, The Spire, The Pyramid, Darkness Visible, Rites of Passage *and its sequel* Close Quarters, *and* The Paper Men. The Scorpion God *is a collection of three long stories, one based on his stage-comedy* The Brass Butterfly, *about a crazy inventor trying to interest a decadent Roman ruler of Egypt in steam power.*

brilliantly-imagined story of the coming of homo sapiens, seen from the standpoint of the gentle ape-people they exterminate).
▶ ▷Hermann Hesse, *Narziss and Goldmund* (which parallels both the good/evil theme and the medieval craft-background of *The Spire*). John Barth, *Giles Goat-boy* (a fantasy, partly satirical, about a professor who brings a child up with no company but goats, trying to avoid contaminating him with human original sin).
▷Anthony Burgess, *Earthly Powers*.
Umberto Eco, *The Name of the Rose*.

GOOD AND EVIL
(the Devil at large)

Mikhail Bulgakov, *The Master and Margarita*
▷John Fowles, *A Maggot*
▷Stephen King, *Carrie*
Ian McEwan, *The Comfort of Strangers*
Neville Shulman, *Exit of a Dragonfly*
▷I.B. Singer, *Satan in Goray*
▷John Updike, *The Witches of Eastwick*

▷Fay Weldon, *The Life and Loves of a She-Devil*

Something Nasty . . . (p 224)

GORDIMER, Nadine • *(1923)*
South African novelist and short-story writer.

Gordimer makes life in South Africa (and especially among the tormented liberal whites who are her main characters) an objective background for subjective choice. Her concerns are the diversity of human nature, and the way our moral and psychological personality is revealed in what we do. She also, magnificently, evokes the vastness and beauty of Africa. Like other South African writers (notably Alan Paton and Laurens van der Post) she gives the continent a kind of mystical identity; its indigenous inhabitants understand this completely, but it gives the incoming whites (who can only dimly perceive it) an unsettling sense of their own inadequacy, as if they are made second-class citizens not by other people's laws but by the very place they live in.

A SPORT OF NATURE • *(1987)*
From adolescence rich, white Hillela is dominated by politics and sex, and combines the two: sex is a source of power, politics give orgasmic satisfaction. She is attracted by, and attracts, powerful men of all professions and races – and progressively moves out of the orbit of whites to a leading position in the black revolutionary movement. The book ends with the success of the revolution, the establishment of majority rule – and with doubts sown in the reader's mind about Hillela herself. Has she really identified as wholly with the blacks as she hoped, or does she remain the 'sport of nature', or freak, of the book's title?

Gordimer's other novels are The Lying Days, A World of Strangers, Occasion for Loving, The Late Bourgeois World, A Guest of Honour, Burger's Daughter, The Conservationist *and* July's People. *Her story-collections include* Not For Publication, Livingstone's Companions *and* A Soldier's Embrace.

READ ON ⟩

● *The Late Bourgeois World* (a grim study of white liberals in a police state. Max, tortured into betraying his friends, commits suicide, and Liz (his divorced wife) is left to choose between continuing in bourgeois complacency, doing nothing about the situation but wring her hands, and joining the black revolutionary movement).

▶ André Brink, *Rumours of Rain* (about redneck Afrikanerdom). J.M. Coetzee, *In the Heart of the Country*. David Caute, *News From Nowhere* (about a liberal journalist covering the events which led to the establishment of Zimbabwe). ▷Isabel Allende, *Of Love and Shadows*. ▷John Le Carré, *The Little Drummer Girl*. Alan Paton, *Cry, the Beloved Country* (a moving book about ancient Zulu culture and the discord brought by invading whites; it is mirrored, from a different point of view, by ▷Chinua Achebe, *Things Fall Apart*).

GORKY, Maxim • *(1868–1936)*
Russian writer of novels, short stories and plays.

'Gorky' (bitter) is the pen name of Aleksei Maksimovich Peshkov – and in view of his childhood, few names could have been more appropriate. He was left to fend for himself at the age of eight, and spent his childhood as a barge-hand, washer-up, thief, beggar, tramp and journalist. This 'apprenticeship', as he called it, affected the style and content of his writing. He saw himself as a colleague and heir of ▷Dostoevsky and ▷Tolstoy, and aimed to write the same kind of panoramic, allegorical works as theirs. But whereas their world was that of landowners and the bourgeoisie, his was one of serfs, vagabonds, criminals and other members of what he called society's 'lower depths'. He despised the middle class, and wrote with contempt of their dependence on money, gentility and religion, the very forces which were destroying them. His preoccupations led him to friendship with Lenin, and to enthusiastic support for the 1917 revolution. Many of his post-1917 books are grandiose and propagandist, and his revolutionary sympathies have diminished his reputation in capitalist countries. But his early work places him squarely in the company of the great 19th-century writers he admired.

FOMA GORDEEV • *(1899)*
Foma, the son of an illiterate barge-owner who has made a fortune conveying goods on the Volga, has been brought up in his godfather's cultured, bourgeois home. His father tries to take him into the business, to educate him in the ways of the world, and for a time Foma thrives. But when the old man dies and he inherits, his head is turned and he lives a life of increasing debauchery, ending up as a lunatic and a drunkard. He is a man without identity: he takes on the moral colouring of the society around him, and is destroyed.

Gorky is known for plays (such as The Lower Depths *and* Smug Citizens*) as well as for prose fiction. His novels include* Mother, Foma Gordeev, The Artamonov Affair, The Life of Klim Samgin *and the post-revolutionary tetralogy* Bystander, The Magnet, Other Fires *and* The Spectre. *His short stories are headed by* 'Twenty-six Men and a Girl', *which normally gives its name to collections. His best-known work, in or out of the USSR, is the autobiographical trilogy* My Childhood, My Apprenticeship *and* My Universities.

READ ON >

● *Yegor Bulitchev and Others* (a black comedy about a dying merchant fawned on by hypocrites who anticipate rich pickings when he dies). *My Childhood* (the first volume of Gorky's autobiography, a scalding account of his life as a barge-hand, the background to Foma Gordeev).
▶ ▷Fyodor Dostoevsky, *The Gambler* (a harsh account of aristocratic folly and obsession in Tsarist Russia, the kind of decadence Gorky vociferously denounced). Jean Genet, *Querelle of Brest* (the story of a boy's brutal upbringing among criminals and gansters in France between the two world wars). ▷Jerome Weidman, *I Can Get It For You Wholesale* (about a young man making his way by guile in the business world of post-Depression New York – and the moral disintegration of character which is the price he pays).

GRAHAM, Winston • *(born 1911)*
British novelist.

Although Graham has written books of many kinds, from historical romances to thrillers, he is best-known for the brooding, atmospheric 'Poldark' saga, about feuding families in 18th and 19th century Cornwall. The first Poldark book was *Ross Poldark/Renegade*, and the series includes *Demelza*, *Jeremy Poldark*, *Warleggan/The Last Gamble* and *The Black Moon*. Graham's best-known thriller is *Greek Fire*.

READ ON ▷

▶ ▷Emily Brontë, *Wuthering Heights*. Arthur Quiller-Couch('Q'), *Troy Town*. ▷Daphne Du Maurier, *My Cousin Rachel*. R.D. Blackmore, *Lorna Doone*.

GRASS, Günter • *(born 1927)*
German writer of novels, plays and non-fiction.

In his twenties Grass worked as a graphic artist, stage designer and jazz musician; he took up writing full-time only after his novel *The Tin Drum* was a best-seller, when he was 32. Politics are the main subject of his books: he grapples with what has happened in Germany over the last half-century, and what is happening now. He uses a framework of absurdity, blending real events with wild black fantasy, collapsing history (so that time is like a well from which you draw not systematically but at random), and making his characters allegorical figures like the people in cartoons. The leading character in *The Tin Drum* (1959), for example, symbolising the German people, is a child who chooses to stop growing at the age of three, and who spends forty years banging a toy drum and giggling as the procession of nazism and post-war reconstruction passes by. For Grass, the human condition is 'absurd': not only ridiculous but morally and philosophically out of focus. His books offer no solutions, but they point out the problems with enormous, malicious glee.

THE FLOUNDER • *(1977)*
The wife and husband from a Grimm fairy-tale move through the entire history of the human race, popping up in this period or that, playing each role by the conventions of its time, and endlessly, affably arguing about gender dominance. They are aided or hindered by a talking fish from the same fairy-tale: it takes now her side, now his. Finally the fish is ordered to defend itself before a late 20th-century feminist tribunal, and the whole male/female business is thrashed out in a hearing as preposterous as the trial in Alice in Wonderland. The fact that this book is about sexual rather than German politics makes it one of Grass's most accessible novels to non-German readers, and it is also wonderfully enlivened with puns, poems, satires

READ ON ▷

▶ *The Tin Drum* is the most accessible of the 'Danzig' novels, and although its theme (nazism) gives it a harsher tone than *The Flounder*, it is equally hilarious and bizarre.

▶ Other books similarly reinventing the human race, tossing all human knowledge and invention into a single fantastic melting-pot: ▷Thornton Wilder, *The Eighth Day*; ▷Kurt Vonnegut, *Galápagos*; ▷J.G. Ballard, *The Unlimited Dream Company*; ▷Michèle Roberts, *The Book of Mrs Noah*.

and recipes. The pleasures of human life have not had such a going-over since ▷Rabelais.

*Grass's other novels include the 'Danzig trilogy' (*The Tin Drum, Dog Years *and* Local Anaesthetic*), From the Diary of a Snail, Cat and Mouse, The Meeting at Telgte, Headbirths *and* The Rat.

GRAVES, Robert • *(1895–1985)*
British novelist, poet and non-fiction writer.

Graves' main interests were myth and poetry. He wrote a best-selling version of the Greek myths, a controversial account of the Bible stories as myth, and *The White Goddess* (1948–52), a study of poetic inspiration. Throughout his life he composed poetry (much of it autobiographical), and his love-poems in particular are much admired. He claimed that his novels were potboilers, written to finance 'real' work, but their quality and craftsmanship belie this description. Most are historical, reimagining characters of the past – from the author of the *Odyssey* to Jesus – as people with markedly 20th-century sensibilities, able to view the events of their own lives, as it were, with hindsight. His books are like psychological documentaries, as if we are looking directly into his characters' minds.

I, CLAUDIUS • *(1934)*
This novel and its sequel *Claudius the God* purport to be the autobiography of the fourth Roman emperor. A spastic and an epileptic, he is regarded by everyone as a fool and ignored; he thus survives the myriad political and dynastic intrigues of the first 50 years of the Roman empire, the reigns of his three dangerous predecessors. He is finally made emperor himself, in a palace coup – and proceeds to rule with a blend of wisdom, guile and ruthlessness which he describes with fascinated relish. The story ends – typically for Graves – with a real document, an account by a Roman satirist of the 'Pumpkinification of Claudius', the arrival of the stammering, limping fool of an emperor in Olympus, home of the gods and of his own terrifying, deified relatives.

Graves' other novels include Count Belisarius *(set in 6th-century Byzantium),* Sergeant Lamb of the Ninth *and* Proceed, Sergeant Lamb *(about the American War of Independence),* Wife to Mr Milton *(set in Puritan England, and written in a brilliant pastiche of 17th-century prose),* Homer's Daughter *(set in prehistoric Greece), and* King Jesus *(about the life and death of Christ).* Seven Days in

READ ON ▷

● *The Golden Fleece/ Hercules My Shipmate* (a novelised account of the expedition of Jason and the Argonauts to find the Golden Fleece, with ingenious, rational explanations of such magic events as the escape from the Clashing Rocks, the yoking of bronze bulls and the sowing of serpents' teeth).

▶ **To *I, Claudius*:** ▷Mary Renault, *The King Must Die*; Marguerite Yourcenar, *Memoirs of Hadrian*; Naomi Mitchison, *The Corn King and the Spring Queen*; Joan Grant, *Winged Pharaoh*.

▶ **Classical works, close to Graves for exuberance of imagination:** Herodotus, *Histories*; Petronius, *Satyricon*.

▶ **Books of similar gusto, on non-classical subjects:** Frederick Rolfe, *Hadrian the Seventh* (about a waspish inadequate – not even a priest – who is elected Pope); Augusto Roa Bastos, *I The Supreme* (the fantasy-

Robert **GRAVES**

Norman **MAILER, ANCIENT EVENINGS**
(memories of charioteer of warrior-pharaoh Rameses II)

Gore **VIDAL, CREATION**
('memoirs' of Persian diplomat who knew Socrates, Buddha and Confucius)

Joan **GRANT, WINGED PHARAOH**
(Grant describes her own previous existence in ancient Egypt)

Joseph **HELLER, GOD KNOWS**
('memoirs' of Old Testament King David)

Marguerite **YOURCENAR, MEMOIRS OF HADRIAN**
(reflections of 14th Roman Emperor and philosopher)

Hilda **DOOLITTLE ('H.D.'), HEDYLUS**
(Samos, 3rd century BC: ex-courtesan, lover and poet-son meditate delicately on life, love, the arts and politics)

John **ARDEN, SILENCE AMONG THE WEAPONS**
('memoirs' of actor's agent mixed up with Roman dictator Sulla in 1st century BC)

Peter **VANSITTART, THREE SIX SEVEN**
(twilight of Roman Britain, late 4th century)

Anthony **BURGESS, THE KINGDOM OF THE WICKED**
(Luke, Paul and other early Christian missionaries)

(4th Roman Emperor's 'memoirs' of his bloodthirsty forebears)

Henry **TREECE, MEDEA**
(powerful evocation of myth-witch, scorned wife who murdered her children)

Mary **RENAULT, THE MASK OF APOLLO**
('memoirs' of actor-spy in 4th century BC Greece)

Peter **GREEN, ACHILLES HIS ARMOUR**
(Alcibiades, the Oscar Wilde of ancient Athens)

Mario **VARGAS LLOSA, THE WAR OF THE END OF THE**
WORLD *(19th-century South American religious community, communist,*
waiting for the Apocalypse)

Augusto Roa **BASTOS, I, THE SUPREME**
('memoirs' of Francia, 19th-century dictator of Paraguay)

Gabriel García **MÁRQUEZ, THE AUTUMN OF THE**
PATRIARCH *(deathbed monologue of fanatical, deranged South*
American dictator)

Nicholas **MONSARRAT, RUNNING PROUD**
(one of Columbus' sailors shipwrecked in New World, is taken for a god)

Carlos **FUENTES, TERRA NOSTRA**
('memoirs' of Philip II of Spain, in deranged old age)

Stephen **MARLOWE, THE MEMOIRS OF CHRISTOPHER**
COLUMBUS *(early disappointments and ironic triumph of unscrupulous*
adventurer-explorer)

New Crete *is an urbane future-fantasy, and* Goodbye to All That *is autobiography, moving from a tormented account of Graves' time as an officer in the first world war to malicious glimpses of Oxford life and the literary London of the 1920s.*

autobiography of a 19th-century Paraguayan dictator deranged by power); ▷Gore Vidal, *Kalki* (about an insane Vietnam veteran who imagines himself Kalki, the last avatar of the god Vishnu whose coming will end the present cycle of human existence).

GREAT DETECTIVES

John Dickson Carr, *Death Watch*
▷Agatha Christie, *Death on the Nile*
▷A. Conan Doyle, *The Hound of the Baskervilles*
▷Dorothy L. Sayers, *Murder Must Advertise*
▷Georges Simenon, *Inquest on Bouvet*
Rex Stout, *Plot it Yourself/Murder in Style*

GREENE, Graham • *(born 1904)*
British writer of novels, plays and non-fiction.

In the 1930s Greene wrote several thrillers influenced by ▷Buchan and by action-films of the time: they include *Stamboul Train* (set on the Orient Express), *A Gun for Sale/This Gun for Sale* (about the manhunt for a political assassin) and *The Confidential Agent* (about left-wing politics in a right-wing state). This work culminated in atmospheric filmscripts, of which the best (later novelised) was *The Third Man*. But thrillers – and, later, comedies such as *Our Man in Havana*, *Travels With My Aunt* and *Monsignor Quixote* – always took second place, at least in Greene's own estimation, to his Catholic novels. These are all concerned with people tormented by their own moral failure and by the longing for God's forgiveness. The settings are often the tropics; the political situations are unstable; the heroes are second-rank functionaries despised by their superiors. Two novels, *Brighton Rock* (1938, about a petty criminal in 1930s Brighton) and *The Human Factor* (1978, about the minor-public-school loyalties and betrayals of the British Intelligence Services), set similar searches for grace in a soulless, down-at-heel

READ ON ▷

● *The Power and the Glory* (a lacerating story, set in Mexico during a left-wing revolution, about a drunken, self-hating priest who struggles against his own fear and the persecution of the revolutionaries to take God to the peasants).
▶ 'Psychic thrillers', similarly showing people driven to the edge of breakdown and beyond, by circumstances, their surroundings or consciousness of their own moral failings:

Britain. Despite the Catholic overtones of these books, which non-believers may find unconvincing, Greene's plots are fascinating, and his evocation of character and place is marvellous.

THE HEART OF THE MATTER • *(1948)*

Scobie, Captain of Police in a God-forsaken African colony during the second world war, is a decent, honest man. His wife Louise, tormented by memories of their dead daughter and by her own isolation from the rest of the British community, begs him to send her away to South Africa – and because of a mixture of pity for her misery and anguish at his inability to make her happy, he breaks police rules and borrows money from a suspected diamond-smuggler. From that lapse onwards, everything Scobie does ends in disaster, and there is nothing he can do but watch himself, appalled but helpless, as he plunges remorselessly towards damnation.

Greene's other novels include The End of the Affair, The Quiet American, A Burnt-out Case, The Comedians, The Honorary Consul *and* Doctor Fischer of Geneva. *His short stories (many of them 'comedies of the sexual life', as he called them) are collected in* Twenty-one Stories *and* May We Borrow Your Husband? *He has also written travel books and plays.*

▷Malcolm Lowry, *Under the Volcano*; ▷Joseph Conrad, *Nostromo*; B. Traven, *The Treasure of the Sierra Madre*; ▷Georges Simenon, *The Stain on the Snow*. ► **Short stories:** ▷Somerset Maugham, *Creatures of Circumstance*; ▷Ernest Hemingway, *Men Without Women*.

GROWING UP: TEENAGERS

Lynne Reid Banks, *The Writing on the Wall*
▷Elizabeth Bowen, *The Death of the Heart*
▷Willa Cather, *The Song of the Lark*
▷Charles Dickens, *David Copperfield*
▷André Gide, *The Counterfeiters*
▷Rose Macaulay, *They Were Defeated*
▷Mary McCarthy, *Birds of America*
▷Iris Murdoch, *The Flight from the Enchanter*
▷J.D. Salinger, *The Catcher in the Rye*

Adolescence (p 3); Children (p 41); Families: All-engulfing (p 72); Growing Up: Young Adults (p 101)

GROWING UP: YOUNG ADULTS

▷Lisa Alther, *Kinflicks*
▷Ford Madox Ford, *Parade's End*
▷Johann Wolfgang von Goethe, *The Apprenticeship of*

Wilhelm Meister
▷Nadine Gordimer, *A Sport of Nature*
▷Marcel Proust, *Within a Budding Grove* (part 2 of
   Remembrance of Things Past)
▷Philip Roth, *Goodbye, Columbus*
   Charles Webb, *The Graduate*

Growing Up: Teenagers (p 101); 'Only Connect'
(p 183); Perplexed by Life (p 190)

H

HAGGARD, H. Rider (Henry Rider) •
(1856–1925)
British novelist.

Haggard's novels are adventure fantasies set in wildly exotic locations: the geysers and glaciers of Iceland (*Erik Brighteyes*), the South American jungle (*Montezuma's Daughter*) or – most commonly of all – Darkest Africa, a continent of the imagination as fabulous as the setting of Sindbad's adventures in *The Arabian Nights*. In *King Solomon's Mines* (1885), Haggard's best-known book, Allan Quatermaine leads a safari in search of the fabulous treasure beyond Africa's Solomon Mountains, a treasure which has already claimed a thousand lives. Desert heat, jungle, hostile warrior-tribes and ice-caves in the mountains must all be faced, to say nothing of black magic, cannibalism and the guile and treachery of members of Quatermaine's own party. Hokum? The best.

> **READ ON**
>
> ● *She*; *Allan Quatermaine*; *Ayesha: The Return of She*.
> ▶ ▷John Buchan, *Prester John*. ▷A. Conan Doyle, *The Lost World*. James Hilton, *Lost Horizon*. ▷Wilbur Smith, *Shout at the Devil*. Edgar Rice Burroughs, *A Princess of Mars*.

HAILEY, Arthur • *(born 1920)*
British/Canadian novelist.

Hailey's books are well-researched, fast-paced adventures set not in jungles or jet-set ski-resorts but in the no less exotic surroundings of a luxury hotel (*Hotel*), an international airport (*Airport*), the US government (*In High Places*) or Wall Street (*The Moneychangers*). In all of them, the fascination is as much in the detail of the location as in action: his books are fly-on-the-wall documentary, thriller and soap opera rolled into one. The hero of *Overload* (1979), a power-company executive, claims that his employers' greed and carelessness will lead to a breakdown of the entire electrical network of California. He becomes involved with ecological fringe-groups, citizen-pro-

> **READ ON**
>
> ▶ Burton Wohl, *The China Syndrome*. John Trenhaile, *The Mahjong Spies*. Paul Gallico, *The Poseidon Adventure*.

tection societies, terrorists, big-business troubleshooters and muck-raking newspaper-reporters – and as the novel pounds towards its climax, he is proved to have been a truer prophet of disaster than even he suspected.

HAMMETT, Dashiell • *(1894–1961)*
US writer of novels, short stories and screenplays.

A former private detective, Hammett wrote stories and serials for pulp magazines, and later became a Hollywood scriptwriter. He perfected the 'private eye' story, in which kidnappings, thefts and murders are investigated by laconic, wisecracking individuals who are always just on the side of the angels and just one step ahead of the police. His best-known detectives are Sam Spade (made famous by Humphrey Bogart), the urbane Nick Charles (made famous in William Powell's 'Thin Man' films) and 'The Continental Op'. Hammett's novels are *The Dain Curse*, *Red Harvest*, *The Maltese Falcon*, *The Glass Key* and *The Thin Man*; his story-collections include *The Continental Op*, *A Man Called Spade* and *A Man Called Thin*.

> **READ ON** >

▶ ▷Raymond Chandler, *The Lady in the Lake*. James M. Cain, *No Orchids for Miss Blandish*. Ross Macdonald, *The Drowning Pool*. Peter Coffin, *The Search for My Great Uncle's Head*. Andrew Bergman, *The Big Kissoff of 1944*. ▷Norman Mailer, *Tough Guys Don't Dance*.

HARDY, Thomas • *(1840–1928)*
British novelist and poet.

As a young man Hardy worked as an ecclesiastical architect, sketching and surveying country churches. This work intensified his love of the old ways of the countryside, patterns of life and customs which dated from feudal times. This is the background to his novels (which are all set in south-western England, the ancient kingdom of Wessex). He describes the minutiae of farming and village life with the exactness of a museum curator, and his characters' habits of mind are rooted in the ebb and flow of the seasons, in the unending cycle of tending for their animals and caring for the land. Life is unhurried but inexorable: Hardy's people are owned by their environment. They are also subject to a range of violent passions and emotions – Hardy thought of human beings as the playthings of destiny – and the placid continuum of existence is the setting for such irrational psychological forces as jealousy, intolerance and revenge. Hardy's bleakness and pessimism were much criticised, and in 1895 he gave up novels to concentrate on poetry. Paradoxically, for all the sombreness of their events, his novels are valued now mainly for their feeling of the harmony between human beings and nature: a kind of rural innocence which has

> **READ ON** >

● *The Mayor of Casterbridge*; *Tess of the d'Urbervilles*.
▶ **Books on similar themes, in a similar style:** ▷George Eliot, *Adam Bede*; ▷Mrs Gaskell, *Ruth*; ▷Edith Wharton, *Ethan Frome*; Melvyn Bragg, *The Hired Man*.
▶ **Further away in period or manner, but equally atmospheric:** ▷John Fowles, *The French Lieutenant's Woman*; ▷Sigrid Undset, *Kristin Lavransdatter*; Oliver Onions, *The Story of Ragged Robyn*.

long since disappeared.

FAR FROM THE MADDING CROWD • *(1874)*

The shepherd Gabriel Oak works for Bathsheba Everdene, and loves her. Bathsheba's head is turned by dashing Sergeant Troy, who marries her and then deserts her, letting her believe that he is dead. Bathsheba now agrees to marry Boldwood, a yeoman farmer, unimaginative and dull, who has secretly loved her for years. Then Troy comes back and claims his wife – provoking a crisis and the resolution of the uneasy relationship between Oak and Bathsheba which has simmered all this time.

Hardy's other novels include Under the Greenwood Tree, A Pair of Blue Eyes, The Return of the Native, The Trumpet-Major, The Mayor of Casterbridge, The Woodlanders, Tess of the d'Urbervilles *and* Jude the Obscure. *He wrote an epic drama set during the Napoleonic Wars,* The Dynasts, *and several books of poetry including* Satires of Circumstance, Moments of Vision *and* Winter Words.

HARRISON, Harry • *(born 1925)*
US novelist and short-story writer.

Although Harrison has written serious SF (eg the fast-moving adventure-series *Deathworld I*, *Deathworld II* and *Deathworld III*), he is best-known for farce, and especially for his books about the Stainless Steel Rat. In a future where technology has made crime all but redundant, James Bolivar di Griz, the Stainless Steel Rat, is a spectacular exception to the rule. He sees himself as a public benefactor, keeping the police on their toes, giving employment to insurance clerks and bringing colour and excitement to TV newscasts. In the first book of the series, *The Stainless Steel Rat*, the galactic police decide that the only way to cope with him is to recruit him and send him to catch the lovely interplanetary criminal Angelina.

The Stainless Steel Rat books include The Stainless Steel Rat's Revenge, The Stainless Steel Rat Saves the World, The Stainless Steel Rat Wants You! *and* The Stainless Steel Rat for President. *Harrison's other novels include* Planet of the Damned, Make Room! Make Room!, Star Smashers of the Galaxy Rangers, Skyfall, Great Balls of Fire *and* Mechanismo. Two Tales and Eight Tomorrows, Prime Number *and* One Step from Earth *are collections of short stories.*

> **READ ON**

● *The Technicolor Time Machine.*
▶ ▷Kurt Vonnegut, *Cat's Cradle.* Robert Sheckley, *The Status Civilization.* Jack Trevor Story, *Morag's Flying Fortress.*

HARTLEY, L.P. (Leslie Poles) •
(1895–1972)
British novelist and short-story writer.

An admirer of ▷James and ▷Forster, Hartley wrote a dozen decorous, restrained novels about emotional deprivation and the way childhood experience shadows a person's whole existence. His best-known books are the 'Eustace and Hilda' trilogy (*The Shrimp and the Anemone, The Sixth Heaven* and *Eustace and Hilda,* 1944–7), about a brother and sister whose emotional interdependence, innocent-seeming when they are children, blights their later lives, and *The Go-Between* (1953), about a boy on holiday during an idyllic Edwardian summer. Carrying messages between two doomed lovers (the daughter of the 'big house' and a tenant farmer), he is emotionally crippled by the passions he senses but hardly understands. *Facial Justice* (1960) is an uncharacteristic but fascinating book, a future-fantasy set in a drab post-nuclear world where there is no fear, no pain, no unkindness – and no room for individuality or emotion.

Hartley's other main novels are The Boat, A Perfect Woman, The Hireling *and* The Brickfield. *His short-story collections include* The Killing Bottle *and* The Travelling Grave.

HAŠEK, Jaroslav • *(1883-1923)*
Czech novelist and journalist.

Hašek spent most of his youth as a dropout and a half-baked political activist (for which, for six months, he was imprisoned by the Russians as a spy). He served, reluctantly, in the first world war, was invalided out and became a satirical journalist. His masterpiece, the 700-page comic novel *The Good Soldier Švejk*, makes hilarious use of all his early experiences. Švejk is the town drunk, a dog-catcher, who is conscripted into the Austrian army as the lowliest of privates. A moon-faced, brainless lump, he obeys every fatuous order and follows every regulation to the letter. The book follows his farcical army career, during which he rises to the dizzy heights of chaplain's batman, takes part in the first world war and sees the first skirmishes of the Russian revolution. He understands nothing of what is going on: food, drink and staying out of trouble are all that interest him. Hašek uses Švejk's blankness like a mirror, showing up officers, politicians and bureaucrats for the fools they are. His nihilistic, iconoclastic farce was quite remarkably ahead of its time. *The*

> **READ ON** ⟩

▶ ▷Henry James, *What Maisie Knew.* ▷Anita Brookner, *Hôtel du Lac.* ▷Edith Wharton, *The Age of Innocence.* ▷Elizabeth Bowen, *The Death of the Heart.* Jane Gardam, *A Long Way from Verona.* Philip Larkin, *Jill.*

> **READ ON** ⟩

▶ ▷François Rabelais, *Gargantua* is the nearest match for Hašek's farcical gusto, and Von Grimmelshausen, *Simplex Simplicissimus* is about a Middle Ages precursor of Švejk. Of more modern books, Eric Linklater, *Private Angelo* is a genial satire on the second world war; Thomas Berger, *Reinhart in Love* is a similarly light-hearted novel about a Švejkish US 'little man'. ▷Thomas

Good Soldier Švejk was banned, or available only in censored form, for over 40 years. It was not until the 1970s, when Absurd Drama and novels like ▷Heller's *Catch-22* had taught us not to take ourselves or our 'betters' so seriously, that it came at last into its own, was published complete, and was recognised as a satirical masterwork in the class of *Gargantua* or ▷Gogol's *Dead Souls*.

All earlier English translations of The Good Soldier Švejk *have been outclassed by Cecil Parrott's, written in the 1970s. Parrott has also published a selection of Hašek's lunatic journalism,* Jaroslav Hašek: the Red Commissar.

HAWTHORNE, Nathaniel • *(1804–64)*
US novelist.

Hawthorne was a descendant of William Hawthorne, one of the Pilgrim Fathers and a notable religious bigot – something which embarrassed Hawthorne himself, as he was a free-thinker, a believer in social equality and a dabbler in the utopian idealism of the mid-1800s USA. Although there was enough family money to pay for his university education, he was forced to earn a living thereafter, and did so as a customs officer, part-time publisher's editor and a newspaper contributor. Much of his early writing was excellent but minor – examples are the short-story collections *Twice-told Tales* and *Mosses from an Old Manse*, for adults, and *A Wonder Book* and *Tanglewood Tales*, sensitive retellings of Greek myth for children. He was triggered into greatness by discovering, in an old chest in Salem, Massachusetts, documents about his family's part in the Salem witchhunts of the mid 17th-century. Soon afterwards, he wrote *The Scarlet Letter* (1850), a novel about intolerance and humbug among the first Puritan settlers in the USA. Hester Prynne has spent two years in Boston, waiting for her elderly husband to join her from England. In the meantime she has borne a love-child, Pearl, and the Puritans pillory her and brand her an adulteress, making her wear the scarlet letter 'A' embroidered on her clothes. Her husband arrives, discovers that her secret lover is a minister of the church, and mercilessly persecutes him for refusing to admit his guilt. Hester's husband and lover pursue their enmity to the end; they ignore Hester herself, who in the meantime lives an unobtrusive but truly Christian life helping the neighbours who once ill-treated her.

Mann, *The Confessions of Felix Krull, Confidence Man* about a confidence-trickster travelling the spas and luxury hotels of Europe in the 1900s, though it lacks Hašek's devastating view of war and politics, exactly parallels his wide-eyed, amiable style.

READ ON ⟩

● *The House of the Seven Gables* (a similarly remorseless novel about a New England family cursed for generations because of their forebears' persecution of an innocent man for witchcraft). *The Blithedale Romance* (a satire, based on Hawthorne's own experience, about life in a Massachusetts utopian community).
▶ ▷Aldous Huxley, *The Devils of Loudon*.
▷I.B. Singer, *Satan in Goray* (set in a medieval community of Polish Jews torn apart by the appearance of a false Messiah).
André Brink, *Rumours of Rain* (about ignorance and intolerance in present-day South Africa).
Robert Coover, *The Origin of the Brunists* (a fascist allegory about the growth of a ruthless religious sect).

HEINLEIN, Robert • *(1907–88)*
US novelist.

Of all SF novelists, Heinlein has always had a most dazzling variety and range, without ever sacrificing literary quality or exuberance of imagination. In the 1940s and 1950s his books were ▷Wellsian, ▷Vernian stories of space exploration and the colonisation of distant planets – still satisfying nowadays for their style and plots, even though much of their science has been overtaken by events. In the 1960s he won a cult hippy following when his book *Stranger in a Strange Land* seemed to be advocating a mystical union of humankind brought about by flower power, free love and hallucinatory drugs. His 1970s and 1980s books were ironical farces, akin to the bleakly hilarious fantasies of ▷Joseph Heller and ▷Kurt Vonnegut. His best known novels, the heart of his achievement, are a series of independent but linked books about Lazarus Long, a man who has the ability to live forever, and who ends up as a kind of universal patriarch: everyone in existence is one of his descendants. Heinlein explores the personal and social problems of such a person, stirring in exotic and fascinating plot ideas. In *Time Enough for Love* (1973), for example, Lazarus Long, bored with life and contemplating suicide, is distracted by being allowed to try the forbidden experience of time-travel: he goes back to 1917, fights in the first world war, meets himself as a six-year-old and falls in love with his own mother.

Other books including Lazarus Long are Methuselah's Children, Number of the Beast *and* The Cat Who Walks Through Walls. *Heinlein's other novels include* I Will Fear No Evil, The Day After Tomorrow *and* Job. *His short stories, including such classics as 'The Man Who Sold the Moon' and 'The Green Hills of Earth', are in the two-volume omnibus* The Past Through Tomorrow.

HELLER, Joseph • *(born 1923)*
US novelist.

Throughout the 1950s, the escalation of the nuclear arms race produced in many people a feeling of desperate impotence. Faced with imminent apocalypse, the only possible option seemed to be hysterical, cynical laughter. By the early 1960s this mood was common in plays, comedians' routines, cartoons and satirical magazines, and Heller's first novel *Catch-22* expressed it perfectly. On the surface a wild farce about airmen in the second world war, it

READ ON

● *Job* (a Bible-inspired story of a human being tormented by a practical-joking, malicious God and finally befriended by the Devil).
▶ ▷Isaac Asimov, *Foundation*. ▷Philip José Farmer, *Riverworld*. ▷Kurt Vonnegut, *Galápagos*.

READ ON

● All Heller's novels centre on characters who are trapped. *Something Happened* (1974) shows a man in thrall to his own boringness; the main character of *Good as Gold* (1979) is

shows human beings as both trapped in a detestable destiny and paradoxically liberated, by the absence of hope or choice, to do exactly as they please, to turn reality into fantasy. Until *Catch-22*, this had been a theme for serious novels (for example those of ▷Camus, ▷Sartre or ▷Hemingway); Heller made it comedy, leading a trend which has since spread from the arts into our general attitude to both our 'leaders' and the way we live.

CATCH-22 • *(1961)*

A group of US bomber-pilots is stationed on a Mediterranean island during the second world war. Every time a man thinks he has flown his quota of bombing-missions, high command doubles the number. There is no escape, and the reason is Catch-22: if you're sane enough to ask to be grounded because what you're doing is crazy, you're sane enough to fly. For all its bleak philosophy, *Catch-22* is brilliantly funny, particularly in its deadpan reporting of the lunatic, gung-ho US top brass, of Milo Minderbinder's extension to infinity of the rules of free-market enterprise (profiteering on everything from eggs to his comrades' lives), and of such pitiful victims of destiny as Major Major Major Major, a man haunted by his name. Robert Altman's film *M*A*S*H*, and the dazzling TV series which followed it, caught an exactly similar mood; *Catch-22* is like all *M*A*S*H*'s most ludicrous, lacerating scenes gathered into one glorious, agonising whole.

Heller's other novels are Something Happened, Good as Gold *and* God Knows. No Laughing Matter *is non-fiction, a blackly funny account of Heller's recovery from near-fatal illness.*

HEMINGWAY, Ernest • *(1898-1961)*
US novelist and short-story writer.

Few great writers provoke such love/hate reactions as Hemingway: it seems impossible to read him without judging him. The reason is that although he wrote some of the most evocative, persuasive prose of the century – as direct and compelling as a journalist's reports – many people find his subject-matter repellent. He believed that creatures, including human beings, are at their noblest when fighting for survival, and his novels and stories are therefore about boxing, big-game hunting, deep-sea fishing, bull-fighting and above all war. Hemingway himself realised that his macho philosophy belonged more to the Middle Ages than the 20th century, and most of his books are tinged with failure. His heroes rarely succeed in 'proving' themselves, their wars are futile, the emphasis is on

oppressed by his New York Jewish family and by hatred of Henry Kissinger; in *God Knows* (1984) the Old Testament King David is shackled by knowledge of the world's whole future history, and by his relationship with a wisecracking, cynical and unhelpful God. ('Where does it say nice?' asks God. 'Where does it say I have to be nice?').
▶ ▷Jaroslav Hašek, *The Good Soldier Švejk.* ▷Wyndham Lewis , *Childermass.* ▷Philip Roth, *Portnoy's Complaint.*

READ ON

● *The Old Man and the Sea* describes a duel to the death between the old Cuban fisherman Santiago and a gigantic marlin, the biggest fish he has ever tried to catch in his life. The book is short, and concentrates on Santiago, struggling not only with the marlin but against his own failing powers,

Joseph **HELLER**

Len **DEIGHTON, BOMBER**
(meticulous planning for a bombing-run over Germany in World War II)

Neville **SHUTE, LANDFALL**
(breakdown of young pilot who sinks 'one of ours' by mistake)

WAR IS HELL

Stephen **CRANE, THE RED BADGE OF COURAGE**
(young volunteer horrified but exhilarated by battle conditions in American Civil War)

Andrew **SINCLAIR, GOG**
(giant from past washed up in Scotland, travels to London, horrified at 20th-century 'civilisation')

IT'S A MAD, MAD WORLD

Günter **GRASS, THE TIN DRUM**
(nazism as an insane circus-parade watched by a gleeful, baby-brained adult)

Budd **SCHULBERG, WHAT MAKES SAMMY RUN?**
(Sammy claws his way to the top; scum always floats)

Richard **CONDON, MILE HIGH**
(US power politics; a farcical orgy of sex, drugs, blackmail and murder)

Jerzy **KOSINSKI, BEING THERE**
(lame-brain gardener taken for political guru and saint)

Terry **SOUTHERN, CANDY**
(virgin innocent abroad — neither innocent nor virgin for long)

(lunacy of war; USAF bomber base on fantasy mediterranean island in World War II)

ANTI-WAR NOVELS

Mario **VARGAS LLOSA, THE CITY AND THE DOGS; THE TIME OF THE HERO**
(farcical tragedy of young cadets in 1950s Peruvian military academy)

Norman **MAILER, THE NAKED AND THE DEAD**
(World War II US conscripts brutalised by conditions of service on a hopeless Pacific mission)

Erich Maria **REMARQUE, ALL QUIET ON THE WESTERN FRONT**
(lives of four young men disrupted and ruined by brutality of World War I trench warfare)

Richard **HOOKER, M*A*S*H**
(US doctors in Korea fighting insane conditions, boredom and gung-ho top brass)

CRAZINESS OF COMMAND

Leslie **THOMAS, THE VIRGIN SOLDIERS**
(over-sexed, bewildered British conscripts in Far East)

Thomas **PYNCHON, GRAVITY'S RAINBOW**
(what is top secret World War II establishment for? What is meaning of life? Should war (and sex) not be more fun that this?)

Jaroslav **HAŠEK, THE GOOD SOLDIER ŠVEJK**
(World War I batman obeys every order, believes every lie, keeps out of trouble)

Herman **WOUK, THE CAINE MUTINY**
(crew court-martialled for mutinying against insane World War II minesweeper captain)

Peter **GEORGE, RED ALERT**
(chain of command follies and failures triggers World War III)

pain, despair and death. But the dream remains, and is Hemingway's own dream. He spent his leisure time in exactly the activities he describes –precise details of how to fight bulls, hunt big game, box or fish are what he does best – and in 1961, feeling too old and sick to continue, he shot himself.

A FAREWELL TO ARMS • (1929)

A US ambulance driver in Italy during the first world war is wounded and taken to hospital, where he falls in love with an English nurse. While he convalesces the couple are deliriously happy, but then he is commanded back to the front. She tells him that she is pregnant, and they decide that their only course is 'a farewell to arms', escaping from the war to neutral Switzerland.

Hemingway's other novels are The Torrents of Spring, The Sun Also Rises/Fiesta *(which includes a superb description of bull-running during the festival at Pamplona),* Death in the Afternoon *(about bull-fighting),* The Green Hills of Africa, To Have and Have Not, For Whom the Bell Tolls *(set during the Spanish civil war),* Across the River and Into the Trees *and* The Old Man and the Sea. *Several unrevised, unfinished books were published posthumously: the best-known is the novel* Islands in the Stream. *His short-story collections include* In Our Time, Men Without Women *and* Winner Take Nothing.

HERBERT, Frank • *(1920–86)*
US novelist.

Herbert's work is dominated by the 2000-page (6-novel) 'Dune' series (1965–85), an SF epic whose scope and complexity dwarf all rivals. Dune is a desert planet, inhabited by gigantic sand-worms which produce mélange, a substance which inhibits aging and gives knowledge of the past and future. The saga (each of whose novels is self-contained) tells how Paul Atreides inherits Dune, has to win it from his enemies and then colonise it. It describes the 'greening' of a planet where water is the most precious of all commodities, and recounts the wars between the Atreides family and other interests (especially the powerful Bene Gesserit sisterhood, which is dedicated to harnessing the pure power of thought and so dispensing with science and technology). The books are partly a swaggering multi-generation saga, the apotheosis of space-opera, and partly a detailed and moving account of the inter-relationship between the colonists and their planet. The effort of controlling but not destroying the environment produces in them a feeling of near-mystic communion with natural

and kept going only by determination and a lifetime's skill.
▶ ▷Graham Greene, *The Power and the Glory.* ▷Norman Mailer, *The Naked and the Dead.* ▷George Orwell, *Homage to Catalonia.* ▷Jack London, *The Sea-wolf.* Hammond Innes, *Campbell's Kingdom.* Alistair Maclean, *The Guns of Navarone.*

> READ ON >

▶ **Good SF follow-ups:** ▷Brian Aldiss, *Helliconia Spring* and its sequels; ▷Ursula Le Guin, *The Left Hand of Darkness.*
▶ **Good non-SF follow-ups:** Frans Bengtsson, *The Long Ships* (about Vikings exploring the surface of our own planet); Jean M. Auel, *Earth Children* (a saga of the distant past, about human beings learning to control their environment and discovering ways of civilisation); Nicholas Monsarrat, *Running*

forces which contrasts strongly with the snarling and bickering of their relations with one another.

The first Dune trilogy is Dune, Dune Messiah *and* Children of Dune; *the second is* God Emperor of Dune, Heretics of Dune *and* Chapterhouse of Dune. *Herbert's many other books, space-opera on a less exalted level, include* The Dragon in the Sea, The Whipping Star, The Dosadi Experiment, The Green Brain *and* The Saratoga Barrier.

HERBERT, James • *(born 1943)*
British novelist.

Herbert's supernatural chillers, among the most frightening in the business, include *The Dark*, *The Domain*, *The Fog*, *The Rats*, *Shrine*, *The Spear*, *The Survivor*, *Sepulchre* and *Moon* (about a boy on an island who dreams of a sadistic, supernatural creature – at the same time as it dreams of him).

HESSE, Hermann • *(1877-1962)*
German/Swiss novelist and non-fiction writer.

A poet and mystic, Hesse was influenced by Jung's ideas of the unconscious and the collective unconscious, and later by Buddhist philosophy. His most famous mystical novel, *The Glass Bead Game/Magister Ludi* (Das Glasperlenspiel), is about a future utopia where all questions about life, morality and personality are covered by a monastic philosophical system centred on a zen-like game involving coloured beads and an abacus. Hesse's reputation for gentle, philosophical woolliness has obscured his true worth. His novels before *The Glass Bead Game* are spare, moving accounts of how people in psychological turmoil reach peace with themselves, either through their own efforts or with the help of friends and loved ones. He is something of a special taste, but few writers' works so reward their devotees.

ROSSHALDE • *(1914)*
Veraguth, a world-renowned painter, is suffering creative block. His marriage is breaking down, and he and his wife

Proud (about one of Columbus' sailors shipwrecked and forced, by the tribe who find him, to invent himself as a godlike personality, with deeds to match).
National Lampoon, *Doon* is a splendid send-up of all Herbert's ideas – replacing mélange, for example, with a wonder-drug called Coke.

READ ON

▶ ▷Stephen King, *It*. Margaret Bingley, *Devil's Child*. Dean R. Koontz, *Whispers*. ▷H.G. Wells, *The Island of Doctor Moreau*.

READ ON

● *Gertrud* (1910, the story of a tragic love-triangle between a girl and two young men who are close friends). *Steppenwolf* (1927) and *Narziss and Goldmund* (1930) are both about the divided self. In *Steppenwolf* a middle-aged recluse has given in to the negative, hopeless side of his nature, and is 'brought back' by the spiritual energy of three young people who may be dream-figures, projections of

stay together out of love for Rosshalde, their beautiful country estate, and devotion to their young son Pierre. Veraguth's problems seem beyond cure – until unexpected tragedy forces him to come to terms with himself, and so to find peace at last.

Hesse's major novels are Gertrud, Peter Camenzind, Under the Wheel/The Prodigy, Siddhartha *(about Buddha),* Steppenwolf, Narziss and Goldmund *and* The Glass Bead Game. *He also published shorter, more mystical fiction (*Knulp; Klingsor's Last Summer*), poetry, short stories, essays and letters.*

his subconscious. In *Narziss and Goldmund* (set in medieval Europe, with a background of monastic and craft-guild life) the conflict between flesh and spirit is symbolised by the two main characters, close friends, one carnal, one spiritual.

▶ **To *Rosshalde*:** ▷André Gide, *The Pastoral Symphony* (*La symphonie pastorale*).

▶ **To *The Glass Bead Game*:** ▷Tom De Haan, *A Mirror for Princes*.

▶ **To *Narziss and Goldmund*:** Georges Bernanos, *Diary of a Country Priest* (about the battle between flesh and spirit in a priest's soul).

▶ **To *Steppenwolf*:** D.M. Thomas, *The White Hotel*.

▶ **To Hesse's work in general:** ▷Heinrich Böll, *The Clown*; ▷Kazuo Ishiguro, *An Artist of the Floating World*.

HEYER, Georgette • *(1902–74)*
British novelist.

Apart from a handful of detective stories (eg *Envious Casca*; *Detection Unlimited*), all Heyer's novels are historical. Some centre on real events (*The Infamous Army*, for example, is about the battle of Waterloo); others, notably *Beauvallet* (1929), *The Tollgate* (1954) and *The Unknown Ajax* (1959), are heady tales of smugglers, highwaymen and other members of the 18th-century underworld. The bulk of her books are light-hearted, frothy romances. A hero and heroine who detest or distrust one another are thrown together by circumstances

> **READ ON**

▶ **To the novels based on real events:** Margaret Irwin, *Young Bess* (first of a trilogy about Queen Elizabeth I of England); ▷Jean Plaidy, *The Spanish Bridegroom*.

▶ **To the adventure novels:** ▷Daphne Du

and fall in love. Often she 'tames' him or he 'tames' her; sometimes masquerade (such as posing as lady's maids or cads) is involved. Heyer's knowledge of Regency ways was exhaustive: every garment, vehicle, gesture and turn of phrase seems exactly and delightfully right. Her novels are fast-moving, uncomplicated entertainment. She perfected the Regency genre, and within it she is unsurpassed.

Heyer's best-known romances are The Masqueraders, These Old Shades, Devil's Cub, Regency Buck, Friday's Child, The Foundling, The Grand Sophy, Bath Tangle, Sprig Muslin *and* Cotillion. Pistols for Two *contains short stories.*

HIBBERT, Eleanor • *(born 1906)*
British novelist.

Hibbert wrote all her books under pseudonyms: Eleanor Burford ▷Philippa Carr, Elbur Ford, ▷Victoria Holt, Kathleen Kellow, ▷Jean Plaidy and Ellalice Tate.

HIGGINS, Jack • *(born 1929)*
British novelist.

'Jack Higgins' is one of the pseudonyms of Henry Patterson, who also writes thrillers as Martin Fallon, James Graham, Hugh Marlow and Harry Patterson. The Higgins books are pacy, violent and full of character. They include *The Last Place God Made*, *A Prayer for the Dying*, *The Eagle Has Landed* (imagining Britain under SS rule), *Hell is Always Today*, *The Dark Side of the Street* and *Solo* (in which a concert pianist, fleeing from the police, kills an assassin's daughter by accident – a mistake which must be punished).

Maurier, *Jamaica Inn*; Jane Aiken Hodge, *Rebel Heiress*; ▷Mary Stewart, *This Rough Magic* (set in modern Greece).

▶ **To the romances:**
▷Jane Austen, *Mansfield Park*; Sheila Walsh, *The Rose Domino*: Clare Darcy, *Eugenia*; Bob Coleman, *The Further Adventures of Tom Jones.*

READ ON ⟩

▶ ▷Len Deighton, *Berlin Game*. Alexander Fullerton, *Regenesis*. Colin Forbes, *Terminal*. Gerald Seymour, *Kingfisher*.

HIGH ADVENTURE

▷Desmond Bagley, *The Golden Keel*
▷Alexandre Dumas, *The Three Musketeers*
▷H. Rider Haggard, *King Solomon's Mines*
▷Anthony Hope, *The Prisoner of Zenda*
　Hammond Innes, *Campbell's Kingdom*
　Rafael Sabatini, *Captain Blood*
▷Wilbur Smith, *Shout at the Devil*
　B. Traven, *The Treasure of the Sierra Madre*

Georgette HEYER

Clare **DARCY, ELYZA**
(plain girl disguises herself as boy to find romance)

Caroline **COURTNEY, DUCHESS IN DISGUISE**
(spurned wife disguises herself to win husband's love)

Jane **AUSTEN, SENSE AND SENSIBILITY**
(love-affairs of two sisters; sensible Elinor and impulsive, romantic Marianne)

Joan **AIKEN, MANSFIELD REVISITED**
(spirited girl 'tames' brother-in-law's snobbish family)

REGENCY ENGLAND

Henry **FIELDING, TOM JONES**
(escapades of foundling wandering 18th-century England to find truth about himself)

P.G. **WODEHOUSE, BILL THE CONQUEROR**
(Percy Pilbeam's havoc-strewn career as editor of 'Society Spice')

Iris **MURDOCH, A SEVERED HEAD**
(sexual merry-go-round in 'swinging' 1960s London)

Mary **WESLEY, THE VACILLATIONS OF POPPY CAREWE** *(rich heiress reviews young men in her life to find the 'best' — i.e. least obviously eligible — husband. Love intervenes.)*

COMEDY OF MANNERS

Mary **STEWART, NINE COACHES WAITING**
(English governess in France, caught in family feud, saves charges from death, finds love)

Helen **MACINNES, RIDE A PALE HORSE**
(US journalist at Prague conference approached by would-be defector)

Anne **BRIDGE, THE GINGER GRIFFIN**
(intrigue and unhappiness in pre-Revolutionary China)

Jane Aiken **HODGE, POLONAISE**
(love and politics in 1810s Poland, caught between Russia and Napoleon)

ROMANTIC MYSTERY

(dislike turns to love in Regency English high society)

PERIOD ROMANCE

Norah **LOFTS, THE BRITTLE GLASS**
(independent girl grows up in 18th-century Fens, a place of smugglers, gipsies and highwaymen)

T.N. **MURARI, TAJ**
(love of Indian Shah Jahan and his wife, for whom he built the Taj Mahal)

Kathleen **WINSOR, FOREVER AMBER**
(love and adventure in 17th-century, Restoration England)

Rosalind **LAKER, WHAT THE HEART KEEPS**
(two immigrants to 1900s USA fall in love, make life together in Wild West and early Hollywood)

M.M. **KAYE, THE FAR PAVILIONS**
(love across the races in dying days of British Raj in India)

Margaret **PEMBERTON, NEVER LEAVE ME**
(successful Californian looks back on doomed wartime love-affair with German officer, when she works for French Resistance)

Caroline **FIRESIDE, GOODBYE AGAIN**
(will heroine sacrifice glamorous film career for love?)

Erich **SEGAL, LOVE STORY**
(two college students fall idyllically, tragically, in love)

20TH-CENTURY ROMANCE

Action Thrillers (p 2); Agents and Double Agents (p 3);
Terrorists/Freedom Fighters (p 234)

HIGHER (?) EDUCATION

▷Robertson Davies, *The Rebel Angels*
▷J.P. Donleavy, *The Ginger Man*
  Richard Gordon, *Doctor in the House*
  Howard Jacobson, *Coming from Behind*
▷Randall Jarrell, *Pictures from an Institution*
▷Alison Lurie, *The War Between the Tates*
▷Mary McCarthy, *The Groves of Academe*
▷Tom Sharpe, *Wilt*

Dreaming Spires (p 66)

HIGHSMITH, Patricia • *(born 1921)*
US novelist and short-story writer.

Except for *The People Who Knock on the Door* (1982,
about the disintegration of an 'ordinary' US family whose
father becomes a born-again Christian) Highsmith's books
are all psychological thrillers. They show the planning and
commission of horribly convincing, 'everyday' crimes,
and the way murder erodes the murderer's moral identity.
Few writers screw tension so tight in such functional,
unemotional prose. Highsmith's most chilling insight is
how close the criminally insane can be to people just like
ourselves.

RIPLEY'S GAME • *(1974)*
Ripley, who appears in several Highsmith books, is a
charming American psychopath who lives in France. In
this book, out of boredom, he sets up circumstances to
snare an entirely innocent man into committing murder.
But the murder-victim is a mafia boss, and soon assassins
begin to hunt down both Ripley and his dupe. The plot is
exciting, but Highsmith's main concern is the comparison
between Ripley's icy amorality and the conscience-racked
flailings of the man he corrupts.

Other Ripley books are The Talented Mr Ripley, Ripley
Under Ground *and* The Boy Who Followed Ripley. *High-
smith's other novels include* Strangers on a Train, The
Two Faces of January, The Story Teller/A Suspension of
Mercy, The Tremor of Forgery, Edith's Diary *and* Found

READ ON ▷

● The central character
of *The Glass Cell* (a
typical non-Ripley
book) is a man
released from prison
after six years during
which his character
has been brutalised
and his moral integrity
destroyed. Tormented
by the possibility of his
wife's unfaithfulness,
he sets out to discover
the truth.
▶ Julian Symons, *The
Man Who Killed
Himself*. ▷Georges
Simenon, *The Hatter's
Ghosts*. Greg
MacDonald, *Running
Scared*. ▷Ruth
Rendell, *Live Flesh*.
▷P.D. James, *The
Skull Beneath the
Skin*. Celia Fremlin,
*Appointment with
Yesterday; Don't Go to
Sleep in the Dark*

in the Street. The Snailwatcher/Eleven, The Animal-lover's Book of Beastly Murder, The Black House, Mermaids on the Golf Course *and* Tales of Natural and Unnatural Catastrophes *contain short stories.*

HILL, Reginald • *(born 1936)*
British novelist.

Hill writes thrillers and adventure stories under the pseudonyms Dick Morland (*Heart Clock*), ▷Patrick Ruell and Charles Underhill (*Captain Fantom*). Under his own name he writes affable, joky detective stories, featuring slobbish Inspector Dalziel and his bushy-tailed, over-eager assistant Pascoe. Hill's books include *A Clubbable Woman, An Advancement of Learning, A Fairly Dangerous Thing, A Very Good Hater* and the cheekily-named *Another Death in Venice.*

HILL, Susan • *(born 1942)*
British writer of novels, short stories and non-fiction.

Except for *The Woman in Black*, a ghost-story in classic 19th-century style, all Hill's novels and stories are about predatory emotional relationships. One partner (spouse, friend, lover or acquaintance) can only survive by engulfing the other, and the process is agonising and deliberate, an erosion of spirit without hope or help. Her least bleak book is *In the Springtime of the Year* (1974), in which a young woman devastated by the death of her husband is rescued from despair by the tranquil daily round of country life. Hill's themes may be sombre, but she writes with delicacy and compassion: in the end, the tears we shed are for the human condition itself, a predicament which is like a third partner in the stories, a malign presence feasting on victims and predators alike.

I'M THE KING OF THE CASTLE • *(1970)*
Mr Hooper, a lonely widower, invites Mrs Kingshaw to be housekeeper of his large Victorian mansion. He hopes that his ten-year-old son and hers will become friends. But the boy Hooper resents Kingshaw's invasion of his psychological kingdom, and torments him. The psychopathic child, possessed by the devil, was a familiar figure in pulp fiction and films of the 1970s (a good example is the 'Omen' film series); Hill turns the same subject into art.

Hill's other main novels are A Change for the Better, Gentleman and Ladies, Strange Meeting *and* The Bird of (short stories).

> **READ ON** ▷

► Colin Watson, *One Man's Meat*. Joyce Porter, *Who the Hell Was Sylvia?*. Ira Wallach, *The Absence of a Cello*.

> **READ ON** ▷

● *The Bird of Night*
► To *I'm the King of the Castle*: ▷Henry James, *The Turn of the Screw*; ▷John Wyndham, *Chocky*; ▷William Golding, *Lord of the Flies*.
► To *In the Springtime of the Year*: Penelope Lively, *Perfect Happiness*. Hill's grim compassion, and her unblinking descriptions of the desolation of the soul, are matched in ▷Carson McCullers, *Reflections in a Golden Eye;* James Agee, *A Death in the Family* and ▷John Updike, *The Centaur*.

Night, *a sombre book about a manic-depressive artist and the friend who tries to help him.* The Albatross *and* A Bit of Singing and Dancing *contain short stories.*

HISTORICAL ADVENTURE

Peter Carter, *The Black Lamp*
Bernard Cornwell, *Sharpe's Regiment*
Frederick Couens, *Gnur Bodi*
▷C.S. Forester, *Mr Midshipman Hornblower*
George Macdonald Fraser, *Flashman*
▷Homer, *Odyssey*
▷R.L. Stevenson, *Kidnapped*

Action Thrillers (p 2); Agents and Double Agents (p 3); High Adventure (p 117)

HOBAN, Russell • *(born 1925)*
US/British novelist.

Hoban first made his name with children's books and with *Turtle Diary* (1976), a novel about two lonely people drawn together by their ambition to return the turtles from the London Zoo to the sea. His chief fame, however, is for *Riddley Walker* (1980). This is a future-fantasy, set in England generations after the nuclear holocaust. The society is primitive – making fire is still a problem, never mind organising the rule of law – and the survivors are haunted by memories of the time before the bomb. Rags of old culture, technology and morality flap in their minds, as inexplicable and as powerful as myth. Their language, similarly – the one the book is written in – is shredded, reconstituted English: words coalesce, grammar has collapsed, new metaphors sprout like weeds. Although this style is difficult at first, it becomes perfectly comprehensible after a few pages, and before long the broken, patched-together words begin to seem like poetry, as Riddley, the story-teller, struggles to find ways to describe the pictures inside his mind.

HOLT, Victoria • *(born 1906)*
British novelist.

'Victoria Holt' is one of the pseudonyms of ▷Eleanor Hibbert. She writes romantic mystery and suspense. In *Secret for a Nightingale*, for example, a 19th-century

READ ON ⟩

● *The Lion of Boaz-Jachin and Jachin-Boaz; The Medusa Frequency.*
▶ ▷William Golding, *Pincher Martin.*
▷George Turner, *Vaneglory.* ▷Anthony Burgess, *A Clockwork Orange.* Robie Macauley, *A Secret History of Time to Come.*

READ ON ⟩

▶ ▷Norah Lofts, *The Wayside Tavern.*
Naomi Jacob,

English girl marries for love in India, and finds out only after her return to England that her husband has not told her everything about himself.

Holt's two dozen other books include Mistress of Mellyn, The Bride of Pendorric, The Shivering Sands, Lord of the Far Islands *and* My Enemy the Queen.

HOMER • *(c 9th century BC)*
Greek epic poet.

Although Homer's *Odyssey* was composed to be declaimed, section by section, at royal feasts, the depth of its character-drawing and its psychological perception transcend such fragmented performances: in a good prose translation (such as E.V. Rieu's) it is as complex and fascinating as any modern novel. Its plot, taken from Greek myth, recounts Odysseus' supernatural adventures on his way home from the Trojan War and his epic battle with the suitors who have plagued his wife Penelope during his absence. But it is also the story of Odysseus' own development, of the way his experiences mould and mature his personality. Each of his encounters – with the flesh-eating giant Polyphemus, the Lotus-eaters, the Sirens, the seductress Calypso, Circe, Nausicaa – changes him, teaches him more about himself, until he is ready to prove himself to his enemies, his people and his patient wife. The *Iliad*, similarly, uses the framework of myth (the quarrel between Achilles and Hector during the Trojan War) to discuss such themes as ambition, pride, courage, the place of destiny in human lives and the glory and futility of war.

'Gollantz' saga.
Cynthia Harrod-Eagles, *'Dynasty' series.*
Caroline Courtney, *Guardian of the Heart.*
Sarah Woodhouse, *The Indian Widow.*

READ ON ▷

▶ **Modern novels drawing on Greek myth:** ▷Robert Graves, *The Golden Fleece/Hercules My Shipmate*; *Homer's Daughter* (a fantasy about the events leading up the composition of the Odyssey); ▷Mary Renault, *The King Must Die*; Henry Treece, *Electra*.
▶ **Books using Homeric style or themes:** Virgil, *Aeneid* (a patriotic Roman epic about the defeated Trojans' voyage to found a new home in Italy); Petronius, *Satyricon* (a parody of the Odyssey set among the pimps, prostitutes, hermaphrodites, fake prophets and sybarites of a fantasy ancient Rome); Miguel de Cervantes Saavedra, *Don Quixote*; ▷Lev Tolstoy, *War and Peace*. The theme of Odysseus' self-discovery, and each individual adventure in turn, inspired ▷James Joyce, *Ulysses*.

HOPE, Anthony • *(1863–1933)*
British novelist.

In *The Prisoner of Zenda* (1894) Hope invented the 'Ruritanian' adventure-story, a colourful escapist yarn set in some fantasy foreign kingdom. Rudolf Rassendyl, an upper-class Englishman on holiday in the middle European country of Ruritania, is astonished to find that he is an exact double of the king, and even more surprised when the king is kidnapped just before his coronation, and Rassendyl is asked to impersonate him. As the story proceeds, the kidnappers (the king's ambitious brother and his henchman Rupert of Hentzau, the finest swordsman in Ruritania) try to foil the coronation-plans, and Rassendyl (who has meanwhile fallen in love with Flavia, the future queen) breaks into Zenda Castle to rescue the imprisoned king. The novel has been filmed a dozen times, and has inspired one of the cinema's favourite clichés: two men, one debonair, one saturnine, duelling up and down the steps of an ancient castle, slicing candles in half, parrying thrusts with three-legged stools and matching each rapier-thrust with a dazzling shaft of wit.

> **READ ON**
>
> ● *Rupert of Hentzau* (the sequel); *Sophy of Kravonia*.
> ▶ Jane Barry, *The Conscience of the King*. Marjorie Bowen, *The Viper of Milan*. Rafael Sabatini, *Captain Blood*. ▷A. Conan Doyle, *The White Company*. P.C. Wren, *Beau Geste*. ▷John Buchan, *John MacNab*. ▷Robert Ludlum, *The Parsifal Mosaic*.

HOUSEHOLD, Geoffrey • *(1909–88)*
British novelist.

Household's thrillers follow squarely in the steps of ▷Buchan, pitting single individuals against the might of sinister corporations, political groups or foreigners, and letting them win by persistence, guts and an invincibly late-Edwardian code of gentlemanly behaviour. Many of his heroes are themselves hunted, and have to 'hole up' either in seedy urban lodgings or in the countryside, where they live by the survival strategies of a commando training manual. The mixture of boys' comic-strip yarns and adult terror is common in English thrillers; in Household's hands it is unsurpassed.

Household's best-known books are Rogue Male, Rogue Justice, The High Place, A Rough Shoot, A Time to Kill, Watcher in the Shadows *and* The Courtesy of Death.

> **READ ON**
>
> ▶ John Welcome, *Run for Cover*. ▷Graham Greene, *A Gun for Sale/This Gun for Hire*. Hugh McCutcheon, *A Hot Wind from Hell*. James Graham, *A Game for Heroes*. William Haggard, *Closed Circuit*. ▷Peter Dickinson, *The Seals*.

HOWATCH, Susan • *(born 1940)*
British novelist.

After a number of atmospheric romances (*The Dark Shore*, *The Waiting Sands*, *April's Grave*, *The Devil on Lammas Night*), Howatch made a second reputation with

> **READ ON**
>
> ▶ Jean Stubbs, *Kits Hill*. Mary Pearce, *The Appletree Saga*.

multi-generation family sagas, setting internal rivalries and alliances against the background of historical events. Her books include *Cashelmara*, *The Rich Are Different* and *Penmarric* (the story of a British family from Victorian times to the second world war).

HUGO, Victor • *(1802–85)*
French novelist, poet and playwright.

Although Hugo was principally a poet and dramatist, he is also remembered for four panoramic historical novels. *Notre Dame de Paris* (1831), set in medieval times, is about the beautiful foundling Esmeralda, the men who try to seduce her, and the deformed Quasimodo, bell-ringer at Notre Dame cathedral, who loves her. The book's detail of Parisian low life is matched in *Les misérables* (1862), about a noble-hearted convict and the corrupt policeman who persecutes him. *The Toilers of the Sea* (1866) allegorises the eternal struggle between human beings and nature into a story of Guernsey fishermen, fighting both the elements and each other. *Ninety-three* (1873) is about royalist resistance in the French Revolution. Hugo's novels are long and prone to philosophising, but they make up for it by the energy of their plots, the melodramatic attraction of their characters – not for nothing is the Hunchback of Notre Dame a Hollywood favourite – and the extraordinary feeling they give that every event, every story, is just one glimpse of the teeming anthill of human life.

HULME, Keri • *(born 1947)*
New Zealand novelist and short-story writer.

Hulme's first novel *The Bone People* was the outsider which won the Booker Prize for 1985. It counterpoints the story of a woman's attemps to 'thaw' an autistic child with an extended reflection on Maori legend and culture. For Hulme, the Maoris are like disabled people in a fit society, and she invests their presence and their culture with the resonance of myth. Her prose-style is uncompromising and experimental, full of fragmented dialogue, stream-of-consciousness narrative and abrupt shifts in time and place. In 1987 *The Bone People* was followed by *The Windeater (Te Kaihau)*, a collection of short stories writ-

Jessica Stirling, *The Spoiled Earth.*

READ ON >

▶ To *Notre Dame de Paris:* Alessandro Manzoni, *The Betrothed* (I promessi sposi).
▶ To *Les misérables:* Heinrich Mann, *The Blue Angel/Small Town Tyrant.*
▶ To *The Toilers of the Sea:* ▷Charles Dickens, *Hard Times.*
▶ To *Ninety-three:* ▷Alexander Solzhenitsyn, *August, 1914.*
▶ To the more swaggering elements of Hugo's style: ▷Lew Wallace, *Ben Hur;* ▷Alexandre Dumas, *The Man in the Iron Mask;* Mika Waltari, *Sinuhe the Egyptian.*

READ ON >

▶ Ian Wedde, *Symme's Hole.* Bruce Chatwin, *The Songlines.* Kathy Acker, *Blood and Guts in High School.* Sheila Watson, *The Double Hook.* Amos Tutuola, *Pauper, Brawler and Slanderer.*

ten over the previous decade. They share the preoccupations, themes and style of *The Bone People* – with an added ingredient, radical feminism – but their shortness makes them easier to read, an excellent introduction to Hulme's work. Despite, or perhaps because of, Hulme's stylistic experiments, the impact of these stories is both overwhelming and unforgettable.

THE HUMAN COMEDY

▷Jane Austen, *Pride and Prejudice*
▷John Cheever, *The Wapshot Chronicle*
▷Peter De Vries, *The Tunnel of Love*
  David Lodge, *The British Museum is Falling Down*
▷Alison Lurie, *Real People*
▷Barbara Pym, *A Glass of Blessings*
▷William Thackeray, *Vanity Fair*
  Angela Thirkell, *High Rising*
▷H.G. Wells, *Tono-Bungay*

Dreaming Spires (p 66); Friends (?) and Neighbours (p 86); Higher (?) Education (p 118)

HUNTER, Evan • *(born 1926)*
US novelist.

Hunter writes under his own name and under the pseudonyms ▷Ed McBain, Richard Marsten (*Rocket to Luna*; *Vanishing Ladies*) and Hunt Collins (*Cut Me In*). As Hunter he has written children's books, plays, screenplays (notably *The Birds*, for Hitchcock), tough novels of New York life (eg *The Blackboard Jungle*, 1954, about an idealistic teacher in a slum high school), and thrillers, many of them agreeably laced with farce. His books (many of them filmed) include *Buddwing*, *The Paper Dragon*, *Last Summer*, *Nobody Knew They Were There*, *Hail to the Chief*, *Where There's Smoke* and *Every Little Crook and Nanny*.

READ ON ▷

▶ Donald Westlake, *The Mercenaries*. ▷Richard Condon, *Prizzi's Honour*. Colin Dunne, *Black Ice*.

HUXLEY, Aldous • *(1894–1963)*
British novelist and non-fiction writer.

Huxley's early books were glittering satires on 1920s intellectual and upper-class life, accounts of preposterous conversations at country-house costume parties and in

READ ON ▷

● *Ape and Essence* (about a California-dwelling group of

such unlikely meeting-places as publishers' offices or the Egyptian Room at the British Museum. His characters are intelligent, creative, fascinating and empty; haunted by the pointlessness of existence, they pass their time flirting, gossiping, swapping philosophical ideas and planning all kinds of japes and pranks. In the 1930s, beginning with *Brave New World*, he changed his approach. Instead of focussing his satire on a single section of British society, he turned on the human race at large, and wrote a series of increasingly bitter books demolishing all our ambitions to make a better society by science, philosophy, religion, socialism or (in the late 1950s, at the germination-stage of flower-power) hallucinatory drugs. His books are a witty, cold dazzle of ideas; enjoyable as you read them, they leave an acid aftertaste.

BRAVE NEW WORLD · *(1932)*

In a soulless future world, genetic engineering programmes people from birth for their status in society, and removes all aggressive or unproductive instincts. Individuality, creativity and personality are sacrificed in the causes of material prosperity, good health and freedom from anxiety. Only a small group of 'savages' – people like us – survives, in a community in New Mexico, and one of them escapes and is brought into the 'real world', with tragic results. As in all his novels, Huxley tells this tale soberly and without comment: the flatness of his prose brilliantly intensifies the horror of what he is saying. Nothing truly terrible happens – and that is the most terrible thing of all.

In chronological order, Huxley's novels are Crome Yellow, Antic Hay, Those Barren Leaves, Point Counter Point, Brave New World, Eyeless in Gaza, After Many a Summer, Time Must Have a Stop, Ape and Essence, The Genius and the Goddess *and* Island. Limbo, Mortal Coils, The Little Mexican, Two or Three Graces *and* Brief Candles *collect short stories, all of them early.*

survivors from the nuclear holocaust, primitives visited by a horror-struck scientist from New Zealand).

▶ **To Huxley's social satires:** ▷F. Scott Fitzgerald, *The Beautiful and Damned* (from the 1920s); ▷Anthony Powell, *Venusberg* (from the 1930s); Martin Amis, *Money* (from the 1980s).

▶ **To *Ape and Essence*:** ▷Paul Theroux, *O-Zone.*

▶ **To Huxley's later books:** Frederick Pohl and C.M. Kornbluth, *The Space Merchants;* ▷L.P. Hartley, *Facial Justice;* Michael Frayn, *Sweet Dreams.*

I

INDIA

▷J.G. Farrell, *The Siege of Krishnapur*
  Valerie Fitzgerald, *Zemindar*
▷E.M. Forster, *A Passage to India*
▷Ruth Prawer Jhabvala, *Heat and Dust*
▷Rudyard Kipling, *Kim*
  T.N. Murari, *Taj*
▷R.K. Narayan, *The Vendor of Sweets*
▷Salman Rushdie, *Midnight's Children*

INNES, Michael • *(born 1906)*
British novelist.

'Michael Innes' is the pseudonym of the Oxford don
J.I.M. Stewart. His 50 detective novels set bizarre puzzles
in the unhurried world of Oxford colleges, English country houses, fine art auction-rooms and elegant Tuscan villas. Well-bred, exquisitely educated people cheat, lie and
kill without ruffling a hair and with a well-turned quota-
tion always on their lips. The blend of privilege and nasti-
ness is brilliant, and the pace of Innes' writing enhances
it. When brutality happens it is fast, unexpected and
breathtaking; when Innes' detectives Appleby or
Honeybath investigate the speed is gentle and unflustered,
allowing plenty of time to savour every epigram, every
devious conversational nuance, every glass of port. Stewart's novels and stories under his own name use similar
locations, the same placid style and an even more twinkly-
eyed cultural affectation, but instead of murders they concern such gentler matters as friendship (especially between
old and young), family feuds, love-affairs and unexpected
inheritances.

> READ ON >

● *The Daffodil Affair*;
  From London Far.
▶ **To Innes' detective
  stories at their
  larkiest:** Edmund
  Crispin, *The Moving
  Toyshop*; Rex Stout,
  Too Many Cooks;
  Carter Dickson, *The
  Ten Teacups*; Gladys
  Mitchell, *Laurels Are
  Poison*.
▶ **To J.I.M. Stewart's
  novels:** ▷C.P. Snow,
  The Masters;
  ▷Anthony Powell,
  Afternoon Men.

OPERATION PAX/PAPER THUNDERBOLT • *(1951)*
In a private clinic in the quiet Oxford countryside something extremely sinister – brainwashing? conditioning by
drugs? plotting world domination? – is going on. A petty
criminal, kidnapped by the experimenters as a human
guinea-pig, escapes and hides in Oxford, where the action
at once involves East European refugees, eccentric dons,
the pupils of a prep school for especially brainy boys, and
John Appleby's pretty young sister Jane. The investigation
climaxes in the 'stacks' of the Bodleian Library, a pile of
eight million books in a cavernous vault under Radcliffe
Square.

*Innes' earlier novels (more convoluted and fantastical
than his later books) include* Death at the President's
Lodgings, Lament for a Maker, Appleby on Ararat, The
Weight of the Evidence, A Night of Errors *and* The
Journeying Boy. *At the heart of Stewart's books is a quin-
tet of novels of Oxford life,* The Gaudy, Young Patullo, A
Memorial Service, The Madonna of the Astrolabe *and*
Full Term. Myself and Michael Innes *is J.I.M. Stewart's*
autobiography.

INTO THE WILDERNESS

▷Willa Cather, *Death Comes for the Archbishop*
▷Joseph Conrad, *Heart of Darkness*
  Fenimore Cooper, *The Last of the Mohicans*
▷Eleanor Dark, *The Timeless Land*
  Brian Moore, *Black Robe*
▷Paul Theroux, *The Mosquito Coast*
▷Patrick White, *Voss*

IRVING, John • *(born 1942)*
US novelist.

At first glance, Irving's novels seem little more than surreal black comedies, magic realism exported from South
to North America. In fact, nothing that happens in his
books is unbelievable: his tales may lose nothing in the
telling, but they are always plausible. The main characters
of *Setting Free the Bears* plot to release the inmates of the
Vienna Zoo. The hero of *The World According to Garp* is
a writer whose creativity is only triggered when terrible
things happen to the women he loves. The family in *The*

READ ON

● *The World According
to Garp.*
▶ ▷Salman Rushdie,
Midnight's Children.
Richard Brautigan,
*Trout Fishing in
America.* ▷Russell
Hoban, *Turtle Diary.*
Gerald H. Morris,

Hotel New Hampshire turns a derelict girls' school into a hotel (complete with dancing bear), and later, when business falls off, moves to Austria where the hotels are smaller, the bears are cleverer, and terrorists are threatening to take over the Vienna Opera. Irving, in his deadpan way, constantly implies – and who can deny it? – that there is nothing eccentric here, that he is recording the bizarreness of life itself.

THE CIDER HOUSE RULES • *(1985)*

Homer Wells, brought up in a rural Maine orphanage and abortion clinic run by the saintly ether-addict Dr Larch, struggles against his destiny, which is to become a gynaecologist and take his mentor's place. He runs away, becomes the manager of a cider-farm, falls in love with his best friend's wife and lives a life of confused obscurity – but he constantly feels the pull back to the clinic and to Melony, a homicidal feminist who hero-worships him and is waiting her chance to murder him.

Irving's other novels are The Water-Method Man *and* The 158-Pound Marriage.

ISHERWOOD, Christopher • *(1904–86)*
British/US writer of novels, screenplays and non-fiction.

Isherwood was a university teacher in California, a writer of plays, films and non-fiction books (chiefly autobiographical or on Hindu mysticism). His novels and stories are all based on personal experience. The best-known (*Mr Norris Changes Trains/The Last of Mr Norris*, 1935; *Goodbye to Berlin*, 1939; *The Berlin Stories*, 1946) are set in 1930s Berlin, a seedy, decadent city haunted by German defeat in the first world war and by the gathering power of nazism. They are first person stories, told by a naive young language teacher amused, perplexed and vaguely terrified by the human tragi-comedy he reports. They have been filmed, made into a stage-play (*I Am a Camera*) and a hit musical (*Cabaret*). In a similarly rueful vein, Isherwood's novel *A Single Man* (1964) describes the emptily busy life of a lonely homosexual teaching English literature at a US university.

ISHIGURO, Kazuo • *(born 1954)*
Japanese/British novelist.

Ishiguro was educated in England and writes in English. His books are gentle, poetic studies of the effects on pre-

---

Doves and Silk Handkerchieves. Jack Trevor Story, *Morag's Flying Fortress*.

> **READ ON**

● *Prater Violet; A Meeting by the River*.
▶ ▷Ruth Prawer Jhabvala, *Heat and Dust*. ▷Mary McCarthy, *Birds of America*. Michael Frayn, *The Russian Interpreter*. Francis King, *The Custom House*. ▷Angus Wilson, *Setting the World on Fire*.

> **READ ON**

▶ ▷R.K. Narayan, *The English Teacher/*

sent-day Japanese of earlier 20th-century events. The central character of *A Pale View of Hills* (1982), a middle-aged woman living in England, is driven by her daughter's suicide to a prolonged reverie about her own childhood in Nagasaki, and her attempt to rebuild her life and her emotional relationships after the city's atomic destruction in 1945. Oni, the elderly protagonist of *An Artist of the Floating World* (1986), was a prominent propagandist for Japanese militarism in the 1930s, and now, in his own 60s, has to come to terms with the collapse of his professional life, his ostracism by younger colleagues, and the way his own children's moral values, typical of the new Japan, seem to deny everything he ever believed in or affirmed.

Grateful to Life and Death. ▷Willa Cather, *The Professor's House.* ▷Graham Greene, *The Quiet American.*

J

JAGGER, Brenda • *(1937–86)*
British novelist.

Jagger wrote historical romances, many of them in series and most set in Yorkshire. Her books include the trilogy *Clouded Hills*, *Flint and Roses* and *Sleeping Sword*, and *A Song Twice Over* (1985, about two early Victorian women, one poor, one rich, who fall in love with the same man).

> **READ ON**

▶ ▷Maeve Binchy, *Light a Penny Candle*. Alice Adams, *Superior Women*. ▷Georgette Heyer, *False Colours*.

JAMES, Henry • *(1843–1916)*
US/British novelist and short-story writer.

As well as novels, James wrote plays, essays, travel-books, literary criticism and a dozen volumes of short stories. In his fiction he returned again and again to the same theme: the conflict between decadence and innocence. James identified decadence with the 'old culture' of Europe, and innocence with the late 19th-century USA; his books often involve visitors from one continent experiencing and coming to terms with the other. Because he was not religious – he was brought up as a rationalist – the moral struggle of his plots is usually less between overt 'good' and 'evil' than between different standards and manners, and he also liked to tease out every strand of meaning in a situation, to explain and theorise about his characters' motives and the possible outcome of each choice they make. Untangling this, especially in his last three, most intricately stylised novels (*The Wings of the Dove*, *The Ambassadors* and *The Golden Bowl*), is one of the chief pleasures of his work.

THE WINGS OF THE DOVE • *(1902)*
Kate Croy lives with her snobbish aunt, who plans to

> **READ ON**

● *Portrait of a Lady* (about the moral and social consequences of a young American's decision to settle in England and Italy); *The Ambassadors* (a long, ironical novel about how Europe changes a group of Americans, young and middle-aged, rich and poor, friends and strangers).

▶ ▷Marcel Proust, *Swann's Way* (part I of *Remembrance of Things Past*). ▷E.M. Forster, *A Room with a View*. ▷Edith Wharton, *The Reef*. ▷Muriel Spark, *The Mandelbaum Gate*.

make a 'great' marriage for her. But Kate is secretly engaged to a penniless journalist, Merton Densher. Millie Theale, a young, rich American, visits Kate's aunt to be introduced to London society, and becomes Kate's friend. Millie is frail, and it is soon apparent that she is dying. She goes to Venice, where she welcomes all her friends in a decaying palazzo on the Grand Canal. Kate persuades Merton to try and comfort Millie's last months by pretending that he loves her; Kate hopes that Millie will then leave money to Merton which will enable them to marry. So everyone will be happy. But another of Millie's suitors, the unprincipled Lord Mark, tells Millie of Merton's and Kate's secret engagement – a revelation which brings tragedy to all three principal characters.

James' other novels include Daisy Miller, Portrait of a Lady, Washington Square, The Bostonians, The Spoils of Poynton *and* The Tragic Muse. *Of his 100 short stories and novellas, the best-known are* The Turn of the Screw *(about two children haunted by a sinister dead couple),* The Real Thing *and* The Lesson of the Master.

JAMES, P.D. (Phyllis Dorothy) •
(born 1920)
British novelist.

Although James is often described as the 1980s 'Queen of Crime', ▷Agatha Christie's heir, she is more like a cross between ▷Sayers and ▷Highsmith. The crimes in her books are brutal, are committed by deranged, psychopathic people, and are described in chilling, unblinking prose as objective as a forensic report. Her detective, Adam Dalgliesh, is a poet and aesthete, combining brilliant detective instincts with a liberal conscience and a dandyish distaste for what he does. Although the books at first seem long and leisurely, James racks tension inexorably tighter until her dénouement: not a cosy Christieish explanation round the library fire, but a scene of pathological, cathartic violence.

A TASTE FOR DEATH • *(1986)*
A lonely spinster, taking flowers to decorate her local church, finds the throat-cut corpses of a tramp, Harry Mack, and a prominent Tory MP, Sir Paul Berowne. Berowne has been the subject of recent slanderous accusations, and Dalgliesh's investigation must begin by deciding whether he was murdered or committed suicide after killing Mack. The story gradually sucks in various members of Berowne's large and mutually hostile family, his servants and his mistress – and as well as showing us this,

▷Stendhal, *Scarlet and Black*. ▷Elizabeth Bowen, *Eva Trout*.

> READ ON >

● *Death of an Expert Witness*.
► ▷Ngaio Marsh, *Surfeit of Lampreys*.
▷Marjorie Allingham, *The Tiger in the Smoke*. ▷Patricia Highsmith, *Ripley Under Ground*. ▷Ruth Rendell, *A Sleeping Life*. Margaret Millar, *Mermaid*.

and describing the police work in exact, unhurried detail, the book also concerns itself with the lives and preoccupations of Dalgliesh's assistants, especially Inspector Kate Miskin, the newest member of the team.

James' other novels are Cover Her Face, A Mind to Murder, Unnatural Causes, Shroud for a Nightingale, An Unsuitable Job for a Woman, The Black Tower, Innocent Blood *and* The Skull Beneath the Skin.

JANSSON, Tove • *(born 1917)*
Finnish novelist and children's writer.

Jansson is best-known for her 'Moomin' books for children: humorous fantasies about gentle balloon-creatures with magic powers. *The Summer Book* (1972), for adults, is a short, beautiful novel about a young child's relationship with her grandmother. The two of them quietly investigate their world – much of the book takes place on a peaceful island in the Gulf of Finland where the family are spending the summer – and share their feelings. They have two kinds of innocence: the child's freshness and the grandmother's paring-down of a lifetime's experience. The mood is placid and evocative, and for all its shortness the book is one of the half-dozen most poetic evocations of childhood composed this century.

> **READ ON** ▷
>
> ● *Sun City.*
> ► **Childhood memoirs of similar poetic intensity:** Laurie Lee, *Cider With Rosie*; Flora Thompson, *Lark Rise to Candleford*; W.H. Hudson, *Far Away and Long Ago*; ▷Vladimir Nabokov, *Speak, Memory*; Gerald Durrell, *My Family and Other Animals.*

JARRELL, Randall • *(1914–65)*
US poet, children's writer and novelist.

Jarrell's main fame is for poetry and a well-loved children's book, *The Animal Family* (1965). His only adult novel, *Pictures from an Institution* (1954), is one of the funniest of all campus comedies. It takes place in a progressive women's college in the 1950s. The girls are dewy-eyed innocents, passionate for life and learning; the faculty-members are wild eccentrics, whether they be Dr Rosenblum the advanced Austrian composer, Jerrold and Flo Whittaker the hippie sociologists, Gertrude the experimental novelist (and her down-trodden husband and greatest fan Sidney) or President Robbins himself, formerly an Olympic swimmer and now a fundraising superman. There is no real plot: the book runs through one eventful year, and the fun is in Jarrell's mixture of malice, magnificent one-liners and affection for even his most absurd characters.

> **READ ON** ▷
>
> ► D.J. Enright, *Academic Year.* ▷Anthony Burgess, *Enderby's Dark Lady.* ▷Kingsley Amis, *Lucky Jim.* Robertson Davies, *The Rebel Angels.*

JEROME, Jerome K. (Klapka) •
(1859–1927)
British novelist and journalist.

Jerome, an actor, wrote humorous pieces while waiting to go on stage; after the success of *Three Men in a Boat* in 1889 he became a full-time writer. *Three Men in a Boat* is the story of a boating holiday on the Thames undertaken by three London clerks (to say nothing of the dog). The book's deadpan humour – what Jerome calls its 'hopeless and incurable veracity' – depends on magnifying life's small problems (such as opening a tin without a tin-opener, or being in the same house as a courting couple without embarrassing them) to epic proportions, and on losing no opportunity for reflections on life, liberty, the pursuit of happiness, and the heroes' invincible conviction that middle-class Victorian young Britons, such as them-selves, are the goal to which all human evolution has been tending.

> **READ ON** >

● *Three Men on a Bummel*; *My Life and Times* (autobiography).
▶ George and Weedon Grossmith, *The Diary of a Nobody.* ▷Max Beerbohm, *Zuleika Dobson.* A.G. Macdonell, *England, Their England.* Stephen Leacock, *Literary Lapses.* Giovanni Guareschi, *The House that Nino Built.*

JHABVALA, Ruth Prawer • *(born 1927)*
British novelist and screenwriter.

In a series of placid, gently ironical novels and screen-plays (beginning with *Shakespeare Wallah* (1965), for the Merchant-Ivory partnership), Jhabvala has become a main European chronicler of India since the Raj. She is less in-terested in public events than in emotions, and particularly in the interface between two mutually uncomprehending cultures, Indian and European. In her best-known book, *Heat And Dust* (1975, filmed 1983), a young Englishwo-man visits modern India to find out about her aunt's un-happy love-affair there 60 years before. The story cuts be-tween the two periods, contrasting the modern character's apparently sophisticated racial and cultural awareness with the aunt's naivety and immaturity, and making points about attitudes (of Indians towards the English and vice versa) both during the Raj and in our own day.

Jhabvala's novels include To Whom She Will, The Na-ture of Passion, Esmond in India, The Householder, Get Ready for Battle, A Backward Glance, A New Dominion, Three Continents *and* In Search of Love and Beauty *(set in the USA, and influenced by her experience scripting* ▷Henry James' The Europeans *for Merchant-Ivory).* Like Birds Like Fishes, A Stronger Climate, An Experience of India, Out of India *and* How I Became a Holy Mother *are collections of short stories.*

> **READ ON** >

● *Esmond in India.*
▶ ▷E.M. Forster, *A Passage to India.* Paul Scott, *Staying On.* Rabindrath Tagore, *The Home and the World.* Anita Desai, *Games at Twilight* (stories).

JONG, Erica • *(born 1942)*
US novelist and poet.

Although Jong is primarily a poet, she became world-famous for two bleak prose satires on our contemporary obsession with sex. The novels are the autobiography of
Isadora. In *Fear of Flying* (1974) she spends her time
cock-hunting: the Holy Grail, she tells us, is the 'zipless
fuck', sex without commitment, and she searches for it in
locker-rooms, on trains and planes, on beaches, in hotel
rooms and wherever else multiple orgasms beckon. In
How to Save Your Own Life (1978) she has fame and
wealth (as the author of a best-selling dirty book), and
walks the treadmill of personal appearances, tours and the
jetset life while still (metaphorically and literally) unzip-
ping every man in sight. But by now the sex is even more
mechanical; the pleasure is no smaller but lasts less long,
and Isadora is increasingly obsessed by the void in her
own life where love should be. Jong's novels have sold
because of their frequent, explicit descriptions of sexual
coupling – no position is left untried – and because they
were at the forefront of the battle to have women's sexuality treated as openly as men's. But they also, chiefly, sa-
tirise contemporary US life and values. The zipless fuck is
a metaphor for instant gratification of every kind, and the
books' insistent theme is that there is much, much more to
life.

*Serenissima is a fantasy about a woman transported back
in time to 16th-century Venice, where she has a passionate affair with a young English playwright and poet who
later immortalises her as 'the dark lady'. Jong's poetry-
collections include* Fruits and Vegetables, Half-Lives,
Loveroot, Here Comes *and* At the Edge of the Body.

JOYCE, James • *(1882–1941)*
Irish novelist and short-story writer.

Although Joyce settled in Italy at 27, and spent the rest of
his life there, he never left the Ireland of his memory: his
work is a ceaseless exploration of Irish scenery, education, history, religion, habits of thought and patterns of
daily life. His early writings – the short stories in *Dubliners* (1914) and the novel *Portrait of the Artist as a
Young Man* (1915), based on his own school and university life – are stylistically straightforward. They are also
notable for precise evocation of sensation and atmosphere.
By giving a mosaic of tiny impressions 'the feel of
wooden desks in a schoolroom, the taste of mud on a

READ ON ▷

► ▷Lisa Alther, *Kinflicks*.
Marilyn French, *The
Women's Room*.
▷Jean Rhys, *Good
Morning, Midnight*.

READ ON ▷

► Ralph Ellison, *Invisible
Man*. ▷Malcolm Lowry,
Under the Volcano.
▷Thomas Wolfe, *Look
Homeward, Angel*.
▷Virginia Woolf, *Mrs
Dalloway*. ▷John
Kennedy Toole, *A
Confederacy of
Dunces* is a kind of
comic Ulysses, set in
New Orleans, and both

rugby field, the smell of gas-lamps in student digs) Joyce builds up a detailed picture which is both factually and emotionally compelling. (▷Proust used a similar idea in the childhood sections of *Remembrance of Things Past*.) In his two long novels, *Ulysses* (1922) and *Finnegans Wake* (1939), Joyce developed this mosaic structure further: *Ulysses* relates the events of a single day, *Finnegans Wake* a man's thoughts and dreams during a single night. Parts of these books are stream-of-consciousness monologues, a tumble of apparently unrelated sentences threading a path through the maze of one person's mind. Joyce often seems to be collapsing language itself: syntax splits apart; words blur into one another; each page is a kaleidoscope of puns, parodies, half-quotations, snatches of song and snippets from half a dozen languages. Some people find this style unreadable; for others it is endlessly rewarding, a mesmeric impression of the jumble of thought itself.

ULYSSES • *(1922)*

The book follows two people, Leopold Bloom and Stephen Dedalus, from dawn to midnight on a single day in Dublin in 1904. At one level what they do is ordinary: they shave, go to the privy, eat, drink, argue in bars, go to a funeral, borrow money, flirt with girls on a beach, visit Dublin's red-light area. But Joyce also shows us their thoughts, the fragmentary responses and impressions evoked by each real incident. The book ends with a 60-page 'interior monologue', the inconsequential, erotic reverie of Bloom's wife Molly as she lies beside him, drifting into sleep.

Joyce's works are Dubliners; Portrait of the Artist as a Young Man *(based on an earlier, unfinished novel,* Stephen Hero, *which has also been published);* Ulysses; Finnegans Wake; Chamber Music *and* Pomes Penyeach *(poetry).*

Joyce's experimental writing and the whole concept of Irishness are spectactularly sent up in Flann O'Brien, *At Swim-Two-Birds*.

James **JOYCE**

James **PLUNKETT, STRUMPET CITY**
(*Dublin life and troubles – of all kinds – before World War I*)

Molly **KEANE, GOOD BEHAVIOUR**
(*large Anglo-Irish family collapsing under its own eccentricity*)

Flann **O'BRIEN, AT SWIM-TWO-BIRDS**
(*homosexual biographer doing research, finds himself being engulfed by his subject and by memories of his own past life*)

IRELAND

Virginia **WOOLF, MRS DALLOWAY**
(*middle-class Englishwoman preparing for dinner-party reviews –and reveals – her whole existence and inner self*)

Marcel **PROUST, THE GUERMANTES WAY**
(*Part III of* Remembrance of Things Past *– the effects of death – of love and the death of the beloved*)

SELF-DISCOVERY

Iris **MURDOCH, THE SANDCASTLE**
(*middle-aged schoolmaster, besotted with young artist, finds his whole life toppling round his ears*)

Joseph **HELLER, SOMETHING HAPPENED**
(*empty man, New York business executive, reviews the reasons for the failure of his career and family life*)

John **FOWLES, THE MAGUS**
(*man seeks true meaning of experience: is our life as real as it seems, or a series of illusions – and if illusion, how well-disposed is the illusionist?*)

(journey of self-discovery on single Dublin day in 1904)

Alexander **THEROUX**, **D'ARCONVILLE'S CAT**
(jilted by sophomore lover, D'Arconville leaves US Deep South to 'find himself' in Venice)

John **BARTH**, **GILES GOAT-BOY**
(US professor tries to bring up child free of original sin)

Salman **RUSHDIE**, **MIDNIGHT'S CHILDREN**
(Saleem and family, 'handcuffed to India', experience the 80-year evolution of independence and self-renewal)

Laurence **STERNE**, **TRISTRAM SHANDY**
('autobiography' of 18th-century English gentleman turns into the longest, richest shaggy-dog story ever told)

'JOYCEAN' NOVELS:

BIG, EXPERIMENTAL, ALL-ENCOMPASSING

Italo **SVEVO**, **THE CONFESSIONS OF ZENO**
(explaining to his psychiatrist why he can't give up smoking, Zeno tells the tale of his extraordinary, inadequate existence)

Joyce **CARY**, **THE HORSE'S MOUTH**
(eccentric artist determines to live bohemian existence, boozy and bawdy, reinventing his own character from day to day)

John Kennedy **TOOLE**, **A CONFEDERACY OF DUNCES**
(self-confessed genius bestrides New Orleans like an anarchic, flatulent colossus, finds it too small to accommodate his appetite for mischief)

Anthony **BURGESS**, **EARTHLY POWERS**
('memoirs' of aged homosexual novelist, who has been at heart of all human betrayal and bitchiness since the 20th century began)

Robertson **DAVIES**, **WHAT'S BRED IN THE BONE**
(odyssey of art-forger, thief and conman, as discovered from his will)

Saul **BELLOW**, **HUMBOLDT'S GIFT**
(Chicago)

J. D. **SALINGER**, **THE CATCHER IN THE RYE**
(New York)

CITIES

Lawrence **DURRELL**, **THE ALEXANDRIA QUARTET**

Eleanor **DARK**, **WATERWAY**
(Sydney)

K

KAFKA, Franz • *(1883-1924)*
Czech novelist and short-story writer.

In the 1920s and 1930s people regarded Kafka as an un-smiling neurotic who depicted the human condition as a bureaucratic hell without explanation or compassion: 'Kafkaesque' was a synonym for 'nightmarish'. Kafka, by contrast, always regarded himself as a humorist, in the line of such surrealist East European jokers as ▷Gogol. Each of his novels and stories develops a single idea to ludicrous, logical-illogical extremes. In 'Metamorphosis' a man has to cope with the fact that he has turned into a gigantic beetle overnight. The prison-camp commander of 'In the Penal Colony' is so eager to show off a newly-invented punishment-machine that he turns it on himself. In 'The Burrow' a creature designs a defence-system of underground tunnels so complex and so perfect that it becomes the whole meaning of existence: it engulfs its own creator. The central figure of *The Trial (Der Prozess)* is arrested one morning although he has done nothing wrong, spends the book trying to discover the charges against him, and is finally executed without explanation. It is easy to treat such tales as psychological or political allegories. But it is also possible to read them as jokes, grimly funny anecdotes invented just for the hell of it. Perhaps keeping his face straight was Kafka's best trick of all.

THE CASTLE (Das Schloss) • *(1926)*
An ordinary, unremarkable man, K, arrives in a strange town to take up the post of Land Surveyor. He finds that no one is expecting him, that the town and the castle which dominates it are a labyrinthine bureaucracy where everyone is responsible only for passing the buck to some-one else, and each favour done, each door opened, leads

READ ON ⟩

● *The Trial*; *America* (the story of a naive young German who goes to the USA thinking that its streets are paved with gold, and goes on believing it despite being cheated and betrayed by everyone he meets).
▶ **Echoing Kafka's humour:** ▷Jaroslav Hašek, *The Good Soldier Švejk*; ▷Joseph Heller, *Catch-22*; ▷Nathanael West, *The Dream Life of Balso Snell*; Joe Orton, *Head to Toe*.
▶ **Echoing the idea of a 'Kafkaesque', nightmare society:** Rex Warner, *The Aerodrome*; Alasdair Gray, *Lanark*; Max Frisch, *I'm Not Stiller*; ▷George Orwell, *1984*.

only to more confusion. K's efforts to reach the heart of the mystery, to be given some official confirmation of his existence, are doomed, hilarious and have the logic not of reality but of a very bad dream indeed.

Kafka's novels are The Trial, The Castle *and* America. *Of the many collections of his stories, the best is* Kafka's Shorter Works, *translated by* Malcolm Pasley.

KENEALLY, Thomas • *(born 1935)*
Australian novelist and playwright.

Although Keneally has written books on many subjects, including the partly-autobiographical *Three Cheers for the Paraclete* (1968), about a young Roman Catholic losing his faith, he is best-known for 'faction': powerful fictional treatments of the issues and personalities behind real events. Apart from *Blood Red, Sister Rose* (1974), about Joan of Arc, his books are set in comparatively recent times, usually at decisive moments in the history of a people or continent – and Keneally gets under the skin of the participants, showing how great events happen for what are usually far smaller and more personal reasons (a quarrel; a cold in the head) than the awareness of grand political or strategic trends which historians would suggest. He is not, however, a 'historical' novelist, simply telling tales about the past. His concentration on issues gives his stories universal resonance: we are constantly shown the relevance of the events he describes to our present-day situation or attitudes. His best-known books are *The Chant of Jimmie Blacksmith* (1971, about racial confrontation in 19th-century Australia), *Gossip from the Forest* (1973, set during the 1918 Armistice negotiations), *Confederates* (1979, about Stonewall Jackson's campaigns in the American civil war) and *The Playmaker* (1987, see right).

SCHINDLER'S ARK • *(1982)*
Schindler is a bragging, boozing opportunist who makes a fortune in Poland during the second-world-war German occupation, buying up the businesses of dispossessed Jews. We read about his black-market deals, his backslapping relationship with the authorities, his parties and his mistresses – and gradually discover that his lifestyle is a façade, that his true activity is saving thousands of Jews from the gas-chambers.

Keneally's other novels include A Dutiful Daughter, Bring Larks and Heroes *(set in 19th-century New South Wales)*, Season in Purgatory *(about Tito and the Yugoslavian par-*

> **READ ON**

● *The Playmaker* (in which convicts transported to 18th-century New South Wales, under the guidance of a confused, would-be liberal army lieutenant, rehearse and perform – of all things – Farquhar's Restoration comedy *The Recruiting Officer*).
▶ E.L. Doctorow, *The Book of Daniel*. Lionel Davidson, *Making Good Again*. William Styron, *Sophie's Choice*.

Thomas KENEALLY

E.L. **DOCTOROW, THE BOOK OF DANIEL**
(lives of children of US immigrants executed for espionage)

John **FOWLES, A MAGGOT**
(witchcraft, murder and possible UFOs in 18th-century England)

Tony **WEEKS-PEARSON, DODO**
(extermination of dodo brings culture-shock to native inhabitants of idyllic Pacific island)

Frederick **FORSYTH, THE DAY OF THE JACKAL**
(plot to assassinate General de Gaulle of France)

Martin Cruz **SMITH, STALLION GATE**
(Mexican magic versus development of first atomic bomb)

NOVELS ARISING FROM REAL EVENTS

Bruce **CHATWIN, THE SONG LINES**
(writer travels modern Australia, investigating Aboriginal sacred places)

William **GOLDING, CLOSE QUARTERS**
(life on 1790s convict-ship sailing from England to Australia)

THE AUSTRALIAN PAST

Eleanor **DARK, THE TIMELESS LAND**
(first white settlers in Australia)

Patrick **WHITE, A FRINGE OF LEAVES**
(shipwrecked 1910s woman learns survival by assimilating Aborigine culture)

Nathaniel **HAWTHORNE, THE SCARLET LETTER**
(religious hysteria and persecution in Puritan New England)

Chinua **ACHEBE, THINGS FALL APART**
(Nigerian tribal life, the rhythms of civilisation, disrupted by coming of white missionaries)

FRONTIERS OF CIVILISATION

Brian **MOORE, BLACK ROBE**
(Jesuit priest in 17th-century Huron Indian country: irreconcilable culture-clash)

(1780s Australia: English officer guides convicts through production of a Restoration comedy)

Victor HUGO, LES MISÉRABLES
(19th-century France: honest man wrongly convicted to the galleys tries to rehabilitate himself)

Alexander SOLZHENITSYN, ONE DAY IN THE LIFE OF IVAN DENISOVICH
(20th-century USSR: unsparing account of life in labour-camp for dissidents)

CONVICTS

Charles DICKENS, LITTLE DORRIT
(19th-century England: corrupting effects of money, and life in the Marshalsea Debtors' Prison)

John CHEEVER, FALCONER
(20th-century USA: life in 'correctional facility' as experienced by mentally unstable, middle-class wife-murderer)

Robertson DAVIES, TEMPEST-TOST
(amateurs in 1950s Canadian university town)

Paul BAILEY, PETER SMART'S CONFESSIONS
(testimony of unsuccessful, mentally unstable actor)

PLAYS AND PLAY ACTORS

Virginia WOOLF, BETWEEN THE ACTS
(thoughts and feelings of everyone involved in village historical pageant)

Roger LANGRIGG, THERE'S A PORPOISE CLOSE BEHIND US *(sour success of 'bright young things' on 1930s London stage)*

AUSTRALIAN LIFE:
THE FUNNY SIDE

Elizabeth JOLLEY, THE FUNNY SIDE

Peter CAREY, ILLYWHACKER

Howard JACOBSON, REDBACK

tisans during and after the second world war), A Victim of the Aurora, A Family Madness, Passenger *and* The Cut-Rate Kingdom. *He has also written films, stage plays, children's books and a fascinating account of his travels in Australia*, Outback.

KING, Stephen • *(born 1946)*
US novelist.

King writes horror-stories: tales of obsession, insanity and the supernatural made even more terrifying by the ordinary US suburbs, schools and factories where they take place. His books (many made into blockbuster films) are *The Dead Zone*, *Carrie*, *Salem's Lot*, *Firestarter*, *The Shining*, *The Stand*, *Christine*, *Pet Sematary*, *Cujo*, *It* and *Misery* (1987), about a best-selling author kidnapped by a maniac. *Night Shift* and *Skeleton Crew* are collections of ghoulish short stories. King also writes as *Richard Bachman* (whose *Thinner*, about a man tormented by a gipsy's curse, is not for readers who find it hard to sleep).

READ ON >

▶ **To King's novels:**
▷James Herbert, *Sepulchre*; Richard Matheson, *The Shrinking Man*; ▷Ruth Rendell, *Live Flesh* – and, from an earlier generation, ▷H.G. Wells, *The Island of Doctor Moreau*.
▶ **To his short stories:**
▷Edgar Allan Poe, *Tales of Mystery and Imagination*; ▷Patricia Highsmith, *Mermaids on the Golf Course*; Roald Dahl, *Kiss, Kiss*; ▷Angela Carter, *Fireworks*.

KIPLING, Rudyard • *(1865–1936)*
British short-story writer and poet.

Kipling learned his craft working for English-language newspapers in India in the 1880s. He wrote reports, stories and poems about the British soldiers and administrators, their servants and the snake-charmers, fortune-tellers and other characters of the towns they lived in. Later, during the Boer War, he worked as a correspondent in South Africa, where he was a friend of Cecil Rhodes. Under the circumstances, it would have been hard for him not to reflect the imperialist attitudes of his age, first sunny confidence and then the jingoistic panic which overtook it in late Victorian times. But he is a more rewarding writer than this suggests. His sympathies were always with subordinates – with private soldiers rather than generals, servants rather than employers, children rather than adults. He wrote well about all three: his stories for and about children, in particular, are magnificent. Something like half of each collection – most books contain both stories

READ ON >

● *Plain Tales from the Hills*; *Debits and Credits*.
▶ **To Kipling's stories about children:**
▷Katherine Mansfield, *Bliss and Other Stories*.
▶ **To his stories about colonial adults:**
▷Somerset Maugham, *Orientations*; the short stories of Noël Coward. ▷John Masters, *Nightrunners of Bengal,* and ▷J.G. Farrell, *The Siege of*

and poems – is nowadays hard to take, not least where he writes in baby-talk (as in the *Just-So Stories*, O best-beloved) or uses funny spellings to evoke Cockney or Irish speech. But every archness is balanced by a gem of insight or sensitivity. In this, too, he was characteristic of his time.

KIM • *(1901)*

This episodic novel is the story of a British orphan brought up as a beggar in Lahore, who becomes first the disciple of a wandering Buddhist priest and then an agent of the British secret service. He travels throughout India, and Kipling uses his adventures as a framework for descriptions of everyday scenes and characters, of 'such a river of life as nowhere else exists in the world'.

Kipling's collections include Barrack-room Ballads, The Seven Seas *and* The Years Between *(verse),* Soldiers Three *(stories), and the mixed prose-and-verse collections* Many Inventions, Traffics and Discoveries, A Diversity of Creatures *and* Debits and Credits. *His novels are* The Light That Failed *and* Captains Courageous, *and his children's books include the* Just-so Stories, *the* Jungle Book, Puck of Pook's Hill *and the public-school yarn* Stalky and Co. Something of Myself *is a guarded autobiography.*

KOSINSKI, Jerzy • *(born 1933)*
Polish/US novelist and non-fiction writer.

Kosinski settled in the USA in his 20s, and all his fiction is in English. He writes of contemporary life with horrified disdain, as if he were a being from an alien planet describing some bizarre and repulsive civilisation – indeed, the SF of such writers as ▷Moorcock or ▷Vonnegut is the closest parallel to his experimental, fantastical style. His best-known book (because of the Peter Sellers film made from it) is *Being There* (1971), about a nonperson, a man of miniscule intelligence whose ideas are received entirely from television or from gardening, and whose monosyllabic mutterings are taken by all around him as profound moral and political philosophy. Chance (the hero) ends up as adviser to the US president, and we are left uncomfortably wondering if he may not also be the only sane person in a lunatic society. Kosinski's other novels also centre on outsiders. The central character of *The Painted Bird* (1965) is a swarthy orphaned child in peasant Poland, regarded by everyone as an alien (a Jew or a gipsy) and rejected. The hero of *The Devil Tree* (1973) is a young man isolated from society both by im-

Krishnapur, about the 1857 Indian 'Mutiny', match Kipling's insight into the heyday of the Raj.

> **READ ON**

● *Steps* (the random thoughts and conversations of a youth growing up in a country he hates and from which he is planning to emigrate as soon as chance allows).
▶ ▷Michael Moorcock, *The English Assassin.* Milan Kundera, *The Book of Laughter and Forgetting.* ▷Saul Bellow, *Mr Sammler's Planet.* Patrick McGinley, *The Trick of the Ga Bolga.* ▷I.B. Singer's short stories, although their subjects are entirely unlike

mense inherited wealth – he could buy and sell whole countries – and by his own adolescent fantasy that he is the only person in the world obsessed by sex. In *Cockpit* (1975) and *Blind Date* (1977) the central characters are secret agents isolated from the real world not only by their trade but by their own burgeoning, uncommunicated thoughts.

KRANTZ, Judith
US novelist.

In the 1970s Krantz took the 'novel of affairs' genre (big-business as sex; sex as big business) perfected a generation earlier by such writers as Harold Robbins, and refurbished it for modern tastes. The businesses of which she writes are multi-national corporations; the wealth is megabucks; the sex is as near pornography as respectable publishers will print. Only the morality remains the same: non-existent. Krantz's books (*Princess Daisy*; *Scruples*; *Mistral's Daughter*; *I'll Take Manhattan*) are like dirtied-up versions of such TV soaps as *Dallas* or *Dynasty*: superb escapism.

Kosinski's, share his feeling that the world is a terrifying, alien environment in which human beings survive – if they do survive – only by chance or because of their own uncompromisingly lateral stance to life.

> READ ON ▷

▶ Shirley Conran, *Lace*. Jackie Collins, *Lucky*. Sally Quinn, *Regrets Only*. Sidney Sheldon, *Bloodlines*.

L

LARGER THAN LIFE

Peter Carey, *Illywhacker*
▷Robertson Davies, *What's Bred in the Bone*
Howard Jacobson, *Redback*
▷Robert Nye, *Falstaff*
Petronius, *Satyricon*
▷François Rabelais, *Gargantua*
▷Laurence Sterne, *Tristram Shandy*

LAWRENCE, D.H. (David Herbert) •
(1885-1930)
British writer of novels, short stories, plays and poems.

For 70 years Lawrence's radicalism has outraged as many people as it has enthralled. He thought that every matter of concern to human beings, and moral and ethical issues in particular, could be settled by rational discussion, if people would only be honest about themselves. His novels deal with such matters as female emancipation, the class struggle, atheism, sexual liberation and pacifism – not explicitly but as part of an ongoing advocacy of nakedness, of people at their best when stripped of inhibition and convention. Lawrence regarded his plain speaking as a way of shedding light in dark corners, a return to the innocence of the Garden of Eden; his enemies thought it shocking. Nowadays, when his rawness seems less threatening, his books stand up not only for moral earnestness – they read at times like humourless, secular sermons – but for their acute presentation of people and society in turmoil, of attitudes to life which the second world war and the dawn of the nuclear age have made seem unimaginably remote.

READ ON ▷

● *The Rainbow.*
▶ ▷George Eliot, *Middlemarch.*
▷Thomas Hardy, *Jude the Obscure* (especially close to *Women in Love* in its treatment of tensions between the sexes). David Storey, *Radcliffe.* Melvyn Bragg, *The Maid of Buttermere.* ▷Thomas Wolfe, *Look Homeward, Angel.* Henry Roth, *Call It Sleep.* ▷James Baldwin, *Go Tell it on the Mountain.*

SONS AND LOVERS • *(1913)*

Paul Morel is the son of ill-matched parents, an ex-school-teacher and an illiterate, alcoholic miner. Morel's mother is determined to help her son escape from the physical grind and intellectual atrophy of pit-village life and fulfil his ambition to be a writer. Her love for him is, however, a force for darkness not liberation. It inhibits both his self-discovery and his relationship with other people (especially the young farm-girl Jessie, who encourages his writing), and it is only when he breaks free of his mother – a protracted, agonising process, a second birth – that he is able to fulfil the destiny she has planned for him.

Lawrence's other novels include The Rainbow *and its sequel* Women in Love, Aaron's Rod, Kangaroo, The Plumed Serpent *and* Lady Chatterley's Lover. *He also published poems, travel books (eg* Sea and Sardinia; Mornings in Mexico*), plays, books on history and literature, and collections of short stories (eg* England, My England; The Woman Who Rode Away*).*

LE CARRÉ, John • *(born 1931)*
British novelist.

For over a century, writers from ▷Verne to ▷Fleming depicted espionage as a swashbuckling, Robin Hood activity with clear rules, absolute moral standards and a penchant for flamboyance. But in the 1960s this view changed. The Cuban missile crisis all but led to world annihilation; the Berlin Wall was built; a series of well-publicised defections revealed that spies were secretive, unremarkable men, morally hesitant and trapped by their own profession. Betrayal, not derring-do, was their stock-in-trade; east, west, north, south, they were as indistinguishable as civil service clerks. This is the atmosphere of Le Carré's books. His characters are not James Bonds, swaggering forth to smash conspiracies of global domination; in dark back streets and rainy woods they nibble away at one another's loyalties, hardly even certain of their own. It is a world of remorseless moral erosion, and Le Carré chillingly shows how it functions entirely for itself, inward-looking and self-perpetuating, with minimal relevance to real life. Since he began writing, every real-life spy-scandal, every revelation of how the 'intelligence' community works, seems to prove his accuracy – unless spies themselves have come to believe the legend he spins.

THE QUEST FOR KARLA • *(1974–80)*
This trilogy (*Tinker Tailor Soldier Spy, The Honourable*

> **READ ON**

● *A Small Town in Germany; A Perfect Spy.*

▶ **To the spy-stories:** ▷Ruth Rendell, *Talking to Strange Men;* ▷Graham Greene, *The Human Factor;* John Lear, *Death in Leningrad.* Julian Semyonov, *Tass is Authorized to Announce* is a cold-war spy-story seen from the Russian side.

▶ **To** *The Naive and Sentimental Lover:* ▷John Fowles, *Daniel Martin;* ▷Frederic Raphael, *April, June and November.*

▶ **To** *The Little Drummer Girl;* ▷Doris Lessing, *The Good Terrorist.*

John LE CARRÉ

THE PERFECT SPY (*'autobiography' of upper-echelon British spy — and double-agent*)

Robert LUDLUM, THE PARSIFAL MOSAIC
(can 'burnt-out' agent's secret knowledge prevent World War III?)

John LEAR, DEATH IN LENINGRAD
(ex-spy Ashweald revels in Leningrad — but there is a price to pay)

John TRENHAILE, THE MAHJONG SPIES
(can Chinese Intelligence stop KGB destabilising Hong Kong?)

Ted ALLBEURY, THE SECRET WHISPERS
(double agent escaping from eastern to western Europe)

Martin Cruz SMITH, STALLION GATE
(can Mexican folk magic halt 1945 race to develop atomic bomb?)

Michael MOLLOY, THE KID FROM RIGA
(can SAS officer give up his career for love? In the meantime . . .)

Walter WAGER, TELEFON
(brainwashed assassins, 'sleepers', await trigger phone-calls to terrorise USA)

Jack HIGGINS, CONFESSIONAL
(KGB agent sent to Belfast to stir things up)

Ian FLEMING, DOCTOR NO
(super-agent 007 outwits psychopathic master-criminal)

Len DEIGHTON, HORSE UNDER WATER
(drugs, spies, master-criminals, all boiled together in Marrakesh)

Eric AMBLER, THE MASK OF DIMITRIOS/COFFIN
FOR DIMITRIOS *(hero tracks down elusive, deadly master-criminal)*

Philip MACDONALD, THE LIST OF ADRIAN MESSENGER
(10 people on list, marked for death. What is the link — and can they be saved in time?)

A. J. QUINNELL, IN THE NAME OF THE FATHER
(who is killing off ageing world leaders, one by one?)

Schoolboy and *Smiley's People*) is about the British Intelligence 'circus', and particularly the role played in it by a
senior official, George Smiley. His task is to investigate
double agents, 'moles', inside the service, while safeguarding his own position and keeping warily in touch
with contacts and rivals in the eastern bloc. His enquiries
uncover treacheries and compromises extending back over
two generations: the corrupt, Kafkaesque 'Circus', with its
links to Oxbridge, the public schools, clubland and government, is a cancer at the throat of British life, and
Smiley is interested less in curing it than in a complex
damage-limitation exercise.

Le Carré's other spy-books are The Spy Who Came in
from the Cold, The Looking Glass War, A Small Town in
Germany *and* A Perfect Spy. *His other books are the
detective stories* Call for the Dead *and* A Murder of Quality, The Naive and Sentimental Lover (*about a bored middle-aged man given the chance to reconstruct his life*) *and*
The Little Drummer Girl (*about a young idealist in the
Middle East who turns to terrorism*).

LE GUIN, Ursula • *(born 1929)*
US novelist.

Le Guin made her name writing space opera (the 'League
of All Worlds' series), and the prize-winning 'Earthsea'
trilogy for children. In the late 1960s and 1970s she
broadened her scope, using the framework of alternative-
world fantasy to discuss social, ecological and political
themes. Although many of her books are still technically
SF, set in the future and on other planets, she also lets
people from the past and the present break through into
magical kingdoms whose values and customs are ironical
variations on our own. *The Word for World is Forest*
(1976) takes place on a planet covered in forests and inhabited (literally) by 'little green people', who shepherd
the trees and spend their lives in placid meditation. Then
earthpeople come to harvest the trees, treat the locals as
mindless and worthless and force them to learn to fight for
their way of life. *The Left Hand of Darkness* (1969) is a
poetic description of Winterworld, of how people cope
with life in an utterly hostile natural environment. The
hero of *Malafrena* (1980) is a landowner's son who becomes a revolutionary leader in a world in which the political ferment of post-Napoleonic Europe is blended with
the religious outlook of Germany in Luther's time and the
psychological and ecological concerns of the late 20th
century; although science and technology are unfailingly
medieval, in all other respects time on Earth has become a

> **READ ON**

● *The Left Hand of
Darkness*.
▶ ▷Tom De Haan, *A
Mirror for Princes*.
▷Stephen Donaldson,
Lord Foul's Bane (first
in the 'Chronicles of
Thomas Covenant'
series). Ian Watson,
*The Gardens of
Delight*. C.S. Lewis,
Perelandra.

continuum, has ceased to be sequential.

THRESHOLD • *(1980)*

The time is the present. Hugh, a supermarket checkout operator, crosses the freeway into a wood and finds himself in another realm, with its own time, its own laws and its own haunting reality, a world away (literally) from his own constricted and unhappy life. He meets a girl who has also broken through, and their explorations lead to a journey, a fight against nameless evil, and the inner peace which will sustain them when they return to everyday reality.

Le Guin's other novels include Rocannon's World, Planet of Exile, City of Illusions, The Lathe of Heaven *and* The Dispossessed. The Wind's Twelve Quarters *and* Orsinian Tales *are collections of short stories. The Earthsea trilogy (as magical as her adult fantasies, but with a child as hero) is* A Wizard of Earthsea, The Tombs of Atuan *and* The Farthest Shore.

LEHMANN, Rosamond • *(born 1901)*
British novelist.

The ideas behind Lehmann's novels were strengthened by reading Jung and by psychic research after her daughter's death in the 1950s. She believes that we are not alone, that each person is part of a greater whole: the experience and knowledge of all human beings who have ever existed. We can enter into that experience, make use of it, during the rites of passage from one stage of existence to another –birth, adolescence, marriage, death – when the subconscious is particularly receptive. Lehmann's heroines are people on the brink of self-discovery; they are either innocents or victims of life, and the novels describe, in a lucid way far removed from the exoticism and mysticism of their events, how self-knowledge is achieved and how it changes the heroine's life, for bad or good.

THE BALLAD AND THE SOURCE • *(1944)*

Ten-year-old Rebecca, picking bluebells in the garden of the old house beside the churchyard, is invited inside by the owner, Mrs Jardine, who knew Rebecca's grandmother and becomes Rebecca's friend. Rebecca listens enthralled to Mrs Jardine's tales of 'the old days' – and the more terrible the stories (they are accounts of passion, adultery, betrayal and hatred in Mrs Jardine's own young life), the more Rebecca is ensnared. Mrs Jardine is not so much like a witch casting a spell – though this is how

READ ON ▷

● In *A Sea-Grape Tree* (the sequel to *The Ballad and the Source*) Rebecca, now grown-up and betrayed by men exactly as Mrs Jardine had been, goes to a Caribbean island to sort out her life and is affected not only by the people she meets there but by spirit-visitors from her past, including Mrs Jardine herself.

► ▷Rose Macaulay, *The World My Wilderness*. ▷Iris Murdoch, *The Philosopher's Pupil*. ▷Virginia Woolf, *Mrs Dalloway*. ▷Alison Lurie, *Imaginary Friends*. Rebecca West, *The Thinking Reed*. Jane Gardam, *Crusoe's Daughter*.

Rebecca's alarmed mother sees her – as a Sibyl from the remote past, revealing the true nature of human emotional existence.

Lehmann's other novels are Dusty Answer, Invitation to the Waltz *and its sequel* The Weather in the Streets, The Echoing Grove *and* A Sea-Grape Tree. The Gipsy's Baby *collects short stories, and* The Swan in the Evening *is an autobiographical memoir centring on her reactions to her daughter's death.*

LEM, Stanislaw • *(born 1921)*
Polish novelist.

Lem's novels are ▷Kafkaesque SF, a blend of black humour and psychological mysticism. His best-known books are *The Cyberiad*, *His Master's Voice*, *The Invincible*, *One Human Minute*, *Fiasco* and – thanks to Tarkovsky's mesmeric film – *Solaris* (1961), about astronauts trapped on a planet which is a thinking organism, able to sense the nerve-impulses of living beings which land on it, and then make clones.

> **READ ON**
>
> ● *The Futurological Congress* (a spoof of his own work).
> ▶ ▷Robert Silverberg, *Tom O'Bedlam*. Jack Vance, *The Blue World*. Robert Irwin, *The Arabian Nightmare*.

LESSING, Doris • *(born 1919)*
British novelist and non-fiction writer.

Lessing was brought up in Rhodesia (now Zimbabwe), but her involvement in progressive politics made it an uncomfortable place to live, and she moved to London in 1949. In the same year she published her first novel, *The Grass is Singing*, about relationships between the races, and followed it in 1952 with the semi-autobiographical *Martha Quest*, the first in a five-book series (the other volumes, published over the next 17 years, are *A Proper Marriage*, *A Ripple from the Storm*, *Landlocked* and *The Four-gated City*). The sequence took her heroine from girlhood to marriage in white Rhodesia, from political virginity to radical activism, from Africa to London, from youth to age. Martha becomes a feminist; she samples and rejects the 'swinging sixties'; she tries religion and mysticism; she watches, and reports on, the last hours of the human race as we writhe towards the apocalypse. The books are in a straightforward 'as-told-to' style: they have the power of documentary rather than fiction. Two other Lessing novels, *The Golden Notebook* (1962, about an unhappy writer coming to terms with herself as a person and with her place in a male-dominated society) and *Briefing for a Descent into Hell* (1971, about nervous breakdown), have

> **READ ON**
>
> ▶ Margaret Laurence, *A Jest of God*. ▷Patrick White, *The Solid Mandala*. ▷Margaret Drabble, *Jerusalem the Golden*. Stanley Middleton, *Harris' Requiem*. Marilyn French, *The Women's Room*. Simone de Beauvoir, *She Came to Stay*. ▷H.H. Richardson, *The Fortunes of Richard Mahony*.

similar intensity. Lessing's (Jungian) psychological interests, and her fascination with Sufi mysticism, influence much of her other work, especially the five-volume sequence 'Canopus in Argus' (1979–83), which uses an SF format to explore ideas not so much of outer as of inner space, the alternative realities inside the mind.

The 'Canopus in Argus' novels are Shikasta; The Marriage Between Zones Three, Four and Five; The Sirian Experiments; The Making of the Representatives for Planet 8 *and* Documents Relating to the Sentimental Agents in the Volyen Empire. *Lessing's other fiction includes the novels* Memoirs of a Survivor, The Summons before the Dark *and* The Good Terrorist, *and the short-story collections* The Habit of Loving, A Man and Two Women *and* African Stories.

LEWIS, Sinclair • *(1885-1951)*
US novelist.

In the 1920s Lewis won prizes for a series of satirical novels on aspects of US life. They are exhaustively researched, and use a fly-on-the-wall technique, reporting actions and speech in an objective-seeming way which conceals Lewis' own devastating authorial point of view. His theme was that the more honest, the more naive people seem, the more they are concealing humbug, and he was especially scathing about the US middle and professional classes. *Main Street* (1920) and *Babbitt* (1922) are slices of life in typical middle US towns: gossip-ridden, bigoted, censorious and unimaginative. *Dodsworth* (1929) is about a wimpish rich businessman trying to discover his soul (and put new life into his flagging marriage) by travelling in Europe. *Arrowsmith* (1925) is a comparatively serious study of a young doctor interested in bacteriological research. *Elmer Gantry* (1927), perhaps the most relevant of Lewis' books today, is about a religious charlatan, a born-again preacher who uses his charms to seduce women and embezzle money.

The best of Lewis' other novels – his later work tends slackly to repeat former themes – are It Can't Happen Here *(about fascism in the late 1930s USA) and* Gideon Planish *(a savage satire about big business and philanthropy).*

READ ON ▷

▶ **To the satires:**
Hamilton Basso, *The View from Pompey's Head*; ▷John Updike, *Rabbit, Run*; ▷Jerome Weidman, *The Centre of the Action*; ▷Thornton Wilder, *Heaven's My Destination*; ▷Heinrich Böll, *Billiards at Half-past Nine*; ▷Saul Bellow, *Mr Sammler's Planet*.

▶ **To *Arrowsmith*:** ▷C.P. Snow, *The Search*.

LEWIS, Wyndham • *(1882-1957)*
British writer and artist.

Lewis spent his life outraging the bourgeoisie, first as a wild avant-garde artist and then as a fiercely opinionated essayist on art and politics, a member of Mosley's British fascist party and an outspoken Hitler-supporter. His novels were prancing satires in the manner of ▷Huxley or ▷Waugh. *Tarr* (1918) and *The Apes of God* (1930) send up art-snobs and the dealers and phoney artists who prey on them. *The Revenge for Love* (1937) is about society people playing at politics but understanding nothing of a real tragedy (the Spanish Civil War) going on under their noses. The hero of *Self-condemned* (1954), a middle-aged professor tired of European life, retreats to a Canadian hotel, only to find it fuller of frauds and fools than the world he has left. Lewis' most stinging satire is the trilogy *The Human Age* (1928–55). It is about Armageddon, and shows the Day of Judgement not in lofty Christian terms but as a dusty, sweaty carnival, human beings prancing or shuffling to their doom at the whim of a cackling, deformed Showman – the gatekeeper of eternity is not St Peter but Mr Punch.

> **READ ON** ▷

> ▶ **To the satires:** Richard Aldington, *Seven Against Reeves*; ▷Anthony Powell, *What's Become of Waring?*; ▷Aldous Huxley, *Antic Hay*; Julian Symons, *The Immaterial Murder Case*.
> ▶ **To Lewis' more apocalyptic comedies:** Joyce Cary, *The Horse's Mouth*; ▷Patrick White, *The Twyborn Affair*; Stuart Evans, *The Caves of Alienation*.

LOFTS, Norah • *(1904–86)*
British novelist.

Lofts wrote historical romances, many set in East Anglia. *The Brittle Glass* (1942) is typical: the story of Sorrel Kingabay, the red-haired, independent daughter of a Norfolk trader in the early 1700s, when smugglers and highwaymen still roamed the English Fens.

Lofts' other novels include many set in romantic or sinister old houses: The Town House, The House at Old Vine, The House at Sunset, Gad's Hall, Haunted House. *Her other romances include* Jassy *and* Day of the Butterfly, *and her thrillers (written under the name Peter Curtis) are* Dead March in Three Keys, Lady Living Alone *and* The Devil's Own.

> **READ ON** ▷

> ▶ Oliver Onions, *The Story of Ragged Robyn*. ▷Daphne Du Maurier, *Jamaica Inn*. Sarah Woodhouse, *Daughter of the Sea*.

LONDON, Jack • *(1879–1916)*
US novelist, short-story and non-fiction writer.

In his teens London worked as a docker, a seal-hunter, an oyster pirate (stealing from other fishermen's oyster-beds) and a customs officer; he also tramped across the United States and took part in the Klondike Gold Rush. At 19 he

> **READ ON** ▷

> ● *White Fang* (a mirror-image of *The Call of the Wild*: the story of a wild dog drawn to the

settled down to writing, aiming to produce 1000 words a day, and began turning out he-man articles and short stories, heavy on adventure and light on character. His human beings (most of them fur-trappers, gold-miners or fishermen) take a two-fisted approach to life. Brutality rules, and survival is only guaranteed until someone stronger or brighter comes along. However blinkered London's view of life – he managed, at the same time, to be a fervent socialist and a fascist convinced that fair-haired, blue-eyed Aryans were the master-race – he wrote of it with breath-taking, blood-hammering effectiveness. His descriptions of fights, and of men battling against enormous natural hazards, set a model which many tough-guy writers have imitated, but none surpassed.

CALL OF THE WILD • *(1903)*

Buck, a St Bernard dog, is stolen from his home in California and taken to the Klondike as a sledge-dog. He passes from owner to owner, each more brutal than the last, until he finds kindness at the hands of John Thornton. But Thornton is killed, Buck's last link with human beings is broken and he escapes to the wild and becomes the leader of a wild-pack.

London's novels include Before Adam *(about the prehistoric ancestors of homo sapiens),* The Sea-wolf *(a ▷Conradian account of the struggle between a brutal sea-captain and the city couple he kidnaps) and* The Iron Heel *(a story of the future, recounting the struggle of a group of urban guerrillas to overthrow a dictatorship which has overrun Chicago). His story-collections include* Children of the Frost, The Road, When God Laughs, The Strength of the Strong *and* Island Tales. John Barleycorn *is an autobiographical novel about a writer battling alcoholism.*

LOWRY, Malcolm • *(1909–57)*
British novelist.

Lowry began experimenting with drugs and drink at Cambridge, and by the time he was 20 he was irretrievably addicted. He spent the rest of his life bumming across the world, in rehabilitation clinics, or in self-imposed isolation while he struggled to turn his experiences into fiction. The only novel published during his lifetime – it took him 20 years to write it – was *Under the Volcano* (1947). This tells of the last two days in the life of an alcoholic British consul in revolution-torn Mexico, and interwines memory, dream and reality in the manner of ▷Joyce's *Ulysses.*

human race, who is betrayed and ill-treated by every owner – the description of his life as a fighting-dog is particularly harrowing – until he ends up at last with a master he can trust).

▶ To *The Call of the Wild*: Richard Adams, *The Plague Dogs*; Romain Gary, *White Dog*; ▷H.G. Wells, *The Island of Doctor Moreau.*

▶ To London's books about humans: ▷Ernest Hemingway, *The Old Man and the Sea*; *To Have and Have Not*; ▷Maxim Gorky, *Foma Gordeev*; ▷Joseph Conrad, *Typhoon.*

▶ To his short stories: Ring Lardner, *Round Up: the Stories/ Collected Short Stories.*

READ ON ▷

● *Lunar Caustic; Dark as the Grave Wherein My Friend is Laid* (about a boozy, doom-ridden tour of Mexico).
▶ ▷Joseph Conrad, *Heart of Darkness.*
▷F. Scott Fitzgerald, *Tender is the Night.*
▷Fyodor Dostoevsky, *The Idiot.* ▷Lawrence

Durrell, *The Black Book*.

LUDLUM, Robert • *(born 1927)*
US novelist.

Ludlum also writes as Jonathan Ryder (*The Cry of the Halidon*; *The Rhineman Exchange*). His thrillers (many based on real-life incidents) are suspenseful, tough-talking and racy: they include *The Scarlatti Inheritance*, *The Gemini Contenders*, *The Matarese Circle*, *The Osterman Weekend* and *The Parsifal Mosaic* (1982, in which a burnt-out, 'disposable' agent holds the knowledge, without realising it, which will prevent a madman code-named Parsifal from triggering world war three).

> **READ ON**

▶ Allen Drury, *The Roads of Earth*. Fred Taylor, *Walking Shadows* (set among German officers during the second world war). ▷John Le Carré, *A Perfect Spy*.

LURIE, Alison • *(born 1926)*
US novelist.

Lurie's streamlined, ivy-league prose, her effortless blend of farce and irony, and the bitchy elegance of her plots link her to such classy US contemporaries as Mary McCarthy, John Updike or Philip Roth – and she has the unsettling ability to lay the human condition bare for our pity even as she sends it up. The people in her novels are all terribly nice: well-educated, well-off, well-dressed, liberal and compassionate. Their lives are like placid pools – and into each of them Lurie drops the acid of discontent (usually something to do with sex) and invites us to smile as the water seethes. Her funniest books are set on university campuses: *Love and Friendship* (1962) is about two people trapped in an affair (and what everyone else thinks about it); *The War Between the Tates* (1974) shows the gradual collapse of a 'perfect' marriage under threat from a combination of adultery and student politics. The heroine of *Imaginary Friends* (1967), finding reality emotionally unfulfilling, seeks to reinvent her personality by psychic experimentation. The narrator of *Only Children* (1979) is a child, who reports on the sexual imbroglios of the adults around her with a wide-eyed gravity which arises less from innocence than from a precocious understanding not only of what is going on but of the sort of butter-won't-melt-in-my-mouth cuteness adults expect from little girls.

FOREIGN AFFAIRS • *(1984)*
Three Americans are visiting England: Vinnie, a 54-year-old professor, Fred, a hunky young academic, and Chuck, a middle-aged, none-too-bright businessman on a package

> **READ ON**

● *The War Between the Tates*.
▶ To *Foreign Affairs*: ▷Mary McCarthy, *The Company She Keeps*; Joan Didion, *A Book of Common Prayer*; ▷Philip Roth, *The Professor of Desire*.
▶ To *The War Between the Tates*: Susan Fromberg Shaeffer, *The Injured Party*.
▶ To *Love and Friendship*: David Lodge, *Small World*.
▶ To *Only Children*: ▷Henry James, *What Maisie Knew*.
▶ To Lurie's work in general: ▷Anita Brookner, *Look at Me*; Alice Thomas Ellis, *The Birds of the Air*.

tour. The novel shows Vinnie's attempts to bring into the two men's lives the same kind of decorous, unflustered order she herself enjoys – and the way her own values crumple under the strain of real emotion.

Lurie's other novels are Real People, *a comedy about artists coping with inspirational blocks and sexual passion in a 'creative colony', and* A Nowhere City, *a serious book about a woman trying to cope with unfocussed psychological panic.*

Alison LURIE

Randall JARRELL, PICTURES FROM AN INSTITUTION
(send-up of life in 'progressive' US women's university, 1950s)

Mary MCCARTHY, THE GROVES OF ACADEME
(political satire: protest-movement when university president tries to sack incompetent lecturer)

Malcolm BRADBURY, STEPPING WESTWARD
(naive Englishman takes up post on 'liberated' Californian campus)

Vladimir NABOKOV, PNIN
(sad Russian émigré tries to adjust to US university ways, while clinging to culture of 'old country')

US CAMPUS LIFE

UNCOMFORTABLE IN AMERICA

Franz KAFKA, AMERICA
(innocent young German immigrant discovers fantasy-land)

William BOYD, STARS AND BARS
(shy Englishman plunged into fast-lane US business life)

Peter DE VRIES, REUBEN, REUBEN
(boozy, hard-wenching poet cuts a swathe through crackerbarrel Massachusetts community)

Evelyn WAUGH, THE LOVED ONE
(the US funeral business will never seem the same again)

John UPDIKE, BECH, A BOOK
(problems of US author: family, publishers, fans, lecture-audiences, reporters, writer's block . . .)

(tragi-comic collapse of 'civilised' marriage on 'liberal' US university campus)

David **LODGE, SMALL WORLD**
(international conference-circuit)

Robertson **DAVIES, THE REBEL ANGELS**
(Canadian Rabelais – researcher raises the Devil)

ACADEMIC FOLLIES

Kingsley **AMIS, LUCKY JIM**
(1950s English culture-snobbery in small-town university)

Howard **JACOBSON, COMING FROM BEHIND**
(English provincial and polytechnic life – as in 'you don't have to be mad to work here, but it helps')

Max **BEERBOHM, ZULEIKA DOBSON**
(life and love among 1910s Oxford dreaming spires)

J.B. **PRIESTLEY, LOW NOTES ON A HIGH LEVEL**
(classical music snobs at 1950s BBC – who will get first performance of famous Scandinavian composer's latest symphony?)

Paul **BRYERS, COMING FIRST**
(trendy TV producer works hard not to be male chauvinist)

NON-ACADEMIC FOLLIES

Hilary **MANTEL, VACANT POSSESSION**
(rollercoaster black satire: 'madwoman' drives yuppie English family crazy)

Patrick **DENNIS, AUNTIE MAME**
(high society – conventional and bizarre – 1950s USA: eccentric aunt takes over 'education' of shy orphan nephew)

M

MACAULAY, Rose • *(1881–1958)*
British novelist.

In the 1920s Macaulay wrote deadpan satires, giving the impression that the British Isles were a rest-home for incurable eccentrics. *Potterism* attacks the gutter press. *Crewe Train* sends up publishing. *Told by an Idiot* features a clergyman who tries on new beliefs – Agnosticism, Anglicanism, Catholicism, Christian Socialism, Dissent, Ethicalism and Unitarianism – like shirts. Unlike many satirists of the time, who treated their characters like puppets, Macaulay always wrote of her people with rueful sympathy, however withering her wit about the foolish things they did. In the 1930s, beginning with *They Were Defeated* (see below), she began to concentrate on the sympathetic side of her art, writing about people (young girls especially) who are racked by the need to choose between the life of the mind and that of the flesh: their intellectual or spiritual ambitions are ambushed by sexual infatuation. The second world war, and a succession of private misfortunes, made Macaulay give up novel-writing for a dozen years, but she returned triumphantly in her mid-70s with *The World My Wilderness* (about a confused girl trying to discover her psychological identity after the second world war) and a riotous, malicious romp about love (sacred and profane), *The Towers of Trebizond*.

THEY WERE DEFEATED • *(1932)*
In 17th-century, Puritan England, Dr Conybeare is determined to educate his 15-year-old daughter Julian as if she were a man. The girl takes lessons from Robert Herrick, rector of the parish, until Herrick is driven out for sheltering an old woman accused of witchcraft. Julian goes to Cambridge, where she has private coaching from the don John Cleveland. Cleveland, however, is more interested in

---

> **READ ON**

● *The Towers of Trebizond*.

▶ **To the satires:** Compton Mackenzie, *Vestal Fire*; Nancy Mitford, *Love in a Cold Climate*; ▷Muriel Spark, *The Ballad of Peckham Rye*.

▶ **To *They Were Defeated*:** ▷Robert Graves, *Wife to Mr Milton*.

▶ **To Macaulay's work in general:** ▷Willa Cather, *The Song of the Lark*; ▷Elizabeth Bowen, *The Death of the Heart*; A.S. Byatt, *The Virgin in the Garden*.

her virginity than in her mind, and seduces her – and she finds herself as entranced by sex as by the heady religious and intellectual atmosphere of Cambridge. Then her brother finds out about the seduction, and tragedy ensues.

Macaulay's other novels include (from the 1920s) Danger-ous Ages, Orphan Island, Keeping Up Appearances *and* Staying with Relations, *and (from the 1930s)* I Would be Private *and* No Man's Wit. *She also wrote poetry, essays on literature and religion, and a book combining travel, archaeology and autobiography,* The Pleasure of Ruins.

MADNESS

▷Richard Condon, *Any God Will Do*
  Margaret Forster, *The Bride of Lowther Fell*
▷Susan Hill, *The Bird of Night*
  Ken Kesey, *One Flew Over the Cuckoo's Nest*
  Sylvia Plath, *The Bell Jar*
▷Jean Rhys, *Good Morning, Midnight*
▷Evelyn Waugh, *The Ordeal of Gilbert Pinfold*

Depression and Psychiatry (p 57); On the Edge of Sanity (p 183)

MAILER, Norman • *(born 1923)*
US writer.

As well as novels, Mailer has published both non-fiction (eg *Marilyn*, about Marilyn Monroe) and 'faction', a blend of real events and fiction (eg *The Executioner's Song*, 1979, an examination of the character and crimes of the murderer Gary Gilmore). Most of his novels are set in the present day, and deal with a single theme: maleness. He regards violence and competitiveness as essential com-ponents of masculinity, related to sexual potency – and claims, further, that capitalist society will only succeed if it models itself on the aggressive, cocky male. The world being what it is, Mailer is often forced – like ▷Hem-ingway before him – to describe the failure of these macho fantasies, and because so many of his books are about the failure of the American dream, despair gives his writing stinging political relevance. *The Naked and the Dead* (1948) is about the brutalisation of a group of bewil-dered young airmen in the second world war. In *Why Are We in Vietnam?* (1967), a savage Hemingway parody, a man takes his son on a bear-hunt as an 18th birthday cele-

> **READ ON**

▶ **To Mailer's contemporary fiction:**
▷Ernest Hemingway, *For Whom the Bell Tolls*; ▷John Cheever, *Falconer*; Henri de Montherlant, *The Bullfighters*; William Styron, *The Long March*.
▶ **To *Ancient Evenings*:**
James Clavell, *Shōgun*; L.P. Myers, *The Near and the Far*; ▷Thomas Mann, *Joseph and His Brothers*.

bration, and this quintessential US manhood-ritual is linked, in a devastating final paragraph, with the mindless, gung-ho crowing of the gook-slaughtering US army in Vietnam, to which the boy will be drafted now that he is adult. *An American Dream* (1965), an equally pungent satire, shows a man at the end of his tether who commits murder and then tries to cudgel from his increasingly insane mind the reasons why his country should have conditioned him to kill, why someone else's violent death should be the outcome of the American dream.

ANCIENT EVENINGS • *(1983)*

Pharaoh Rameses IX of Egypt, perplexed by his failure as a ruler, asks his minister Menenhetet to think back to a former existence as charioteer to the great warrior pharaoh Rameses II, and to explain the secrets of Rameses' success. Menenhetet's account is the bulk of the book, a dazzling description of a society dependent on belief in magic and on a (not unconnected) view of its own powers of rejuvenation, of constantly being able to deconstruct and reconstruct its past.

A good sampler of Mailer's work is Advertisements for Myself, *an anthology of his early writings with a fascinating autobiographical commentary. His other novels include* Barbary Shore, The Deer Park *and the thriller* Tough Guys Don't Dance.

MANN, Thomas • *(1875–1955)*
German novelist and non-fiction writer.

Although Mann was not a political writer, the themes of his work reflect northern European politics of the last 100 years. His first great novel, *Buddenbrooks* (1901), shows the decline of a powerful German industrial family over three decades – and although it is superficially a Forsyte-like family saga, its strength comes from the persistent impression that the Buddenbrooks are characteristic of the decadent 'old Germany' as a whole. The hero of *The Magic Mountain* (1924) spends much of the book learning about Europe's moral, artistic and philosophical heritage – and then goes to fight in the first world war. In *Joseph and His Brothers* (1933–43), based on the Bible and written under the shadow of nazism, Joseph, the figure symbolising progress, is a plausible rogue, a Hitler-figure, and his brothers, symbolising barbarism, are as gullible as they are honest. The composer-hero of *Doctor Faustus* (1947) can unlock his creativity only by entering ever deeper into the morass of his own mind, and by accepting

READ ON ⟩

● *Buddenbrooks*; *The Confessions of Felix Krull, Confidence Man.*
▶ To *The Magic Mountain*: ▷Johann Wolfgang von Goethe, *The Apprenticeship of Wilhelm Meister*; Robert Musil, *The Man Without Qualities.*
▶ To *Buddenbrooks*: ▷I.B. Singer, *The Family Moskat*; ▷Honoré de Balzac, *Cousin Bette.*
▶ To *Joseph and His Brothers*: ▷Gustave Flaubert, *Salammbô.*
▶ To *Dr Faustus*:

that to be 'ordinary' is to opt not for cultural calm but for chaos. The con-man central character of *The Confessions of Felix Krull, Confidence Man* (1954), Mann's only comic novel, preys on the expectations of those who still believe in the old rules of religion, society and politics.

THE MAGIC MOUNTAIN (Der Zauberberg) • (1924)

Castorp, a rich, unimaginative young man, spends seven years in a Swiss TB sanatorium. The sanatorium is full of endlessly talkative intellectuals, who educate Castorp in music, philosophy, art and literature. The book shows him growing in both knowledge and moral stature, until at last he is cured both of TB and of the greater disease (in Mann's eyes) of ignorant complacency. As the novel ends, however, he strides out to fight in the first world war – and Mann invites us, in the light of hindsight, to ponder his probable fate and that of the European culture he has so laboriously acquired.

Mann's shorter works include Mario the Magician *(about demonic possession),* Death in Venice *(Tod in Venedig) (about a dying writer galvanised by longing for a beautiful boy),* Lotte in Weimar *(a historical novel about the young ▷Goethe), and* The Holy Sinner *(a beautiful – and poker-faced, despite the ridiculousness of its events – re-telling of a medieval religious legend involving incest, communion with angels and magical transformations).* Stories of a Lifetime *is a collection of short stories.*

MANNING, Olivia • *(1908–80)*

British novelist.

Manning is best known for the 6-novel sequence *Fortunes of War* (*The Balkan Trilogy*, 1960–65 and *The Levant Trilogy*, 1977–80). The central characters, Guy and Harriet Pringle, are English expatriates during the early years of the second world war. They settle in Bucharest, where Guy teaches English; then, as the Axis powers advance, they move to Athens and from there to Cairo, where they 'hole up' during the desert campaign of 1942. Like the rest of Manning's characters, English, Middle Eastern or European, the Pringles dwell on the fringes, not at the centre, of great events; their lives are bounded by bread-shortages, electricity-cuts and squabbles over status. The civilisation which bred them is collapsing, and they are themselves symbols of its decadence: they are effete and powerless, able only to run before events. None the less, Harriet's character does contain the seeds of change. When she marries Guy she is an unawakened personality, a genteel 1930s 'English rose'. Events draw from her

---

Hermann Broch, *The Death of Virgil*; ▷Susan Hill, *The Bird of Night.*
▶ To *Death in Venice*: ▷Hermann Hesse, *Peter Camenzind.*
▶ To *The Holy Sinner*: Hilda Doolittle ('H.D.'), *Hedylus.*

READ ON

▶ ▷Elizabeth Bowen, *The Heat of the Day.* Jennifer Johnston, *The Captains and the Kings.* Isabel Colegate, *The Shooting Party.* ▷Evelyn Waugh, *Sword of Honour.*

emotional and intellectual strength she never knew she had – and the effects are to alienate the rest of the stuffy British community and to put stress on her marriage to Guy, an honourable, unimaginative man trapped in pre-war attitudes. He wanted a wife who was a companion not an equal, a pupil not a friend; although he is the same age as Harriet, he is as typical of the 'old' generation as she is of the 'new'. None of this is openly declared. At first sight Manning seems to be offering no more than a series of artless anecdotes about the muddle and horror of life in exotic cities engulfed by war. It is not till the mosaic is complete that her underlying scheme becomes apparent: the description of a whole culture in a state of unwished-for, panic-stricken change.

The novels in The Balkan Trilogy *are* The Great Fortune, The Spoilt City *and* Friends and Heroes; *those in* The Levant Trilogy *are* The Danger Tree, The Battle Lost and Won *and* The Sum of Things. *Manning's other novels are* Artist Among the Missing, School for Love, A Different Face, The Doves of Venus, The Play Room *and* The Rain Forest. Growing Up *and* A Romantic Hero *are collections of short stories.*

MANSFIELD, Katherine • *(1888–1923)*

New Zealand short-story writer.

Mansfield went to London at 14, and spent the rest of her life in Europe. When she wrote of New Zealand it was either with childhood nostalgia (for example in 'Prelude' and 'At The Bay') or with distaste for the lives its adults led in the outback ('Ole Underwood'; 'The Woman at the Store') or in dingily genteel suburbs ('Her First Ball'; 'How Pearl Button was Kidnapped'). She admired ▷Chekhov's stories, and sought to write the same kind of innocent-seeming anecdotes distilling single moments of human folly or aspiration. Many of her stories are about small children. In 'Sixpence', for example, she describes a little boy's sudden inexplicable naughtiness, and the guilt his father feels when he beats him; in 'The Little Girl', she shows a young child's feelings for her father. Her favourite characters were shallow, silly and desperate people: an unemployable film-extra ('Pictures'), a snob-bish mother and her unmarried daughters ('The Garden-party'), a hen-pecked singing-teacher ('Mr Reginald Peacock's Day'), expatriates on the continent ('The Man Without a Temperament'; 'Je ne parle pas français'). She polished and refined her prose, often spending months on a single story – and the feeling of craftsmanship in her

READ ON ▷

▶ ▷Anton Chekhov, *The Lady With the Little Dog and Other Stories*. ▷John Cheever, *Collected Stories*. Jean Stafford, *Collected Stories*. William Saroyan, *Best Stories of Saroyan*. ▷Elizabeth Bowen, *The Dream Lover*. Dorothy Parker, *Here Lies*.

work, of slightly self-conscious artistry, greatly enhances the impression she seeks to give, that tragedies are not diminished because the lives they affect are small.

Mansfield's story-collections are In A German Pension, Bliss, The Garden Party, The Dove's Nest *and* Something Childish. *Her* Journals *give fascinating glimpses both of her character and of the events and conversations which she drew on in her work.*

MÁRQUEZ, Gabriel García • *(born 1928)*
Colombian novelist and short-story writer.

In Márquez' invented South American town of Macondo, a place isolated from the outside world, 'magic realism' rules: there is no distinction between magic and reality. At one level, life is perfectly ordinary: people are born, grow up, work, cook, feud and gossip. But there is a second, irrational and surrealist plane to ordinary existence. The Macondans (unless they murder each other for reasons of politics, sex or family honour) live for 100, 150, 200 years. Although they are as innocent of 'real' knowledge as children – they think ice miraculous and they are amazed to hear that the world is round – they know the secrets of alchemy, converse with ghosts, remember Cortez or Drake as 'uncles'. Macondo is a rough-and-tumble Eden, a paradise where instinct rules and nothing is impossible – and Márquez spends his time either describing its enchantment or detailing the savage results when people from the outside world (jackbooted generals; con-men; lawyers; bishops) break through to 'civilise' it. For Márquez, Macondo stands for the whole of South America, and his stories are barbed political allegories. But he seldom lets this overwhelm the books. Instead of hectoring, he opens his eyes wide, puts his tongue in his cheek and tells us wonders.

ONE HUNDRED YEARS OF SOLITUDE • *(1967)*
As Colonel Aurelio Buendia faces the firing squad, the whole history of his family flashes before his eyes. They begin as poor peasants, in a one-roomed hut on the edge of a swamp. They proliferate like tendrils on a vine: Aureliano himself has 17 sons, all called Aureliano. The family-members absorb knowledge, people and property until they and Macondo seem indissoluble. Finally, led by Aureliano senior, they defend the old, innocent values against invasion by a government which wants to impose the same laws in Macondo as everywhere else, and the dynasty disappears from reality, living on only in fantasy,

> **READ ON** ▷

► ▷Salman Rushdie, *Shame.* ▷Isabel Allende, *The House of the Spirits.* Carlos Fuentes, *The Old Gringo.* ▷Virginia Woolf, *Orlando.* ▷Italo Calvino, *Our Ancestors.* Gerald H. Morris, *Doves and Silk Handkerchieves.*

as a memory of how human beings were before the whole world changed.

Márquez' other novels are No One Writes to the Colonel, In Evil Hour, Chronicle of a Death Foretold *and* The Autumn of the Patriarch *(the stream-of-consciousness monologue of a dying dictator). His short stories are collected in* Leaf-storm and other Stories, Big Mama's Funeral *and* Innocent Erendira and other Stories.

MARSH, Ngaio • *(1899–1982)*
New Zealand novelist.

Few writers use 'classic' detective-story ingredients as magnificently as Marsh. Her murder-methods are ingenious and unexpected. Her locations are fascinating: backstage (and onstage) at theatres; during a village-hall concert; in the shearing-shed of a sheep-farm; at a top-level diplomatic reception. Her characters are exotic and her detection is scrupulously fair, with every clue appearing to the reader at the same time as to Alleyn, Marsh's urbane and hawk-eyed sleuth. Above all, her books move at a furious pace, fuelled by her effervescent glee at the follies of humankind.

FINAL CURTAIN • *(1947)*
Shortly after the second world war, Agatha Troy (Alleyn's artist wife) is persuaded to spend a week painting the portrait of Sir Henry Ancred, a distinguished actor now retired. She goes to his country mansion, and finds it a lowering old house in the best whodunnit tradition. One wing has been taken over by an evacuated prep school, and the rest is filled with eccentric relatives who have been plunged into twittering alarm by the arrival of Sir Henry's young, vulgar and nubile mistress, who may just become his wife and cut the rest of the family off from their inheritance. Sittings for the painting proceed – Sir Henry is costumed as for his most famous role, Macbeth – and are interrupted first by a series of unpleasant practical jokes, and then by the old man's murder. Scotland Yard must be called in, and Alleyn arrives back from war-service just in time to take the case and sort out the murderer from half a dozen candidates, each with a cast-iron alibi and a very good reason for wishing Sir Henry dead.

Marsh's three dozen novels include Hand in Glove, Died in the Wool, Clutch of Constables, Vintage Murder, Spinsters in Jeopardy, Surfeit of Lampreys, Black as He's Painted *and* Death in Ecstasy. Black Beech and Honey-

---

READ ON ▷

● *Enter a Murderer*;
  Overture to Death.
▶ ▷Marjorie Allingham,
  The Beckoning Lady.
  H.R.F. Keating, *Zen
  There Was Murder*.
  Emma Lathen, *When
  in Greece*. Jean Potts,
  Go, Lovely Rose.
  ▷Peter Dickinson, *The
  Poison Oracle*.

dew *is an autobiography, especially interesting on her childhood and her fascination with theatre.*

MASTERS, John • *(born 1914)*
British novelist.

Masters, an army officer in India, wrote a series of books setting fictional characters in the context of real historical events. The Raj background and the interplay between two incompatible cultures are brilliantly evoked, and the foreground action is fast, thrilling and plausible. The best-known books in the sequence are *Nightrunners of Bengal* (1951), set during the Indian 'Mutiny', and *Bhowani Junction* (1954), about the plot to blow up a train during the struggle for independence.

Masters' other books include Far, Far the Mountain Peak, The Road Past Mandalay, The Breaking Strain, Thunder at Sunset *and* The Himalayan Concerto.

> **READ ON**

▶ **Equally sensitive to India and its history during the last 150 years:** Paul Scott, *The Raj Quartet*; ▷J.G. Farrell, *The Siege of Krishnapur*.
▶ **Similar books, about different periods and continents:** James Clavell, *Shôgun* (set in 17th-century Japan); ▷Robert Graves, *Sergeant Lamb of the Ninth* and ▷Gore Vidal, *1776* (both about the American War of Independence); ▷C.S. Forester, *The Gun* (set in the Peninsular War); Timothy Mo, *An Insular Possession* (about the British and Hong Kong).

MAUGHAM, W. Somerset (William) •
(1874–1965)
British writer of novels, short stories and plays.

A tireless traveller (especially in the Far East), Maugham wrote hundreds of short stories based on anecdotes he heard or scenes he observed en route. Many of them were later filmed: 'Rain', for example (about a missionary on a cruise-liner in Samoa struggling to reform a prostitute, and losing his own soul in the process), was made half a dozen times. Maugham's novels used true experience in a similar way, shaping it and drawing out its meaning but keeping close to real events. *Liza of Lambeth* (1897) is about a London slum girl tormented by her neighbours for conceiving a bastard child. *Of Human Bondage* (1915) is the story of an orphan, bullied at school because he has a club foot, who struggles to find happiness as an adult, is

> **READ ON**

▶ **To *Liza of Lambeth*:** ▷Émile Zola, *The Boozer* (L'Assommoir).
▶ **To *Of Human Bondage*:** ▷C.P. Snow, *Strangers and Brothers*; ▷Jerome Weidman, *Fourth Street East*.
▶ **To *The Moon and Sixpence*:** Joyce Cary, *The Horse's Mouth*.
▶ **To *Cakes and Ale*:** ▷Rose Macaulay, *Crewe Train*; ▷J.B.

ravaged by love for a worthless woman, and settles at last to become a country doctor. The stockbroker hero of *The Moon and Sixpence* (1919) gives up career, wife and family to become a painter in the South Seas, as Gauguin did. *Cakes and Ale* (1930) is an acid satire about the 1930s London literary world; Maugham avoided libel suits only by claiming that every writer it pilloried was just another aspect of himself.

Maugham's other novels include The Trembling of a Leaf, The Casuarina Tree, The Razor's Edge *and* Catalina. *His* Complete Short Stories *and* Collected Plays *(from 1907–32 he wrote two dozen successful plays, mainly comedies) were published in the 1950s. A Writer's* Notebook *and* The Summing Up *give fascinating insights into the balance between his life and work.*

MAURIAC, François • *(1885–1970)*
French novelist.

Mauriac's books, all set among rich families in the Bordeaux wine country at the start of this century, are based on Roman Catholic doctrines of guilt and repentance. They show people tormented by conscience (often quite justified: his characters include murderers, embezzlers, adulterers and family tyrants). Some are never challenged; others are outcasts, reviled by neighbours and relatives as unpleasant as they are themselves. A few repent, and the move from moral darkness to light irradiates their souls. The quest for redemption is, however, always left to the individual: no one is saved against his or her own will. Despite the religious starting-point of Mauriac's books, they are anything but churchy: they are psychological case-studies rather than religious tracts. Like ancient Greek tragedy, his work can seem remorselessly gloomy – and it has a similar hypnotic power.

THE NEST OF VIPERS (Le nœud de vipères) • *(1932)*
The book is the confession of a dying man, trying to explain to his grown-up children how his wife's infidelity, many years before, shrivelled his soul and led him to hate both her and them. For 30 years he has plotted to rob them of their inheritance, taking pleasure in the prospect of their distress when he dies and leaves them penniless. Then his wife unexpectedly dies, and he begins a reassessment of his moral situation, and a painful process of rehabilitation.

Mauriac's other novels include Thérèse Desqueyroux *(a*

Priestley, *The Image Men.*
▶ **To the short stories:** Guy De Maupassant, *Boule de Suif*; ▷R.L. Stevenson, *Island Nights' Entertainment*; ▷Rudyard Kipling, *Wee Willie Winkie*; ▷Paul Theroux, *World's End.*

READ ON ▷

▶ ▷Carson McCullers, *Reflections in a Golden Eye.* ▷Graham Greene, *Brighton Rock.* Theodore Dreiser, *Sister Carrie.* ▷Patricia Highsmith, *The People Who Knock on the Door.* John Hergesheimer, *The Three Black Pennies.*
▶ The idea of the stifling, overbearing family is sent up in ▷Ivy Compton-Burnett, *Brothers and Sisters* and ▷Tom Sharpe, *Ancestral Vices.*

chilly investigation of the mind of a woman who has poisoned her husband), Genetrix (about a young couple whose love is blighted by the man's monstrous, possessive mother), The Desert of Love (in which a father and son fall in love with the same woman), and The Woman of the Pharisees (about religious bigotry, and the way the middle-aged resent the young).

McBAIN, Ed • *(born 1926)*
US novelist.

'Ed McBain' is one of the pseudonyms of ▷Evan Hunter. He writes fast, tough police-procedurals set in New York; many of them (including the 87th Precinct series) are woven out of several simultaneous investigations, in the manner of such TV series as *Hill Street Blues*. McBain also describes the private lives of his hard-talking, street-wise cops: this humanises the violence. His books include *Cop Hater*, *Give the Boys a Great Big Hand*, *Calypso* and *Eighty Million Eyes*.

> **READ ON** ⟩
>
> ▶ Chester Himes, *Blind Man With a Pistol*. Dell Shannon, *Date With Death*. Lesley Egan, *The Hunters and the Hunted*. Joseph Wambaugh, *The Choirboys*. Martin Cruz Smith, *Gorky Park* is an intriguing variation on the formula: a police-procedural set in Moscow and involving corruption and departmental infighting in the Kremlin itself.

McCAFFREY, Anne • *(born 1926)*
US novelist.

Although McCaffrey has written novels, romances, a thriller and books on music and cookery, she is best-known for SF (often, eg in *The Crystal Singer*, with a musical background) and fantasy. Her most substantial work is the 'Pern' sequence of novels. Pern is a distant, medieval world where the élite ride and telepathically control – or are controlled by –dragons; the dragons are the only beings which can destroy Thread, a devastating space-virus which would otherwise engulf all other life. The series details the fragile balance of society on Pern, and in particular the symbiosis – by turns comic, tragic and movingly poetic – between humans and dragons on which all life depends.

The Pern books (self-contained but linked) are Dragonflight, Dragonquest, The White Dragon, Dragonsong, Dragonsinger, Dragondrums *and* Moreta. *McCaffrey's other SF books include* The Ship Who Sang, Restoree *and*

> **READ ON** ⟩
>
> ● *The Crystal Singer*.
> ▶ ▷Piers Anthony, *Vicinity Cluster*. ▷Robert Heinlein, *Glory Road*. ▷Ursula Le Guin, *The Word for World is Forest*.

Dinosaur Planet. Get off the Unicorn *is a collection of short stories*.

McCARTHY, Mary • *(born 1912)*
US novelist and non-fiction writer.

As well as novels, McCarthy has published books on Venice and Florence, political essays (especially on the US involvement in Vietnam) and an admired – and fictionalised – autobiography, *Memoirs of a Catholic Girlhood*. (She set the record straight in 1987 with the more factual *How I Grew*.) Each of her half-dozen novels simultaneously discusses and satirises major issues of its day. The heroine of *The Company She Keeps*, from the 1940s, tries to reconcile being a free spirit with her longing to find Mr Right. *The Group*, a 1960s best-seller, is about eight women making their way in society and demanding equal shares in the sexual and social revolution. The hero of *Birds of America* (1971) is a naive young American in Europe, worrying himself sick over small matters like dirty toilet-bowls, and over such large ones as ecological balance, the awfulness of US package-tourists and the fact that no one in Europe seems to share America's high opinion of itself. In *Cannibals and Missionaries* (1980) a group of wealthy, cultured people is held hostage by terrorists. One US critic (Brady Nordland) called *Birds of America* 'sweet, funny and very clever'; the description fits all McCarthy's work.

THE GROVES OF ACADEME • *(1952)*
Henry Mulcahy is an inefficient, unreliable teacher in the English Department of Jocelyn College. He is also a married man with children, and a left-wing activist. The President of the College decides not to renew Mulcahy's tenure, and the department immediately starts politicking in Mulcahy's defence. The book's once-topical background (it was published during the anti-left witch-hunts of Senator Joe McCarthy – no relation of Mary McCarthy, and certainly no soul-mate) has faded, leaving a sparkling, malicious campus comedy in which everyone gets their due come-uppance; the final irony, discomforting Mulcahy's woolly liberal colleagues, is particularly neat.

McCarthy's other novels are The Oasis/A Source of Embarrassment *and* A Charmed Life. Cast a Cold Eye *is a collection of short stories*.

> READ ON

● *Birds of America.*
▶ **To *The Groves of Academe:*** D.J. Enright, *Academic Year*; Howard Jacobson, *Coming from Behind.*
▶ **To *The Group:*** Rona Jaffe, *Class Reunion* (and its sequel *Mazes and Monsters*).
▶ **To McCarthy's novels generally:** Alice Thomas Ellis, *The Other Side of the Fire*; A.N. Wilson, *The Sweets of Pimlico*; ▷Frederic Raphael, *The Graduate Wife*; ▷Alison Lurie, *The War Between the Tates.*

McCULLERS, Carson • (1917–53)
US novelist.

Reading McCullers is like visiting a freak-show: her characters are repulsive but fascinating, kin to the more macabre human figures in modern pop and horror videos. The hero of *The Heart is a Lonely Hunter* (1940) is a deaf-mute, distracted by his inability to communicate either his sensitivity or his generosity of spirit. The awkward, ugly heroine of *The Ballad of the Sad Café* (1951) runs a haven in the Georgia swamps for tramps, lunatics and other social misfits – and her world is shattered when she falls in love with a malign homosexual dwarf. *Reflections in a Golden Eye* (1941) describes boredom and sexual obsession among the wives in a wartime army camp. *Clock Without Hands* is about racism. Only in one book, *The Member of the Wedding*, does McCullers transcend such nightmarish imaginings. Her heroine is a young adolescent in a household bustling with preparations for a wedding: fascinated but totally ignorant about what is going on, she feels as locked out of 'real' (ie adult) society as the freaks and emotional cripples of McCullers' other books.

MELVILLE, Herman • (1819–91)
US novelist.

As a teenager, Melville educated himself by reading the Bible, Shakespeare, Milton and Sir Thomas Browne. He served at sea until he was 23, and later worked as a customs officer. His books take their style from the grand literature he read, and their stories from his own seafaring adventures or from travellers' tales. His novels are long, and read at times as if Genesis or Job had been revised to include whaling, smuggling, shipwreck and naval war. But their epic thought and style easily match the magnificence of the books which influenced him.

MOBY-DICK • (1851)
Moby Dick is a huge sperm-whale, and the novel tells of Captain Ahab's obsessive attempts to hunt it down and kill it. Melville's whaling-lore is exhaustive, his action-scenes are breath-taking, and he gives an unforgettable picture of Ahab: lonely, driven, daunting as an Old Testament patriarch, a fitting adversary for the monster he has vowed to kill.

Melville's other novels include Typee *and* Omoo, *based on his own experiences after being shipwrecked among cannibals in Polynesia;* Redburn: his First Voyage; White-

---

> **READ ON**

▶ **To McCullers' more freakish books:** Ian McEwan, *The Comfort of Strangers*; Iain Banks, *The Wasp Factory*; Deborah Moggach, *Porky*; Paul Bailey, *At The Jerusalem*; ▷Émile Zola, *Nana*.
▶ **To *The Member of the Wedding*:** ▷Eudora Welty, *Delta Wedding*; ▷Katherine Anne Porter, *The Leaning Tower* (short stories).

> **READ ON**

▶ ▷Nathaniel Hawthorne, *The Scarlet Letter*. ▷Victor Hugo, *Toilers of the Sea*. ▷Joseph Conrad, *The Nigger of the Narcissus*.
▶ **Novels about dark obsessions of other kinds:** ▷Thomas Mann, *Doctor Faustus*; ▷Norman Mailer, *An American Dream*; ▷John Fowles, *The Collector*.

jacket, or The World in a Man-o'-War; *the bitter satire*
The Confidence Man *and* Billy Budd, *the story of an inar-*
ticulate young sailor who kills a sadistic petty officer.

THE MIDDLE AGES

▷Italo Calvino, *Our Ancestors*
  Umberto Eco, *The Name of the Rose*
▷William Golding, *The Spire*
▷Victor Hugo, *Notre Dame de Paris*
  Pär Lagerkvist, *The Dwarf*
▷Thomas Mann, *The Holy Sinner*
▷Jean Plaidy, *The Bastard King*
  Helen Waddell, *Peter Abelard*

Other Peoples, Other Times (p 186); Renaissance
Europe (p 201)

MILLER, Walter M. • *(born 1922)*
US novelist.

In Miller's best-known novel, *A Canticle for Leibowitz*
(1960), the human race has survived the nuclear holocaust
(or 'Great Fallout') at the expense of having to retrace its
steps towards civilisation. In the twelfth century of the
new era, the curators of knowledge are a group of monks,
the Blessed Order of Leibowitz. They pore over their sacred writings, Leibowitz's jottings and research-notes, and
try to turn what they read into actuality. Their experiments
– which even they view with alarm, tampering with powers beyond their comprehension – will (we know from
hindsight) parallel the discoveries of alchemists and scientists from our own time, repeating the cycle which led to
the Great Fallout in the first place. In the meantime, in all
ignorance, the monks are just making their first experiments with electricity.

READ ON ▷

● *The Darfsteller.*
▶ ▷Russell Hoban,
Riddley Walker.
▷James Blish, *Black*
Easter. Bamber
Gascoigne, *Cod*
Strewth (a similar, but
comic story: the
surviving book is not
science but scraps of
▷Rabelais).

MITCHELL, Margaret • *(1900–49)*
US novelist.

Gone with the Wind, Mitchell's only book (published in
1936; filmed three years later with Clark Gable and
Vivien Leigh) was aptly described in its day as 'the greatest love-story ever told'. In Atlanta, Georgia, at the outbreak of the 1860s American civil war, Scarlett O'Hara

READ ON ▷

▶ ▷Boris Pasternak,
Doctor Zhivago.
▷Daphne Du Maurier,
Rebecca. Colleen
McCullough, *The Thorn*

falls in love with Ashley Wilkes, the foppish son of a neighbouring plantation-owner, only to discover that he is having an affair with her sister. Heartbroken, she turns to other men, including the cynical, rakish Rhett Butler. The civil war proceeds, the South loses, Atlanta is burned and Scarlett's beautiful house, Tara, is plundered. The devastation of war mirrors the suffering in her heart. She tells Rhett of her hopeless love for Ashley, Rhett leaves her (with a blunt 'Frankly, my dear, I don't give a damn'), and she realises that he was really the man she loved all the time.

Birds. M.M. Kaye, *The Far Pavilions.*

MONEY

▷John Galsworthy, *The Forsyte Saga*
 Brian Glanville, *The Financiers*
▷Maxim Gorky, *Yegor Bulitchev and Others*
▷Judith Krantz, *Scruples*
 Emma Lathen, *Banking on Death*
▷Christina Stead, *House of All Nations*
▷Jerome Weidman, *A Family Fortune*
 Donald Westlake, *Bank Shot*

MOORCOCK, Michael • *(born 1939)*
British novelist.

In the 1960s Moorcock edited the SF magazine New Worlds, pioneering and encouraging 'new wave' writing. The underlying ideas of this are traditional: time-travel, space-opera, sword-and-sorcery. But the literary style is freewheeling, psychedelic, experimental and poetic. Moorcock's own 'new wave' work is at its peak in his Jerry Cornelius books (eg *The English Assassin*; *The Final Programme*), which are less straightforward novels than firework displays of ideas, magical mystery tours round one man's overheated brain. In later books Moorcock returned to a more sober style, still crammed with ideas but much easier to read. Many of his novels offer alternative versions of the present (*Warlord of the Air*, for example, imagines a 20th century where the first world war never happened and the old 19th century empires, British, Austrian, Russian and German, are still jockeying for power). Others (*Gloriana*; *The Jewel in the Skull*) are satires about societies which are dark and decadent perversions of our own. A good starting-point to his multifarious, dazzling work is the 1970s series 'Dancers at the End of Time' (*An*

> **READ ON** >

● *The Jewel in the Skull.*
▶ ▷Robert Heinlein, *The Number of the Beast.* Robert E. Vardeman and Victor Milan, *The War of Powers.* ▷J.G. Ballard, *The Day of Creation.* ▷Robert Silverberg, *Tom O'Bedlam.*

Alien Heat, *The Hollow Lands*, *The End of All Songs* and a cluster of less closely related novels). The time is the very last days of the universe. The few hundred surviving members of the human race control vast energies: anything desired can be obtained by twisting a 'power ring'. Jerek Cornelian (the last human being ever to be born, an avatar of Jerry Cornelius from the earlier novels) falls in love with a strait-laced Victorian time-traveller, Mrs Amelia Underwood. He follows her back in time, and is promptly stranded in the slums of Victorian London: a typical Moorcock idea, allowing him to collapse history, fantasy, social comment and literary parody – Cornelian gives ▷H.G. Wells the idea for The Time Machine – into a single mesmeric and unpredictable experience.

Many of Moorcock's novels are grouped in series: The Chronicles of the Black Sword, The High History of the Runestaff, The Chronicles of Castle Brass, The Books of Corum, The History of the Eternal Champion. *His single novels include* The Ice Schooner, Breakfast in the Ruins *and* Condition of Muzak. The Singing Citadel, Voyage on a Dark Ship *and* The Time Dweller *are collections of short stories.*

MOORHOUSE, Frank • *(born 1938)*
Australian short-story writer.

Moorhouse's stories are character-sketches: he is less interested in plot than in showing states of feeling, emotion and (particularly) psychological disturbance. His complex style (short scenes, jump-cut as in films; dialogue with little indication of who is speaking; no distinction between the description of thoughts and actions, the subjective and the objective), quickly builds up a sense of randomness, of disorientation. Some of his 1960s stories were published in girlie magazines, and their sexual explicitness was considered shocking at the time. His collections are *Futility and Other Animals* (1969, anthropologist's reports on the 'urban tribe' of small-town Australia), *The American Baby* (1972, parodying Australia's infatuation with US culture), *Conference-ville* (1976, set among university students and teachers), *Tales of Mystery and Romance* and *The Everlasting Secret Family and Other Secrets*, both about the obsessions and rituals of 'ordinary' family life.

> **READ ON** ⟩
>
> ▶ Robert Coover, *Pricksongs and Descants*. ▷J.D. Salinger, *Nine Stories/ For Esmé, with Love and Squalor*. ▷Keri Hulme, *The Windeater*. Anaïs Nin, *Under a Glass Bell*. Richard Brautigan, *Willard and His Bowling Trophy* (novel).

MORRIS, William • *(1834–96)*
British craftsman and writer.

At the end of his life Morris (hitherto an artist, designer and philosopher) turned to fiction, writing historical novels and two future-fantasies, *A Dream of John Ball* (1888) and *News From Nowhere* (1891). *News from Nowhere* has the distinction of being one of the very few fantasies to predict a happy future for the human race. Its hero drifts off to sleep during a political meeting in the 1890s, and wakes up to find that he has been transported 60 years forwards in time, and that every socialist dream has been fulfilled. The worker's paradise exists: war, fear, disease and poverty have been eradicated, along with money, prisons and politicians. Everyone is equal, and the harmony between human beings and their environment (the banks of the Thames) is as perfect as it was in Eden before the arrival of the Serpent. Morris' vision is poetic rather than sickly-sweet, and he writes without a twitch of irony. Whatever our hindsight-programmed cynicism a century later, *News from Nowhere* is still a fascinating and remarkable read. If its optimism had been based on Christian rather than humanist beliefs, it might be universally recognised as a major work of visionary literature – which is exactly what it is.

Morris' historical novels (influenced by Icelandic sagas and northern European legends such as Beowulf) include The House of the Wolfings, The Wood Beyond the World *and* The Sundering Flood.

MOSCO, Maisie
British novelist.

Mosco, a prolific romantic novelist, is best-known for the saga of a Jewish family, refugees from early 20th-century European pogroms, who make a new home in northern England. Her detail of Manchester slum existence in the first half of this century, and of the closeness of Jewish family and community life, is particularly admired. The books in the sequence (all written in the 1980s) are *Almonds and Raisins*, *Scattered Seed* and *Children's Children*.

> **READ ON**

● *A Dream of John Ball.*
▶ ▷Robert Graves, *Seven Days in New Crete.* Sarah Scott, *Millenium Hall.* ▷Hermann Hesse, *The Glass Bead Game.* Michael Frayn, *Sweet Dreams* (a satire on exactly the kind of liberal-socialist paradise Morris describes – but literal: Frayn's leading character is exploring Heaven itself).

> **READ ON**

▶ Thomas Armstrong, *The Crowther Chronicles.* Claire Rayner, *'Performers' series.* ▷Bernice Rubens, *The Brothers.* ▷Mrs Gaskell, *Mary Barton* and *North and South* give an earlier, even robuster, view of life in industrial Manchester.

MUNRO, Alice • *(born 1931)*
Canadian short-story writer.

Many of Munro's stories are set in the villages and small towns of British Columbia and Ontario, places she depicts as genteel, culturally negligible and bigoted, stagnant since the days of the Model T Ford. Many of her characters are young people of spirit (usually women or girls), stretching the bounds of this environment. Although her themes are modern – feminism, for example – her careful descriptions of the streets, houses, rooms and clothes of her people give the stories a strong nostalgic appeal. She is like one of the gentler Southern US writers (▷Eudora Welty, say) transported north.

Munro's story-collections include Lives of Girls and Women, Something I've Been Meaning to Tell You, The Moons of Jupiter *and* Who Do You Think You Are?/The Beggar Maid, *in which the stories are linked to form an episodic novel.*

► ▷Eudora Welty, *The Golden Apples.* ▷Katherine Mansfield, *The Dove's Nest and Other Stories.* Sherwood Anderson, *Winesburg, Ohio.* Edna O'Brien, *A Scandalous Woman and Other Stories.*

READ ON ▷

MURDER MOST MIND-BOGGLING

John Franklin Bardin, *Devil Take the Blue-Tail Fly*
Edmund Crispin, *The Moving Toyshop*
▷Peter Dickinson, *The Lively Dead*
Umberto Eco, *The Name of the Rose*
H.R.F. Keating, *A Rush on the Ultimate*
Cameron McCabe, *The Face on the Cutting-room Floor*
Josephine Tey, *The Singing Sands*

Classic Detection (p 46); Great Detectives (p 100); Private Eyes (p 196)

MURDOCH, Iris • *(born 1919)*
Irish/British novelist and philosopher.

The subject of Murdoch's two dozen novels is personal politics: the ebb and flow of relationships, the way we manipulate others and are ourselves manipulated. The time is now; the people are middle-class, professional, usually from the English Home Counties – and they are all bizarre, possessed by a demon which blurs reality and dream into a single, mesmeric state. Seduction, mysticism and moral disintegration are favourite themes, and the in-

READ ON ▷

● *The Book and the Brotherhood.*
► ▷Mary McCarthy, *A Charmed Life.* Alice Thomas Ellis, *The 27th Kingdom.* D.M. Thomas, *Birthstone.* Mary Flanagan, *Trust.*

Iris MURDOCH

AN UNOFFICIAL ROSE *(nine people, all looking for love; nine intertwined, entangled lives)*

WOMEN ALONE

Anita BROOKNER, A MISALLIANCE
(divorced woman, keeping up façade of busy, fulfilled existence, is troubled by chaotic emotional life of people she meets)

Jenni DISKI, RAINFOREST
(professor tries to stop intellectual meticulousness destroying emotional life)

Bernice RUBENS, OUR FATHER
(archaeologist's meeting with God in Sahara triggers a search of her past and the relationship between her charismatic, enigmatic parents)

Susan HILL, IN THE SPRINGTIME OF THE YEAR
(young widow 'rehabilitated' from grief by calm rhythms of country life)

Jane GARDAM, CRUSOE'S DAUGHTER
(Robinson Crusoe gives lonely woman purpose in life and grasp on sanity)

D.M. THOMAS, THE WHITE HOTEL
(case-history of disturbed woman, erotic and violent, reflects nightmarish psychic experience of all 20th-century humanity)

SEARCHING FOR SELF

Lisa St Aubin de TERAN, THE BAY OF SILENCE
(apparently happy, successful film actress haunted by schizophrenia)

Lawrence DURRELL, THE DARK LABYRINTH/CEFALÙ
(group of tourists enter Cretan labyrinth in search of psychic identity – and each quest is unexpectedly fulfilled)

Virginia WOOLF, TO THE LIGHTHOUSE
(thoughts and memories of large close family on holiday: projected day-trip to a lighthouse focuses each of their lives)

Eleanor DARK, RETURN TO COOLAMI
(four people motoring in Australian outback discover themselves)

Christopher ISHERWOOD, A MEETING BY THE RIVER
(two brothers, estranged and 'lost', find Buddhism, true love and tranquility of soul)

Hermann HESSE, STEPPENWOLF
(lonely middle-aged recluse 'rehabilitated' spiritually by three mystical, possibly fantasy young people)

LURE OF THE EXOTIC

Olivia MANNING, THE RAIN FOREST
(young couple, psychically 'lost', seek solace on magical, sinister tropical island)

Paul THEROUX, THE MOSQUITO COAST
(tired of US civilisation, man takes family 'back to nature' in Ecuadorian jungle)

Rosamond LEHMANN, A SEA-GRAPE TREE
(deserted wife seeks spiritual and psychic reassurance on Caribbean island)

Patrick WHITE, VOSS
(explorers 'find' themselves by trekking across Australia; at home in Sydney, girl waits breathlessly for news)

Isabel ALLENDE, THE HOUSE OF THE SPIRITS
(Trueba family women, over four generations, order their lives by magic, fantasy and psychic communion rather than as their patriarch ordains)

Angus WILSON, THE MIDDLE AGE OF MRS ELIOT
(widow seeks happiness by surrendering to impulse, going on haphazard Far Eastern odyssey)

nocent late adolescent (whose effect on other people's lives is often devastating) is a standard character.

THE BELL • *(1958)*

Should we live our lives by the conventions of society or moment by moment, defining ourselves by our own changing moods and enthusiasms? This question perplexes every character in *The Bell*: all are waiting for a sudden inspiration or discovery which will define their existence, show them how they should behave. The setting is a lay community housed in a former convent, a refuge for an eccentric collection of inmates whose peace is disturbed by the mechanics of replacing the convent bell and by the arrival of two amoral 'innocents', Dora and Toby. *The Bell* was popular in the hippie 1960s, and still seems to catch the wide-eyed, distracted mood of those times. But its story and characters are fascinating and its images (for example that of the nude, startlingly white-bodied Toby diving, like a fallen angel, into the murky convent lake to investigate a sunken bell) are as disturbing as they are unforgettable.

Murdoch's other novels include The Flight from the Enchanter, The Sandcastle, A Severed Head, The Red and the Green, The Time of the Angels, The Sea, The Sea *and* The Book and the Brotherhood.

Irene Handl, *The Sioux*.

MUSIC

▷Anthony Burgess, *The Piano Players*
▷Willa Cather, *The Song of the Lark*
▷Hermann Hesse, *Gertrud*
  Jack Higgins, *Solo*
▷Thomas Mann, *Doctor Faustus*
▷H.H. Richardson, *The Getting of Wisdom*
  Joseph Skvorecky, *Dvořák in Love*

N

NABOKOV, Vladimir • *(1899–1977)*
Russian/US novelist and short-story writer.

Nabokov wrote in Russian until 1940, when he settled in the USA; thereafter, he worked in English, and also translated and revised his earlier works. He was fascinated by language, and his books are firework displays of wit, purple-prose descriptions, ironical asides and multi-lingual puns: for his admirers, style is a major pleasure of his work. Several of his novels take the form of teasing 'biographies', revealing as much about their dogged biographers as their subjects. The hero of *The Defence* (1929) is a chess-champion, crippled emotionally both by his profession and by his feeling of identity with the whole Russian cultural tradition. The heroes of *The Real Life of Sebastian Knight* (1941) and *Look at the Harlequins!* (1974) play ironical games with their would-be biographers: the more they seem to reveal themselves, the more elusive they become. *Pnin* (1957) is a sad comedy about an accident-prone Russian professor at a US university, trying to keep the customs of the Old Country in a baffling new environment. *Invitation to a Beheading* (1935) and *Bend Sinister* (1947), Nabokov's most political books, are stories of oppression and nightmare in harsh totalitarian regimes. *Despair* (1934) is a dream-like psychological thriller about a man who hunts down and murders his double, only to find that he has destroyed himself. Humbert Humbert, the tragi-comic hero of *Lolita* (1955), is led by sexual infatuation for a twelve-year-old girl into a farcical kidnapping, a flight from the police through the motels and diners of grubby middle America, and finally to murder. The book's tone of obsessive erotic reverie is repeated in *Ada* (1969), about an incestuous love-affair between two rich, spoiled people in a mysterious country midway between 19th-century Russia and the 1930s USA.

> **READ ON**

● *Pnin*.
▶ **To Nabokov's elegant, games-playing style:** ▷Muriel Spark, *The Abbess of Crewe*; John Barth, *Giles Goat-boy*; ▷Frederic Raphael, *California Time*; Julian Barnes, *Flaubert's Parrot*.
▶ **To his darker novels:** ▷Franz Kafka, *The Trial*; ▷Jerzy Kosinski, *The Painted Bird*; Martin Amis, *Success*.
▶ **To his short stories:** Richard Barthelme, *City Life*.

PALE FIRE • *(1962)*
Few novels can ever have had such an original form: a
999-line poem with introduction and commentary. The
poet is an exiled Eastern European king; the commentator
is a fool who fantasises that he is the real heir to the
throne, and that he is writing under the shadow of an as-
sassination-plot. The effect is as if ▷Anthony Hope had
beefed up someone's PhD thesis: *Pale Fire* is funny,
clever – and, despite its bizarre form, a delightfully easy
read.

Nabokov's other novels include King, Queen, Knave*;*
Glory*;* Camera Obscura/Laughter in the Dark *and* The
Gift*.* Nabokov's Dozen, Nabokov's Quartet, A Russian
Beauty, Tyrants Destroyed *and* Details of a Sunset *are
short-story collections.* Speak, Memory *is a poetic account of his privileged, pre-Revolutionary Russian childhood.*

NAIPAUL, V.S. (Vidiadhar Surajprasad)
(born 1932)
Trinidadian novelist and non-fiction writer.

A Trinidadian Indian who settled in England in his early
20s, Naipaul identifies exclusively with none of these
three communities, and has written about all of them. His
early novels (culminating in *A House for Mr Biswas*) were
gentle tragi-comedies, but from the late 1960s onwards his
books grew darker. He wrote savage non-fiction about the
West Indies, India, South America and the Middle East, a
mixture of travel and harsh political and social analysis,
and his novels dealt with totalitarian oppression and despair. *In a Free State* is about cultural alienation: its central characters are an Indian servant in Washington, a
Trinidadian in racist London and two whites in a fanatical
black-power Africa. *Guerrillas* is set in a Caribbean dictatorship, *A Bend in the River* in a 'new' African country,
emerging from centuries of colonial exploitation into a
corrupt, Orwellian state. For most of the 1980s Naipaul
wrote no fiction, but in 1987 he published *The Enigma of
Arrival*, synthesising most of his earlier themes. Its hero,
a Trinidadian writer living near Salisbury, reflects ruefully
on the passing of 'old England' and the breakdown of the
existing order of things.

A HOUSE FOR MR BISWAS • *(1961)*
Mr Biswas is a free spirit shackled by circumstance. He is

> **READ ON** ▷

● *The Mystic Masseur.*
▶ **To the social
comedies:** ▷R.K.
Narayan, *Mr Sampath/
The Printer of Malgudi*;
Amos Tutuola, *The
Palm-wine Drinkard*;
Timothy Mo, *Sour
Sweet.*
▶ **To Naipaul's political
novels:** ▷Joseph
Conrad, *Nostromo*;
Christopher Hope,
Black Swan.

a poor Hindu in Trinidad, an educated man among illiterates, a good-natured soul who irritates everyone. He marries into an enormous extended family, the Tulsis, and spends the next 20 years trying to avoid being engulfed by their lifestyle, which he finds vulgar and ridiculous. The conflict – critics see it as an allegory about the absorption of political or ethnic minorities – is chiefly expressed in comedy. Mr Biswas is desperate to escape from the Tulsis' rambling mansion, thronged with disapproving relatives; his ambition is to live decently with his family in a home of his own. Although he succeeds, the book ends ironically and tragically: his victory, the vindication of all he stands for, turns to ashes even as he savours it.

Naipaul's other novels include The Suffrage of Elvira, Mr Stone and the Knights Companion *and* The Mimic Men. *His non-fiction books include* The Middle Passage *(on the West Indies and South America),* An Area of Darkness *and* India: a Wounded Civilisation *(two studies, a decade apart, of Indian life and politics) and* Among Believers: an Islamic Journey. The Overcrowded Barracoon *is a collection of essays and articles;* Miguel Street *and* A Flag on the Island *are collections of short stories.*

NARAYAN, R.K. (Rasipuran Krishnaswami) • *(born 1907)*
Indian novelist.

Narayan's stories are set in the imaginary southern Indian town of Malgudi, or in the villages and farms of the nearby Mempi Hills. His characters are shopkeepers, peasant farmers, craftsmen, priests, money-lenders, teachers and housewives, and his theme is the way Hindu belief sustains them in the face of the bewildering or ridiculous events of daily life. Many of his books are comedies. In *The Maneater of Malgudi* (1961) a demented taxidermist works on a series of creatures of ever-increasing size until, to universal panic, he suggests killing and stuffing the town's sacred elephant. The narrator of *A Tiger for Malgudi* (1983) is a worldly-wise tiger who becomes a circus performer, a film star and a travelling guru. *The Painter of Signs* (1976) recounts the farcical relationship between Raman, an ambitious but under-employed sign-painter, and Daisy from the Family Planning Centre, a New Woman whose life is dedicated not to love-affairs but to preventing over-population. Other books replace knockabout with gentler, more bitter-sweet scenes from the human comedy. *The English Teacher/Grateful to Life and Death* (1945) is a beautiful story about a husband

READ ON ▷

● *The Financial Expert.*
▶ Rabinadrath Tagore, *The Home and the World.* Anita Desai, *The Clear Light of Day.* S.N. Ghose, *And Gazelles Leaping.*
▷Kazuo Ishiguro, *An Artist of the Floating World.* ▷Tove Jansson, *The Summer Book.* Giovanni Guareschi, *The Little World of Don Camillo* (short stories).

coping with grief after the death of his beloved wife. In
The Guide (1958) a pushy young man sets himself up as a
tourist-guide, becomes the manager of a brainless dancer,
and finally finds fulfilment not in any such secular enterprise but as a prophet.

THE VENDOR OF SWEETS • *(1967)*

The sweet-manufacturer Jagan is a devout Hindu, a fol-
lower of Gandhi. He lives an austere, uncomplicated and
self-sufficient life. Then his wastrel son Mali arrives from
Delhi with a non-Indian wife and a scheme for enriching
himself by marketing a machine for writing novels. Mali
and his wife take up residence in Jagan's house, and the old
man is torn between love for his son, exasperation, and distress at the contrast between what Mali is doing (which he
claims to be in the spirit of the 'new India') and the beliefs
and rituals which have sustained Jagan all his life.

Narayan's other novels include Swami and Friends *and*
The Bachelor of Arts *(which with* The English Teacher
form a trilogy), Mr Sampath/The Printer of Malgudi, The
Financial Expert *and* The Talkative Man. A Horse and
Two Goats, An Astrologer's Day, Lawley Road *and*
Malgudi Days *are short-story collections;* My Days *is a
placid autobiography.*

NEWBY, P.H. (Percy Howard) • *(born 1918)*
British novelist.

READ ON ▷

▶ Michael Frayn, *The
Russian Interpreter.*
▷Alison Lurie, *Foreign
Affairs.* ▷Evelyn
Waugh, *Scoop.*

The people in Newby's satires have neither the power nor
the will to influence events. They are content to let things
happen – and those things are unpredictable, dreamlike
and bizarre. *Leaning in the Wind* (1986), set in the leafy
English countryside, treats its characters like pieces in a
surreal board-game. The protagonists are an insurance
man who is also a poet, and the daughter of a nazi couple
who emigrated to Cincinatti; he loves her, but she loves a
Kenyan white settler who may or may not be descended
from Shakespeare's sister. The plot revolves with remorseless, inconsequential logic round hauntings, forged
manuscripts, betrayals and adulteries – and when the climax of the book demands a rabbit from the hat, out pops
Idi Amin, that unlikeliest of conjurer's props.

Newby's other novels include A Journey to the Interior,
Picnic at Sakkara, A Season in England, Revolution and
Roses, A Guest and his Going, Something to Answer For
and A Lot to Ask. Ten Miles from Anywhere *is a collection of short stories.*

NEWSPAPERS

▷Heinrich Böll, *The Lost Honour of Katherina Blum*
Max Davidson, *Wellington Blue*
Michael Frayn, *Towards the End of the Morning*
George Gissing, *New Grub Street*
▷Rose Macaulay, *Potterism*
▷William Thackeray, *Pendennis*
▷Evelyn Waugh, *Scoop*

NINETEENTH-CENTURY ENGLAND

Caryl Brahms and S.J. Simon, *Don't, Mr Disraeli*
Richard Cobbold, *Margaret Catchpole*
▷David Cook, *Sunrising*
▷Charles Dickens, *Hard Times*
▷John Fowles, *The French Lieutenant's Woman*
George and Weedon Grossmith, *The Diary of a Nobody*
▷William Thackeray, *Pendennis*
▷Anthony Trollope, *The Warden*

NYE, Robert • *(born 1939)*
British writer of novels and children's books.

As well as novels, Nye has written prize-winning children's books and poetry. His best-known adult novel, *Falstaff* (1976), is the autobiography of Shakespeare's fat knight, written as a series of two-or-three-page meditations on such subjects as 'Honour', 'Sherry Sack' and 'Sir John Falstaff's Prick'. Falstaff feels that he has been comprehensively betrayed – by his times, by his family, by his king and above all by his own aging flesh. He looks back on the successes (and excesses) of his life, reshaping awkward facts and warming himself on the memory of gargantuan meals, orgies, pranks and confidence tricks. Nye's wonderful flights of language are sometimes his own, sometimes shameless Shakespeare-borrowings, and his view of late Middle Ages life as a glorious, uninhibited romp – 'eat, drink, fuck, for tomorrow we die' – is swaggering and seductive, so long as you can stay the pace.

READ ON ▷

● *Merlin*; *The Voyage of the Destiny*.
▶ ▷François Rabelais, *Gargantua*. Petronius, *Satyricon*. Bamber Gascoigne, *Cod Strewth*. Stephen Marlowe, *The Memoirs of Christopher Columbus*. ▷John Kennedy Toole, *A Confederacy of Dunces*.

O

OGNIBLAT L'ARTSAU, MRS: see Franklin, Miles

O'HARA, John • *(1905–1970)*
US novelist and short-story writer.

In 18 novels and no less than 374 short stories, O'Hara created a one-person archive of US life and thought in the first half of this century. He wrote of ordinary middle Americans coping with financial, social, religious and family crises. Many of his stories are told in the first person or in the form of letters, and are strong on irony, revealing the teller's mind or attitudes despite the words he or she uses. The prevailing mood is desperation. O'Hara's people feel that their lives and their country are like monsters out of control; all that can be done is to try to live a decent life, and even that ambition is ambushed by poverty, drink, sex, ambition or politics. This concentration on the darker side of life sometimes leads, in O'Hara's longer books, to melodrama: they deal in a soap-opera style with such issues as abortion, alcoholism or incest. His short stories, by contrast, are well-controlled, single anecdotes, remarkable for their restraint.

O'Hara's story-collections include Files on Parade, Here's O'Hara, The Great Short Stories of O'Hara, 49 Stories, The O'Hara Generation *and* Pal Joey *(which he, Rodgers and Hart made into a successful musical, about an amoral, cynical 1930s night-club owner). His novels include* BUtterfield 8, Ten North Frederick, A Rage to Live *and* The Lockwood Concern.

READ ON >

▶ **To O'Hara's novels:** Ellen Glasgow, *The Sheltered Life*; Jean Stafford, *Boston Adventure*; John Braine, *Room at the Top*; Alberto Moravia, *The Woman of Rome*; Joyce Carol Oates, *Do With Me What You Will.*

▶ **To O'Hara's short stories:** Sherwood Anderson, *Winesburg, Ohio*; Ring Lardner, *You Know Me, Al*; Peter Taylor, *The Old Forest*; V.S. Pritchett, *When My Girl Comes Home.*

OLD AGE

▷Kingsley Amis, *Ending Up*
▷Honoré de Balzac, *Old Goriot*
  Julian Barnes, *Staring at the Sun*
▷David Cook, *Missing Persons*
▷Tove Jansson, *Sun City*
▷Muriel Spark, *Memento Mori*

OLD DARK HOUSES

▷Jane Austen, *Northanger Abbey*
  Robert Bloch, *Psycho*
▷Charlotte Brontë, *Jane Eyre*
▷Daphne Du Maurier, *Rebecca*
  Dinah Lampitt, *Sutton Place*
▷Mervyn Peake, *Gormenghast*
  Horace Walpole, *The Castle of Otranto*

Country Houses (p 51)

'ONLY CONNECT'
(people emotionally ill-at-ease)

▷Anita Brookner, *Look at Me*
▷George Eliot, *Middlemarch*
▷Gustave Flaubert, *Madame Bovary*
▷E.M. Forster, *Howards End*
▷Rosamond Lehmann, *The Ballad and the Source*
▷Mary McCarthy, *The Company She Keeps*
▷John Updike, *Marry Me*

Against the Stream (p 3); Perplexed by Life (p 190)

ON THE EDGE OF SANITY

▷Djuna Barnes, *Nightwood*
▷Lawrence Durrell, *The Dark Labyrinth/Cefalù*
▷Graham Greene, *Brighton Rock*
▷Hermann Hesse, *Steppenwolf*
▷Franz Kafka, *The Trial*
▷Malcolm Lowry, *Under the Volcano*

▷Vladimir Nabokov, *Despair*
▷R.K. Narayan, *The English Teacher/Grateful to Life and Death*

Depression and Psychiatry (p 57); Madness (p 59)

ORWELL, George • *(1903–50)*
British writer.

'George Orwell' was the pseudonym of Eric Blair. In his 20s he worked for the Colonial Police in Burma (an experience he later used in the novel *Burmese Days*). He returned to England disgusted with Imperialism and determined never again to work for or support 'the system'. In fact most of his work thereafter was literary: articles, essays and books taking a jaundiced view of British society and attitudes. Commissioned to report on the industrial north of England, he wrote *The Road to Wigan Pier* (1937), an indictment not only of unemployment and poverty but also of the failure of idealists, of all political parties, to find a cure. *Down and Out in London and Paris* (1933) is a description of the life of tramps and other derelicts; *Homage to Catalonia* (1938) is a withering account of the failure of the International Brigade in the Spanish Civil War. During the 1930s Orwell published three ▷Wellsian novels, about people dissatisfied with the constricting middle-class or lower-middle-class lives they led. It was not until 1945, when the second world war seemed to have blown away forever the humbug and complacency which Orwell considered the worst of all British characteristics, that he published his first overtly political book, *Animal Farm*. In this Stalinist 'fairy story', pigs turn their farm into a workers' democracy in which 'all animals are equal, but some are more equal than others', and the rule of all quickly degenerates into the tyranny of the few. The success of *Animal Farm* encouraged Orwell to write an even more savage political fantasy, *1984*.

1984 • *(1949)*
In the totalitarian future, Winston Smith's job is to rewrite history, adding to or subtracting from the record people who are in or out of Party favour. He falls in love – a forbidden thing, because it arises from freewill and not by order of the Party – and is betrayed to the Thought Police. He is tortured until he not only admits, but comes to believe, that the Party is right in everything: if it says that 2 + 2 = 5, then that is so. The book ends, chillingly, with the idea that Winston has won the victory over himself: he is happy because he has chosen, of his own free will, to have no choice.

READ ON

▶ **To the savage politics of *1984*:** Victor Serge, *The Case of Comrade Tulayev*; Arthur Koestler, *Darkness at Noon*; ▷Franz Kafka, *The Trial*; ▷Vladimir Nabokov, *Bend Sinister*.
▶ **Future-fantasies of a similarly bleak kind:** ▷Aldous Huxley, *Brave New World*; ▷Anthony Burgess, *A Clockwork Orange*.
▶ ▷Mario Vargas Llosa. *The City and the Dogs/The Time of the Hero,* set in a Peruvian military academy, is that rare thing, an Orwellian political allegory which is also funny.

George ORWELL

1984 *(repression and oppression in grim totalitarian future)*

Alexander **SOLZHENITSYN, ONE DAY IN THE LIFE OF IVAN DENISOVICH** *(repression of dissidents in Stalinist labour-camp)*

Maxim **GORKY, FOMA GORDEEV**
(underbelly of Tsarist Russia in decline)

Nathaniel **HAWTHORNE, THE SCARLET LETTTER**
(religious bigotry in Pilgrim Fathers America)

Margaret **ATWOOD, THE HANDMAID'S TALE**
(grim future: totalitarian, religious oppression, anti-women)

Fay **WELDON, LIFE AND LOVES OF A SHE-DEVIL**
(betrayed wife takes macabre, comic revenge)

William **GOLDING, LORD OF THE FLIES**
(schoolboys revert to barbarism after being marooned from civilisation)

Joseph **CONRAD, HEART OF DARKNESS**
(wilderness as a satanic, engulfing force, human evil symbolised)

Paul **THEROUX, O-ZONE**
(efforts to make a viable post-nuclear society in US wilderness)

Patrick **WHITE, A FRINGE OF LEAVES**
('civilised' woman in distress, rehabilitated by contact with aboriginal, 'primitive' people)

Willa **CATHER, DEATH COMES FOR THE ARCHBISHOP**
(Catholic missionaries test their faith in 1870s Mexican wilderness)

Anthony **BURGESS, A CLOCKWORK ORANGE**
(crime and class-war in future Britain)

Graham **GREENE, BRIGHTON ROCK**
(crime and redemption in 1930s England)

Georges **SIMENON, THE MURDERER**
(criminal psychologically destroyed by guilt)

Orwell's 1930s novels are A Clergyman's Daughter, Keep the Aspidistra Flying *and* Coming Up for Air. *A collection of his essays, articles and letters was published in 1968.*

OTHER PEOPLES, OTHER TIMES
(historical novels set in remote or unusual times)

Jean M. Auel, *Clan of the Cave Bear* (prehistoric Europe)

James Clavell, *Shôgun* (17th-century Japan)

▷Eleanor Dark, *The Timeless Land* (18th-century Australia)

▷Gustave Flaubert, *Salammbô* (ancient Carthage)

▷Norman Mailer, *Ancient Evenings* (ancient Egypt)

Naomi Mitchison, *Early in Orcadia* (prehistoric Orkneys)

▷Robert Silverberg, *Gilgamesh the King* (ancient Sumeria)

▷Sigrid Undset, *Kristin Lavransdatter* (14th-century Norway)

▷Mario Vargas Llosa, *The War of the End of the World* (19th-century Peru)

Ancient Greece (p 9); Bible: Old Testament (p 23)

P

PARENTS AND CHILDREN

Samuel Butler, *The Way of All Flesh*
Margaret Forster, *Private Papers*
▷Hermann Hesse, *Rosshalde*
▷D.H. Lawrence, *Sons and Lovers*
▷Ivan Turgenev, *Fathers and Sons*
▷John Updike, *The Centaur*

Adolescence (p 3); Families: All-engulfing (p 72); Families: Eccentric (p 72); Families: Many Generations (p 72); Growing Up: Teenagers (p 101)

PASTERNAK, Boris • *(1890-1960)*
Russian poet and novelist.

In the USSR Pasternak is remembered chiefly as a poet and translator (of ▷Goethe and Shakespeare). Western readers know him for his 1957 novel *Doctor Zhivago*, and for the savage reaction of the Soviet authorities of the time, who banned the book and made Pasternak renounce his Nobel prize. *Doctor Zhivago* is about a doctor, Zhivago, and a teacher, Lara, caught up in the civil war which followed the 1917 Revolution. Although each is married to someone else and has a child, they fall in love – and the feverishness of their affair is increased by knowledge that neither it nor they will survive the war, since they come from a doomed class, the bourgeoisie. Horrified and powerless, they witness the brutality, class hatred and fury which precede the establishment of the USSR. Despite the reaction of the late-1950s authorities to all this, Pasternak was not really concerned with politics. He was more interested in the idea of people out of step

READ ON ▷

▶ ▷Lev Tolstoy, *Anna Karenina*. ▷Ernest Hemingway, *A Farewell to Arms*. ▷Elizabeth Bowen, *The Heat of the Day*. ▷Margaret Mitchell, *Gone With the Wind*. ▷Iris Murdoch, *The Red and the Green*.

with their time, star-crossed by destiny, and in the way Zhivago's and Lara's relationship was an emotional counterpart to the chaos and destruction all round them. The book ends with Zhivago's poems about Lara, like faded love-letters plucked from the rubble of the past.

PEAKE, Mervyn • *(1911–68)*
British novelist and artist.

Peake earned his living as an artist, drawing cartoons and grotesque, sombre illustrations to such books as *Treasure Island* and *The Hunting of the Snark*. He also made portraits of the main characters in his own novels: unsmiling freaks with distorted limbs and haunted eyes, violently cross-hatched as if with giant cobwebs. He admired ▷Poe and ▷Kafka, and his own work lopes gleefully – and hilariously – down the same dark passages of the imagination, peering into every corner and detailing the horrors that wait behind every moss-grown, slime-streaked door.

GORMENGHAST • *(1946–59)*
The 'Gormenghast' trilogy *Titus Groan*, *Gormenghast* and *Titus Alone* takes place in a mist-shrouded, monstrous kingdom surrounding the crumbling Gothic castle of Gormenghast. Evil broods, waiting to pounce; it is kept at bay only if everyone, from Lord Sepulchrave himself to the physician Prunesquallor, from Nanny Slagg to the demented, crippled scullion Steerpike, lives every second of each day by a precise, bizarre ritual, as compulsive and pointless as the movements of the insane. *Titus Groan* describes the fearful consequences when Steerpike, to further his own dark ambitions, starts fomenting social revolution. *Gormenghast* is about the growing-up of Titus, 77th Earl of Groan: how he learns about his inheritance, uncovers the castle's secrets and begins to chafe against the rituals which choke its people's lives. In *Titus Alone* Titus breaks free of the castle and explores the country outside, an arrogant knight-errant on a terrifying, pointless quest.

Peake's only other novel, Mr Pye, *is a gentler story about a man on Sark in the Channel Islands who shows distressing signs of turning into an angel.*

READ ON ⟩

▶ **To *Gormenghast***;
▷Mary Shelley, *Frankenstein*; ▷Edgar Allan Poe, *The Fall of the House of Usher*; ▷Tom De Haan, *A Mirror for Princes*; ▷J.R.R. Tolkien, *Lord of the Rings*..
▶ **To *Mr Pye*:** Paul Gallico, *Flowers for Mrs Harris*.

Mervyn PEAKE

GORMENGHAST (*Titus Groan uncovers his destiny in sinister castle-kingdom*)

Dennis **WHEATLEY, THE KA OF GIFFORD HILLARY**
(*while Hillary sleeps, 'other self' leads malign independent life*)

James **HERBERT, THE MAGIC COTTAGE**
(*young couple move into macabre haunted house*)

Bram **STOKER, DRACULA**
(*vampire Count*)   **SUPERNATURAL TERROR**

Stephen **KING, PET SEMETARY**
(*ghosts walk in rural Maine*)

Edgar Allan **POE, TALES OF MYSTERY AND IMAGINATION** (*madness, burial alive, and living dead*)

Sylvia **PLATH, THE BELL JAR**
(*treatment for suicidal depressive mania*)

Patricia **HIGHSMITH, THE GLASS CELL**
DERANGEMENT AND MADNESS   (*man driven mad by prison, has wife been faithful?*)

Ken **KESEY, ONE FLEW OVER THE CUCKOO'S NEST**
(*lunatics take over the asylum*)

Robert **SILVERBERG, TOM O'BEDLAM**
(*are Tom's visions madness or manifestations of genuine alien gods?*)

Tom **DE HAAN, A MIRROR FOR PRINCES**
(*disturbed family of 'medieval' dictator wait for his death*)

Ursula **LE GUIN, MALAFRENA**
(*Napoleonic Europe – or its mirror*)

Robert **SILVERBERG, LORD VALENTINE'S CASTLE**   **FANTASY SOCIETIES**
(*young man – good – gathers followers to battle usurper*)

Robert **IRWIN, THE ARABIAN NIGHTMARE**
(*man on medieval pilgrimage is trapped in his own dreams*)

Jack **VANCE, THE BLUE WORLD**
(*floating worlds in water-paradise – but beware sea-monsters*)

Daphne **DU MAURIER, REBECCA**
(*what is the secret of Manderley?*)

Angela **CARTER, THE MAGIC TOYSHOP**
(*adolescent orphan goes to live with deranged puppeteer-uncle*)

Michael **INNES, LAMENT FOR A MAKER**
OLD, DARK HOUSE AND   (*who killed the mad Laird of Erchany? What is the meaning*
CASTLES   *behind the curse?*)

Susan **HILL, THE WOMAN IN BLACK**
(*ghosts walk in rural England*)

Henry **JAMES, THE TURN OF THE SCREW**
(*who can exorcise the ghosts which haunt the children?*)

PERPLEXED BY LIFE
(people battling to understand and control their destiny)

▷Saul Bellow, *Humboldt's Gift*
▷Albert Camus, *The Fall*
▷Erica Jong, *Fear of Flying*
▷Hermann Hesse, *Rosshalde*
▷Iris Murdoch, *The Sandcastle*
▷V.S. Naipaul, *A House for Mr Biswas*
▷Italo Svevo, *The Confessions of Zeno*
▷Angus Wilson, *Anglo-Saxon Attitudes*

PIRANDELLO, Luigi • *(1867-1936)*
Italian writer of novels, short stories and plays.

Although Pirandello is chiefly known for such experimental plays as *Six Characters in Search of an Author*, he was
also a prolific short-story writer and the author of six
novels about aristocratic and peasant life in late 19th-cen-
tury Sicily. His 250 stories take as their starting-point the
kind of mundane crimes – adultery, fraud, murder –
which figure in the 'news in brief' columns of tabloid
newspapers: lip-smacking gossip about total strangers, But
Pirandello regards each sensational event as the release of
a long build-up of tension or psychological panic – and
that build-up is his subject. He shows us people trapped
by convention, by their own passions and longings, and
by the malevolence of others. If you stripped the music
from Puccini's operas and boiled their plots and motiva-
tion down to half a dozen pages of lucid, implacable
prose, the results might be very similar.

Pirandello's novels include The Late Mattia Pascal, The
Old and the Young *and* One, None and a Hundred Thou-
sand. *A good, representative story-collection is* Better
Think Twice About It.

> **READ ON** ▷

► Alberto Moravia,
Roman Tales. Cesare
Pavese, *Nice Summer*.
Ivan Klíma, *My First
Loves*. William
Saroyan, *The
Insurance Salesman
and Other Stories*.
George Moore,
Celibate Lives.
▷Vladimir Nabokov,
*The Real Life of
Sebastian Knight*
(novel).

PLACES

Melvyn Bragg, *The Maid of Buttermere* (English Lake
District)
▷Emily Brontë, *Wuthering Heights* (Yorkshire moors)
▷Graham Greene, *The Comedians* (Haiti)
▷Thomas Hardy, *Jude the Obscure* (rural Wessex)

▷John Irving, *The Cider House Rules* (rural Maine)
▷Rudyard Kipling, *Kim* (rural India)
▷R.K. Narayan, *The Painter of Signs* (small-town India)

Cities: New World (p 44); Cities: Old World (p 44); Deep South, USA (p 55); Into the Wilderness (p 127); US Small Town Life (p 246)

PLAIDY, Jean • *(born 1906)*
British novelist.

'Jean Plaidy' is one of the pseudonyms of Eleanor ▷Hibbert. She is the author of over 80 light historical novels, most of them based on the intrigues surrounding European royal marriages, accessions and other political and dynastic events. Several of her best-known books are grouped in series, including the 'Norman Trilogy' (beginning with *The Bastard King*, 1975, about William the Conqueror), the 'Plantagenet Saga' (based on the Wars of the Roses) and the 'Mary Queen of Scots' series.

Plaidy's other books include The Spanish Bridegroom, A Health Unto his Majesty, Flaunting Extravagant Queen, Perdita's Prince, Sweet Lass of Richmond Hill *and* The Prince and the Quakeress.

> READ ON

▶ Margaret Irwin, *Young Bess*. Tyler Whittle, *The Young Victoria*. Anya Seton, *Katherine*. Caryl Brahms and S.J. Simon, *No Bed for Bacon* (an Elizabethan spoof).

POE, Edgar Allan • *(1809–49)*
US short-story writer.

Poe's miserable life is almost as well-known as his stories. He was an orphan whose foster-father hated him; he was thrown out of university, military college and half a dozen jobs because of the instability of his character; in order to earn a living he suppressed his real ambition (to be a poet) in favour of hack journalism and sensational fiction; he gambled, fornicated, and finally drank himself to death. He was like a man haunted by his own existence – and this is exactly the feeling in his macabre short stories, which are less about the supernatural than about people driven crazy by their own imagination. 'The Fall of the House of Usher' and 'The Premature Burial' recount the terrifying results when people are accidentally entombed alive. The murderer in 'The Tell-tale Heart' buries his victim under the floorboards, only to be haunted by what he takes to be the thud of the dead man's heartbeat. The hero of 'The Pit and the Pendulum' is psychologically tortured by the Spanish Inquisition, first by fear of a

> READ ON

▶ **To Poe's stories of the macabre:** H.P. Lovecraft, *Dagon and Other Macabre Tales*; M.R. James, *Ghost Stories of an Antiquary*; Roald Dahl, *Switch Bitch*; ▷Stephen King, *Night Shift*; ▷James Herbert, *Moon* (novel).
▶ **To the detection-stories:** ▷A. Conan Doyle, *The Adventures of Sherlock Holmes*; Edgar Wallace, *The Four Just Men*; ▷Isaac Asimov, *Tales of the Black Widowers*.

swinging, ever-approaching blade and then by the way the walls of his cell move inwards to crush him. In 'The Black Cat' a murderer is given away by the mewing of a cat which he has accidentally walled up with his victim's body. As well as stories of this kind, Poe occasionally wrote lighter mysteries. The best-known of all ('The Murders in the Rue Morgue'; 'The Mystery of Marie Roget') centre on an eccentric investigator who solves crimes by meticulous reconstruction according to the evidence: they are the first-ever detective-stories.

Poe's stories are normally collected nowadays as Tales of Mystery and Imagination. *His other writings include poetry (*The Bells; The Raven*) and vitriolic literary criticism, savaging such contemporaries as Longfellow.*

POLICE PROCEDURAL

Wilkie Collins, *The Woman in White*
Freeman Wills Crofts, *Death of a Train*
Nicholas Freeling, *Cold Iron*
▷Ed McBain, *Lightning*
▷Ruth Rendell, *A Guilty Thing Surprised*
Maj Sjöwall and Per Wahlöo, *The Laughing Policeman*
Martin Cruz Smith, *Gorky Park*

POLITICS (1)

▷Chinua Achebe, *Anthills of the Savannah*
Jorge Amado, *The Violent Land*
David Caute, *News from Nowhere*
▷Richard Condon, *Mile High*
Benjamin Disraeli, *Coningsby*
Martha Gellhorn, *A Stricken Field*
Arthur Koestler, *Darkness at Noon*
▷Mary McCarthy, *The Groves of Academe*

POLITICS (2)

▷George Orwell, *Animal Farm*
Amos Oz, *A Perfect Peace*
▷Salman Rushdie, *Shame*

Victor Serge, *The Case of Comrade Tulayev*
Howard Spring, *Fame is the Spur*
▷C.P. Snow, *The Corridors of Power*
▷Gore Vidal, *Burr*

PORTER, Katherine Anne • *(1890-1980)*
US novelist and short-story writer.

Many of Porter's short stories, set in Texas, are accounts
of ordinary matters – the relationship of old and young,
swimming, the conversation of farm-workers, the coming
of a circus – seen through the eyes of a child. They are
wistful and nostalgic, depicting human existence as both
beautiful and transient. Her major work, the 500-page
novel *Ship of Fools* (1962), is in a harsher, allegorical
vein. The ship of fools is the world, and the passengers
are the human race, cruising to disaster. Porter's ship is
sailing from Vera Cruz to Bremerhaven in 1931. The crew
and most of the passengers are German; the other travellers are Mexican, Swedish, Swiss, American, and above
all Spanish: 870 plantation-workers being sent home because of a slump in the sugar trade, and a troupe of sinister dancers. At the start of the voyage, the people are determined to be friendly; but soon divisions of class, race,
nation and politics begin to surface, and the outcome is
war. The lumpishness of this allegory is offset by the re-
finement of Porter's writing: the book reads like a collaboration by ▷Chekhov and ▷Conrad, unlikely but persuasive.

Porter's story-collections are Flowering Judas; Pale
Horse, Pale Rider *(three short novels);* The Leaning
Tower *and* The Old Order. *Her* Collected Stories *ap-
peared in 1967.*

POWELL, Anthony • *(born 1905)*
British novelist.

In the 1930s Powell wrote half a dozen novels in a similar
vein to those of Rose Macaulay and Evelyn Waugh, satirising the British intellectual and upper classes of the
time. The optimistic, aimless young people of *Afternoon
Men* drift from party to party, trying to summon up
enough willpower to make something of themselves.
From a View to a Death/Mr Zouch: Superman sets the arts
and foxhunting at each other's throats. The hero of *What's
Become of Waring?* has to find someone to write the biog-

READ ON ▷

▶ **To Porter's stories:**
▷Eudora Welty, *The
Golden Apples*; ▷Willa
Cather, *The Troll
Garden*; Seán
O'Faoláin, *Foreign
Affairs*.
▶ **To *Ship of Fools*:**
▷Joseph Conrad,
Typhoon; ▷Patrick
White, *Voss*.

READ ON ▷

▶ **To Powell's 1930s
books:** ▷Evelyn
Waugh, *Vile Bodies*;
Henry Green, *Party
Going*; ▷Rose
Macaulay, *Crewe
Train*.
▶ The mood of elegiac,
upper-class malice

raphy of a best-selling travel-writer who has disappeared in circumstances which grow more mysterious, and more unsavoury, by the minute. After the second world war, during which he produced no fiction, Powell abandoned single books for a 12-novel sequence, *A Dance to the Music of Time*, a satirical portrait of 70 years of English high society and establishment life.

A DANCE TO THE MUSIC OF TIME • *(1951–75)*

The sequence follows its characters from Edwardian schooldays to nostalgic, worldly-wise old age. The narrator, Nick Jenkins, discreet as a civil servant, goes everywhere, knows everyone, and writes of his contemporaries (notably the ambition-racked Widmerpool) in elegant, ironic prose. The books move imperturbably from farce to seriousness, from knockabout to reverie. The first three novels, *A Question of Upbringing*, *A Buyer's Market* and *The Acceptance World*, concern the characters' schooldays, their Oxbridge careers and their entry into the glittering smart set of 1920s London. *At Lady Molly's*, *Casanova's Chinese Restaurant* and *The Kindly Ones* are about first jobs, marriages and the establishment of a network of sexual, social, financial and political alliances which will bind their lives. *The Valley of Bones*, *The Soldier's Art* and *The Military Philosophers* take the characters through two world wars, and *Books Do Furnish a Room*, *Temporary Kings* and *Hearing Secret Harmonies* show them coming to terms with post-war austerity, the white heat of the technological revolution and flower-power, reflecting on the change not only in themselves but in every aspect of British establishment life since their schooldays 50 years before.

Powell's other 1930s novels are Venusberg *and* Agents and Patients. *After finishing* A Dance to the Music of Time *he wrote an autobiography,* To Keep the Ball Rolling, *and two other (unrelated) novels,* O, How the Wheel Becomes It! *and* The Fisher King.

POWYS, John Cowper • *(1872–1963)*
British novelist and non-fiction writer.

A university professor, Powys wrote books on ▷Dostoevsky, ▷Homer and ▷Rabelais, dozens of articles, reviews and other non-fiction works, and a lively autobiography. His early novels (*Ducdame*; *Rodmoor*; *Wolf Solent*, all written before 1930) are sombre, ▷Hardyish stories about the farmers and fishermen of the English West Country. After he retired from teaching Powys wrote a series of

characteristic of *A Dance to the Music of Time* is repeated in three other novel sequences – ▷Marcel Proust, *Remembrance of Things Past* (*A la recherche du temps perdu*). Simon Raven, *Alms for Oblivion*; Stuart Evans, *Windmill Hill* – and in the single novels Edward Candy, *Scene Changing*; Emma Tennant, *The House of Hospitalities* and ▷Frederic Raphael, *Orchestra and Beginners*.

READ ON ▷

▶ **To Powys' early novels:** ▷Victor Hugo, *Toilers of the Sea*; ▷George Eliot, *Silas Marner*; ▷Nathaniel Hawthorne, *The Scarlet Letter*.

completely different novels: long, mystical books influenced by Homer and the Old Testament and drawing on English legend and dark ages history. In *A Glastonbury Romance* modern inhabitants of the Glastonbury area (including worshippers and clergy at the Abbey) find their lives mysteriously affected by local legends of King Arthur and of the Holy Grail. In a similar way, *Maiden Castle* describes how unearthing the distant past – some of the characters are archaeologists working on a prehistoric site – disturbs the present. *Owen Glendower* and *Porius* are historical romances, full of wizards, giants and ancient magic. *The Bronze Head* is about Roger Bacon, the first scientist (or last alchemist). In *Atlantis* the hero of Homer's *Odyssey* embarks on a quest to find the lost continent.

▶ **To *A Glastonbury Romance*:** ▷Lawrence Durrell, *The Dark Labyrinth/Cefalù*; Charles Williams, *War in Heaven*.

▶ **To the late historical novels:** ▷Sigrid Undset, *Kristin Lavransdatter*; Peter Vansittart, *Three Six Seven*; Pär Lagerkvist, *The Sibyl*; ▷Gore Vidal, *Creation*.

PRICHARD, Katharine Susannah •
(1883-1969)
Australian novelist.

Prichard was a political activist, and her best-known novels deal with matters of social concern, mainly in the 1920s and 1930s. *Working Bullocks* is the study of a community of timber workers in Western Australia, fighting the introduction of streamlined methods which will destroy their employment prospects. *Coonardoo* is about the confrontation of white people and aborigines. The 'goldfields trilogy' *The Roaring Nineties*, *Golden Miles* and *Winged Seeds* (1946–50) is a densely-organised multi-generation saga, also set in Western Australia, from the goldrush days of the 19th century, through the industrialisation and political confrontation of the 1920s to post-second-world-war decline.

▶ ▷Émile Zola, *Germinal*. Mrs Gaskell, *Mary Barton*. Upton Sinclair, *The Jungle*. ▷John Steinbeck, *The Grapes of Wrath*.

Prichard's other novels include Black Opal *(about a mining community threatened by big-business takeovers),* Intimate Strangers *(about a bickering couple whose marriage is saved by their shared political enthusiasms) and* Haxby's Circus *(about a husband-and-wife team struggling to run a travelling circus).* The Wild Oats of Han, *a children's book, is based on her idyllic childhood in Tasmania.*

PRIESTLEY, J.B. (John Boynton) •
(1894-1984)
British novelist and playwright.

As well as plays and non-fiction books, Priestley wrote

▶ *Lost Empires* (a darker

over 60 novels. They range from amiable satire (eg *Low Notes on a High Level*, 1956, sending up egghead BBC musicians) to sombre social realism (eg *Angel Pavement*, 1936, about a sleepy 1930s business firm galvanised into new activity and then destroyed by a confidence trickster). His best-loved novel, *The Good Companions* (1929), tells of three people who escape from humdrum lives to join the Dinky Doos concert party in the 1920s. The novel follows the concert party's career in theatres and seaside resorts all over England, and ends with each of the main characters finding self-fulfilment in an entirely unexpected way. The book bulges with show-biz cliché – brave little troupers; lodging-house keepers with hearts of gold; leading ladies and their tantrums; cynical, hung-over leading men – and with warm-hearted nostalgia for the provincial England of the Good Old Days. It is an armchair of a novel, a book to wallow in – and if life was never really like that, so much the worse for life.

story, about a group of music-hall performers in the year of feverish jingoism and imperialist posturing which led up to the first world war); *The Image Men* (a satire about advertising and television).

► **To *The Good Companions:*** Bamber Gascoigne, *The Heyday*; Noel Langley, *There's a Porpoise Close Behind Us*. Budd Schulberg, *What makes Sammy Run?* and ▷Len Deighton, *Close Up* give beadier-eyed views of the entertainment business (perhaps because their subject is not music-hall but films).

► **To Priestley's books in general:** ▷H.G. Wells, *Tono-Bungay*; James Hilton, *Goodbye, Mr Chips*; Eric Linklater, *Poet's Pub*.

PRIVATE EYES

PROUST, Marcel • *(1871-1922)*
French novelist.

Proust's *Remembrance of Things Past* (A la recherche du temps perdu) (1913–27; magnificently translated by C.K.

▷ **READ ON**

► **Good parallels to the sensuous childhood-**

Scott Moncrieff and Terence Kilmartin) is in seven sections: *Swann's Way*, *Within a Budding Grove*, *The Guermantes Way*, *Cities of the Plain*, *The Captive*, *The Fugitive*, *Time Regained*. Each is as long as a normal novel and each can be read both on its own and as part of the whole huge tapestry. The book is a memoir, told in the first person by a narrator called Marcel, of a group of rich French socialites from the 1860s to the end of the first world war. It shows how they react to outside events – the Dreyfus case, women's emancipation, the first world war – and how, as the world moves on, their power and social position wane. Above all, it shows them reacting to each other, to friends, acquaintances and servants: the book is full of love-affairs, parties, alliances and betrayals. Through it all moves Marcel himself, good-natured, self-effacing, fascinated by beauty (both human and artistic: his accounts of music and literature are as deeply-felt as those of people), and with a sharply ironical eye for social and sexual absurdity. Proust developed for the book a system of 'involuntary memory', in which each sensual stimulus – the smell of lilac, the taste of cake dipped in tea – unlocks from the subconscious a stream of images of the past. Though this technique has structural importance in the novel – Proust believed that our present only makes sense when it is refracted through past experience – its chief effect for the reader is to provide pages of languorous, detailed descriptions, prose poems on everything from the feel of embroidery to garden sounds and scents on a summer evening. Proust likes to take his time: at one point Marcel spends nearly 100 pages wondering whether to get up or stay in bed. But only the length at which he works allows him scope for the sensuous, malicious decadence which is the main feature of his work.

Proust's other writings include translations of Ruskin's The Bible of Amiens *and* Sesame and Lilies, *a collection of short stories and literary parodies,* The Pleasures and the Days *(Les Plaisirs et les jours), and* Jean Santeuil, *a draft of part of* Remembrance of Things Past.

evocations of the first part of *Remembrance of Things Past:* Alain Fournier, *The Lost Domain* (Le grand Meaulnes); ▷James Joyce, *Portrait of the Artist as a Young Man.*

▶ **Echoing the hedonism and decadence of some of Proust's later sections:** Joris-Karl Huysmans, *Against Nature* (A rebours).

▶ **Good on 'the texture of experience':** Dorothy Richardson, *Pilgrimage*; ▷Virginia Woolf, *The Waves*; John Dos Passos, *Manhattan Transfer.*

▶ **Novel-sequences of comparable grandeur:** ▷Anthony Powell, *A Dance to the Music of Time*; Henry Williamson, *The Flax of Dream.* (Williamson's later sequence *A Chronicle of Ancient Sunlight* starts well, but is hijacked half-way through by the author's fascist sympathies.)

PUBLISH AND BE DAMNED
(writers; publishers; agents; readers; fans)

▷Marjorie Allingham, *Flowers for the Judge*
▷Erica Jong, *How To Save Your Own Life*
▷Wyndham Lewis, *The Apes of God*
▷Rose Macaulay, *Crewe Train*
▷Anthony Powell, *What's Become of Waring?*
▷Philip Roth, *Zuckerman Unbound*
▷Tom Sharpe, *The Great Pursuit*

PUZO, Mario • *(born 1920)*
US novelist and screenwriter.

Puzo began his career as a writer of children's books, but in 1969 turned to adult fiction and had one of the biggest commercial successes in publishing history with *The Godfather*. The story concerns the New York mafia family the Corleones. It centres on Don Vito Corleone's handover of authority to his son Michael – a gift akin to being made successor to Genghis Khan – and on the power-struggle, both with outsiders and between members of the family, to which this leads. Present-day events are intercut with flashbacks to Don Vito's Sicilian childhood and his early days in the USA. The plot of *The Godfather* is in a direct line from those of such multi-generation family and big-business sagas as the novels of Harold Robbins. But Puzo's detail of mafia life is as exhaustive and compelling as a government research report. As ▷Le Carré does with spies, he seems to be spilling 'insider' secrets in every line, and his inventions (if they are inventions) are so plausible that it is hard to imagine how the real mafia could be run in any other way. After the 1970s success of the two Godfather films, Puzo turned to screenwriting (among other things, he co-wrote the first Superman film), and his later novels *Las Vegas*, *Fools Die* and *The Sicilian*, though fast-moving and exciting, are like novelised movies, airport-bookstall fodder lacking the documentary earnestness which makes *The Godfather* so compulsive.

PYM, Barbara • *(1913–80)*
British novelist.

Only ▷Jane Austen and ▷Ivy Compton-Burnett wrote about worlds as restricted as Pym's – and she is regularly compared to both of them. Her books are high-Anglican high comedies; she is tart about the kind of pious middle-class ladies who regard giving sherry-parties for the clergy as doing good works, and she is merciless to priests. Much of the charm of her books lies in their ornate, formal dialogue: her characters all speak with the same prissy, self-conscious elegance, like civil servants taught light conversation by Oscar Wilde.

A GLASS OF BLESSINGS • *(1958)*
Wilmet Forsyth is rich, well-bred, happy and dim. She fills her mind with fantasies about the priests and parishioners at her local church, imagining that their lives are a

READ ON ▷

▶ **Good mafia follow-ups:** ▷Richard Condon, *Prizzi's Honour*; Donald Westlake, *The Mercenaries*; Elmore Leonard, *Glitz*.
▶ **Blockbusters about big business and/or politics:** John Gregory Dunne, *The Red White and Blue*; ▷Jerome Weidman, *I Can Get it for you Wholesale*; Sally Quinn, *Regrets Only*.

READ ON ▷

● *Quartet in Autumn*.
▶ ▷Ivy Compton-Burnett, *Pastors and Masters*. A.N. Wilson, *Kindly Light*. Edward Candy, *Scene Changing*. Alice Thomas Ellis, *The Twenty-seventh Kingdom*. J.F. Powers, *Morte d'Urban*. ▷Anita Brookner, *Look at Me*.

whirl of hidden passions, ambitions and frustrations. She imagines herself in love with a handsome evening-class teacher, and assumes that he adores her too. As the book proceeds, every one of these assumptions is proved spectacularly, ludicrously mistaken.

Pym's other novels are Some Tame Gazelle, Excellent Women, Jane and Prudence, Less than Angels, Quartet in Autumn, The Sweet Dove Died, Crampton Hodnett *and* An Academic Question.

PYNCHON, Thomas • *(born 1937)*
US novelist.

Reading Pynchon's satires is like exploring a maze with an opinionated and eccentric guide. He leads us lovingly up every blind alley, breaks off to tell jokes, falls into reverie, ridicules everything and everyone, and refuses to say where he's going until he gets there. *The Crying of Lot 49* (1967) begins with Oedipa Maas setting out to discover why she has been left a legacy by an ex-lover, and what it is; but it quickly develops into a crazy tour of hippie 1960s California, an exploration of drugs, bizarre sex, psychic sensitivity and absurd politics, centring on a group of oddball characters united in a secret society determined to subvert the US postal system. *Gravity's Rainbow* (1973) is a much darker fable, a savage anti-war satire set in a top-secret British centre for covert operations during the second world war. In a mad world, where actions have long ceased to have any moral point, where nothing – on principle – is ever explained or justified, the characters spend their working hours alternately doing what they're told and trying to find out the reason for their existence, and pass their leisure hours in masochistic, joyless sex. On the basis of his short stories and *The Crying of Lot 49*, Pynchon is sometimes claimed as a comic writer. But although *Gravity's Rainbow* is satirical, its jokes are knives, its farce makes us scream with despair not joy.

Pynchon's first and most experimental novel was V *(1963).* Mortality and Mercy in Vienna *is a novella, and* Low-lands *is a collection of short stories.*

READ ON ▷

▶ The satirical fury of *Gravity's Rainbow* is most nearly matched in: ▷Joseph Heller, *Catch-22* and William Gaddis, *J.R.* (about a deranged 10-year-old genius in a reform school who trades in stocks and shares and exploits other people's greed).

▶ Pynchon's more genial, loonier side is parallelled in: ▷Mario Vargas Llosa, *Aunt Julia and the Scriptwriter*; Terry Southern, *The Magic Christian* and ▷Kurt Vonnegut, *Breakfast of Champions*.

▶ Midway between despair and farce, recommended follow-ups are: ▷John Irving, *The Hotel New Hampshire* and ▷Jerzy Kosinski, *The Devil Tree*.

R

RABELAIS, François • *(c 1494–1553)*
French satirist.

At heart Rabelais' *Gargantua* (1534) and *Pantagruel* (1532–3) are simple fairy-tales: accounts of the birth and education of the giant Gargantua and of his son Pantagruel. But Rabelais was really writing satire, sending up the whole of medieval knowledge and belief. The giants study philosophy, mathematics, theology and alchemy; they build an anti-monastery whose rules are not poverty, chastity and obedience but wealth, fornication and licence. Pantagruel's mentor is no dignified greybeard but the conman Panurge, and the two of them go on a fantastic journey (through countries as fabulous as any of those visited by Sinbad or Gulliver) to find the answer to the question 'Whom shall Pantagruel marry?'. Because Rabelais' heroes are giants, every human appetite is magnified a thousand-fold. It takes 17,913 cows to provide enough milk to feed the infant Gargantua, and when he is learning to wipe his bottom he experiments with so many different substances that it takes two pages just to list them. Much of *Gargantua*'s first half is taken up with a fierce battle between the giants and their neighbours, and in particular with the exploits of the roistering, apoplectic Friar John of the Funnels and Goblets, who is later rewarded by being made Abbot of the Monastery of Do As You Like. Rabelais described his books as a 'feast of mirth', and their intellectual satire is balanced by celebration of physical pleasure of every kind: not for nothing has the word 'rabelaisian' entered the dictionary. The original French, already engorged with puns, jokes, parodies and over-the-top lists of every kind, was inflated to nearly twice the length by the 17th-century translator Thomas Urquhart. His English is funnier, filthier and even more fantastical

READ ON

▶ ▷Laurence Sterne, *Tristram Shandy*. ▷Jonathan Swift, *Gulliver's Travels*. Giovanni Boccaccio, *Decameron* (short stories). Anon, *The Thousand and One Nights/The Arabian Nights*. Alexander Theroux, *D'Arconville's Cat*. ▷J.P. Donleavy, *The Ginger Man*.

than Rabelais' French: Rabelais would have loved (and stolen back) every word of it.

RAPHAEL, Frederic • *(born 1931)*
US/British novelist and screenwriter.

Raphael's sourly witty TV plays and series, showing the hollow husks that brilliant Oxbridge graduates become in later life, have diverted attention from his 16 novels. These walk in darker, more sinister paths. His subject is the power of evil, whether political, moral or social. Sometimes (as in *Lindmann*, about guilt for a second-world-war atrocity, or in *Like Men Betrayed*, set in the 1940s Greek civil war), evil is an external force, the result of perverted idealism; in other books (*Richard's Things*, about erotic possession and betrayal; *Heaven and Earth*, about artistic and personal integrity) we are ourselves corrupt, battling our own urges and ambitions. The heart of darkness in Raphael's work is concealed by a firework-display of satirical, witty dialogue which some readers find intrusive, others a symptom of his characters' inability to cope with their own despair.

APRIL, JUNE AND NOVEMBER • *(1972)*
Daniel Meyer, a film-director, has spent his youth in a dazzle of artistic, social and sexual triumph. Now, as middle age looms, he begins to suspect that under the Byronic façade his true self has all but disappeared. Affairs follow, with a younger and an older woman; he lets himself be seduced by different life-styles, in grubby, rainy London and on a sun-bleached Greek island, a rich man's paradise. Like all Raphael's main characters, Meyer is a battle-ground between genuineness and the role he plays in life – and the question of which side of him wins is left a cliffhanger until the book's last, most ironical line of all.

Raphael's other novels include The Limits of Love, Orchestra and Beginners *and* Two for the Road. The Glittering Prizes *and* After the War *are novels linked to TV series.* Sleeps Six *and* Oxbridge Blues *are collections of short stories.*

RENAISSANCE EUROPE

Caryl Brahms and S.J. Simon, *No Bed for Bacon*
▷Alexandre Dumas, *The Three Musketeers*
▷Dorothy Dunnett, *Niccolò Rising*
Carlos Fuentes, *Terra Nostra*

> **READ ON**

● *Heaven and Earth.*
▶ ▷F. Scott Fitzgerald, *The Great Gatsby.* Vita Sackville-West, *The Edwardians.* ▷Philip Roth, *Zuckerman Unbound.* Rona Jaffe, *Class Reunion.*

Stephen Marlowe, *The Memoirs of Christopher Columbus*
▷Jean Plaidy, *Queen of the Realm*
Irving Stone, *The Agony and the Ecstasy*

The Middle Ages (p 170)

RENAULT, Mary • *(1905–83)*
British novelist.

In her 30s and 40s Renault wrote several novels about hospital and wartime life, culminating in *The Charioteer*, the moving story of a homosexual serviceman. In the 1950s she began writing historical novels about ancient Greece. *The King Must Die* and *The Bull from the Sea* are based on the myth of King Theseus of Athens, who killed the Cretan Minotaur; *Fire From Heaven*, *The Persian Boy* and *Funeral Games* are about Alexander the Great. Like ▷Robert Graves, Renault treats people of the past as if they were psychologically just like us, so that even the most bizarre political or sexual behaviour seems both rational and credible.

THE MASK OF APOLLO • *(1966)*
Niko, a Greek actor of the 4th century BC, is used as a go-between by politicians trying to replace the despotic régime in Sicily with an ideal state ruled by a philosopher-king. Political intrigue is interwoven with Niko's own complicated private life, and with his (brilliantly described) theatrical personality: he is as vulnerable, as self-centred, as dedicated and as nervously extrovert as any Broadway or National Theatre star today.

Renault's other Greek books are The Last of the Wine *and* The Praise Singer. *Her novels with 20th-century settings are* Purposes of Love/Promise of Love, Kind Are Her Answers, The Friendly Young Ladies/The Middle Mist, Return to Night, North Face *and* The Charioteer.

RENDELL, Ruth • *(born 1930)*
British novelist.

Rendell's Chief Inspector Wexford novels are atmospheric murder mysteries in traditional style, set in the small towns and villages of the English Home Counties. Like ▷P.D. James, she spends much time developing the character of her detective, a liberal and cultured man appalled at the psychological pressures which drive people to

READ ON >

● *The Last of the Wine*.
▶ Helen Waddell, *Héloise and Abelard*. John Arden, *Silence Among the Weapons*. Naomi Mitchison, *The Corn King and the Spring Queen*. ▷Gore Vidal, *Creation*. Pär Lagerkvist, *The Sibyl*. Henry Treece, *Oedipus*.

READ ON >

▶ **To the Wexford books:** ▷P.D. James, *Shroud for a Nightingale*; Nicholas Freeling, *Love in Amsterdam*.

crime. Those pressures are the subject of Rendell's other books: grim stories of paranoia, obsession and inadequacy. In *Judgement in Stone* (1978), for example, an illiterate housekeeper is terrified that if her problem is discovered she will be sacked – and her cunning, desperate attempts to conceal it begin a ladder of consequences which leads inexorably to murder.

Rendell's Wexford books include A New Lease of Death, Wolf to the Slaughter, A Guilty Thing Surprised, Some Lie and Some Die *and* An Unkindness of Ravens. *Her psychological novels include* The Face of Trespass, The Killing Doll, The Tree of Hands, Live Flesh *and* Talking to Strange Men. The Fallen Curtain, Means of Evil *and* The Fever Tree *are collections of short stories. Rendell also writes as Barbara Vine (*A Dark-Adapted Eye*).*

▶ **To the psychological thrillers:** Joan Fleming, *Young Man I Think You're Dying*; ▷Patricia Highsmith, *The Glass Cell*; John Katzenbach, *The Traveller*.

REVISITING ONE'S PAST

▷Margaret Atwood, *Surfacing*
▷Anita Brookner, *A Start in Life*
▷Bernice Rubens, *Our Father*
▷Graham Swift, *Waterland*
▷Paul Theroux, *Picture Palace*
▷Virginia Woolf, *Mrs Dalloway*

RHYS, Jean • *(1894–1979)*

British novelist.

All Rhys' novels and stories are about the same kind of person, the 'Jean Rhys woman'. She was once vivacious and attractive (an actress, perhaps, or a dancer) but she fell in love with some unsuitable man or men, was betrayed, and now lives alone, maudlin and mentally unhinged. In Rhys' first four novels (published in the 1920s and 1930s), the heroines are casualties of the Jazz Age, flappers crushed by life itself. In her last, 1960s, book *Wide Sargasso Sea* the central character is a victim of the way men think (or fail to think) of women: she is a young Caribbean heiress in the early 1800s, who marries an English gentleman, Mr Rochester, and ends up as the demented creature hidden in the attics of Thornfield Hall in *Jane Eyre*.

GOOD MORNING, MIDNIGHT • *(1939)*

Deserted by her husband after the death of their baby,

READ ON

● *Wide Sargasso Sea.*
▶ **To *Good Morning Midnight*:** Brian Moore, *The Doctor's Wife*; ▷Doris Lessing, *The Golden Notebook*; ▷Mary McCarthy, *The Company She Keeps*; ▷Anita Brookner, *Hôtel du Lac*; Marguerite Duras, *The Lover*; ▷Christopher Isherwood, *A Single Man*.
▶ **To *Wide Sargasso Sea*:** Lisa St Aubin de Terán, *Slow Train to Milan*.

Sasha would have drunk herself to death if a generous friend had not rescued her and paid for her to spend a fortnight in Paris. She 'arranges her little life', as she puts it: a cycle of solitary meals and drinks, barren conversations with strangers, drugged sleep in seedy hotel-rooms. She is a damned soul, a husk – and then a gigolo, mistaking her for a rich woman, begins to court her, and she has to gather the rags of her sanity and try to take hold of her life once more.

Rhys' other novels are Quartet/Postures, After Leaving Mr Mackenzie *and* Voyage in the Dark. The Left Bank, Tigers are Better-looking *and* Sleep it off, Lady *are collections of short stories.*

THE RHYTHM OF NATURE
(people in tune with or in thrall to the land)

Pearl S. Buck, *The Good Earth*
Erskine Caldwell, *God's Little Acre*
Neil M. Gunn, *The Well at the World's End*
▷Thomas Hardy, *Far From the Madding Crowd*
▷Susan Hill, *In the Springtime of the Year*
Mikhail Sholokhov, *Virgin Soil Upturned*

The Countryside (p 51)

RICHARDSON, Henry Handel •
(1870–1946)
Australian novelist.

'Henry Handel Richardson' was the pseudonym of Ethel Robertson. She was born and educated in Australia, but went to Europe in her late teens and remained there, with one three-month break, for the rest of her life. Her best-known books, however (*The Getting of Wisdom*, 1910, and the Richard Mahony trilogy: see below) are set in Australia and reflect her own or her parents' experience. She was interested in 'psychic outsiders', people who felt that heightened awareness or sensibilities set them apart from their fellows. *The Getting of Wisdom* is about a gifted, unhappy adolescent in a late 19th-century boarding school, who uses love of the arts as an escape from the oppressive narrowness of the régime. The battle against depressive illness is a major theme of the Mahony trilogy. *The Young Cosima* is about Liszt's daughter Cosima, her husband Hans von Bülow and her lover Wagner – all of

> **READ ON** ▷

● *Maurice Guest*
(another study of depression, this time about a man ambitious to be a professional musician who finds that he has talent but no genius, and who is then further distracted by falling unhappily in love).
▶ To *The Fortunes of Richard Mahony*:
▷Gustave Flaubert, *Madame Bovary*;
▷Malcolm Lowry, *Under the Volcano*.

them exemplars (at least in their own fevered imaginations) of Nietzschean 'superbeings', who are nevertheless racked by feelings and emotions as uncontrollable as anyone else's.

THE FORTUNES OF RICHARD MAHONY •
(1915–29)

In this trilogy of novels (*Australia Felix*, *The Way Home*, *Ultima Thule*) Mahony, a British doctor, goes to Australia to make his fortune in the 1850s gold rush, marries and settles. His gold-prospecting fails, and he turns first to store-keeping and then back to medicine, before making a sudden fortune from shares he thought were worthless. Unable to cope with wealth, he dissipates his money, impoverishes his family and begins a long, anguished slide into depressive mania. His devoted wife takes a job as postmistress in a remote area, nursing her husband and bringing up her uncomprehending, sorrowing family. Although the trilogy is chiefly concerned with Mahony's complex character and his relationship with his family, it is also a compelling account of 19th-century Australian pioneer and outback life.

Richardson's only other novel is Maurice Guest. Two Studies *contains a pair of long short stories;* The End of a Childhood *and* The Adventures of Cuffy Mahony *are collections of short stories;* Myself When Young *is autobiography.*

RICHARDSON, Samuel • *(1689–1761)*
British novelist.

A successful printer, Richardson was compiling a book of sample letters for all occasions when he had the idea of writing whole novels in letter-form. He produced three, *Pamela*, *Clarissa* and *Sir Charles Grandison*. They are enormously long (over a million words each), and readers even at the time complained of boredom. But the books were still best-sellers, not, as Richardson imagined, because of their high moral tone, but because his sensational theme (the way some people are drawn irresistibly to debauch the innocent) guaranteed success.

CLARISSA, OR THE HISTORY OF A YOUNG LADY
(1748)

To escape from her parents, who have shut her in her room until she agrees to marry a man she loathes, the hapless Clarissa Harlowe elopes with Mr Lovelace, a rake. He tries every possible way to persuade her to sleep with

▶ **To *Maurice Guest*:**
▷Hermann Hesse, *Steppenwolf*.
▶ **To *The Getting of Wisdom*:** ▷Antonia White, *Frost in May*.

> **READ ON**

● *Pamela*.
▶ Pierre Choderlos de Laclos, *Dangerous Alliances* (Les liaisons dangereuses) is another letter-novel about moral predation, but shorter, wittier and less sentimental. This book apart, Richardson's work has been more pilloried than parallelled. John Cleland, *Fanny Hill* is the memoirs of a prostitute, combining a dismissive view of men with detailed

him, and when she refuses he puts her into a brothel, drugs and rapes her. She goes into a decline and dies of shame. The story is told by means of letters from the main characters, to one another, to friends, relatives and acquaintances. One of Richardson's triumphs – which some critics claim justifies the book's inordinate length – is to reveal Lovelace's villainy only gradually, as Clarissa herself discovers it.

descriptions of life and gossip in an 18th-century, high-society London brothel.
▷Henry Fielding, *Tom Jones* mocks Richardson's moral earnestness: far from shrinking from the pleasures of seduction, Tom lives for them. Aphra Behn, *Love-letters between a Nobleman and his Sister,* pre-dating Richardson by 75 years, is the no-holds-barred account of an incestuous affair.

RICHLER, Mordecai • *(born 1931)*
Canadian novelist.

The heroes of Richler's vitriolic black satires are 'outsiders' (for example Jews in a gentile society), poor (they come from big-city slums) or inept (too guileless for their own good). They face a hostile world of crooks, cheats, extortionists, poseurs (often film makers or tycoons) and bullies. Sometimes, like the hero of *The Apprenticeship of Duddy Kravitz* (1959), Richler's men fight back, using the enemies' weapons and winning the battle at the expense of their own souls; others, like the middle-aged hero of *Joshua Then and Now* (1980), are so humbled by the sense of their own inadequacy that instead of fighting the slings and arrows of outrageous fortune (in Joshua's case, the false accusation that he is a sexual deviant), they welcome them. *Joshua Then and Now* and *Cocksure* (1968) (a violent farce about an honest man bewildered by the permissiveness of the 'swinging sixties') are Richler's most savage books, written to lacerate as well as to amuse.

Richler's other novels include A Choice of Enemies, The Incomparable Atuk/Stick Your Neck Out *and* St Urbain's Horseman. Shovelling Trouble *and* Home Sweet Home *are collections of essays and articles, many of them about Canada and its attitude to 'culture'.* The Street *is a memoir of his childhood in the backstreets of Montreal, a fascinating parallel to the opening chapters of* The Apprenticeship of Duddy Kravitz.

READ ON ▷

▶ To *The Apprenticeship of Duddy Kravitz:* ▷Jerome Weidman, *I Can Get It for You Wholesale;* ▷Saul Bellow, *The Adventures of Augie March.*

▶ To *Cocksure:* Budd Schulberg, *What Makes Sammy Run?;* ▷Gore Vidal, *Myra Breckinridge.*

▶ To Richler's work in general: ▷Nathanael West, *Miss Lonelyhearts;* ▷F. Scott Fitzgerald, *The Great Gatsby.*

ROBERTS, Michèle • *(born 1949)*
British poet and novelist.

Much of Roberts' work has a feminist edge, and her latest novel in particular, *Mrs Noah* (1987), is likely to leave the male half of the human race feeling distinctly uncomfortable. It is a dazzling fantasy, set in the present day. A woman visiting Venice with her preoccupied husband fantasises that she is Mrs Noah. The Ark is a vast library, a repository not only of creatures but of the entire knowledge and experience of the human race. She is its curator (or Arkivist), and her fellow-voyagers are five Sibyls and a token male, the Gaffer, a bearded old party who once wrote a best-selling book (the Bible) and has now retired to a tax-heaven in the sky. Each Sibyl tells a story, and each story is about the way men have oppressed women down the centuries. For all its feminist anger, the book is a witty, imaginative tour de force.

READ ON >

● *The Wild Girl* (the Gospel according to Mary Magdalene, a stunning reworking of familiar New Testament themes)
▶ ▷Margaret Atwood, *The Handmaid's Tale*. ▷Joseph Heller, *Catch-22*. Joe Orton, *Head to Toe*.

ROMAN CATHOLICISM (1)

▷Kingsley Amis, *The Alteration*
  Georges Bernanos, *Diary of a Country Priest*
▷Anthony Burgess, *Earthly Powers*
  Rumer Godden, *A Candle for St Jude*
▷Graham Greene, *Monsignor Quixote*
  Nikos Kazantzakis, *The Greek Passion*
▷Thomas Keneally, *Three Cheers for the Paraclete*

ROMAN CATHOLICISM (2)

  David Lodge, *How Far Can You Go?*
  Brian Moore, *The Colour of Blood*
  J.F. Powers, *Morte d'Urban*
  Frederick Rolfe, *Hadrian the Seventh*
▷Muriel Spark, *The Abbess of Crewe*
▷Morris West, *The Devil's Advocate*
▷Antonia White, *Frost in May*

ROSSNER, Judith • *(born 1935)*
US novelist.

Rossner's novels, whether serious, ironical or farcical, are all fuelled by the same polemical, feminist rage against male-oriented society. They treat human life as a straight-forward battle of wits between emotional predators and their quarry – a struggle which always ends in psychological mutilation or destruction. In some books, for example *Nine Months in the Life of an Old Maid* (1969, about a ghastly family who get on each others' nerves) the chase is funny and the mode is farce. In others, for example *Looking for Mr Goodbar* (1975, about a woman cruising singles bars in search of love) the events are grim and the mode is tragedy. The theme of emotional depredation has been popular with recent US writers of all kinds, from 'serious' novelists to the authors of big-business and family sagas. Rossner is one of its wittiest exponents.

ROTH, Philip • *(born 1933)*
US novelist.

One of the wryest and wittiest of all contemporary US novelists, Roth writes of Jewish intellectuals, often authors or university teachers, discomforted by life. Their marriages fail; their parents behave like joke-book stereotypes (forever making chicken soup and simultaneously boasting about and deploring their sons' brains); sexual insatiability leads them from one farcical encounter to another; their career-success attracts embarrassing fans and inhibits further work; their defences of self-mockery and irony wear ever thinner as they approach unwanted middle age. In his best-known book, *Portnoy's Complaint* (1969), Roth treated this theme as farce, heavy with explicit sex and Jewish-mother jokes. The majority of his novels are quieter, the tone is more rueful, and he generalises his theme and makes it symbolise the plight of all decent, conscience-stricken people in a world where barbarians make the running. His major 1980s work was a series of novels about a New York Jewish author, Nathan Zuckerman, who agonises over his trade, writes an immensely successful (dirty) book and is immediately harrassed by the way his fame both forces him to live the life of a celebrity and makes him even more of an enigma to his family and friends.

> **READ ON**

● *Attachments; August.*
▶ Joyce Carol Oates, *The Poisoned Kiss.*
▷Angela Carter, *The Infernal Desire Machines of Doctor Hoffman.* Robert Bloch, *Psycho.* ▷Susan Hill, *The Bird of Night.*
▶ **Similar novels from an earlier period:** ▷Djuna Barnes, *Nightwood;* ▷Christina Stead, *The Man Who Loved Children.*

> **READ ON**

● *When She was Good.*
▶ Bernard Malamud, *Dubin's Lives.*
▷Bernice Rubens, *Our Father.* ▷John Fowles, *Daniel Martin.*
▷John Updike, *Marry Me.*

THE PROFESSOR OF DESIRE • *(1977)*

David Kepesh, a brilliant young literature teacher, is trying to sort out his life. His views on art and literature, which once seemed the last word in wit and wisdom, now appear to him to have been engulfed by the subjects he studies: he feels like a dwarf trying to shift a mountain. His emotional life is dominated by an insistent craving for physical pleasure which he finds degrading but irresistible and which he longs to replace by love. His mother and father are elderly, tetchy and horrified by the way their son the genius has betrayed his Jewish roots. Kepesh's circumstances seem to him like a maze, as bewildering and terrifying as anything in ▷Kafka – and the book shows him gradually, painfully, discovering the key.

Roth's other books include Letting Go, The Great American Novel *(which uses baseball as a farcical symbol for every red-blooded US tradition or way of thought),* My Life as a Man *and* Our Gang *(a* ▷Swiftian *satire about the Nixon presidency).* Goodbye Columbus *collects an early novella and five short stories. The Zuckerman books are* The Ghost Writer, Zuckerman Unbound, The Anatomy Lesson, The Prague Orgy *and* The Counterlife.

RUBENS, Bernice • *(born 1927)*
British novelist.

Rubens' heroes and heroines are people at the point of breakdown: her novels chart the escalation of tension which took them there or the progress of their cure. Some of the books are bleak: in *The Elected Member/The Chosen People* (1969), for example, a man is driven mad by feeling that he is a scapegoat for the entire suffering of the Jewish people throughout history, and the story deals with his rehabilitation in a mental hospital. In other books, Rubens turns psychological pain to comedy, as if the only way to cope with the human condition were to treat it as God's black joke against the human race. God is even a character in *Our Father* (1987): he pops up in the Sahara, in the High Street, in the parlour, in bed with the heroine and her husband, constantly nagging her to make up her mind about herself – and his persistence leads her to rummage through childhood memories (where it becomes clear that she completely misunderstood her parents' emotional relationship) and to redefine her life.

Rubens' other novels include Madame Sousatzka, I Sent a Letter to my Love, The Ponsonby Post, Sunday Best, The

> **READ ON**

● *Birds of Passage.*
▶ ▷Paul Theroux, *Picture Palace.*
▷David Cook, *Missing Persons.* ▷Anita Brookner, *Hôtel du Lac.* Susan Fromberg Shaeffer, *Worldly Goods.* ▷Susan Hill, *A Bit of Singing and Dancing* (short stories).

Brothers, A Five Year Sentence, Birds of Passage, Favours, Spring Sonata *and* Mr Wakefield's Crusade.

RUELL, Patrick • *(born 1936)*
British novelist.

'Patrick Ruell' is one of the pseudonyms of ▷Reginald Hill. His fast-moving, uncomplicated adventure stories include *The Castle of the Demon*, *Red Christmas*, *Death Takes the Low Road*, *Urn Burial* and *The Long Kill* (1986, about a marksman stalking human quarry in the English Lake District).

RUSHDIE, Salman • *(born 1947)*
Indian/British novelist and non-fiction writer.

Rushdie writes magic realism, a mesmeric entwining of actuality and fantasy. *Midnight's Children* (1981) is the story of a rich Indian family over the last 80 years, and especially of Saleem, one of 1001 children born at midnight on 15 August 1947, the moment of India's independence from Britain. Saleem's birthtime gives him extraordinary powers: he is, as Rushdie puts it, 'handcuffed' to India, able to let his mind float freely through its history and to share in the experience of anyone he chooses, from Gandhi or Nehru to the most insignificant beggar in the streets. He represents India's own awareness of itself, and his family story (which he himself tells) is the account of a whole people and a continent. Its filters, his perception and personality, make it mysterious and magical: time coalesces, 'real' politics blur with fantasy, a child's memories and magnifications are just as valid as newspaper accounts. The effect is to change reality to metaphor – and Rushdie uses this to make several sharp political points. In *Shame* (1983) he goes still further. This novel is set in a dream-country, Peccavistan ('Sinned' rather than Sind), whose geography and history are like Pakistan's seen in a distorting mirror. We witness a power-struggle between members of the Harappa dynasty and their friends/rivals/enemies the Hyders. Interwoven with it all is the story of Omar Khayyam Shakil, a bloated, brilliant physician, and his wife Sufiya Zinobia, a mental defective inhabited by a demon which periodically breaks out in homicidal fury. Describing Rushdie's books is like summarising dreams: the telling bleaches them of wit, poetry and compulsion. Like ▷Márquez, he reinvents reality and makes fantasy seem more plausible than truth itself.

> **READ ON** ▶ Nelson De Mille, *The Cathedral*. Derek Lambert, *Touch the Lion's Paw*. Russell Braddon, *The Finalists*.

> **READ ON** ▶ ▷Gabriel García Márquez, *One Hundred Years of Solitude*. Augusto Roa Bastos, *I, The Supreme*. ▷Angela Carter, *Nights at the Circus*. Lisa St Aubin de Terán, *The Keepers of the House*. ▷Günter Grass, *The Tin Drum*.

Salman **RUSHDIE**

SHAME *(feud between ruling families in
fantasy-state 'Peccavistan')*

Jeanette **WINTERSON, THE PASSION**
(Napoleon)

Augusto **ROA BASTOS, I THE SUPREME**
(Francia, dictator of Paraguay)

Evelyn **WAUGH, BLACK MISCHIEF**
(England-educated 1930s black African ruler)

Miguel **ASTURIAS, THE PRESIDENT**
(corruption and jackboot evil in South America)

Michael **MOORCOCK, GLORIANA**
(state and ruler one gross, monstrous entity)

DICTATORS

Chinua **ACHEBE, ANTHILLS OF THE SAVANNAH**
(emerging African totalitarian state)

Nadine **GORDIMER, A SPORT OF NATURE**
(white girl joins South African freedom fighters)

Gore **VIDAL, BURR**
('traitor' who tried to set up rival republic to Jeffersonian America)

POLITICS

Timothy **MO, AN INSULAR POSSESSION**
(British imperialism and Hong Kong)

Authur **KOESTLER, DARKNESS AT NOON**
(treason-trial of old-guard revolutionary in unnamed but Stalinist dictatorship)

George **ORWELL, ANIMAL FARM**
(animals declare republic which degenerates into dictatorship)

Isabel **ALLENDE, THE HOUSE OF THE SPIRITS**
*(political and personal evolution in rich South American family
over 100 years.)*

Gabriel García **MÁRQUEZ, ONE HUNDRED YEARS OF
SOLITUDE** *(sprawling family dominate small town in fantasy South America)*

Peter **CAREY, ILLYWHACKER**
(132-year-old Australian conman tells his story)

MANY GENERATIONS

Gerald H. **MORRIS, DOVES AND SILK
HANDKERCHIEVES** *(magic and realism in 1900s English mining village)*

Günter **GRASS, THE FLOUNDER**
(fisher-couple and talking fish live through all German history)

John **IRVING, THE WORLD ACCORDING TO GARP**
(evolution of writer in fantasy New England town)

Rushdie's other works include Grimus *(an early, experimental novel) and* The Jaguar Smile *(non-fiction: a report on Nicaragua and on the effect of US policies in central America).*

S

SALINGER, J.D. (Jerome David) •
(born 1919)
US novelist and short-story writer.

Salinger's only novel, *The Catcher in the Rye* (1951), is a rambling monologue by 17-year-old Holden Caulfield. He has run away from boarding school just before Christmas, and is spending a few days drifting in New York City while he decides whether to go home or not. He feels that his childhood is over and his innocence lost, but he detests the phoney, loveless grown-up world (symbolised by plastic Christmas baubles and seasonal fake goodwill). He thinks that to be adult is a form of surrender, but he can see no way to avoid it. He wanders the city, talking aimlessly to taxi-drivers, lodging-house keepers, bar-tenders, prostitutes and his own kid sister Phoebe, whom he tries to warn against growing up. Finally, inevitably, he capitulates – or perhaps escapes, since we learn that what we have just read is his 'confession' to the psychiatrist in a mental home. Salinger pursued the question of how to recover moral innocence in his only other publications, a series of short stories about the gifted, mentally unstable Glass family. 'Franny and Zooey', the most moving of the stories, shows Zooey Glass, an actor, talking his sister Franny out of a nervous breakdown. It is a performance of dazzling technical brilliance and full of loving-kindness, but – and this is typical of Salinger's grim view of human moral endeavour – although it helps Franny momentarily, it contributes nothing whatever to the good of the world at large.

The Glass family stories are collected in Franny and Zooey; Nine Stories/For Esmé, with Love and Squalor *and* Raise High the Roofbeam, Carpenters.

READ ON

▶ **To *The Catcher in the Rye:*** ▷Carson McCullers, *The Member of the Wedding*; ▷Willa Cather, *My Antonia*; ▷John Updike, *The Centaur*; Truman Capote, *Breakfast at Tiffany's*; Alan Sillitoe, *Saturday Night and Sunday Morning*.
▶ **To 'Franny and Zooey':** Sylvia Plath, *The Bell Jar*; ▷Susan Hill, *The Bird of Night*.

SARTRE, Jean-Paul • *(1905–80)*
French novelist, poet and philosopher.

The philosophy of existentialism, which Sartre developed
in essays, plays, novels and monographs, says that Nothingness is the natural state of humanity: we exist, like animals, without ethics or morality. But unlike beasts we
have the power to make choices, and these give moral status: they are a leap from Nothingness to Being. For some
people, the choice is the leap of faith, and belief in God
gives them moral status; for others the choice is to make
no choice at all, to drift the way the world leads them
without taking moral initiatives. For Sartre's characters,
the leap into being involved taking responsibility, making
moral decisions from which there was no turning back.
His vast novel *The Roads to Freedom* (1945–9; in three
volumes, *The Age of Reason*, *The Reprieve* and *Iron in
the Soul/Troubled Sleep*) tackles this theme exactly: the
questions of what moral decisions to make and how to
make them. It describes a group of young people trying to
sort out their personal lives and at the same time to cope
with the moral and intellectual challenges of fascism,
communism, colonialism and the second world war. The
book is packed with intellectual, political and philosophical discussion and argument: a complex read. But few
writings better give the intellectual 'feel' of the 1930s and
1940s, the matrix from which so many of today's ideas
were born.

Sartre's main philosophical monograph is Being and
Nothingness. *His plays include* The Flies, The Victor/Men
Without Shadows, Crime Passionel *and* Huis Clos/No
Exit/In Camera. Nausea/The Diary of Antoine Roquentin
*is an autobiographical novel about a young intellectual in
the 1920s and 1930s.* The Wall/Intimacy *is a collection of
short stories.*

SAYERS, Dorothy L. (Dorothy Leigh) •
(1893–1957)
British novelist.

The writer Colin Watson cruelly but accurately described
Sayers' kind of crime fiction as 'snobbery with violence'.
The fascination of her books is not only in the solving of
bizarre crimes in out-of-the-ordinary locations (an advertising agency; an Oxford women's college; an East An-
glian belfry), but also in the character of her detective, the
super-sleuth Lord Peter Wimsey. He is a languid, mono-
cled aristocrat, whose foppish manner conceals the facts

> **READ ON**

● *Nausea.*
▶ ▷Albert Camus, *The
Plague.* Arthur
Koestler, *Darkness at
Noon.* ▷Frederic
Raphael, *Like Men
Betrayed.*
▶ **Novels discussing
similar personal
dilemmas, but with
different
backgrounds and
cultural conditions:**
▷Lev Tolstoy, *War and
Peace*; ▷Ford Madox
Ford, *The Good
Soldier*; ▷Olivia
Manning, *The Levant
Trilogy.*

> **READ ON**

● *Gaudy Night.*
▶ Amanda Cross, *No
Word from Winifred.*
▷Michael Innes,
Hamlet, Revenge!
Robert Robinson,
*Landscape with Dead
Dons.* John Dickson
Carr, *Poison in Jest.*

that he has a first-class Oxford degree, was in army intelligence during the first world war, collects rare books, plays the piano like Rubinstein, dances like Astaire and seems to have swallowed a substantial dictionary of quotations. He is aided and abetted by his manservant Bunter, a suave charmer adept at extracting confidences from the cooks, taxi-drivers, waitresses, barbers and vergers who would collapse in forelock-tugging silence if Wimsey himself ever deigned to speak to them. Seldom have detective stories been so preposterous or so unputdownable.

HAVE HIS CARCASE · (1932)

In a sleepy seaside resort, someone has cut the throat of a gigolo – and the plot thickens when it is discovered that he was romantically involved with a lonely, rich and foolish widow. But where do the men with the patently-false hair and beards come into it? Why are there no footprints in the sand? What connects the crime with the Russian ex-royal dynasty? All these mysteries are as nothing compared to the greatest cliffhanger of all: will Wimsey's persistent charm ever wear down Harriet Vane, the best-selling crime-novelist, until she agrees to marry him?

The Wimsey/Vane romance is also featured in Strong Poison, Gaudy Night *and* Busman's Honeymoon. *Sayers' other Wimsey books – which some admirers prefer to those involving Harriet Vane – include* Murder Must Advertise, Hangman's Holiday *and* The Nine Tailors.

Rex Stout, *Fer de Lance*. ▷Ruth Rendell, *Some Lie and Some Die*.

SCHOOLS

Nicholas Best, *Tennis and the Masai*
▷Charles Dickens, *Nicholas Nickleby*
James Hilton, *Goodbye, Mr Chips*
▷James Joyce, *Portrait of the Artist as a Young Man*
▷John Le Carré, *Call for the Dead*
▷H.H. Richardson, *The Getting of Wisdom*
▷John Updike, *The Centaur*
▷Evelyn Waugh, *Decline and Fall*

Adolescence (p 3)

SCOTT, Walter · *(1771–1832)*
British novelist and poet.

Scott began his career not with novels but with poems, in a style similar to Scottish folk-ballads and the lyrics of Robert Burns. In 1814, piqued because his verse was out-

READ ON ⟩

● *Ivanhoe; The Heart of Midlothian.*
▶ Harrison Ainsworth,

sold by Byron's, he turned instead to historical novels, and wrote 29 in the next 18 years. They are swaggering tales of love, bravery and intrigue, many of them centred on events from Scottish history and set in the brooding landscapes of the highlands and islands.

ROB ROY • (1817)

In the 1710s, Osbaldistone and Rashleigh are rivals for the hand of Diana Vernon. Rashleigh embezzles money and frames Osbaldistone. Osbaldistone escapes to the highlands of Scotland, where he seeks help from Rob Roy, an outlaw who (like Robin Hood centuries before him) robs the rich to help the poor, rights wrongs and fights a usurping power (in his case, the English) on behalf of an exiled, true royal prince (James Stuart, the Old Pretender). Osbaldistone's quest to clear his name becomes inextricably bound up with the Jacobite Rebellion, and it is not until Rashleigh (who, not unexpectedly, supports the English and betrays Rob Roy to them) is killed that justice prevails and Osbaldistone and Diana at last find happiness.

Scott's other novels include Waverley, Guy Mannering, Old Mortality, The Heart of Midlothian, The Bride of Lammermoor, Ivanhoe, Kenilworth, The Fortunes of Nigel, Quentin Durward, Redgauntlet *and* Castle Dangerous.

The Tower of London. James Fenimore Cooper, *Last of the Mohicans.* ▷Victor Hugo, *Notre-Dame de Paris.* ▷Alexandre Dumas, *The Man in the Iron Mask.* Nigel Tranter, *Montrose: the Captain General.*

SEGAL, Erich • *(born 1937)*

US novelist and non-fiction writer.

Love Story (1970), Segal's first novel, was one of the most affecting romances of the century. A true three-handkerchief weepie, it tells of the idyllic, doomed love-affair between two college students, one of whom falls terminally ill. The book, and the film made from it, moved audiences to tears from Manchester to Melbourne, from Peking to Peoria. In a later romance, *Oliver's Story* (1977), Segal took up the life of one of the young people from the earlier book, eight years later. Oliver falls in love again, only to be haunted by the thought that he is betraying his earlier, 'eternal' love.

> **READ ON**

▶ *Love Story*'s ecstatic sadness is matched in ▷Boris Pasternak, *Doctor Zhivago* and ▷Margaret Mitchell, *Gone With the Wind* and Philip Roth, *Letting Go.* *Love Story*'s unselfconscious sentimentality is parallelled in Richard Bach, *Jonathan Livingstone Seagull,* though its plot (an 'outsider' allegory about a bird longing to fly free) could hardly be more different.

SHARPE, Tom • *(born 1928)*
British novelist.

If, as many foreigners maintain, British humour is obsessed with the functions of the lower body, then Sharpe is our comic Laureate. In each of his books he chooses a single target – polytechnic life, publishing, Cambridge University, the landed gentry – and demolishes it magnificently, comprehensively, by piling slapstick on crudity like a demented circus clown. Sharpe's heroes live in a state of unceasing, ungovernable panic, and are usually crippled by lust, forever tripping over their own erections. His old men are gluttonous, lecherous and senile, prone to perversion and prey to strokes and heart attacks; his matrons are whooping whip-wielding Boadiceas, scything down every bedable male in sight. If your humorous fancy is for penises trapped in briar-patches, condoms ballooning above Cambridge spires or maniacs burying sex-dolls in wet cement, Sharpe's books are for you.

RIOTOUS ASSEMBLY • *(1973)*
Kommandant van Heerden, police chief of the sleepy South African town of Piemburg, wants a quiet life and an invitation to join the exclusive British Country Club. His assistant Verkramp wants van Heerden's job. Konstabel Els wants to keep on playing with his electrodes and fucking kaffirs. But Miss Hazelstone phones to say that she has just shot her black cook – and that it was not a 'garbage-disposal operation' but the result of a lovers' tiff. Van Heerden, thinking that she must be covering up for her brother the bishop, sets out on an investigation which spirals into an orgy of transvestism, voyeurism, bestiality and murder. The South African setting gives this book devastating point: given the situation, even Sharpe's most slapstick satirical excess seems a model of self-restraint.

Sharpe's other books include Wilt *and its sequels* The Wilt Alternative *and* Wilt on High; The Throwback; Porterhouse Blue; Ancestral Vices *and* Vintage Stuff.

SHELLEY, Mary • *(1797–1851)*
British novelist.

After the death of her husband (the poet) in 1822, Shelley began a literary career of her own, editing her husband's work, writing essays, journals and travel-books, and publishing short stories and novels, many on what would now be considered SF themes. Her best-known book is *Frankenstein, or the Modern Prometheus* (1818), about a man

---

READ ON ⟩

● *Indecent Exposure*; *Blott on the Landscape*.
▶ Colin Douglas, *The Houseman's Tale*. Thorne Smith, *The Bishop's Jaegers*. Howard Jacobson, *Peeping Tom*. ▷J.P. Donleavy, *The Ginger Man*.

READ ON ⟩

▶ **To *Frankenstein*:** ▷H.G. Wells, *The Island of Doctor Moreau*; Bram Stoker, *Dracula*; Gerald Du Maurier, *Trilby*.

who tries to prove the superiority of scientific rationality to the supernatural by usurping God's function and creating life. Although, thanks to Hollywood, Frankenstein's monster has nudged his creator from centre-stage, even the worst Frankenstein films keep to one of Shelley's most fascinating ideas: that the monster is an innocent, as pure as Adam before the Fall, and that its ferocity is a response learned by contact with 'civilised' human beings. Shelley developed the theme of the contrast between innocence and the corruption of civilisation in other books, most notably the future-fantasy *The Last Man* (1826), set in a world where all human beings but one have been destroyed by plague, and the survivor wanders among the monuments of the glorious past like a soul in Hell.

▶ **To *The Last Man*:**
▷Daniel Defoe, *Robinson Crusoe*; Bernard Malamud, *God's Grace*.

SHIPS AND THE SEA

John Dickson Carr, *The Blind Barber*
▷Joseph Conrad, *The Nigger of the Narcissus*
Paul Gallico, *The Poseidon Adventure*
▷Herman Melville, *Moby-Dick*
Nicholas Monsarrat, *The Cruel Sea*
▷Katherine Anne Porter, *Ship of Fools*
Paul Rodgers, *To Kill a God* (Captain Cook's voyages)
▷Jules Verne, *Twenty Thousand Leagues Under the Sea*
▷Herman Wouk, *The Caine Mutiny*

SHIPWRECK

Martin Boyd, *Nuns in Jeopardy*
▷Daniel Defoe, *Robinson Crusoe*
Nicholas Monsarrat, *Running Proud*
▷Muriel Spark, *Robinson*
▷Kurt Vonnegut, *Galápagos*
▷Patrick White, *A Fringe of Leaves*

SHUTE, Neville • *(1899–1960)*
British/Australian novelist.

'Neville Shute' was the pseudonym of Neville Shute Norway. In the 1920s he worked as an aeronautical engineer, and he later served as a second-world-war naval com-

▶ **READ ON**

● *A Town Like Alice* (about two survivors from the Japanese

mander – experiences which inspired two of his finest books, *Pied Piper* (1942), about a mild-mannered man who rescues a group of children from the nazis and *No Highway* (1948), about an aircraft engineer trying desperately to warn sceptical superiors and politicians of the existence of metal fatigue. In 1950 Shute settled in Australia, and made it the setting for most of his later books. He wrote of ordinary people in a self-effacing style; his books have the immediacy of 'in-depth' newspaper reporting. But the characters of each story are in crisis, and the plot shows them working out moral or ethical dilemmas which have implications far beyond the novel's bounds. Several of his books were filmed, and inspired a whole genre of documentary-style drama about 'issues', now also common on television. Some of Shute's themes (for example the horrific effects of bombing on civilians, the theme of his 1939 novel *What Happened to the Corbetts*, or the existence of metal fatigue) have been overtaken by events, and his once-slangy dialogue has dated. But few popular writers have treated serious themes so grippingly. Despite their age, his novels are unputdownable.

ON THE BEACH • *(1957)*

The book is set in the Melbourne suburbs at some unstated time in the near future. We see perfectly ordinary people (a young couple with a baby; a woman and her US sailor-lover) bustling about their mundane lives. But the background is anything but ordinary: the whole human race is facing imminent annihilation from the nuclear fallout of World War III. As the novel proceeds, and Shute explores the implications of this theme, his characters' attempts to preserve everyday decencies are shown to be not so much survival strategy as a pitiable, pointless evasion of reality.

Shute's early books include So Disdained, Lonely Road *and the excellent war-story* Landfall. *His later novels include* The Far Country, In the Wet, Requiem for a Wren *and* Trustee from the Toolroom. Slide Rule *is an autobiography up to 1938.*

SILVERBERG, Robert • *(born 1934)*
US novelist.

Many of Silverberg's single SF novels are set on Earth in the near future, and – like ▷Ballard's – involve escalation towards catastrophe of trends and ideas of the present day. The theme of *Master of Life and Death* is over-popula-

occupation of Malaya who decide to develop one small settlement in the Australian outback).
▶ **To *On the Beach*:** John Christopher, *The Death of Grass*; ▷George Turner, *The Sea and Summer*.
▶ **To Shute's books involving technology and research:** Nigel Balchin, *The Small Back Room*; ▷C.P. Snow, *The New Men*.
▶ **To Shute's work in general:** H.E. Bates, *The Purple Plain*; ▷Morris West, *The Navigator*; Ernest K. Gann, *The High and the Mighty*; ▷Elizabeth Bowen, *The Heat of the Day*.

> READ ON >

▶ **To the single novels:** ▷Robert Heinlein, *Job*; Frederick Pohl, *The*

tion. *Recalled to Life* imagines a medical advance which allows us to bring the dead back to life. The hero of *Stochastic Man* is a psychic adviser to presidents who finds that he can genuinely predict the future. *A Time of Changes* imagines human society entirely controlled by drugs. Silverberg is also known for fantasy-series set in worlds of the far future. Majipoor, for example, is a giant planet where magic and science, medieval politics and high technology, aliens and humans, co-exist. In *Lord Valentine's Castle* (first volume of the 'Majipoor' Trilogy, 1979–83), a wandering juggler discovers, by chance use of his psychic powers, that he is the rightful Coronal, or ruler, of the planet, and gathers a company of warriors to unseat the usurper and win back his inheritance. In *The Majipoor Chronicles* a boy discovers the planet's computer-archives, and embarks on a psychic exploration of its teeming, magical history. In *Valentine Pontifex* the Coronal of Majipoor has to undertake his most demanding task yet, a battle against the shape-changers (or Metamorphs) who are destroying crops, trying to starve Majipoor's people into submission and take over Valentine's throne.

Silverberg's other books include Lord of Darkness, Capricorn Games *and two inspired by Biblical and other ancient myth*, Shadrach in the Furnace *and* Gilgamesh the King.

SIMENON, Georges • *(born 1903)*
Belgian novelist.

Simenon is best-known for some 150 crime-stories featuring the pipe-smoking, calvados-drinking Commissaire Maigret of the Paris Police. The books are short and spare; they concentrate on Maigret's investigations in bars, lodging-houses and rain-soaked Paris streets, and on his casual-seeming, fatherly conversations with suspects and witnesses. But Simenon is a far more substantial writer than this suggests. His non-Maigret novels – several hundred, since for 50 years he averaged a book every six or seven weeks – are compelling psychological studies of people distracted by fear, obsession, despair or hate. *Act of Passion* (1947) is the confession of a madman who kills his lover to keep her pure, to prevent her being contaminated by the evil which he feels has corroded his own soul. The hero of *The Man Who Watched the Trains Go By* (1938), outwardly placid and controlled, is in fact so gnawed by the sense of his own inadequacy that he chooses murder as the best way to make his mark on the

Reefs of Space; Ray Bradbury, *The Illustrated Man*.

▶ **To the fantasies:**
▷Piers Anthony, *Vicinity Cluster*; Ian M. Banks, *Consider Phlebas*; ▷Anne McCaffrey, *Dragonflight*.

READ ON ▷

▶ **To** *Pedigree*:
▷Jerome Weidman, *Fourth Street East*.
▶ **To Simenon's non-Maigret novels:** Julian Symons, *The 31st of February*.
▶ **To the Maigret books:** Nicholas Freeling, *Love in Amsterdam*; Maj Sjöwall and Per Wahlöö, *The Laughing Policeman*; Friedrich Dürrenmatt, *The Quarry*.

world. In *The President* (1958) a politician, brooding in enforced retirement, is unexpectedly offered the chance to revenge himself both politically and personally on the man who wronged him. *Ticket of Leave* (1942) is about a woman who falls in love with a paroled murderer. All these books are written in a sinewy, unemotional style, as plain as a police report. Only in one novel, *Pedigree* (1948), does Simenon break out of his self-imposed limits. It is a 500-page account of a boy's growing-up in Belgium in the first 15 years of this century, an evocation not only of trams, gaslight, cobble-stones and teeming back-street life, but of an emerging personality. A fictionalised autobiography, it is one of Simenon's most unexpected and rewarding works.

SINGER, I.B. (Isaac Bashevis) •
(born 1904)
Polish/US novelist and short-story writer.

Singer writes in Yiddish, and maintains that even when he translates his work himself, English dilutes its force. His characters are also Yiddish-speakers, either Middle European Jews – merchants, yeshiva-students, gravediggers, rabbis, drunks – from the ghettos and peasant villages of the 17th-19th centuries, or (in several of his finest stories) present-day settlers in Israel or the USA. They struggle to lead decent lives, uplifted or oppressed by the demands of orthodox Jewish belief and ritual. They are haunted by outside forces beyond their control: supernatural beings – several stories are narrated by dybbuks, ghosts and even the Devil himself – or mindless, vicious anti-semitism. Only one of Singer's novels is contemporary: *The Penitent* (1974), about a Polish-American Jew who returns to Israel and tries to come to terms with his own belief and with the tragic history of his people. The rest have historical settings – except that no Singer fiction is really historical, since everything he writes is a fable, with universal resonance. *Satan in Goray*, *The Magician of Lublin* and *The Slave* are about dark forces, demonic evil breaking out in small, closed communities. In *The Manor*, *The Estate* and *Enemies, a Love Story* the destructive forces are internal, as people's orthodox beliefs are challenged by love-affairs, business-deals, friendships and other such worldly claims.

THE FAMILY MOSKAT • *(1950)*
This is a warm, multi-generation story about a large Jewish family in Warsaw, and Singer's finest novel. The focus is on the human relationships within the family, mag-

> **READ ON**

▶ **To the short stories:** S.Y. Agnon, *The Bridal Canopy*; Isaac Babel, *Odessa Tales*; ▷Nikolai Gogol, *Arabesques*.
▶ **To *The Family Moskat*:** I.J. Singer (I.B.'s brother), *The Brothers Ashkenazy*.
▶ **To Singer's other novels:** Bernard Malamud, *The Fixer*; Nikos Kazantzakis, *The Greek Passion*; ▷Mario Vargas Llosa, *The War of the End of the World*; ▷Jerzy Kosinski, *The Painted Bird*.

nificently and movingly described; but the novel's edge comes from the constant intrusion of grim outside reality, the tormented history of Poland between the Congress of Vienna in 1815 and the second-world-war nazi storming of the Warsaw Ghetto. Counterpoint between inner and outer reality, between public and private life, between flesh and spirit, makes this book not just another family saga but a statement about Jewish (and non-Jewish) humanity at large. In that, *The Family Moskat* is characteristic of Singer's work – it is his universality, not his particularity, which makes him one of the most respected writers of the century.

Singer's short-story collections are Gimpel the Fool, The Spinoza of Market Street, Short Friday, The Séance, A Friend of Kafka, A Crown of Feathers, Passions, Love and Exile *and* Old Love. Collected Stories *is a fat anthology.* In My Father's Court *is a memoir of Singer's Warsaw days as the son of a rabbi, a theological student and a budding writer.*

SMITH, E.E. 'Doc' (Edward Elmer Smith, PhD) •
(1890-1965)
US novelist.

Smith's books are the quintessence of space-opera. Good guys in powerful spaceships battle villains, explore new worlds, use entire planets as weapons, arrange the rise and fall of galactic civilisations. Although his scientific invention has been overtaken by events, and his plots and situations have been endlessly pirated in trashy films and TV series, no SF writer has surpassed him as a teller of straightforward, edge-of-the-seat space yarns. *First Lensman*, the first novel of the 'Lensman' series (1950–60; *Triplanetary*, 1948, is a prologue) is a splendid introduction to his work. Faced with the ever-growing power of criminals, from space pirates to intergalactic drug barons, the police are falling further and further behind until Virgil Samms, head of the Triplanetary Service, receives word that he will find help on Arisia, a ghost-planet hitherto shunned by space-travellers.

> READ ON

● *Skylark of Space* (first of the 4-novel 'Skylark' series); *The Imperial Stars* (first of the 10-novel 'Family d'Alembert' series).
▶ David A. Kyle, *The Dragon Lensman* (first of a trilogy of Lensman sequels authorised by the Smith estate). Vonda N. McIntyre, *Enterprize – the First Adventure* (a powerful book using characters from the TV series *Star Trek*). ▷Harry Harrison, *Star Smashers of the Galaxy Rangers* (a merciless spoof).

SMITH, Wilbur • *(born 1933)*
South African novelist.

Smith's novels, set in South Africa, are swaggering adventure yarns in the tradition of ▷H. Rider Haggard. Their backgrounds are war (especially the Boer War), mining and jungle exploration; their heroes are free spirits, revelling in the lawlessness and vigour of frontier life. (John Wayne played their US equivalents in a hundred films.) *Shout at the Devil* (1968) is typical: the story of lion-hunting, crocodile-wrestling, ivory-poaching Flynn O'Flynn, whose Robin Hood humiliations of the sadistic German commissioner Fleischer take a serious turn when war is declared – this is 1914 – and he falls into a German trap.

> **READ ON** ▷
>
> ● *The Diamond Hunters* (about a safari to find hidden diamonds); *Gold Mine; A Sparrow Falls*.
> ▶ ▷Desmond Bagley, *Running Blind*. John Gardner, *The Secret Generation*. Hammond Innes, *Campbell's Kingdom*. ▷H. Rider Haggard, *King Solomon's Mines*.

SNOW, C.P. (Charles Percy) • *(1905–80)*
British novelist.

Snow's main work is the novel-sequence 'Strangers and Brothers' (1940–74). Though many characters recur, each book is self-contained. As the series proceeds, Lewis Eliot (the narrator of all 11 novels) rises from humble provincial beginnings to become a barrister, a civil servant and a senior government official. Snow's preoccupation was power: how people influence each other, the working of committees and hierarchies, the morality of office. He coined the phrase 'the corridors of power' – and he offers unrivalled glimpses of the people who tramp those corridors, of real individuals behind the establishment façade. *The Masters*, one of the key books in the sequence, describes the alliances and compromises required to elect a new master for a Cambridge college. *The New Men*, about scientists working on the first atomic bomb, is a study of responsibility: should we use our skills for ends we feel are wrong? In *The Conscience of the Rich*, about family loyalty, a rich young man rejects the future his father plans for him and becomes a doctor. *The Sleep of Reason*, the bleakest of all Snow's books, discusses our moral responsibility for others' evil; it was based on a horrific real 1960s case of multiple child-murder. Snow's themes are large, but his books are blander and less agonised than this suggests. His characters – especially the imperturbable committee-men (never women) who keep things going and the mavericks who let feelings interfere with common sense – are fascinating, and his scenes of discussion and persuasion are brilliantly done: he keeps us on the edge of our seats about such apparently trivial matters as whether

> **READ ON** ▷
>
> ▶ ▷Anthony Trollope, *Can You Forgive Her?* (the first novel in the 'Palliser' sequence). ▷Angus Wilson, *The Old Men at the Zoo*. Pamela Hansford Johnson (Lady Snow), *Error of Judgement*. ▷Gore Vidal, *Washington, D.C.* ▷Neville Shute, *No Highway*.

someone will end up saying 'yes' or 'no'.

The books in the sequence are Strangers and Brothers, The Light and the Dark, A Time of Hope, The Masters, The New Men, Homecomings, The Conscience of the Rich, The Affair, The Corridors of Power, The Sleep of Reason *and* Last Things. *Snow's other novels include two thrillers,* Death Under Sail *and* A Coat of Varnish, *and a fascinating study (*The Search*) of the excitement and passion of scientific research.*

SOLZHENITSYN, Alexander • *(born 1918)*
Russian novelist and non-fiction writer.

Denounced for treason in 1945 (he was a Red Army soldier who criticised Stalin), Solzhenitsyn spent eight years in a labour camp where he developed stomach cancer, and after nine months in a cancer hospital was sent into internal exile. He turned this bitter experience into novels – the prison-camp books *One Day in the Life of Ivan Denisovich* (1961) and *The First Circle* (1968); *Cancer Ward* (1968) – and their publication outside the USSR made him one of the most famous of all 1960s Soviet dissidents. He was finally expelled from the USSR in 1974, for writing an exhaustive description of the location, history and methods of the Russian prison-camp system, *The GULAG Archipelago* (1974–8). Few writers have ever surpassed him as a chronicler of human behaviour at its most nightmarish: his personal history authenticates every word he wrote.

Solzhenitsyn's only other novel is August 1914, *about the stirrings of the Russian Revolution.*

SOMETHING NASTY...

  Roald Dahl, *Kiss Kiss* (short stories)
▷James Herbert, *Moon*
▷Stephen King, *Pet Sematary*
▷Ruth Rendell, *Live Flesh*

Good and Evil (p 94)

> READ ON

► ▷Fyodor Dostoevsky, *Notes from the House of the Dead*. Arthur Koestler, *Darkness at Noon*. ▷Vladimir Nabokov, *Bend Sinister*. André Brink, *Looking on Darkness*. ▷Thomas Pynchon, *Gravity's Rainbow*. William Styron, *Sophie's Choice*.

SOUTH AFRICA

J.M. Coetzee, *In the Heart of the Country*
▷Nadine Gordimer, *Burger's Daughter*
Dan Jacobson, *A Dance in the Sun*
David Karp, *The Day of the Monkey*
Alan Paton, *Cry, The Beloved Country*
▷Tom Sharpe, *Riotous Assembly*
Carolyn Slaughter, *The Innocents*
▷Wilbur Smith, *Rage*

SPARK, Muriel • *(born 1918)*
British novelist.

Spark made her name in the 1960s: her tart black come-dies seemed just the antidote to the fey optimism of the time. Her books' deadpan world is a distorted mirror-im-age of our own, a disconcerting blend of the bland and the bizarre. In *Memento Mori* old people are mysteriously tel-ephoned and reminded that they are about to die. In *Robinson* a plane-load of ill-assorted people (among them the standard Spark heroine, a Catholic with Doubts) crashes on an island where laws and customs are hourly remade at the whim of the sole inhabitant. In *The Prime of Miss Jean Brodie* an Edinburgh schoolmistress tries to brainwash her pupils into being nice, conforming gels. *The Abbess of Crewe* reworks convent politics in terms of Watergate; the hero of *The Only Problem*, a scholar work-ing on the Book of Job, finds its events parallelling those in his own life. Spark develops these ideas not in farce but in brisk, neat prose, as if they were the most matter-of-fact happenings in the world. The results are eccentric, unsettling and hilarious.

THE GIRLS OF SLENDER MEANS • *(1963)*
A group of young ladies lives in a run-down London club for distressed gentlefolk. It is 1945, and there is rumoured to be an unexploded bomb in the garden. The girls are excited by the possibility of imminent destruction: they find it almost as thrilling as the thought of sex. They bus-tle about their busy, vapid lives: pining after film stars, writing (unanswered) letters to famous writers, bargaining for black-market clothing coupons. The book is an alle-gory about seedy-genteel, self-absorbed Britain under the threat of nuclear extinction; for all Spark's breezy hu-mour, the novel is haunted by the questions of where

READ ON

● *The Ballad of Peckham Rye*; *The Bachelors*.
▶ Ronald Firbank, *The Eccentricities of Cardinal Pirelli*. ▷Rose Macaulay, *The Towers of Trebizond*. Alice Thomas Ellis, *The 27th Kingdom*. ▷Anita Brookner, *Look at Me*. ▷John Updike, *The Witches of Eastwick*.

we'll be and how we'll behave when the bomb goes up.

Spark's other novels include The Mandelbaum Gate *(her most serious book, about a half-Jewish Catholic convert visiting Jerusalem at the height of Arab-Israeli tension),* The Driver's Seat, Not to Disturb, The Takeover *and* Territorial Rights. The Stories of Muriel Spark *is a generous short-story collection.*

STEAD, Christina • *(1902–83)*
Australian novelist.

Although Stead was born in Australia, she lived most of her life, and set many of her books, in Europe (especially Paris) and the USA. She writes of these places, however, not as a native but as a visitor, in a detached, ironic tone as if she were an anthropologist describing the behaviour of some unlikely, uncongenial tribe. In *The Beauties and Furies*, a savage moral tale about adultery, a young wife runs off to 1930s Paris and has an affair with a handsome but ruthless sexual adventurer; in the end he drops her and goes in search of younger prey. *House of all Nations*, an 800-page blockbuster about the insidious corruption of money, centres on the customers, staff and owners of a private European bank, and especially on its chief Jules Bertillon, a man whose moral sense and conscience have atrophied in the face of 'market forces'. Stead was a socialist, and this book is a devastating, if covert, assault on the pre-second-world-war European capitalist system. *The Man Who Loved Children*, set in the USA but based on Stead's own experience, is a story of stifling family life at the turn of the century, presided over by a monstrous, bullying father; the whole thing is seen through the eyes of his daughter, Louise, as she grows from terrified, adoring childhood to rebellious adolescence and adulthood.

Stead's other novels include For Love Alone, Dark Places of the Heart/Cotter's England, The People With the Dogs, Miss Herbert (The Suburban Wife) *and the long, ironic 'romance'* Letty Fox, Her Luck. The Salzburg Tales *is a collection of macabre, satirical and bawdy short stories modelled on Chaucer's* Canterbury Tales.

STEEL, Danielle
US novelist.

If there can be such a thing as feminist romance, that is what Steel writes. Her young women are briskly in charge

---

READON ⟩

▶ To *The Beauties and Furies:* ▷Jean Rhys, *After Leaving Mr Mackenzie*; Patrick Hamilton, *Hangover Square*; ▷Djuna Barnes, *Nightwood*.
▶ To *House of All Nations:* ▷John Galsworthy, *The Forsyte Saga*; ▷Jerome Weidman, *A Family Fortune*.
▶ To *The Man Who Loved Children:* ▷Ivy Compton-Burnett, *A Family and a Fortune*; ▷Angela Carter, *The Magic Toyshop*.

READON ⟩

▶ Helen Van Slyke, *The Rich and the*

of their own destinies, and regard men not as knights in shining armour but as equal partners – an attitude which some of her men find hard to take. Melting femininity is present, in that the books are about love-affairs, but so is melting masculinity: where emotion and sentiment are concerned, all human beings are one. Her books include *Crossings*, *Loving*, *The Promise* and *Full Circle* (1985), whose heroine is involved with the 1970s protest movement in the USA, fighting for civil rights and the end of the Vietnam war.

STEINBECK, John • *(1902–68)*
US novelist.

Until Steinbeck settled to writing in 1935, he moved restlessly from one job to another: he was a journalist, a builder's labourer, a house-painter, a fruit-picker and the caretaker of a lakeside estate. This experience gave him first-hand knowledge of the dispossessed, the unemployed millions who suffered the brunt of the US Depression of the 1930s. Their lives are his subject, and he writes of them with ferocious, documentary intensity and in a style which seems exactly to catch their habits of both mind and speech. The ruggedness of his novels is often enhanced by themes borrowed from myth or the Old Testament. *To A God Unknown* (1933) is about an impoverished farmer who begins worshipping ancient gods and ends up sacrificing himself for rain. *Tortilla Flat* (1935) about 'wetbacks' (illegal Mexican immigrants to California) uses the story of Arthur, Guinevere and Lancelot from British myth. *East of Eden* (1952) is based on the story of Cain and Abel. Though Steinbeck never thrusts such references down his readers' throats, they add to the grandeur and mystery which, together with documentary grittiness, are the overwhelming qualities of his work.

THE GRAPES OF WRATH • *(1938)*
The once-fertile Oklahoma grain-fields have been reduced to a dust-bowl by over-farming, and the Joad family are near starvation. Attracted by leaflets promising work in the fruit-plantations of California, they load their belongings into a battered old car and travel east. In California they find every plantation surrounded by destitute, desperate people: there are a thousand applicants for every job. The plantation-owners pay starvation-wages and sack anyone who objects; the workers try to force justice by strike action – and are beaten up by armed vigilantes. When Tom Joad, already on the run for murder, is caught up in the fight for justice and accidentally kills a man; it is time for Ma to gather the family together again and move on.

Righteous. Mary Wesley, *The Camomile Lawn*. Charlotte Vale Allen, *Promises*.
▷Alice Walker, *Meridian*.

READ ON ⟩

● *Of Mice and Men* (a tragedy about the friendship between two ill-matched farmworkers, Lennie – a simple-minded giant of a man – and the weedier, cleverer George).
▶ Erskine Caldwell, *God's Little Acre*.
▷Edith Wharton, *Ethan Frome*. ▷William Faulkner, *The Hamlet*. Upton Sinclair, *The Jungle*. ▷Victor Hugo, *Toilers of the Sea*. ▷Somerset Maugham, *Liza of Lambeth*.

There must be a place for them somewhere; there must be a Promised Land.

Steinbeck's shorter novels include Cannery Row, The Pearl *and* The Short Reign of Pippin IV. *His short stories, usually about 'wetbacks', share-croppers and other victims of the US system, are in* The Red Pony *and* The Long Valley. The Acts of King Arthur and his Noble Knights *is a straightforward retelling of British myth;* The Portable Steinbeck *is a packed anthology.*

STENDHAL • *(1783-1842)*
French novelist and non-fiction writer.

'Stendhal' was a pseudonym used by the French diplomat Henri-Marie Beyle. As well as fiction (four novels; a dozen short stories) he published essays on art, literature and philosophy and several autobiographical books. Unlike most early 19th-century writers – even ▷Balzac and ▷Dickens – who concentrated on surface likenesses, painting word-pictures of events, people and places without introspection, Stendhal was chiefly interested in his characters' psychology. The main theme of his novels was the way outsiders, without breeding or position, must make their way in snobbish, tradition-stifled society by talent or personality alone. His books give the feeling that we are watching the evolution of that personality, that we are as intimate with his people's psychological development as if they were relatives or friends.

SCARLET AND BLACK (Le rouge et le noir) •
(1830)
The book is a character-study of Julien Sorel, a carpenter's son who rises in the world by brains, sexual charm and ruthlessness. He becomes first tutor to the children of the local Mayor, then the Mayor's wife's lover, and finally secretary to an aristocratic diplomat whose daughter falls in love with him. In ten years he has travelled from humble origins to the verge of a dazzling marriage and a brilliant career. But then the Mayor's wife writes a letter denouncing him as a cold-hearted adventurer, his society acquaintances reject him, and he returns to his native town to take revenge.

Stendhal's other completed novels are Armance, The Abbess of Castro *and* The Charterhouse of Parma. The Life of Henri Brulard *and* Memoirs of an Egoist *are fictionalised autobiography.*

READ ON ⟩

● *The Charterhouse of Parma.*
▶ **To *Scarlet and Black*:** ▷André Gide, *Strait is the Gate*; ▷Nikolai Gogol, *Dead Souls*; ▷George Eliot, *Middlemarch*; ▷Honoré de Balzac, *Lost Illusions*: John Braine, *Room at the Top*; ▷Jerome Weidman, *I Can Get it for You Wholesale.*
▶ **To *The Charterhouse of Parma*:** Umberto Eco, *The Name of the Rose.*

STERNE, Laurence • *(1713–68)*
British novelist.

Sterne's only novel, *The Life and Opinions of Tristram Shandy, Gentleman* (1760–7) is less a story than a gloriously rambling conversation. Tristram sets out to tell his life-story (beginning with the moment of his conception, when his mother's mind is less on what she is doing than on whether his father has remembered to wind the clock). But everything he says reminds him of some anecdote or wise remark, so that he constantly interrupts himself. It takes 300 pages, for example, for him to get from his conception to the age of seven, and in the meantime we have had such digressions as a treatise on what the size and shape of people's noses tells us about their characters, an explanation of how the boy came to be called Tristram by mistake for Trismegistus (and what each name signifies), accounts of the Tristapaedia (the system devised for Tristram's education), the curse of Ernulphus of Rochester and the misfortunes of Lieutenant le Fever; we have also had the novel's preface (placed not at the beginning but as the peroration to Book III), and many musings on life, love and the pursuit of happiness by Tristram's father, Uncle Toby and Corporal Trim. The reader is constantly exhorted, nudged and questioned; there is even a blank page in case you have urgent thoughts of your own to add. We never know how Tristram's life turns out; instead, we are copiously informed about Uncle Toby's love-affair, Tristram's travels in France and the adventures of the King of Bohemia. Sterne himself called *Tristram Shandy* 'a civil, nonsensical, good-humoured book'; it is the most spectacular shaggy-dog story ever told.

Sterne's other writings include sermons – he was a Yorkshire parson – and A Sentimental Journey, *a discursive, half-fictionalised account of the towns and people he saw and the tales he heard during six months' travelling in France.*

STEVENSON, R.L. (Robert Louis) •
(1850–94)
British writer of novels, short stories and non-fiction.

Apart from the brief psychological thriller *Dr Jekyll and Mr Hyde* (1886, about a man who uses drugs to change himself from kindly family doctor to deformed killer and back again), Stevenson's chief works are historical adventure-stories. They have been hijacked by child readers, but (except perhaps in *Treasure Island*, 1883) there is also

> READ ON ▷

▶ ▷François Rabelais, *Gargantua*. Miguel de Cervantes Saavedra, *Don Quixote*. Tobias Smollett, *The Expedition of Humphrey Clinker*.
▷John Kennedy Toole, *A Confederacy of Dunces*. Flann O'Brien, *At Swim-Two-Birds*.
▷Saul Bellow, *Henderson the Rain King*.

> READ ON ▷

▶ **To *Dr Jekyll and Mr Hyde:*** ▷H.G. Wells, *The Invisible Man*; Gaston Leroux, *The Phantom of the Opera*; James Hogg,

plenty to interest adults: Stevenson's evocation of scenery (especially Scotland), the psychological complexity of his characters, and the feeling (which he shared with ▷Tolstoy) that each human life is part of a vast historical, moral and cultural continuum.

Stevenson's historical novels include The Black Arrow *(a story of the Wars of the Roses),* Weir of Hermiston *(about an Edinburgh 'hanging-judge' in the early 19th century) and the Jacobite trilogy* Kidnapped, Catriona *and* The Master of Ballantrae. *His lighter fiction includes* The Wrong Box, The Wrecker *and* The Ebb-tide. *The Merry Men and* Island Nights' Entertainment *contain short stories. He also wrote poetry, travel books (eg* Travels with a Donkey*) and plays.*

STEWART, Mary • *(born 1916)*
British novelist.

Stewart's romantic adventure stories are set in magnificently-evoked, exotic parts of Europe and the Mediterranean. Her books include *Madam Will You Talk?*, *Wildfire at Midnight*, *Thunder on the Right*, *Nine Coaches Waiting*, *The Moon-spinners*, *Airs Above the Ground*, *The Gabriel Hounds*, *Touch Not the Cat* and *This Rough Magic* (1964), in which a girl, holidaying on Corfu, is caught up not only in sorcery – Corfu is the 'magic island' of Shakespeare's *The Tempest* – but in a gun-running conspiracy between Greece and Albania. Stewart also wrote a trilogy based on the legends of Merlin and King Arthur; the first volume is *The Crystal Cave* (1970).

SVEVO, Italo • *(1861-1928)*
Austrian/Italian novelist.

Svevo was a businessman in Trieste; his firm made underwater paint. Despite encouragement from his friend ▷James Joyce, he never took his writing seriously until the last year of his life, when a French translation of *The Confessions of Zeno* (1922) brought him European fame. His books are ironical comedies. Their ineffective, bewildered heroes blunder about in society, looking for some point to their existence – and the chief irony is that they are genuinely the 'zeros' they think they are, their existence has no point at all. *The Confessions of Zeno* is the autobiography of a man who wants to give up smoking. He explains that his addiction is actually psychological, since every cigarette he smokes reminds him, in ▷Prous-

---

Confessions of a Justified Sinner.
▶ **To the adventure stories:** ▷Daniel Defoe, *Robinson Crusoe*; ▷Walter Scott, *The Heart of Midlothian*; John Masefield, *Jim Davis*; ▷John Buchan, *Castle Gay*; ▷A. Conan Doyle, *The Valley of Fear*; ▷Desmond Bagley, *Running Blind*.

> **READ ON**

● *The Gabriel Hounds.*
▶ Anne Bridge, *Illyrian Spring.* Helen MacInnes, *The Venetian Affair.* ▷Dorothy Dunnett, *Dolly and the Cookie Bird.*

> **READ ON**

▶ ▷Franz Kafka, *The Castle.* ▷Saul Bellow, *Herzog.* Alberto Moravia, *The Conformist.* Joaquin Machado de Assis, *The Heritage of Quincas Borba.* William Cooper, *Scenes from Married Life.* William Boyd, *The New Confessions.*

tian fashion, of some past experience, so that to give up smoking would be to surrender his own history; he writes of his Oedipal relationship with his father (whom he accidentally killed), of his prolonged, ludicrous courtship of the wrong woman, and of his treatment by a psychiatrist sicker than himself. The book is as dreamlike and terrifying as ▷Kafka's novels – indeed, Svevo exactly shared Kafka's vision of the world as an absurd, endless and sinister labyrinth.

Svevo's other novels are A Life, As A Man Grows Older *and the shorter* Tale of the Good Old Man and the Pretty Girl.

SWIFT, Graham • *(born 1949)*
British novelist.

Swift's novels centre on apparently ordinary people – shopkeepers, housewives, clerks – under psychological stress. They have reached turning-points in what have seemed boring, routine lives, and the novels show them mentally rerunning the past to find explanations for their feelings, either to themselves or to others. In *Waterland* (1983) the main character is an elderly history teacher, and the event he is remembering is the discovery, forty years before, of a boy's body in a drainage-ditch in the English Fens. In front of a bored, cheeky class, he begins thinking aloud about the reasons for the boy's death – and his monologue ranges through the history of the Fens (one of the remotest and most mysterious English regions), the story of several generations of his own family, and, not least, an account of the rivalry between his mentally subnormal brother Dick and Freddie Parr, the boy found drowned.

Swift's other novels are The Sweet Shop Owner, Shuttlecock *and* Out of This World. Learning To Swim *is a collection of short stories.*

SWIFT, Jonathan • *(1667-1745)*
British/Irish satirist and journalist.

Swift was a savage satirist, pouring out poems, articles

> **READ ON**

● *Out of This World* (in which, in alternate monologues, the son and grand-daughter of a first-world-war hero, an arms manufacturer, reflect on the way the old man's obsessive love for them has poisoned both their lives).

▶ Peter Benson, *The Levels* (also set in Fen-country). Gerald H. Morris, *Doves and Silk Handkerchieves* and ▷John Irving, *The Cider House Rules* are similarly multi-layered, mysterious stories, set respectively in a Yorkshire mining village at the turn of the 20th century and in rural Maine before, during and after the second world war.

> **READ ON**

▶ Voltaire, *Candide*.

and essays attacking the follies of his time. *Gulliver's Travels* (1726) differs from his other work only in that the edge of its satire is masked by fairy tale – indeed, the satire is often edited out so that the book can be sold for children. Gulliver is a compulsive explorer, despite the moral humiliation he suffers after every landfall. In Lilliput the people (who are six inches high) regard him as an uncouth, unpredictable monster – particularly when he tells them some of the ideas and customs of his native England. In Brobdignag he becomes the pet of giants, and tries without success to convince them of the value of such civilised essentials as law-courts, money and guns. He visits Laputa and Lagado, cloud-cuckoo-lands where science has ousted common sense; on the Island of Sorcerers he speaks to great thinkers of the past, and finds them in despair at what has become of the human race. Finally he is shipwrecked among the Houynhyms, horses equipped with reason who regard human beings as degenerate barbarians, and who fill him with such distaste for his own species that when he returns to England he can hardly bear the sight, sound or smell of his own family. Throughout the book, Gulliver doggedly preaches the glories of European 'civilisation' (that is, the customs and beliefs of the Age of Enlightenment), and arouses only derision or disgust.

Samuel Butler, *Erewhon*. ▷Nathanael West, *A Cool Million*.
▶ **Equally lacerating satires on aspects of late 20th-century life:** Michael Frayn, *A Very Private Life*; ▷Thomas Pynchon, *The Crying of Lot 49*; ▷Angela Carter, *The Passion of New Eve*.

T

TAYLOR, Elizabeth • *(1912–75)*
British novelist and short-story writer.

A large part of Taylor's art consists in appearing to have no art at all: few authors have ever seemed so self-effacing in their work. As each novel or story begins, it is as if a net curtain has been drawn aside to reveal ordinary people in a normal street. The setting is the outskirts of some large English town; the people are housewives, bus-conductors, labourers, schoolchildren; there seems to be no drama. But as the story proceeds, an apparently unfussy chronicle of ordinary events and conversations builds up enormous psychological pressure, which Taylor then releases in a shocking or hilarious happening which opens speculation wide about whatever will happen when the book is closed. Her artistry – subtle, gentle and unsettling – is at its peak in short stories; her novels, thanks to larger casts, more varied settings and longer time-schemes, tend more to wry social comedy than to the sinister.

THE DEVASTATING BOYS • *(1972)*
The people in this story collection are typical Taylor characters: an elderly couple in the countryside who decide to offer a holiday to two black children from the city slums; a young West Indian, utterly alone in London on the eve of his birthday; an ll-year-old child taking a bus home from a hateful piano lesson; a blue-rinsed widow with an orderly routine of life. Something unexpected happens to each of them, a psychological bombshell. They were as unremarkable as our neighbours – but after these stories, our neighbours will never seem the same again.

Taylor's short stories are collected in Hester Lilly, The Blush *and* A Dedicated Man. *Her novels include* At Mrs Lippincote's, A View of the Harbour, A Game of Hide-

> **READ ON**

● *Hester Lilly; The Wedding Group* (novel).
▶ **To the stories:** V.S. Pritchett, *The Camberwell Beauty and Other stories*; William Trevor, *Angels at the Ritz*; Mary Gordon, *Temporary Shelter*; Joyce Carol Oates, *Crossing the Border.*
▶ **To the novels:**
▷Susan Hill, *A Change for the Better*;
▷Barbara Pym, *Excellent Women*;
▷Angus Wilson, *Late Call*; Theodore Fontane, *Effi Briest.*

and-seek, The Wedding Group, Blaming, A Wreath of
Roses, Mrs Palfrey at the Claremont *and* The Soul of
Kindness.

TERRORISTS/FREEDOM FIGHTERS

Jerzy Andrzeyewski, *Ashes and Diamonds*
▷Joseph Conrad, *Under Western Eyes*
Rosalind Laker, *This Shining Land*
▷John Le Carré, *The Little Drummer Girl*
▷Doris Lessing, *The Good Terrorist*
Primo Levi, *If Not Now, When?*
▷Frederic Raphael, *Like Men Betrayed*
Idries Shah, *Kara Kush*

War: Behind the Lines (p 253)

THACKERAY, William Makepeace •
(1811-63)
British novelist and journalist.

Until the success of *Vanity Fair*, when he was 36, Thackeray earned his living as a journalist and cartoonist (especially for Punch magazine) and as a humorous lecturer.
His first intention in his novels was to write 'satirical biographies', letting the reader discover the follies of the
world at the same time as his naive young heroes and heroines. But the characters took over, and his books now
seem more genial and affectionate than barbed. He invented characters as grotesque as ▷Dickens', caricatures
of human viciousness or folly, but he wrote of them with
a kind of disapproving sympathy, a fellow-feeling for
their humanity, which Dickens lacks. Humbug, ambition
and the seven deadly sins are Thackeray's subjects – and
so are friendship, kindness and warm-heartedness. At a
time when many English novels were more like sermons,
clamorous for reform, he wrote moral comedies, showing
us what fools we are.

VANITY FAIR • *(1847–8)*
The book interweaves the lives of two friends, gentle
Amelia and calculating, brilliant Becky Sharp. Becky is
an impoverished orphan determined to make her fortune;
Amelia believes in love, marriage and family life. Each of
them marries; Amelia's husband has an affair with Becky,
and dies at Waterloo with her name on his lips; Becky's
husband finds her entertaining a rich, elderly admirer and

READ ON

● *Pendennis.*
▶ ▷Jane Austen, *Emma.*
▷Arnold Bennett, *The
Card*. ▷H.G. Wells,
Tono-Bungay.
▷Eudora Welty, *The
Ponder Heart*.
▷Barbara Pym, *No
Fond Return of Love.*

abandons her. In the end, each girl gets what she longed for, but not in the way she hoped. Amelia, after ten years pining for her dead husband, is cruelly told by Becky of his infidelity, and turns for comfort to a dull, kind man who has worshipped her from afar, and who now offers her marriage, a home and all the comforts of obscurity. Becky's son inherits his father's money and gives her an annuity on condition that she never speaks to him again; we see her at the end of the book, queening it in Bath, an idle, rich member of the society she has always aspired to join and whose values Thackeray sums up in the title of the book.

Thackeray's other books include Pendennis *(the story of a selfish young man, spoilt by his mother, who goes to London to make his fortune as a writer) and its sequel* The Newcomes, Henry Esmond *and its sequel* The Virginians, *and a number of shorter tales and stories including* Barry Lyndon, The Great Hoggarty Diamond *and the spoof fairy-tale* The Rose and the Ring.

THEROUX, Paul • *(born 1941)*
US novelist and non-fiction writer.

Some of Theroux's most enjoyable books are about travelling. *The Great Railway Bazaar* takes him by a succession of weird and wonderful old steam trains from London to Tokyo and back again. In *The Old Patagonian Express* he takes public transport from Boston to the southernmost tip of South America. *The Kingdom by the Sea* is the waspish account of a journey round the coastal resorts of seedy 1980s Britain. In all of them the narrator, the writer himself, feels detached, an observer of events rather than a participant – and the same is true of the people in Theroux's novels. They live abroad, often in the tropics; like the heroes of ▷Graham Greene (the author Theroux most resembles) they feel uneasy both about the society they are in and about themselves; they fail to cope. The hero of *Saint Jack* (1973), a US pimp in Singapore, hopes to make a fortune providing R and R for his servicemen compatriots, but the pliability of his character makes him the prey for every conman and shark in town. In *The Mosquito Coast* (1981) an ordinary US citizen, depressed by life, uproots his family and tries to make a new start in the Honduran jungle, with tragic, farcical results. *Picture Palace* (1978) is the life-story of a famous photographer who has hidden all her life behind her camera, reduced existence to images on film, and now, in withered old age, agonisingly contrasts her memories of youth, warmth and

READ ON ▷

▶ **To O-Zone:** ▷Russell Hoban, *Riddley Walker*; Robie Macauley, *A Secret History of Time to Come*; Keith Roberts, *Kiteworld*.
▶ **To Theroux's novels in general:** ▷Graham Greene, *Our Man in Havana*; Timothy Mo, *Sour Sweet*.
▶ **To the short stories:** ▷Lawrence Durrell, *Antrobus Complete*.
▶ **To the travel-books:** Gordon Meyer, *The River and the People*; Jonathan Raban, *Coasting*.

affection with the dusty prints which are all she has to show for them.

O-ZONE • (1986)

The O-Zone or Outer Zone is an American county evacuated after a nuclear accident and left as a no-go area. After 15 years a group of New Yorkers visits it on a sensation-seeking spree – and finds not desert but a self-contained society of mutant, brutalised human beings. Later, two of the New Yorkers return to the O-Zone, seeking to come to terms with the nightmare as their ancestors once tried to tame the wilderness.

Theroux's other novels include Waldo, Fong and the Indians, The Black House, The Family Arsenal *and* Doctor Slaughter. Sinning With Annie, The Consul's File *and* The London Embassy *are collections of short stories.*

TOLKIEN, J.R.R. (John Ronald Reuel) •
(1892–1973)
British novelist.

In 1939 Tolkien, a teacher of Anglo-Saxon literature at Oxford University, published a children's book (*The Hobbit*), about a small furry-footed person who steals a dragon's hoard. Bilbo Baggins was a hobbit, and his quest was the prologue to an enormous adult saga in which elves, dwarves, wizards, ents, human beings and hobbits unite to destroy the power of evil (embodied by the Dark Lord Sauron and his minions the Ring-wraiths and the orcs). The three volumes of *The Lord of the Rings*, published in the mid-1950s, started a vogue for supernatural fantasy-adventure which has spread world-wide and taken in films, quiz-books and role-play games as well as fiction. Tolkien outstrips his imitators not so much because of his plot (which is a simple battle between good and bad, with the moral issues explicit on every page) as thanks to his teeming professorial imagination. He gave his made-up worlds complete systems of language, history, anthropology, geography and literature. Reading him is like exploring a library; his invention seems inexhaustible.

Although The Hobbit *and* The Lord of the Rings *are self-contained, Tolkien published several other volumes filling in chinks of their underlying history, explaining matters only sketched in the main narrative, and adding even more layers of linguistic, historical and anthropological fantasy. The chief books are* The Silmarillion *and* Unfin-

READ ON

▶ ▷Stephen Donaldson, *The Chronicles of Thomas Covenant.*
▷Piers Anthony, *A Spell for Chameleon.*
▷David Eddings, *The Belgariad Quintet.*
Terry Pratchett, *The Colour of Magic* is a spectacular spoof, hardly less fantastical and engrossing than Tolkien's original.

ished Tales. Lost Tales *(three volumes) contain notes and drafts, chiefly of interest to addicts.* Farmer Giles of Ham *and* The Adventures of Tom Bombadil *are short stories for children.*

TOLSTOY, Lev Nikolaevich • *(1828–1910)*
Russian novelist.

In his 60s and beyond Tolstoy became famous as a kind of moral guru or secular saint: he preached the equal 'value' of all human beings, and suited actions to words by giving away his wealth, freeing his serfs and living an austere life in a cottage on the edge of his former estate. A similar view underlies his fiction. His ambition was to enter into the condition of each of his characters, to show the psychological complexity and diversity of the human race. His books are not tidily organised, with every event and emotion shaped to fit a central theme, but reflect the sprawl of life itself. The result was a psychological equivalent of ▷Balzac's 'snapshots' in *The Human Comedy*. Whether Tolstoy is showing us a coachman who comes and goes in half a page, or a major character who appears throughout a book, he invites us to feel full sympathy for that person, makes us flesh out his or her 'reality' in terms of our own.

WAR AND PEACE • *(1869)*
The book begins with people at a St Petersburg party in 1805 discussing the political situation in France, where Napoleon has just been proclaimed emperor. Tolstoy then fills 100 pages with seemingly random accounts of the lives and characters of a large group of relatives, friends, servants and dependants of three aristocrats, Andrey Bolkonsky, Pierre Bezuhov and Natasha Rostov. Gradually all these people become involved both with one another and with the gathering storm as Napoleon's armies sweep through Europe. The story culminates with the 1812 French invasion of Russia, Napoleon's defeat and his retreat from Moscow. The war touches the lives of all Tolstoy's people, and in particular resolves the triangle of affection between his central characters. The effects of war are the real subject of *War and Peace*. It contains 539 separate characters – the range is from Napoleon to the girl who dresses Rostov's hair, from Bolkonsky to an eager young soldier sharpening his sword on the eve of battle – and Tolstoy shows how their individual nature and feelings are both essential to and validated by the vast

READ ON ▷

● *Anna Karenina*.
▶ **To *War and Peace*:**
▷Émile Zola, *The Downfall*, (La débâcle).
▷I.B. Singer, *The Family Moskat*; André Malraux, *Man's Estate*.
▶ **To *Anna Karenina*:**
▷Ivan Turgenev, *On the Eve*; ▷George Eliot, *Romola*;
▷Gustave Flaubert, *Madame Bovary*;
▷Boris Pasternak, *Doctor Zhivago*.

Lev TOLSTOY

Jeanette **WINTERSON, THE PASSION**

Anthony **BURGESS, THE NAPOLEON SYMPHONY**

NAPOLEON

'ALL HUMAN LIFE IS HERE'

STENDHAL, SCARLET AND BLACK (*middle- and upper-class life in Napoleonic France*)

Miguel de **CERVANTES SAAVEDRA, DON QUIXOTE** (*fantasy knight-errantry in Renaissance Spain*)

Johann Wolfgang von **GOETHE, THE APPRENTICESHIP OF WILHELM MEISTER** (*young man travels 18th-century Europe, learning about life and love*)

Charles **DICKENS, DAVID COPPERFIELD** (*English city society in the 1830s*)

Mark **TWAIN, THE ADVENTURES OF HUCKLEBERRY FINN** (*small-town life on Mississippi before American Civil War*)

Ivan **TURGENEV, FATHERS AND SONS** (*landed class resist fashionable revolutionary ideas, 1860s*)

Nicolai **GOGOL, DEAD SOULS** (*conman tours rural estates, buying up dead serfs' 'souls'*)

Fyodor **DOSTOEVSKI, THE IDIOT** (*psychological disintegration of count dismissed by family as simpleton*)

Maxim **GORKY, FOMA GORDEEV** (*brutal upbringing in barge-owning family on 19th-century Volga*)

TSARIST RUSSIA

WAR AND PEACE *(tapestry of Russian life during Napoleonic Wars)*

NAPOLOENIC WARS

Bernard **CORNWELL, SHARPE'S REGIMENT**

C.S. **FORESTER, THE GUN**

William **THACKERAY, VANITY FAIR**

Boris **PASTERNAK, DOCTOR ZHIVAGO**
(tragic love in chaos of Russian revolution)

Ernest **HEMINGWAY, A FAREWELL TO ARMS**
(love-affair overshadowed by World War I)

Olivia **MANNING, FORTUNES OF WAR**
(World War II: effects on civilians in Balkans and Egypt)

William **STYRON, SOPHIE'S CHOICE**
(US woman haunted by memory of nazi concentration camps)

Kazuo **ISHIGURO, A PALE VIEW OF HILLS**
(Japanese woman coping with memories of Hiroshima)

FALLOUT OF WAR

tapestry of human affairs of which they are part.

Tolstoy's other novels include Anna Karenina *(in which an adulterous and tragic love-affair is used to focus a picture of the stifling, morally incompetent aristocratic Russian society of the 1860s),* The Death of Ivan Illich, The Kreutzer Sonata, Master and Man *and* Resurrection. *His autobiographical books include* Childhood, Boyhood, Youth *and* A Confession.

TOOLE, John Kennedy • *(1937–69)*
US novelist.

A Confederacy of Dunces (1980), Toole's only novel, was published posthumously: it had collected so many rejection-slips that he killed himself. It is a no-holds-barred comic grumble against the 20th-century world in general and the city of New Orleans in particular. Its anti-hero, Ignatius J. Reilly, is a narcissistic, hypochondriacal, towering genius who regards himself as too good for the world. He has successfully avoided working for 30 years, living in a fetid room in his mother's house and alternately masturbating, playing the lute and scribbling brilliant thoughts on a succession of supermarket notepads. At last his mother sends him out to find a job – with catastrophic results. Bored after one hour in a trouser-factory, he sets about destabilising staff-management relations; hired to sell hot-dogs, he eats his stock; in all innocence, he takes up with drug-addicts, whores and corrupt police. If Ignatius were likeable (say, like Voltaire's Candide), the satire might seem more genial and sympathetic; but he is a revolting example of how, in Toole's view, there is no excuse for the clinical brilliance of the brain being shackled to such a bag of guts as the human body. *A Confederacy of Dunces* is witty, slapstick, Rabelaisian, Falstaffian – and offers the human species no reason at all for self-congratulation or for hope.

READ ON >

▶ Robert Coover, *The Universal Baseball Association*. Frederick Rolfe, *Hadrian the Seventh*. Peter Carey, *Illywhacker*. B.S. Johnson, *Christie Malry's Own Double-Entry*. Martin Amis, *The Rachel Papers*.

TRAINS

▷Agatha Christie, *Murder on the Orient Express*
  Freeman Wills Crofts, *Death of a Train*
▷Graham Greene, *Stamboul Train*
▷Jaroslav Hašek, *The Good Soldier Švejk*
▷Patricia Highsmith, *Strangers on a Train*
▷John Masters, *Bhowani Junction*

TROLLOPE, Anthony • *(1815–82)*
British novelist.

Until Trollope was 52 he worked for the Post Office, travelling in Europe, the USA, north Africa and all over the British Isles. He turned his foreign experience into travel books, and used his British observations in 47 novels, many of them written, in the fashion of the time, for serial publication in magazines. His style is genial and expansive, and his books deal with such characteristic Victorian themes as class, power, money and family authority. His favourite characters are the upper-middle class of small towns and the surrounding estates. His plots involve the exercise of authority by the older generation and, by the young, all kinds of pranks, kicking over the traces, unsuitable love-affairs and mockery of their elders' stuffiness. Trollope's best-loved novels are in two six-book series, the 'Barsetshire' books (1855–67), about intrigue and preferment in a cathedral city, and the 'Palliser' books (1864–80), about politics on the wider stages of county and country. Each novel is self-contained, but recurring characters and cross-references between the books, added to Trollope's easy-going style, give the reader a marvellously comfortable sensation, as of settling down to hear about the latest scrapes of a group of well-loved friends.

BARCHESTER TOWERS • *(1857)*
The second novel in the Barsetshire sequence is high comedy. Imperious Mrs Proudie, wife of the timid new Bishop of Barchester, brings the Reverend Obadiah Slope into the Palace to help dominate her husband and run the diocese. But Slope is a snake in the grass, determined to make a rich marriage for himself, to win preferment in the church, even to defy Mrs Proudie if that will advance his cause. Their power-struggle is the heart of the book, a stately but furious minuet which soon sweeps up all Trollope's minor characters: rich, pretty Widow Bold, apoplectic Archdeacon Grantly, flirtatious Signora Vesey-Negroni, saintly Mr Harding, bewildered Parson Quiverful and his 14 squalling brats.

The Barsetshire novels are The Warden, Barchester Towers, Doctor Thorne, Framley Parsonage, The Small House at Allington *and* The Last Chronicle of Barset. *The Palliser novels are* Can You Forgive Her?, Phineas Finn, The Eustace Diamonds, Phineas Redux, The Prime Minister *and* The Duke's Children. *Trollope's other novels include* The Bertrams, Orley Farm, The Belton Estate, The Way We Live Now *and* Mr Scarborough's Family.

READ ON ▷

▶ **To the Barsetshire books:** Angela Thirkell, *High Rising* (first of a series set in Barsetshire and borrowing Trollope's characters); Elizabeth Goudge, *Cathedral Close*; Hugh Walpole, *The Cathedral*; ▷Barbara Pym, *Crampton Hodnett*.

▶ **To the Palliser books:** ▷John Galsworthy, *The Forsyte Saga*; Benjamin Disraeli, *Coningsby*; ▷Christina Stead, *House of All Nations*.

▶ **To Trollope's work in general:** Oliver Goldsmith, *The Vicar of Wakefield*; Louis Auchincloss, *The Great World and Timothy Colt*; ▷Barbara Taylor Bradford, *A Woman of Substance*.

TURGENEV, Ivan Sergeevich • *(1818–83)*
Russian novelist and playwright.

A rich man, Turgenev spent much of his life travelling in Europe, and was welcomed abroad as the leading Russian writer of his time. He was less popular in Russia itself. Although his limpid style (influenced by his friend ▷Flaubert) and his descriptions of nature were admired, his wistful satire, treating all human endeavour as equally absurd, won favour with neither conservatives nor radicals. His favourite characters are members of the leisured class, and his stories of disappointed ambition, failed love-affairs and unfocussed dissatisfaction anticipate not so much later revolutionary writings as the plays of ▷Chekhov.

FATHERS AND SONS • *(1861)*
Arkady, a student, takes his friend Bazarov home to meet his father. The old man is impressed by Bazarov's vigorous character and outspoken views – which are that none of the old moral and social conventions have intrinsic validity, and that people must decide for themselves how to live their lives. (This attitude to life, 'nihilism', was widespread among Russian intellectuals in the 1860s and 1870s.) The novel soon leaves politics to explore the effects of Bazarov's character on his own life. He falls in love, and disastrously misinterprets his beloved's wish for friendship as the proposal of a 'free' liaison; he visits his parents, who cannot reconcile their admiration for their son with bewilderment at his ideas; he quarrels with the traditionalist Pavel, Arkady's uncle, and fights an absurd duel with him; he nurses serfs during a typhus epidemic and becomes fatally infected. Although Bazarov always regarded his own existence as futile, after his death it becomes apparent that he has changed the lives and attitudes of every other person in the story.

Turgenev's novels include Rudin, A Nest of Gentlefolk, On the Eve, Smoke *and* Virgin Soil. A Hunter's Notes/A Sportsman's Sketches *contains short stories and poetic descriptions of country scenes.* A Month in the Country, *a Chekhovian comedy, is his best-known play.*

TURNER, George • *(born 1916)*
Australian novelist.

The Sea and Summer (1987), Turner's best-known novel, is set in New Melbourne, Australia, three generations from now. The human race has pillaged the environment

---

> **READ ON** ▷

● *Torrents of Spring* (the story of a man torn by love for two women, a beautiful girl and the wife of an old school friend).
▶ ▷Gustave Flaubert, *Sentimental Education*. George Moore, *The Lake*. ▷L.P. Hartley, *The Go-Between*. ▷Willa Cather, *The Professor's House*. ▷Anton Chekhov, *The Lady With the Little Dog* (and other short stories).

> **READ ON** ▷

● *Beloved Son*.
▶ ▷Anthony Burgess, *A Clockwork Orange*.

to the point where the atmosphere itself is in revolt: the ice-caps are melting and water is lapping at the lower floors of the kilometre-high tower-blocks where the Swill live. The Swill make up ninety per cent of the population; they are unemployed and unemployable, an urban underclass surviving on state handouts, denied education and kept in check by army patrols and razor-wire. The Sweet, by contrast, have privilege, wealth and culture – so long as they keep their jobs. The book is about the relationship between Billy Kovacs, a Swill 'tower boss' (gang-ruler) and a Sweet family fallen on hard times. Although the situation suggests SF, *The Sea and Summer* is, rather, a novel about character and relationships. The quality of Turner's writing, the harshness of his judgements and his depiction of people coping with a horrifying, doomed society, are ▷Dickensian in both range and rage.

Turner's other novels include The Cupboard Under the Stairs, Vaneglory *and* Yesterday's Men.

TWAIN, Mark • *(1835–1910)*
US novelist and journalist.

'Mark Twain' was the pseudonym of Samuel Clemens. A former steam-boat captain on the Mississippi, soldier, gold-miner and traveller, he wrote breezy, good-humoured accounts of his experiences, with an eye for quirky customs, manners and characters. His favourite form was the short story or comic, factual 'sketch' of half a dozen pages, and several of his books are collections of such pieces. He wrote three historical novels, *Personal Recollections of Joan of Arc* (serious: the biography of Joan by a former page and secretary), *The Prince and the Pauper* (about a beggar-boy changing places with King Edward VI of England, his exact double) and *A Connecticut Yankee in King Arthur's Court* (in which a man, transported back in time, startles Camelot with such 'magic' items as matches, a pocket watch and gunpowder). In Twain's best-loved books, *The Adventures of Tom Sawyer* (1876) and *The Adventures of Huckleberry Finn* (1886), he wove reminiscences of boyhood and of life on the Mississippi into an easy-going, fictional form. *Tom Sawyer* is about the scrapes, fancies and fears of boyhood. The heroes of *Huckleberry Finn*, a boy and a runaway slave, pole a raft down the Mississippi, beset by conmen, bounty-hunters and outraged citizens, and fall into slapstick adventures each time they land. Twain is regarded in the USA as a founding father of American literature, and dismissed in Europe as a children's author; he offers far slyer, far

Keith Roberts, *Kiteworld*. Ray Bradbury, *Fahrenheit 451*. ▷Paul Theroux, *O-Zone*. ▷David Cook, *Sunrising*.

READ ON ▷

▶ **To *Huckleberry Finn*:** Alphonse Daudet, *Tartarin of Tarascon*; ▷Henry Fielding, *Tom Jones*; H.E. Bates, *The Darling Buds of May*.
▶ **To Twain's travelbooks:** ▷Robert Louis Stevenson, *Travels With a Donkey* (and its sibling, ▷John Steinbeck, *Travels with Charlie*); ▷Laurence Sterne, *A Sentimental Journey*; Laurie Lee, *As I Walked Out One Midsummer Morning*.

gentler, pleasures than either view suggests.

Twain's satires include Pudd'nhead Wilson *and* Extract from Captain Stormfield's Visit to Heaven *(funny) and* The Mysterious Stranger *(serious).* Tom Sawyer Abroad *and* Tom Sawyer Detective *are novels, following Tom's adventures in adult life. Twain's short stories are collected in* The Celebrated Jumping Frog of Calaveras County and Other Sketches *and* The Man That Corrupted Hadleyburg. *His books of travel and reminiscence include* The Innocents Abroad, Roughing It, A Tramp Abroad *and* Life on the Mississippi.

U

UNDSET, Sigrid • *(1882–1949)*
Norwegian novelist.

Outside Norway, Undset is best-known for *Kristin Lavransdatter* (1920–22), a novel-trilogy set in medieval times. It follows the life of Kristin, a landowner's daughter who flies in the face of convention by insisting on marrying the man she loves. He is arrogant and unyielding, even when his political enemies imprison him and strip him of wealth and lands. Only Kristin stands by him: the book's subject is the growth of her soul, the way her Christian devotion transcends humiliation and despair. The book's bleak subject-matter is offset by Undset's warm feeling for her characters, and by her detailed, perceptive picture of 14th-century life and thought.

READ ON >

● *The Master of Hestviken.*
▶ Helen Waddell, *Héloise and Abelard.* Umberto Eco, *The Name of the Rose.* Janet Lewis, *The Trial of Sören Kvist.*

UNLOOKED-FOR FRIENDSHIPS

▷David Cook, *Winter Doves*
▷Tove Jansson, *The Summer Book*
▷Alison Lurie, *Foreign Affairs*
▷Joseph Olshan, *A Warmer Season*
▷C.P. Snow, *The Light and the Dark*
▷John Steinbeck, *Of Mice and Men*
▷Morris West, *The World is Made of Glass*

UPDIKE, John • *(born 1932)*
US novelist and short-story writer.

Updike's short stories (most of them written for the *New Yorker*) are witty anecdotes about the snobberies and love-affairs of ambitious Long Island couples, or single, bril-

READ ON >

● *Of the Farm.*
▶ ▷Philip Roth, *The*

liant jokes (for example treating bacteria under a microscope as if they were guests at a trendy cocktail party). Some of his novels are in a similarly glittering, heartless style. In *Couples* (1968) a small group of bored Connecticut commuters changes sex-partners as carelessly as if playing a party game. In *The Witches of Eastwick* (1984) three bored young widows set themselves up as a coven of amateur witches, only to become sexually ensnared by a devilishly charming man. The hero of *A Month of Sundays* is a 'progressive' clergyman tortured by lust. Updike's other novels are deeper, concentrating more on the underlying pain than on the ludicrous surface of his characters' lives. The 'Rabbit' trilogy (*Rabbit, Run*; *Rabbit Redux*; *Rabbit is Rich*, 1960–81) tells the life of an ex-school sports champion who finds emotional maturity and happiness almost impossible to grasp. The hero of *Roger's Version*, a middle-aged professor, is thrown into moral turmoil by the possibility of devising a computer-program to prove the existence of God. *Marry Me*, one of Updike's most moving books, is a tragi-comedy about an adulterous affair.

THE CENTAUR · *(1963)*

George Caldwell, an eccentric, ineffective science teacher at Olinger High School in the 1950s, deflects his feelings of inadequacy by fantasising that he is Chiron, the centaur who taught the heroes of Greek myth (which makes his headmaster Zeus and his colleagues Athene, Hephaestus and Hercules), and that he has terminal stomach cancer. The book describes three days in his life, during which he is forced to come to terms with himself and with his adolescent son Peter, who idolises him. Myth-reminiscences start and end the book; its heart is more straightforward, a moving account of small-town life and of the inarticulate love between Peter and his perplexed, exasperating father.

Updike's other novels include The Poorhouse Fair, Of the Farm, The Coup *and two made from stories about a neurotic writer,* Bech, a Book *and* Bech is Back. *His story-collections include* The Same Door, Pigeon Feathers, Museums and Women, The Music School *and* Trust Me.

Ghost Writer. Arthur Laurents, *The Way We Were.* ▷Frederic Raphael, *Heaven and Earth.* ▷Angus Wilson, *Hemlock and After.* Brian Moore, *The Great Victorian Collection.*

US SMALL TOWN LIFE

Sherwood Anderson, *Winesburg, Ohio*
▷John Cheever, *Bullet Park*
▷John Irving, *The Cider House Rules*

Garrison Keillor, *Lake Wobegon Days*
Arthur Laurents, *The Way We Were*

Deep South, USA (p 55)

V

VARGAS LLOSA, Mario • *(born 1936)*
Peruvian novelist.

An admirer of ▷Márquez, Vargas Llosa uses magic realism to give a similarly mordant view of South American life and politics. His books with contemporary settings are his sharpest: *Aunt Julia and the Scriptwriter* (1983) sends up big-city life; *The City and the Dogs/The Time of the Hero* (1962) is a satire on fascism set in a gung-ho, brutal military academy. His finest book, *The War of the End of the World* (1981), is quieter. Ostensibly a historical novel about the setting-up (and savage dismantling by the authorities) of a religious community for drop-outs and derelicts – the kind of people Christ himself might have chosen to wait for the apocalypse at the turn of the 19th/20th centuries – it spreads tendrils of fantasy into every area of social, religious, military and political life.

Vargas Llosa's other novels include The Green House, Conversation in the Cathedral *and* Captain Pantoja and the Special Service. The Cubs *is a collection of short stories.* The Perpetual Orgy *is a book-length musing about* ▷Flaubert's Madame Bovary, *part literary criticism, part reconstruction, part anthology: it is magic realism and non-fiction, hand in hand.*

VERNE, Jules • *(1828–1905)*
French novelist.

Verne began writing in the 1860s, the heyday of both exploration and popular science – and his inspiration was to mix the two. His stories mimic the memoirs of real-life explorers of the time, fabulous adventures narrated in sober, business-like prose – and, by stirring in scientific

READ ON ▷

▶ **To Vargas Llosa's fiction:** ▷Isabel Allende, *Of Love and Shadows*; ▷Gabriel García Márquez, *The Autumn of the Patriarch*; Augusto Roa Bastos, *I the Supreme*.
▶ **To *The Perpetual Orgy*:** Julian Barnes, *Flaubert's Parrot*.

READ ON ▷

▶ ▷A. Conan Doyle, *The Lost World*. ▷H.G. Wells, *The First Men in the Moon*. ▷H. Rider Haggard, *She*.

wonders impossible or unlikely at the time, he tips them into fantasy. His heroes are not tethered to the surface of the Earth: they tunnel towards its core (*Journey to the Centre of the Earth*), live underwater (*Twenty Thousand Leagues Under the Sea*) and ride rockets into space (*From the Earth to the Moon*; *Round the Moon*). Alternately with these 'scientific' adventure-stories, Verne produced tales of more orthodox derring-do: *Michel Strogoff*, for example, is a gentleman-adventurer whose bravery saves Civilisation as We Know It; in *Round the World in Eighty Days* Phileas Fogg embarks on a crazy balloon-journey to win a bet. Modern science has outstripped most of Verne's inventions, but few later SF writers have bettered him in straight-down-the-line, thrill-in-every-paragraph adventure.

C.S. Lewis, *That Hideous Strength*. Edgar Rice Burroughs, *Pirates of Venus*. ▷E.E. 'Doc' Smith, *The Imperial Stars*. ▷Kurt Vonnegut, *The Sirens of Titan*.

VIDAL, Gore • *(born 1925)*
US novelist and non-fiction writer.

Vidal made his name as a tart-tongued, witty commentator on 1960s and 1970s life, a favourite chat-show guest. Whatever the topic, from the rotation of crops to the horror of nazi concentration camps, from zen to flower-arranging, he had something interesting to say. The same protean brilliance fills his novels. Whether their subject is homosexuality (*The City and the Pillar*, 1948/65), the excesses of the film industry (*Myra Breckinridge*, 1968) or US politics (the tetralogy *Burr*, *1876*, *Washington DC* and *Empire* 1967–86), they are original, stimulating and engrossing. This is particularly so in his historical novels, where he makes his alternative view of past events seem more attractive than reality itself. *Julian* is a study of the last pagan Roman emperor, who tried to stop the rush of Christianity in the name of (as Vidal sees it) the more humane, more generous Olympian religion. *Creation* is the memoirs of an imaginary Persian nobleman of the 5th century BC, who went as ambassador to India, China and Greece and knew Confucius, Buddha and Socrates. *Lincoln* refocuses our view of the thoughts and achievements of the 16th US president.

KALKI • *(1978)*
Teddy Ottinger, a test pilot, is summoned to the Tibetan ashram of the mysterious Kalki. Born an American, James Kelly, Kalki has settled in the Himalayas after the Vietnam war and announced that he is the tenth avatar of the god Vishnu and that his coming to earth means the end of the present cycle of human existence. The book, a witty intellectual thriller, shows how Kalki's prophecy is ful-

> ## READ ON

● *Duluth*.
▶ **To *Kalki*:** ▷Richard Condon, *Winter Kills*; ▷Kurt Vonnegut, *Galápagos*.
▶ **To Vidal's historical novels:** Peter Green, *The Sword of Pleasure* (set in republican Rome); John Hersey, *The Wall* (about US missionaries in China); John Barth, *The Sotweed Factor* (set in Maryland in the time of the Pilgrim Fathers).
▶ **To Vidal's novels in general:** ▷Kingsley Amis, *The Alteration*; ▷Patrick White, *The Twyborn Affair*; ▷Muriel Spark, *The Ballad of Peckham Rye*.

filled, and what happens to Teddy and the few other survivors in a world left unchanged except that all human life has ceased.

Vidal's other novels include Williwaw, In a Yellow Wood, The Season of Comfort, Two Sisters, Myron *and* Duluth. *He also wrote detective stories (including* Death in the Fifth Position*) under the name* Edgar Box. A Thirsty Evil *is a collection of short stories.*

VONNEGUT, Kurt • *(born 1922)*
US novelist.

SF ideas shape Vonnegut's novels – and so do autobiography, political and social satire, loonish humour and a furious, nagging rage at the way the human race is pillaging the world. *Galápagos* (1985) begins at the moment of nuclear apocalypse (which is triggered by a bomber-pilot fantasising that firing his missile is like having sex). A group of people, gathered in Ecuador for the 'Nature Cruise of the Century', find that their ship has become a Noah's Ark: they are the sole survivors of humankind. They land in the Galápagos Islands, equipped with no technology except a computer whose memory is stuffed with 1000 dead languages and a million quotations from the world's great literature, and set about survival. At first they are hampered, as (Vonnegut claims) the human race has been handicapped throughout its existence, by the enormous size of their brains, attics of unnecessary thought. But Galápagos is the cradle of the evolutionary theory – and that may be humanity's last hope.

Vonnegut's other novels are Player Piano; The Sirens of Titan; Mother Night; Cat's Cradle; God Bless You, Mr Rosewater; Slaughterhouse Five; Breakfast of Champions; Slapstick; Jailbird; Palm Sunday *and* Deadeye Dick. Canary in a Cathouse *and* Welcome to the Monkeyhouse *contain short stories.*

READ ON >

● *Cat's Cradle; The Sirens of Titan.*
▶ ▷Brian Aldiss, *The Primal Urge.* Frederick Pohl, *The Coming of the Quantum Cats.*
▷Michael Moorcock, *The Final Programme.*
▷Russell Hoban, *Riddley Walker.*
▷Walter M. Miller, *A Canticle for Leibowitz.*
Bamber Gascoigne, *Cod Strewth.*

W

WALKER, Alice • *(born 1944)*
US novelist, poet and non-fiction writer.

The background to Walker's books is the struggle for equal rights in the US over the last 30 years, first by blacks and then by women. Radical politics are not, however, her main concern. She writes wittily, ironically, about the follies of human life, and she is as merciless to her idealistic, college-educated activists as she is to their slobbish, mindless opponents. If ▷Mary McCarthy or ▷Alison Lurie had written about black, feminist politics, these might have been their books. *Meridian* (1976), Walker's second novel, is the splendidly ironical study of a southern black activist, educated to be a 'lady' (in the 1920s white meaning of the term), who becomes a leader in the equal-rights movements of the 1960s. When we see Meridian years later, all battles won, holed up in the small southern town of Chickokema where apart from the coming of equality nothing momentous has ever happened, she is totally confused about where all her energy, her driving-force, has gone. Was this really what her life was for?

Walker's other novels are Third Life of Grange Copeland *and* The Color Purple *(also a film). In* Love and Trouble *and* You Can't Keep a Good Woman Down *are short-story collections. She has also published poetry (*Once; Revolutionary Petunias; Willie Lee, I'll See You in the Morning) *and a book of essays,* In Search of Our Mother's Garden.

READ ON ▷

- ● *The Color Purple.*
- ▶ **To Walker's elegant, tart style:** ▷Mary McCarthy, *The Group*; ▷Muriel Spark, *The Girls of Slender Means.*
- ▶ **To her view of the bizarreness lurking inside perfectly ordinary-seeming human beings:** ▷John Irving, *The World According to Garp*; ▷Tove Jansson, *Sun City.*
- ▶ **To her politics:** ▷Lisa Alther, *Kinflicks*; Ralph Ellison, *Invisible Man.*

Lew **WALLACE**

BEN-HUR *(Christian and pagan antagonism
in ancient Rome)*

Jeanette **WINTERSON, BOATING FOR BEGINNERS**
(Noah's flood)

Thomas **MANN, JOSEPH AND HIS BROTHERS**
(– seen as allegory of 1930s fascist Europe)

Joseph **HELLER, GOD KNOWS**
('memoirs' of King David)

BIBLE OLD TESTAMENT

George **MOORE, THE BROOK KERITH**
(Joseph of Arimathea)

Pär **LAGERKVIST, BARABBAS**
(– before, during and after Christ's crucifixion)

Lloyd C. **DOUGLAS, THE ROBE**
*(effects on Roman centurion and others who inherit Christ's robe at
crucifixion)*

THE FIRST CHRISTIANS

Frank **SLAUGHTER, THE SHOES OF THE FISHERMAN**
(Peter)

Henryk **SIENKIEWYCZ, QUO VADIS?**
(first Christian converts, first martyrs)

Anthony **BURGESS, THE KINGDOM OF THE WICKED**
(missionary journeys of Paul, Luke and Barnabas)

Pasquale Festa **CAMPANILE, FOR LOVE, ONLY FOR
LOVE** *(Joseph)*

Severia **HURÉ, I, MARY, DAUGHTER OF ISRAEL**
(Mary)

Robert **GRAVES, KING JESUS**
(fulfilment of all Old Testament prophecy)

Michèle **ROBERTS, THE WILD GIRL**
(Gospel according to Mary Magdalene)

JOSEPH, MARY AND JESUS

WALLACE, Lew • *(1827-1905)*
US novelist.

Ben-Hur (1880), the best-known of Wallace's historical romances, is set in Palestine in the reign of the Roman Emperor Nero. The Jewish aristocrat Judah Ben-Hur and the Roman general Messala, once friends, quarrel over politics. Messala falsely accuses Ben-Hur of treason; Ben-Hur's lands are confiscated, his wife and mother are thrown into prison (where they contract leprosy) and he himself is condemned to the galleys. He escapes, leads a resistance-movement against the Romans, wreaks vengeance on Messala during a chariot-race in the Coliseum (the book's action-climax), rescues his mother and wife and takes them to be healed by the preacher Jesus. They are converted to Christianity, and the book ends with a moving scene as they witness Christ's crucifixion. Wallace's Christianity is somewhat preachy, but his depiction of the grandeur and decadence of ancient Rome, of the resistance-movement in Palestine and of the fervour of early Christian converts is unsurpassed.

Wallace's other novels include The Fair God, *a novel of Cortez' invasion of Mexico, and* The Prince of India, *which culminates in a magnificent description of the Turkish siege of Constantinople in 1453. Wallace's Autobiography is almost as swaggering as his fiction, particularly about his time as a general during the American Civil War.*

READ ON ▷

▶ **To *Ben-Hur*:** Henryk Sienkiewycz, *Quo Vadis?*; Lord Lytton, *The Last Days of Pompeii.*
▶ **To Wallace's work in general:** ▷Walter Scott, *Ivanhoe*; ▷Victor Hugo, *Notre-Dame de Paris.*

WAR: BEHIND THE LINES

▷Noel Barber, *A Woman of Cairo*
▷Elizabeth Bowen, *The Heat of the Day*
　Elizabeth Darrell, *At the Going Down of the Sun*
▷Jaroslav Hašek, *The Good Soldier Švejk*
▷Ernest Hemingway, *A Farewell to Arms*
▷Thomas Keneally, *Schindler's Ark*
▷Neville Shute, *What Happened to the Corbetts*
▷Lev Tolstoy, *War and Peace*

Terrorists/Freedom Fighters (p 234); War: Front Line (p 254)

WAR: FRONT LINE

▷Len Deighton, *Bomber*
  Emma Drummond, *Forget the Glory*
  William Fairchild, *The Poppy Factory*
▷Joseph Heller, *Catch-22*
▷Ernest Hemingway, *For Whom the Bell Tolls*
  Alistair Maclean, *The Guns of Navarone*
▷Norman Mailer, *The Naked and the Dead*
  Erich Maria Remarque, *All Quiet on the Western Front*

WAUGH, Evelyn • *(1903–66)*
British novelist.

Waugh's main work was a series of tart satires on 1930s attitudes and manners. His vacuous, amiable heroes stumble through life, unsurprised by anything that happens. By chance, they land in the centre of affairs (political, business and sexual) and their presence triggers a sequence of ever more ludicrous events. Innocence is their only saving grace: Waugh's views were that the world is silly but dangerous, and that those who think they understand it are the most vulnerable of all. He was particularly venomous about British high society, depicting the ruling class as a collection of alcohol-swilling Hooray Henries or Henriettas, whose chief pastimes are partying (if young) and interfering in public life (if old). That class apart, the range of his scorn was vast. *Decline and Fall* sends up (among other things) the English prep school system, *Black Mischief* mocks tyranny in an African state emerging from colonialism, *Scoop* satirises gutter journalism and *The Ordeal of Gilbert Pinfold* (1957) mercilessly details the hallucinations of an alcoholic author on a detestable ocean cruise. The second-world-war trilogy *Sword of Honour* (1965) sets Waugh's foolish heroes in the context of truly dangerous, genuinely lunatic real events, and *Brideshead Revisited* (1945) is a more serious book still, the study of an aristocratic Catholic family collapsing under the weight of centuries of unconsidered privilege.

A HANDFUL OF DUST • *(1934)*
The book begins with standard Waugh farce: a pin-headed society wife, Brenda Last, takes a lover to occupy her afternoons. But the effect on her husband Tony and son John is devastating, and the book moves quickly from

READ ON ⟩

● *Scoop*.
▶ William Boyd, *A Good Man in Africa*.
▷Malcolm Bradbury, *Eating People is Wrong*. David Lodge, *How Far Can You Go?*
▷P.H. Newby, *The Picnic at Sakkara*.
▷John Updike, *The Coup*.

farce to tragedy. Waugh never abandons the ridiculous –
no one else would have placed his hero in impenetrable
tropical jungle, the slave of a megalomaniac who makes
him read *Edwin Drood* aloud – but he also writes with
compassion for his characters, involving us in their loneliness as his shallower novels never do.

Waugh's other novels are Vile Bodies, Put Out More
Flags *and* The Loved One. *His travel-books include* Remote People *and* Waugh in Abyssinia. *His* Diaries *and his
autobiography* A Little Learning *are a revealing blend of
pity for himself and mercilessness to others.*

WEBSTER, Jan • *(born 1924)*
British novelist.

Webster writes family sagas, spanning many generations.
Her best-known books are the sequence *Colliers Row*,
Saturday City and *Beggarman's Country*, set in the Glas-
gow slums.

READ ON ▷

► ▷Maisie Mosco,
Almonds and Raisins.
Helen Forrester,
*Twopence to Cross
the Mersey*. Sarah
Shears, *Louise*.

WEDDINGS

  Elizabeth Colegate, *Statues in a Garden*
▷Carson McCullers, *The Member of the Wedding*
  Elizabeth North, *Worldly Goods*
▷Eudora Welty, *Delta Wedding*

WEEPIES

▷Charlotte Brontë, *Jane Eyre*
▷Daphne Du Maurier, *Rebecca*
▷Brenda Jagger, *A Song Twice Over*
▷Norah Lofts, *The Brittle Glass*
▷Margaret Mitchell, *Gone With the Wind*
▷Boris Pasternak, *Doctor Zhivago*
▷Erich Segal, *Love Story*
  Mrs Henry Wood, *East Lynne*

WEIDMAN, Jerome • *(born 1913)*
US novelist.

The typical Weidman hero is a successful banker or businessman. Forced by some crisis to look back over the past, he recounts the story of his life and the influences which have made him what he is. Many of the men are Jewish, the sons of poor European immigrants in the early years of the century; the novels are warm-hearted, Dickensian stories of the struggle for existence in the sweatshops and back-streets of 1930s New York, and of young men rising, by brains, luck or adroitness – some of them are crooks – to the positions they hold today. Without exception, Weidman's characters are creations of the American dream – and every one of them feels compromised, as if material success has eroded the moral value-system which helped their parents in their first years in the USA, and which supported their own childhood and growing up.

OTHER PEOPLE'S MONEY • *(1967)*
In 1915, three-year-old Victor is made the foster-son of rich Walter Weld and his wife. Five years later another orphan, Philip Brandwine, joins the household. The novel recounts the boys' childhood, their young manhood, their service in the second world war – and their rivalry for the love of Harriet Weld, their foster-sister. Its subsidiary theme is the character-clash between the two men: Philip is charismatic, dazzling and untrustworthy, Victor is meticulous, earnest and unquestioningly loyal. Their relationship collapses during the second world war, only to be rebuilt afterwards, in the agonising reunion which starts and ends the book. Over everything hovers an enigma, unsolved until the book's last page: what was there about the boys that made the Welds take them as foster-sons in the first place?

Weidman's novels include I Can Get it for You Wholesale, Your Daughter Iris, The Enemy Camp, The Center of the Action, The Temple *and* A Family Fortune. *His short-story collections include* The Horse That Could Whistle Dixie, My Father Sits in the Dark *and* The Death of Dickie Draper. Praying for Rain *is autobiography.*

WELDON, Fay • *(born 1933)*
British novelist and screen-writer.

A TV dramatist, Weldon writes novels in short, screenplay-like scenes full of dialogue: her books are like sinis-

READ ON

● *Fourth Street East* (and its sequels *Last Respects* and *Tiffany Street*).
▶ Budd Schulberg, *What Makes Sammy Run?*.
▷ Mordecai Richler, *The Apprenticeship of Duddy Kravitz*. ▷ Saul Bellow, *The Adventures of Augie March*. E.L. Doctorow, *World's Fair*. Louis Auchincloss, *Venus in Sparta*.

READ ON

● *The Hearts and Lives of Men*.

ter sit-coms turned into prose. In the 1970s she was re-garded as a leading feminist writer, and 'women's experience' is a major theme. Her heroines are ordinary people resisting the need to define themselves as someone else's wife, lover or mother, and missing the traditional cosiness such roles afford. Individuality can only be bought at the cost of psychic discomfort – and this is often intensified by the malice of others and by the hostility of the environment: witchcraft and the venomousness of na-ture add spice to Weldon's plots. Her books are fast, funny and furious; but their underlying ideas, especially for male chauvinist pigs, are no joke at all.

PUFFBALL · (1980)

Liffey, married to boring, ambitious Richard, longs to live in a country cottage; Richard wants a child. They strike a bargain, move to the wolds near Glastonbury and do their best to get Liffey pregnant. Almost at once the idyll turns to nightmare. The cottage has few facilities; there are no commuter-trains to London; their neighbour is a child-beater and an amateur witch. As the baby grows in Lif-fey's womb and Richard, alone in London for five days a week, consoles himself, Mabs (the neighbour) tries every trick of witchcraft, from potions to pin-stuck wax models, to make Liffey abort her child. *Puffball* is a romantic novel for grown-up people – and the games Weldon plays with our longing for a happy ending give the plot some of its most devastating, satisfying twists.

Weldon's other novels include Down Among the Women, Female Friends, The President's Child, Little Sisters, Praxis, Watching Me Watching You, The Life and Loves of a She-Devil, The Shrapnel Academy *and* The Heart of England. The Rules of Life *is an SF novella.*

WELLS, H.G. (Herbert George) ·
(1866–1946)
British writer of novels, short stories and non-fiction.

Wells' early novels were science fantasies, imagining what it would be like if people could travel in time (*The Time Machine*, 1895) or space (*The First Men in the Moon*, 1901), or how the Earth might defend itself against extra-terrestrial attacks (*The War of the Worlds*, 1898). Like ▷Verne, Wells predicted many inventions and dis-coveries now taken for granted: in *The War in the Air* (1908) for example, he forecast fleets of warplanes and bombers in the days when the Wright brothers were still headline news. For all their scientific wonders, these novels are full of pessimism about society: wherever peo-

▶ ▷Margaret Atwood, *Life Before Man.* Marge Piercy, *The High Cost of Living.* Mary Gordon, *The Company of Women.* Penelope Mortimer, *Long Distance.* Alice Thomas Ellis, *Unexplained Laughter.* Maggie Gee, *Light Years.*

> **READ ON**

▶ **To Wells' SF:** ▷Jules Verne, *Twenty Thousand Leagues Under the Sea*; C.S. Lewis, *Out of the Silent Planet*; H.P. Lovecraft, *The Shadow over Innsmouth.*
▶ **To his social comedies:** ▷Arnold Bennett, *The Card*; Hugh Walpole, *Mr*

ple go, they find barbarism, oppression and misery. *The Island of Doctor Moreau* (1896), about a mad scientist hybridising humans and animals on a lonely island, brings the pessimism nearer home. Side by side with such morbid fantasies, Wells wrote a series of utterly different books. They are genial social comedies, about ordinary people (shop-assistants, clerks) who decide that the way to find happiness is to break out and 'make a go of things'. Sometimes (as in *Ann Veronica*, about a 1910s girl determined on emancipation despite the wishes of her family) Wells' message is polemical; but most of the books – *Love and Mr Lewisham, Kipps, The History of Mr Polly* – replace propaganda with an indulgent, enthusiastic view of human enterprise.

TONO-BUNGAY • *(1909)*

George Ponderevo goes to live with his uncle Toby. He helps Toby market a marvellous new elixir, Tono-Bungay: it is the answer to the world's problems, the health, wealth and happiness of humankind in a bottle. The Tono-Bungay fortune swells by the minute – and then George discovers that the product is 99% distilled water. The discovery presents George with unresolvable moral dilemmas of all kinds. Does it matter what Tono-Bungay is made of, if it does what it claims to do? Is Toby a crook or does he genuinely believe he is benefiting humankind? How can George bankrupt those he loves – and in the process destroy his own chances of a happy marriage and a prosperous home? He puts off the decision, and in the meantime continues his hobby: pioneer aviation. In the end, technology – the lighter-than-air-machine itself – comes to the rescue: a charming example of Wells' view that all moral and social dilemmas can be solved by science.

Wells' other science-fantasies include When the Sleeper Wakes, The Food of the Gods *and the story-collections* Tales of Space and Time *and* The Country of the Blind and Other Stories. *His other novels include* Mr Blettsworthy on Rampole Island, *a savage anti-totalitarian satire.*

WELLS, Eudora • *(born 1909)*
US novelist and short-story writer.

Unlike such writers as ▷Faulkner or ▷McCullers, who saw the southern United States as a kind of hell tenanted by freaks and degenerates, Welty treated them as paradise. The countryside is lush; birds and animals teem; all nature is in harmony. Human beings are at the heart of the

Perrin and Mr Traill; ▷David Cook, *Missing Persons.*

> **READ ON**

● *Losing Battles* (more farcical, set not among cotton barons but in a sleepy, dim-witted farming-community, but

idyll – and Welty shows them as uncomprehending innocents. The 'Negroes' – she is writing about times long gone – are children of nature, at peace with their environment. The 'White Folks', by contrast, feel edgy. They sense that they are corrupt, that their presence threatens Eden; but they have no idea what the matter is, and all they can do is live as they always have and hope that things will be all right, that nothing will change. The surface events in Welty's books are a mosaic of ordinariness – parties, children's games, chance meetings in town or at the bathing-station – but underlying them all is a sense of fragility, of impending loss. Her characters are living in a dream, comfortable and comforting, but it is only a dream, and already we, and they, sense the first chill of wakefulness.

DELTA WEDDING • (1946)

In the 1920s, nine-year-old Laura travels to her uncle's plantation in the Mississippi Delta, to help in preparations for her cousin's wedding. She revels in the eccentric, affectionate rough-and-tumble of cousins, great-aunts, visitors (and dozens of blacks, as friendly and unconsidered as household pets); she climbs trees, bakes cakes, guesses riddles, listens to gossip as the wedding-dress is sewn. Welty also shows the preparations through the eyes of the bride's parents, the bride and groom themselves, and an assortment of servants, friends and neighbours. The wedding brings a whole community into focus – and we are shown, with persistent, gentle irony, that it is not just the bride and groom who must undergo a rite of passage, but the South itself.

Welty's other novels are The Robber Bridegroom, The Ponder Heart, The Optimist's Daughter *and* Losing Battles. *Her short stories are collected in* A Curtain of Green, The Wide Net, The Golden Apples *and* The Bride of Innisfallen.

WEST, Morris • *(born 1916)*
Australian novelist.

West's books are fast-moving moral thrillers, stories not of espionage or crime but of the solution of ethical dilemmas. The hero of *The Shoes of the Fisherman* is a saintly iron-curtain prelate who is elected Pope. *The Clowns of God* is about another Pope forced to abdicate because he has seen a vision predicting the imminent end of the world, and proposes to publicise the fact. In *The Navigator* (1981) a group of people sails to find the Polynesian

with the same undertone of devastating moral condemnation).
► ▷Randall Jarrell, *Pictures from an Institution.* ▷L.P. Hartley, *The Go-Between.* ▷Colette, *The Ripening Seed.* ▷Evelyn Waugh, *Brideshead Revisited.* Robert Penn Warren, *All the King's Men.* Lillian Hellman, *Pentimento.*

> **READ ON**

● *The Devil's Advocate.*
► ▷Jerome Weidman, *The Temple.* Frank Slaughter, *Epidemic.* ▷Neville Shute, *Requiem for a Wren.* ▷C.P. Snow, *The Sleep of Reason.* ▷Thomas Keneally,

paradise to which all human souls, the myth says, go after death; they are led by a man who is either a visionary, a charlatan or mad. *The Ambassador* (1965) is about a conscientious US ambassador who resigns over his country's policy in South Vietnam. Moral dilemmas like these are nowadays more common in films than in novels – and anyone who enjoyed *Platoon*, say, or *The Killing Fields* will find the experience of West's novels much the same.

THE WORLD IS MADE OF GLASS · *(1983)*

In Vienna in 1913, the psychiatrist Jung treats a woman who regards him more as a confessor than a healer – and the experience brings him hard up against his sense of his own moral failure, both as a doctor and as a man.

West's other novels include Children of the Sun, The Devil's Advocate, Daughter of Silence, The Tower of Babel, Summer of the Red Wolf, The Salamander *and* Harlequin.

Three Cheers for the Paraclete. Brian Moore, *The Colour of Blood*.

WEST, Nathanael · *(1906–40)*
US novelist and screenwriter.

West wrote rubbishy films for a living: their titles include *Rhythm in the Clouds, Born to be Wild* and *Hallelujah I'm a Bum*. To please himself, he wrote four satirical novels, dark black comedies a million miles from Hollywood. The hero of *Miss Lonelyhearts* (1933) is a cynical newspaperman assigned to the agony column. He begins by despising the wretches who write for advice, but soon begins to pity them and finally leaves his desk to intervene in one case personally, with fatal but farcical results.

West's other novels are The Dream Life of Balso Snell, A Cool Million *and* The Day of the Locust.

> **READ ON** ⟩

● *The Day of the Locust* (a bleakly funny send-up of Hollywood).
▶ Joe Orton, *Head to Toe*. Budd Schulberg, *What Makes Sammy Run?*. ▷Aldous Huxley, *After Many a Summer*. ▷Mordecai Richler, *Cocksure*. Thorne Smith, *The Bishop's Jaegers*.

WHARTON, Edith · *(1862–1937)*
US writer of novels, short stories and non-fiction.

A society hostess, Wharton caused outrage by writing with ironical rage about the complacency and shallowness of her own class. (She later described high society as 'frivolous..., able to acquire dramatic significance only through what its frivolity destroys'.) In 1907 she moved to Europe and broadened her scope, writing two Hardyesque rural tragedies (*Ethan Frome, Summer*), several books set in Europe (including *The Reef*, which her friend ▷Henry James admired) and some atmospheric ghost stories. But she regularly returned to her favourite theme, the stifling

> **READ ON** ⟩

● *The Custom of the Country*.
▶ Ellen Glasgow, *Barren Ground*. Louis Auchincloss, *A World of Profit*. ▷George Eliot, *Middlemarch*. ▷William Thackeray, *Vanity Fair*. ▷Elizabeth Taylor, *The Wedding*

Edith WHARTON

THE HOUSE OF MIRTH *(woman rebels against 1900s New York high society)*

Thomas **HARDY**, **FAR FROM THE MADDING CROWD**
(tragic life and love in 19th-century rural England)

William **THACKERAY**, **VANITY FAIR**
(two girls' ambitions to conquer 1810s English high society)

Theodore **DREISER**, **AN AMERICAN TRAGEDY**
(ambition, crime and punishment in lower-class 1920s New York)

Nathaniel **HAWTHORNE**, **THE HOUSE OF THE SEVEN GABLES** *(New England family cursed for generations because of religious intolerance)*

'PLAYTHINGS OF DESTINY'

Gustave **FLAUBERT**, **MADAME BOVARY**
(mid-19th-century small-town France)

Margaret **ATWOOD**, **THE HANDMAID'S TALE**
(21st-century fundamentalist Republic of Gilead)

Olivia **MANNING**, **THE RAIN FOREST**
(retreat for psychological misfits on island 'paradise')

Alison **LURIE**, **THE WAR BETWEEN THE TATES**
('progressive' US university)

STIFLING COMMUNITIES

Emily **BRONTË**, **WUTHERING HEIGHTS**
(1800s Yorkshire: a woman loves brutal, 'child-of-nature' foster-brother)

Helen **WADDELL**, **HÉLOÏSE AND ABELARD**
(12th-century Paris: a monk falls in love with beautiful pupil)

Victor **HUGO**, **NOTRE DAME DE PARIS**
(14th-century Paris: hunchback tries to protect beautiful gipsy from men who would debauch her)

Hermann **HESSE**, **GERTRUD**
(1890s German university: two students, friends, love the same woman)

AGAINST THE ODDS

Anthony **TROLLOPE**, **DOCTOR THORNE**
(snobbery, illegitimacy and inheritance among 19th-century English landed gentry)

Sinclair **LEWIS**, **BABBITT**
(wealthy, morally empty merchant tries to break free of sterile small-town conformity)

Angus **WILSON**, **LATE CALL**
(widow lives with uncongenial son in soulless 1960s British 'new town')

John **UPDIKE**, **RABBIT, RUN**
(ex-high-school sports star tries to adjust to adult mediocrity)

PRESSURE TO CONFORM

conventions of 1870s-1920s New York high life – and it is on this that her reputation rests. Her enemies put her down as a clumsy imitator of James. But whereas he showed his characters' psychological innerness, she was interested in manners, in events. She also wrote shorter, wittier sentences, and crisper dialogue. Except that her subject-matter is so sombre, she is more like Oscar Wilde than James.

THE HOUSE OF MIRTH • *(1905)*

Lily Bart, a beautiful, sharp-witted girl, has been conditioned to luxury from birth. Unfortunately she is an orphan, living on a small allowance. She gambles at cards, loses, and because of her moral scruples (she refuses to work off her debts by becoming the mistress of a wealthy creditor), she ends up poorer and more desperate than ever. Faced with the choice of marrying either a rich man she despises (not least because he is a Jew, something her WASPish upbringing has taught her to abhor) or the penniless man she loves, she chooses neither – and soon afterwards, as the result of scandalous accusation, loses her position in society. She moves into cheap lodgings and sinks into despair. She has achieved moral integrity, broken free of her upbringing, but in the process, because of that upbringing, she has destroyed herself.

Wharton's other New York books include the novels The Custom of the Country, The Age of Innocence *and* Old New York, *and the short-story collections* The Descent of Man, Xingu, Certain People *and* Human Nature. Ghosts *contains ghost-stories, and* A Backward Glance *is autobiography, interesting on her friendship with Henry James.*

WHITE, Antonia • *(1899-1979)*
British novelist.

A journalist and translator (notably of ▷Colette), White is remembered for four deeply-felt autobiographical novels. *Frost in May* (1933) is the story of a child at a grim convent boarding school. The nuns' mission is to 'break' each pupil like a horse – to tame her for Christ – and the book remorselessly charts the series of small emotional humiliations they inflict on the heroine, which have entirely the opposite effect to the one they planned. In the later novels White's heroine works as an actress (*The Lost Traveller*, 1950), tries to combine serious writing with work as a copy-writer (*The Sugar House*, 1952), and finally (*Beyond the Glass*, 1954), in the course of a terrifying mental illness, exorcises the ghosts of Catholicism and her relationship with her father, the influences which have both de-

Group. Mary Wesley, *Not That Sort of Girl.*

READ ON ▷

▶ **To *Frost in May*:**
▷James Joyce, *Portrait of the Artist as a Young Man*; Jane Gardam, *Bilgewater*; ▷Thomas Keneally, *Three Cheers for the Paraclete.*

▶ **To *Beyond the Glass*:** Sylvia Plath, *The Bell Jar.*

▶ **To White's work in general:** ▷Rosamond Lehmann, *Dusty Answer*; ▷Rose

fined and deformed her life.

White's other books include the short-story collection
Strangers, *and* The Hound and the Falcon, *an account in
letter-form of her return to Catholicism.*

WHITE, Patrick • *(born 1912)*
Australian novelist and playwright.

White was interested in Nietzsche's idea of 'superbeings',
people endowed with qualities or abilities which set them
apart from the rest of the human race. But White's characters are cursed, not blessed, by difference: their chief attri-
bute is a cantankerous individuality which makes it impossible for them to adjust to society or it to them. In some
books (eg *Riders in the Chariot*, about anti-semitism, or
The Vivisector, about a convention-defying painter) the
'enemy' is the stifling gentility of lower-middle-class Sydney suburbanites. In others (eg *The Tree of Man*, about a
young farmer in the 1900s, or *A Fringe of Leaves*, 1976,
see right), the battle is more symbolic, against the wilderness itself. But wherever conflict takes place, it is of epic
proportions: White's craggy prose puts him in the company of such past writers as ▷Melville or ▷Conrad, and
in the 20th century only ▷Golding equals his blend of
fast-paced story-telling and brooding philosophical
allegory.

VOSS • *(1957)*
In 1857, financed by a group of Sydney businessmen, a
group of explorers sets out to cross Australia. The expedition is led by the German visionary Voss: physically awkward, ill-at-ease in towns and houses, speaking a tortured,
poetic English which sounds as if he learned it by rote,
phrase by painful phrase. The other members include an
ex-convict and a dreamy aboriginal boy, Jackie, torn between the white people's culture and his own. White bal-
ances reports of the expedition's struggle against the desert and to understand one another with accounts of the life
of Laura Trevelyan, a young woman fascinated by Voss
(at first as a larger-than-life character, an epic personality,
and then as a vulnerable human being) as she waits in
Sydney, like a medium hoping for spirit-messages, for
news of him.

White's other novels are Happy Valley, The Living and
the Dead, The Aunt's Story *(a comedy about an indomita-
ble spinster travelling alone),* The Solid Mandala, The
Eye of the Storm *and* The Twyborn Affair. The Burnt
Ones *and* The Cockatoos *are collections of short stories.*

Macaulay, *The World
My Wilderness.*

> **READ ON**

● *A Fringe of Leaves*
(about a woman
shipwrecked in
Queensland in the
1840s, who is captured
by aborigines and
brought to terms not
only with an alien
culture but with her
feelings about the
'civilisation' she knew
before).
▶ **To** *Voss:* ▷William
Golding, *Darkness
Visible;* ▷H.H.
Richardson, *The
Fortunes of Richard
Mahony;* Paul Bowles,
The Sheltering Sky;
▷Joseph Conrad, *The
Nigger of the
Narcissus.*
▶ **To** *A Fringe of
Leaves:* ▷D.H.
Lawrence, *The Plumed
Serpent;* ▷Katharine
Susannah Prichard,
Coonardoo.
▶ **To White's work in
general:** ▷Christina
Stead, *The Man Who
Loved Children;* Joyce
Cary, *The Horse's
Mouth;* ▷Elizabeth
Taylor, *Blaming.*

Flaws in the Glass *is an autobiography, good on White's own battles against the wilderness (he was an outback farmer) and against convention (he is homosexual).*

WILDER, Thornton • *(1897–1975)*
US novelist and playwright.

Wilder is known for plays as well as novels: *The Matchmaker* (source of the musical *Hello, Dolly*), *Our Town*, *The Skin of Our Teeth* and many others. His works explore an idea he called 'simultaneity'. Time is not progressive but circular, our destinies move in cycles, and when people's cycles coincide (like the overlapping Olympic rings), that is the moment of simultaneity, of crisis, in all their lives. In his best-known novel, *The Bridge of San Luis Rey* (1927), the moment of simultaneity is the collapse of a bridge in 18th-century Peru; the book tells the lives of each of the five people killed in the disaster, reaching a climax at the exact instant when the bridge falls in.

THE IDES OF MARCH • *(1948)*
This historical novel charts, in a series of imaginary letters, the converging destinies of a group of people in ancient Rome; it ends on the morning of the Ides of March, 44 BC, as Julius Caesar leaves for the senate-house where (history tells us) he was due to be assassinated. The letter-writers are Caesar himself, Brutus, Cassius, Mark Antony, the poet Catullus, the dissolute aristocrats Clodius and Clodia (symptomatic of the decadent old ruling families Caesar was hoping to replace), and Wilder's purpose is to show how, given those people and circumstances, Caesar's death and the ensuing civil war were inevitable.

Wilder's other novels are The Cabala, The Woman of Andros, Heaven's My Destination, The Eighth Day *and* Theophilus North.

WILSON, Angus • *(born 1913)*
British novelist and short-story writer.

Wilson is a nuclear-age successor to the great Victorian novelists. His plots are expansive, his pages teem with characters and his style is pungently satirical. His middle-class heroes and heroines, often members of the professions, have large, quarrelsome families; adultery, homosexuality, shady dealing and the conflict between public

READ ON ▷

● *The Bridge of San Luis Rey.*
▶ To *The Ides of March:* Marguerite Yourcenar, *Memoirs of Hadrian*; John Arden, *Silence Among the Weapons*; ▷Mary Renault, *The Last of the Wine*; Hilda Doolittle ('H.D.'), *Hedylus.*
▶ **Other books, of different periods and on different themes, but all concerned with our perception of time:** ▷James Joyce, *Ulysses*; ▷Lawrence Durrell, *Tunc* and *Numquam*; ▷Salman Rushdie, *Midnight's Children.*
▶ **To Wilder's work in general:** ▷Günter Grass, *The Flounder*; Osbert Sitwell, short stories.

READ ON ▷

● *As If By Magic.*
▶ **To Wilson's novels:** ▷Iris Murdoch, *The Sandcastle*; ▷Willa Cather, *The Professor's House*;

and private duty shape their lives. The 'public' plot of *Hemlock and After* (1952) is about a novelist trying to establish a writers' centre in a large, old house; the 'private' plot concerns his anguish about his own homosexuality. *The Old Men at the Zoo* (1961) is a satire set in a future Britain threatened by a united Europe and defeated by its own penchant for replacing action with committee rhetoric. The heroine of *The Middle Age of Mrs Eliot* (1958), unexpectedly widowed, throws off the home-counties mask and embarks on a raffish odyssey across the world, a quest to find herself. In *Late Call* (1964) another lower-middle-class matron, forced to live with her widowed, unloved son, has to come to terms with the soulless New Town he lives in, a reflection both of his own inner desolation and of the emotional wasteland between them where once was love. *Setting the World on Fire* (1980) is a study of the lives and relationships of two brothers, one a finicky lawyer, the other an artist (an experimental theatre director). As well as his novels, Wilson's short stories are much admired. They are sharp anecdotes of emotional ineptness, often involving the clash between middle-aged parents and their children or between ill-matched lovers.

ANGLO-SAXON ATTITUDES · (1956)
Gerald Middleton is a rich, successful academic (a historian of Anglo-Saxon England). His personal life is a shambles: he lives apart from his wife, dislikes his children and grandchildren, squabbles with his colleagues and has lost touch with his friends. Faced with the need to accept or reject an important academic task, he begins to think again about the greatest, and oddest, archaeological discovery of his youth 50 years before: an obscene pagan statue in the tomb of a 7th-century Christian missionary. Was it a hoax – and if so, if this is yet another lie on which he has built his life, what can he do now to set things right?

Wilson's other novels are No Laughing Matter *and* As If By Magic. The Wrong Set, Such Darling Dodos *and* A Bit Off the Map *are collections of short stories.*

WODEHOUSE, P.G. (Pelham Grenville) ·
(1881–1975)
British novelist.

In the 1920s and 1930s Wodehouse wrote Broadway shows, and he once described his novels as 'musical comedy without the music'. There are over 100 of them, gloriously frivolous romps set in high society 1920s England

Peter Taylor, *A Summons to Memphis.*
▶ **To the short stories:**
V.S. Pritchett, *The Camberwell Beauty*;
Mary Gordon, *Temporary Shelter.*

READ ON

● *Summer Lightning.*
▶ Ben Travers, *Rookery Nook* (novel version).
Richard Gordon,

or among dyspeptic US newspaper magnates and film tycoons. Wodehouse's gormless heroes are in love with
'pips' and 'peacherinos'. Before they can marry they must
persuade dragon-like relatives (usually aunts) to give reluctant consent or to part with cash – and the persuasion often involves stealing valuable jewels (to earn undying
gratitude when they are 'found' again), smuggling the girl
into the house disguised (so that the radiance of her personality will charm all opposition) or blackmail (threatening to reveal embarrassing secrets of the relative's miss-
pent youth). There are two main novel-series, the Jeeves
books (in which Bertie Wooster consistently makes an ass
of himself, usually by being the fall-guy in Jeeves' machi-
avellian schemes), and the Blandings books (in which
Lord Emsworth's prize pig bulks large). Other books tell
of the multifarious members of the Mulliner family and
the Drones Club, of golfers, cricketers and incompetent
crooks; in all of them the season is high summer, every
cloud is lined with silver, and happy endings are distributed 'in heaping handfuls' (to quote Wodehouse's own
immortal phrase).

LEAVE IT TO PSMITH • *(1923)*

Before Eve Halliday will marry him, Freddie Threepwood
needs £1000 to start a bookmaker's business. He goes to
Blandings Castle to ask his father Lord Emsworth. But
Lord Emsworth has no access to his own fortune: that
route is guarded by Lady Constance Keeble and her side-
kick the Efficient Baxter. The plot spirals to include poets
who are not everything they seem, stolen jewels, a pur-
loined pig – and above all the machinations of the endlessly, irritatingly good-humoured Psmith.

Wodehouse's Blandings books include Galahad at Blandings, Heavy Weather, Pigs Have Wings *and* Uncle Fred in
the Springtime. *His Jeeves books include* Joy in the Morning, The Inimitable Jeeves, Jeeves in the Offing *and* The
Code of the Woosters. *His other novels include* Money in
the Bank, Uncle Dynamite, The Luck of the Bodkins *and*
Quick Service. The Man Upstairs, The Clicking of
Cuthbert, Eggs and Crumpets *and* Meet Mr Mulliner *are
short-story collections, and* Performing Flea *is autobiography.*

WOLFE, Thomas • *(1900–38)*

US novelist.

Wolfe's life's work was an incoherent, multi-million-word
torrent of autobiographical prose, an attempt to make epic

Doctor in the House.
Patrick Dennis, *Auntie
Mame*. The same kind
of gormless farce,
transplanted to
California, updated to
the 1980s and set
among incompetent
crooks and gangsters
is in Donald
Westlake's Dortmunder
books, eg *Bank Shot*
or *Who Stole Sassi
Manoon?*.

READ ON ▷

▶ ▷John O'Hara, *From
the Terrace.*

fiction of ordinary US life. His models were ▷Homer, Shakespeare and ▷Dickens – and his work is every bit as grand as that suggests. He and his publishers organised some of the material into two long novels, telling the story of Eugene Gant, a young Carolina writer, from boyhood to first success. The first and most accessible book, *Look Homeward, Angel* (1929), tells of Eugene's childhood as the youngest member of a sprawling, bickering slum family, of his awakening to culture and of his heart-breaking realisation that to 'follow art' he must abandon his family and everything it stands for and chop off his own roots. *Of Time and the River* (1935) continues the story, following Eugene through college and to Paris, charting his artistic friendships, his learning about sex and love, and his first attempts at writing. After Wolfe's death two other novels, *The Web and the Rock* and *You Can't Go Home Again*, were assembled from his manuscripts. They follow another writer, George Weber – an adult version of Eugene Gant – through marriage, divorce, disillusion with the USA and hostility to European fascism in the 1930s.

WOOLF, Virginia • *(1882-1941)*
British novelist and non-fiction writer.

As well as novels, Woolf published two dozen non-fiction books: biographies (one of Flush, Elizabeth Barrett Browning's pet dog), diaries, essays on feminism and on literature. She was fascinated by psychology, and her nine novels set out to show, in prose, the workings of the subconscious mind. Instead of narrating strings of events she lets her characters run on in a 'stream-of-consciousness' style which gradually builds a clear picture of their personalities. She developed the technique from Freud's case-histories, but her characters are not psychologically damaged, as Freud's patients were: she tells us the jumble of thoughts and memories in ordinary men and women, and she is particularly good at showing moments of radiant inner happiness. *Mrs Dalloway* (1925), the interior monologue of a middle-class woman preparing to give a dinner-party, reveals her feelings about herself and her past as well as the urgent claims of the coming evening. In *To the Lighthouse* (1927) a group of adults and children is shown on a summer holiday – the trip to the lighthouse is a promised birthday treat for one of the children – and then in the same place ten years later, when the trip is finally made. Despite war and death in the intervening years, the influence of the dead mother is as strong as in her lifetime. *The Waves* (1931), Woolf's most complex book, traces six people's reactions to experience from childhood to maturity, showing how apparently small 'real' past

▷Lawrence Durrell, *The Black Book*. ▷H.H. Richardson, *The Fortunes of Richard Mahony*. James Jones, *From Here to Eternity*.

> READ ON

▶ ▷Marcel Proust, *Swann's Way* (the first part of *Remembrance of Things Past*). ▷Jean Rhys, *Good Morning, Midnight*. D.M. Thomas, *The White Hotel*. Dorothy Richardson, *Pilgrimage*. Anaïs Nin, *Seduction of the Minotaur*. ▷Margaret Atwood, *Surfacing*. Gertrude Stein, *Three Lives*. ▷Iris Murdoch, *The Sea, the Sea*.

events continue to affect the personality as waves shape and reshape the shore.

Woolf's other novels are The Voyage Out, Night and Day, Jacob's Room, Orlando, The Years *and* Between the Acts. Haunted House *and* Mrs Dalloway's Party *are collections of short stories.*

WOUK, Herman • *(born 1915)*
US novelist and playwright.

Wouk's best-known novel, *The Caine Mutiny* (1951), is a tense study of life on a second-world-war US minesweeper whose crew judge the captain unfit for command. Its culminating sequence, a court-martial of the mutineers during which the captain is tricked into revealing his paranoia, was made into a hit Broadway play and a Humphrey Bogart film – and the book itself inspired a score of other novels, films and plays about the craziness not only of war but of the hierarchies of command: they range from the James Cagney/Henry Fonda film comedy *Mr Roberts* to ▷Heller's novel *Catch-22*. Wouk himself wrote two other powerful second-world-war books, *The Winds of War* and *War and Remembrance*. His other novels, several made into blockbuster films, include *Marjorie Morningstar* (1955, the story of a young woman who goes to New York to make her way in show-business and who finds romance instead), *Youngblood Hawke* (1962, a tragic-comic satire about a genius-novelist – based on ▷Thomas Wolfe – who is corrupted as soon as he begins meeting agents, publishers and publicists), and *The City Boy* (1948, a wisecracking story about a poor but cheerful New York Jewish family during the Depression).

WYNDHAM, John • *(1903–69)*
British novelist and short-story writer.

Wyndham's novels are less SF than thrillers, set on Earth, with SF overtones: he called them 'logical fantasies'. In

> READ ON

▶ To *The Caine Mutiny*: Erich Maria Remarque, *All Quiet on the Western Front* (set before, during and after the first world war); Nicholas Monsarrat, *The Cruel Sea* (a powerful thriller about British anti-submarine warfare in the second world war); Pierre Boulle, *The Bridge Over the River Kwai* (set in a Japanese labour camp in Burma during the second world war); ▷Norman Mailer, *The Naked and the Dead* (set in a US training camp during the second world war).
▶ To *Marjorie Morningstar*: ▷Willa Cather, *The Song of the Lark*.
▶ To *The City Boy*: ▷Jerome Weidman, *Fourth Street East*; ▷Mordecai Richler, *The Apprenticeship of Duddy Kravitz*.

> READ ON

▶ Bob Shaw, *Night Walk*.

The Midwich Cuckoos (1957) an alien race seeks to colonise Earth not by force of arms but by fertilising women – and the story begins, in the quiet English countryside (a favourite Wyndham location), as the half-alien children approach puberty. In *Chocky* (1968) a small boy has an invisible confidant – not a figment of his imagination, but a being from outer space. *The Day of the Triffids* (1951) begins with two simultaneous disasters, the sudden blinding of all human beings and the growth of enormous, mobile, predatory plants; the novel concerns the hero's attempts to organise resistance and save the human race.

Wyndham's other novels include The Chrysalids, The Kraken Wakes *and* Trouble With Lichen. *His short stories are collected in* The Seeds of Time, Consider Her Ways *and* Web.

▷James Herbert, *The Magic Cottage*. ▷H.G. Wells, *The Time Machine*.

Y

YERBY, Frank • *(born 1916)*
US novelist.

Yerby's early books, serious novels about racism, were published in the second world war, and found few readers. In 1945 he changed his style, began to write historical romances – and became one of the best-selling authors of the century. Superficially his books are straightforward 'bodice-rippers', passion-and-crinoline melodramas set in the American Deep South. But his persistent underlying theme is the equality of all people, white or black, and this gives his work an edge unusual in romance. In the 1960s he broadened his scope, writing books set in ancient Greece, Biblical Palestine, Victorian England and present-day Washington, D.C.

Yerby's romances include The Foxes of Harrow, The Golden Hawk, Floodtide, A Woman Called Fancy, The Devil's Laughter, Bride of Liberty, Griffin's Way *and* A Darkness at Ingraham's Crest. *His other novels include* The Saracen Blade, The Serpent and the Staff, Goat Song, Judas My Brother *and* Hail the Conquering Hero.

READ ON

▶ **To the romances:** ▷Margaret Mitchell, *Gone With the Wind*; Kathleen Winsor, *Forever Amber*; Colleen McCullough, *The Thorn Birds*.
▶ **To Yerby's other books:** Lloyd C. Douglas, *The Big Fisherman*; ▷John Galsworthy, *The Man of Property*; Allen Drury, *A Shade of Difference*.

Z

ZOLA, Émile • *(1840-1902)*
French novelist and non-fiction writer.

Zola won scandalous fame at 27 with his novel *Thérèse Raquin*, about a pair of lovers who murder the woman's husband. The book's financial success let him take up fiction full-time, and he began a 20-novel series designed to show – in a scientific way, he claimed, as species are described – every aspect of late 19th-century French life. Although each novel is self-contained, their main characters are all members of the two families which give the series its name, *The Rougons and the Macquarts*. Zola's scheme echoed ▷Balzac's in *The Human Comedy*, and like Balzac he was interested in exact description, what he called 'naturalism'. But his morbid and pessimistic nature led him to concentrate on the harsher aspects of human existence, so that his characters often seem less like real human beings than the people dragged into sermons to illustrate the effects of drink, lust or poverty. Outside France, Zola's best-known books are *Germinal* (1885, about conditions in the coal-mines, and including a strike and a major accident), *Earth* (La Terre) (1887, about subsistence farming), *The Belly of Paris* (Le ventre de Paris) (1873, about the food-markets of the city), *The Boozer* (L'assommoir) (1871) and *For Women's Delight* (1883, about the staff and customers of a department store).

NANA • *(1880)*
The subject is sex. Nana's mother was a country girl who went to Paris to seek her fortune, became a laundress but was destroyed by drink – this is the story of *The Boozer*. Nana grows up as a street-urchin, and later becomes an actress and singer. She is beautiful but corrupt, morally brutalised by her childhood. She sets out systematically to destroy men: Zola thinks of her first as one of the Sirens

> **READ ON** ▷
>
> ● *Thérèse Raquin.*
> ▶ ▷Somerset Maugham, *Liza of Lambeth.* Theodore Fontane, *Effi Briest.* Frank Norris, *The Pit.* Theodore Dreiser, *An American Tragedy.* ▷John Steinbeck, *The Grapes of Wrath.* George Gissing, *New Grub Street.*

in myth, drawing men irresistibly to her by the beauty of her voice, and then as a spider, preying on them even as she mates with them. He pities neither Nana nor her victims: like his other novels, this panorama of big-city life is painted entirely in shades of black.

Other books in the series include The Human Beast *(La* bête humaine*) (about the gangs of navvies who built railroads),* Money *(set among financiers) and* The Downfall *(La débâcle) (a devastating picture of the 1870 Commune and siege of Paris, which Zola saw as a cleansing operation, ridding the city of the corruption which had led to the misery described in his other books). In his last years he finished the first three books of another series,* The Four Gospels*: their titles are* Fertility, Work *and* Truth.

INDEX

Bold type indicates main entries.

B

G

O

P

T